INFLATION

TARGETING

in the world economy

INFLATION

TARGETING

in the world economy

Edwin M. Truman

INSTITUTE FOR INTERNATIONAL ECONOMICS
Washington, DC
October 2003

Edwin M. Truman, senior fellow, was assistant secretary of the US Treasury for international affairs (1998–2000). He directed the Division of International Finance of the Board of Governors of the Federal Reserve System 1977 to 1998. From 1983 to 1998, he was one of three economists on the staff of the Federal Open Market Committee. He has been a member of numerous international groups working on international economic and financial issues, including the Financial Stability Forum's Working Group on Highly Leveraged Institutions (1999–2000), the G22 Working Party on Transparency and Accountability (1998), the G10-sponsored Working Party on Financial Stability in Emerging Market Economies (1996–97), the G10 Working Group on the Resolution of Sovereign Liquidity Crises (1995–96), and the G7 Working Group on Exchange Market Intervention (1982–83). He has published on international monetary economics, international debt problems, economic development, and European economic integration.

INSTITUTE FOR INTERNATIONAL ECONOMICS
1750 Massachusetts Avenue, NW
Washington, DC 20036-1903
(202) 328-9000   FAX: (202) 659-3225
www.iie.com

C. Fred Bergsten, *Director*
Valerie Norville, *Director of Publications and Web Development*
Brett Kitchen, *Director of Marketing and Foreign Rights*

Typesetting by BMWW
Printing by Kirby Lithographic Company, Inc.

Printed in the United States of America

05 04 03   5 4 3 2 1

Library of Congress Cataloging-in-Publication Data

Truman, Edwin M.
  Inflation targeting in the world economy / Edwin M. Truman.
      p. cm.
  Includes bibliographical references and index.
    ISBN 0-88132-345-4
  1. Inflation (Finance)—Government policy.
  2. Monetary policy.   3. International finance.   I. Title.

HG229.T768 2003
339.5′3—dc22   2003061260

With love and appreciation to my mother, Elinor G. Truman,
and to my father, David B. Truman, who died on August 28, 2003.
For more than sixty years,
they supported and encouraged me in every project,
large or small, that I undertook, including this study.

Contents

Tables

Figures

Boxes

Preface

The international monetary system has been a focal point at the Institute for International Economics throughout its existence. John Williamson, in particular, developed several pioneering concepts on the issue in the 1980s, especially *The Exchange Rate System* (1983) and *Targets and Indicators: A Blueprint for the International Coordination of Economic Policy* (1987, with Marcus H. Miller). More recently, Morris Goldstein has produced a series of studies on the topic including *Managed Floating Plus* (2002), *Assessing Financial Vulnerability: An Early Warning System for Emerging Markets* (2000, with Graciela Kaminsky and Carmen Reinhart), and *Safeguarding Prosperity in a Global Financial System: The Future International Financial Architecture* (as project director of an Independent Task Force Report sponsored by the Council on Foreign Relations). We have also published comprehensive analyses by two outstanding visiting fellows, *Toward a New International Financial Architecture* by Barry Eichengreen (1999) and *The International Financial Architecture: What's New? What's Missing?* by Peter Kenen (2001).

Monetary policy of course plays a central role in each country's participation in the international financial system. Over the past decade or so, inflation targeting has become a leading concept for management of monetary policy and more than 20 countries in both the industrial and developing world have now adopted that approach. This book breaks new ground by integrating the analysis of inflation targeting, as a framework for the conduct of national monetary policy, with the functioning of the international financial system. In particular, it asks whether more widespread adoption of inflation targeting—especially by the leading economies of the United States, Euroland, and Japan—could enhance the effectiveness and stability of the global economy, and reaches a positive conclusion that could have significant implications for the future of both monetary management in those key areas and the functioning of the international system itself.

This is the first major Institute study by Edwin M. Truman, who became a senior fellow here in early 2001 after completing a distinguished career of more than 25 years in official positions in the United States. For most of that period, he was director of the Division of International Finance of the Board of Governors of the Federal Reserve System and one of three economists on the staff of the Federal Open Market Committee. He concluded his public service as assistant secretary of the Treasury for international affairs during 1998–2001. In these positions, he participated actively and with considerable authority in the evolution of both US and global monetary and international economic policies over an extended period. He thus brings unparalleled experience and knowledge to the issues addressed in this book.

The Institute for International Economics is a private nonprofit institution for the study and discussion of international economic policy. Its purpose is to analyze important issues in that area and to develop and communicate practical new approaches for dealing with them. The Institute is completely nonpartisan.

The Institute is funded largely by philanthropic foundations. Major institutional grants are now being received from the William M. Keck, Jr. Foundation and the Starr Foundation. A number of other foundations and private corporations contribute to the highly diversified financial resources of the Institute. About 18 percent of the Institute's resources in our latest fiscal year were provided by contributors outside the United States, including about 8 percent from Japan.

The Board of Directors bears overall responsibilities for the Institute and gives general guidance and approval to its research program, including the identification of topics that are likely to become important over the medium run (one to three years), and which should be addressed by the Institute. The director, working closely with the staff and outside Advisory Committee, is responsible for the development of particular projects and makes the final decision to publish an individual study.

The Institute hopes that its studies and other activities will contribute to building a stronger foundation for international economic policy around the world. We invite readers of these publications to let us know how they think we can best accomplish this objective.

C. FRED BERGSTEN
Director
October 2003

Acknowledgments

I have incurred many debts during the completion of this study about inflation targeting as a means of achieving reasonable price stability. My first debt is to C. Fred Bergsten, who supported the project, took my word that it fit the research program of the Institute for International Economics, and encouraged me to press on.

Second, I owe tremendous debts to the central banking community. I thank Arminio Fraga, Ilan Goldfajn, Marcelo Kfoury Muinhos, and their colleagues at the time at the Central Bank of Brazil for their hospitality and education about inflation targeting in Brazil where I presented earlier versions of this study. I thank Ian Macfarlane, Stephen Grenville, Guy Debelle, Glenn Stevens, and their colleagues for similarly hosting me at the Reserve Bank of Australia. In particular, I thank Don Brash, Murray Sherwin, David Archer, and their colleagues for four extraordinary, stimulating weeks of discussions at the Reserve Bank of New Zealand. Finally, I thank Kazuo Ueda and his colleagues for inviting me to speak at the Bank of Japan.

In the same spirit, I acknowledge the essential support of each of the 22 inflation-targeting central banks for their assistance in getting the facts straight about their inflation-targeting frameworks, and often in other ways as well. Rafael Buenventura, Mervyn King, Lars Heikensten, Carlos Massad, and Miguel Urrutia are among those who provided important assistance and support at several critical points. I also have benefited from the assistance of nontargeting central banks, the European Central Bank, the Swiss National Bank, and in particular, many former colleagues at the Federal Reserve, in addition to the Bank of Japan.

I acknowledge the hospitality of Toshihiko Fukui and the Fujitsu Research Center and Ambassador Arafune and the Institute for International Economic Studies, both in Tokyo, in providing me venues to present my study. I thank all the participants in two lively study groups at the Institute for International Economics.

I also incurred debts to three groups of colleagues. First, I thank my colleagues at the Institute for International Economics, each of whom encouraged me to stay the course with the project and, in particular, Martin Baily, William Cline, Morris Goldstein, Randall Henning, Michael Mussa, Adam Posen, and John Williamson for their advice, comments, and assistance at crucial stages. Second, I acknowledge the advice, comments, and assistance of a group of friends and colleagues outside the Institute— Laurence Ball, Ralph Bryant (long one of my most constructive critics), William Dickens, Barry Eichengreen, Stanley Fischer, Robert Flood, Richard Freeman, Joseph Gagnon, Timothy Geithner, Edward Gramlich, Dale Henderson, Karen Johnson, Stephen Kamin, Donald Kohn, Jose Luis Machinea, Laurence Meyer, Fredric Mishkin, Athanasios Orphanides, Vincent Reinhart, Mark Stone, Lars Svensson, and Onno Wijnholds. Third, I acknowledge the critical support of a group of more distant colleagues: Edmar Bacha, Leo Bartolini, Steve Cecchetti, Andrew Haldane, Thomas Jordan, Eduardo Levy-Yeyati, Georg Rich, Klaus Schmidt-Hebbel, and Federico Sturzenegger.

Turning to the really heavy lifters, this project would not have been successfully completed without the support of key individuals at the Institute for International Economics. Yifan Hu helped me get started on the project and conducted some of the empirical analyses, Frank Gaenssmantel assisted during the critical composition stage, and Fabrizio Iacobellis supplied the energy to push the project through to its final completion. Shannon Skupas and Tracy Gary provided essential secretarial assistance. Valerie Norville and her team of Marla Banov, Katie Sweetman, and in particular, Madona Devasahayam applied their magic vastly to improve the final product.

Finally, this study would not have been completed without the support and encouragement of my family, my wife Tracy, our children David and Christine, and my parents, to whom this book is dedicated.

Thus, I acknowledge my large debts to many institutions and individuals. Any errors, flaws, and omissions are mine alone.

What Is the Fuss All About?

In December 1989, the New Zealand parliament passed the Reserve Bank of New Zealand Act, completing the first codification of inflation targeting as a framework for the conduct and evaluation of monetary policy. The New Zealand authorities had been searching since April 1988 for a monetary policy framework in which the policy objective was well defined and the central bank or its governor, as was the case in the end, could be held accountable for achieving that objective (Brash 2002).

In the following 13 years, 22 countries have formally adopted inflation targeting as their preferred monetary policy framework.[1]

Many commentators have urged the central banks of the G3 economies (the United States, Euroland,[2] and Japan) to adopt inflation targeting, and

1. The 22 are Australia, Brazil, Canada, Chile, Colombia, the Czech Republic, Finland, Hungary, Iceland, Israel, Korea, Mexico, New Zealand, Norway, Peru, the Philippines, Poland, South Africa, Spain, Sweden, Thailand, and the United Kingdom. Finland and Spain dropped off the list when their monetary regimes were absorbed into the European System of Central Banks in January 1999 (table 2.3). The inflation-targeting frameworks of these countries are far from identical. (Moreover, inflation performance of some nontargeters in recent years has been better than a number of inflation targeters.) Nevertheless, the authorities of the countries and the policy community generally accept that these 22 countries are or were inflation targeters. Some authors—Carare and Stone (2003), for example—categorize these countries as full-fledged inflation targeters. I make no such distinction.

2. Euroland or the euro area includes the 12 members of the 15-member European Union that are full participants in the European System of Central Banks, using the euro as their currency and with the European Central Bank (ECB) as their central bank. The 12 countries are Austria, Belgium, Finland, France, Germany, Greece, Ireland, Italy, Luxembourg, the Netherlands, Portugal, and Spain. The three current EU members not in Euroland are Denmark, Sweden, and the United Kingdom.

at least three countries—Argentina, Russia, and Turkey—are aspiring inflation targeters. The 22 countries—a significant number—make up more than 10 percent of the membership of the International Monetary Fund (IMF) and more than 20 percent of world GDP measured on a purchasing power parity basis. The list of actual inflation targeters includes industrial, emerging, developing, and transition economies located in Africa, Asia, Europe, and North and South America. Therefore, even though historical experience with inflation targeting remains short, the widespread use of the framework justifies this study's focus on the challenges and opportunities inflation targeting offers for the world economy.

Inflation targeting as a framework for the conduct of monetary policy is not a panacea for the difficulties facing policymakers. But a sound monetary policy—along with appropriate fiscal, financial, and structural policies—is an important pillar for economic success. So, what is the best monetary policy framework for each country given its economic and financial circumstances? Is it pure discretion (no framework); a focused, hierarchic, or multipart mandate with or without an inflation target; a monetary aggregate; a (more or less hard) exchange rate target to achieve some goal (normally low inflation); or subcontracting monetary policy to another central bank by adopting its currency (dollarization or euroization)? The authorities and ultimately the citizens of the relevant jurisdiction have to choose. As in the case of exchange rate regimes, it is highly unlikely that any one framework for monetary policy will be the best for all countries, at all times, in all circumstances. Nevertheless, choices of monetary policy frameworks are normally treated as permanent, even if they are not, because the economic and financial costs of switching frameworks (or regimes) are normally substantial.

Inflation targeting as a framework for the conduct of monetary policy places some demands and requirements on central banks. This study addresses how extensive and consequential they are. Moreover, if inflation targeting is to benefit a large number of adopting economies and the world economy, the challenge will be whether the framework can accommodate differences in the wide-ranging circumstances of those economies.

Some proponents of inflation targeting argue that there is substantial convergence in practice among inflation targeters and that differences in practices can provide insights into what works and does not (Bernanke et al. 1999, chapter 11). Experience offers insights, but at this early stage, sufficient experience may not exist to firmly guide countries about how best to implement an inflation-targeting framework. Chapter 3 details that inflation targeting in practice exhibits considerable variety.

Controversies about monetary policy frameworks date back at least to the 19th century, when debates and international conferences were held about which countries were on a gold standard and whether gold and silver could coexist as monetary standards. Today, most observers agree on three basic points. First, policies matter for economic success or failure; a sound monetary policy is a necessary, but not a sufficient, condition for success. No country has successfully developed without a disciplined monetary policy, which can be reasonably defined as avoiding high inflation, more than 10 percent per year, for an extended period.[3]

Second, a successful economy needs a robust monetary policy framework. One candidate is inflation targeting, a main attraction of which is its focus on an ultimate target—control of inflation—which is crucial to long-run economic success. In the words of Lars Svensson (2003b, 426), one of the gurus of inflation targeting, "Successfully stabilizing inflation around a low average with some concern for stabilizing output around potential output" is nothing more than the definition of "good monetary policy." However, that definition contains much of the debate about the appropriateness and advantages of inflation targeting as a framework for monetary policy: just how low should the target rate of inflation be? How much emphasis should be placed on stabilizing output as well? What if there is no generally accepted measure of potential output or its growth rate? These are among the classic questions about monetary policy in modern market economies.

Third, rigid frameworks may promise quick results, but they involve higher risk, especially in the context of a volatile global economic and financial environment, as Argentina, Brazil, and Turkey have recently learned. The challenge is to find a robust framework that contributes to sound economic performance in a range of circumstances for a particular country that can only anticipate that it may over time face a range of unpredicted and unpredictable supply as well as demand disturbances.

Thus, the central bank of a country adopting inflation targeting as its framework for the conduct and evaluation of monetary policy is not buying into a formula for instant, painless success and popularity. It is not doing away with the classic questions of monetary policy. As described by Lars Heikensten and Anders Vredin (1998, 12) of the Riksbank, Sweden's central bank, "central banks [adopting inflation targeting] accordingly face the challenge of winning credibility for a low inflation target while conducting a monetary policy that is sufficiently flexible to dampen short-run fluctuations in output and employment without jeopardizing the long-term goal."

Inflation targeting offers a quantitative monetary policy framework. It is an open question whether inflation targeting is more demanding than other monetary policy frameworks or whether its successful application

---

3. Turkey had high inflation for an extended period, averaging more than 60 percent a year from 1990 to 2002, and positive real growth of almost 2 percent per capita per year throughout that period (see appendix tables A.2 and A.3). However, in 1999 the authorities adopted an exchange rate–based disinflation strategy to bring inflation down to single digits. The strategy was unsuccessful, but the point is that the authorities decided it was appropriate to Turkey's circumstances and that Turkey needed to address its chronic inflation problem to help boost growth on a sustained basis.

absorbs more central bank or other government resources. However, in part, inflating targeting may tend in that direction because of the transparency aspects of the framework.[4] The central issue is whether the payoffs for the adoption of such an approach are worth it, compared with the alternative.

In their influential volume on inflation targeting, Ben S. Bernanke, Thomas Laubach, Frederic S. Mishkin, and Adam S. Posen (1999, 308) "conclude that inflation targeting is a highly promising strategy for monetary policy, and . . . predict that it will become the standard approach as more and more central banks and governments come to appreciate its usefulness."[5] In 1998, when they wrote the volume, only 11 countries were formal inflation targeters.[6] It is noteworthy that most central banks that practice inflation targeting are actively involved in the political economy of improving and solidifying their frameworks and that, aside from those countries (Finland and Spain) that practiced inflation targeting before the European System of Central Banks absorbed their central banks, no country has abandoned the framework.

It is also important to appreciate that inflation targeting has not yet swept alternative monetary policy frameworks in major economies. In particular, none of the G3 monetary authorities (Bank of Japan, European Central Bank, and US Federal Reserve) has adopted the framework despite considerable urging to do so. As Edward Gramlich (2000, 8) wrote, "For the United States, given the strong aversion to inflation already apparent in policy responses, there are various pros and cons, but it is not obvious that a more formal regime of inflation targeting will lead to very great differences in actual monetary policies." Later, Gramlich's then colleague on the Federal Reserve Board, Laurence Meyer (2001), advocated that the Federal Reserve adopt a formal inflation target, but he stopped short of endorsing a full inflation-targeting framework for the United States.[7]

---

4. See Carson, Enoch, and Dziobek (2002) on the statistical implications of inflation targeting. Along the same lines, the Czech National Bank cooperated with the IMF (Coats, Laxton, and Rose 2003) to produce and publish an analytical review of the bank's system for forecasting and policy analysis.

5. See also Bernanke and Mishkin (1997) for an earlier summary of inflation targeting and Sterne (2002) and Schmidt-Hebbel and Tapia (2002) for more recent summary treatments.

6. The 11 were Australia, Canada, Chile, the Czech Republic, Finland, Israel, New Zealand, Poland, Spain, Sweden, and the United Kingdom.

7. Laurence Meyer (2001) argues that "full inflation targeting," as he uses the term, should include an advance commitment about the objectives of central bank policy if it were to miss its target, and he does not see such a commitment as being in the economic interests of the United States because of the uncertainty associated with the disturbances or policy errors that may have contributed to the miss, including the size and circumstances of the miss.

The objective of this study is not simply to consider whether the United States or any other economy would perform better using an inflation-targeting framework to guide and evaluate its monetary policy, but rather to consider more generally in what respects the functioning of the international financial system might or might not improve if, for example, each of the G3 monetary authorities or a larger number of emerging-market economies adopted such frameworks.

What Is Inflation Targeting?

The absence of complete agreement on the definition of inflation targeting as a monetary policy framework should not surprise observers of political processes or policymakers, especially those advised by economists. It is useful, initially, to think in generic terms.

First, monetary policy focuses on inflation because that is where monetary policy primarily has its influence over the medium term. A stronger version of this proposition is that monetary policy has little or no influence on the level or growth rate of economic activity over the medium term.

Second, however, in the short run, monetary policy also can and does influence output or the rate of expansion of economic activity.

Third, these two dimensions (inflation and growth) point to an underlying tension in any monetary policy framework between (a) the policy's short-term influence on output or growth and limited—if not nonexistent—longer-term influence on output or growth and (b) much greater influence on the price level or inflation.

Fourth, in this context, inflation targeting offers a framework of "constrained discretion" (Bernanke and Mishkin 1997; Bernanke et al. 1999; King 1997a, 1997b, and 2002; and Kuttner and Posen 2000). The constraint is the inflation target, and the discretion is the scope to take account of short-run economic and financial considerations. In the best of circumstances and in many theoretical presentations, the constraint and discretion act together like a pair of scissors, cutting through thickets of economic disturbances to produce a happy combination of low inflation and strong economic activity. It is not surprising that in debates about the merits of inflation targeting, many supporters emphasize the discretion while many critics emphasize the constraint.

This study does not focus on strict inflation targeting (SIT), which Svensson (2001a, 16) characterizes as "completely disregarding the real consequences of monetary policy in the short and medium term and focusing exclusively on controlling inflation at the shortest possible horizon." No central bank today practices SIT, although it can be and has been argued (Bryant 1996) that in the early days of inflation targeting, some countries such as New Zealand used something quite close to an SIT framework.[8] Instead, inflation-targeting central banks generally practice flexible inflation targeting (FIT), which Svensson (2001a, 16) characterizes as a framework in which "the primary goal of monetary policy is to achieve price stability in the form of an inflation target, but it is recognized that some weight should be given to stabilizing the business cycle and, consequently, stabilizing output movements around potential output."

Nevertheless, even under FIT, there is potential tension both in practice and in theory between missing the inflation target and the credibility or reputation of the central bank. There is also the risk that an inflation-targeting central bank is not serious about its policy, resulting in a framework that in practice is not only flexible but also looks more like mush. As Bernanke (2003a) stresses, in the view of some proponents, inflation targeting exerts a constructive constraint on central bank flexibility by influencing the expectations and behavior of economic agents. Finally, inflation targeting does not solve many perennial judgment questions facing central banks, particularly with respect to supply disturbances that push inflation in one direction and economic activity in the other.

For purposes of this study, inflation targeting as a framework for the conduct and evaluation of monetary policy contains four main elements:

- price stability—a principal, if not the sole, explicit or implicit goal of monetary policy;
- numerical target or sequence of targets—to make the goal of price stability operational;
- time horizon—to reach the inflation target or to return to the target; and
- evaluation—an approach for ongoing review of whether the inflation target will be or has been met.

In practice, no two countries and their central banks construct or implement their inflation-targeting frameworks identically. Moreover, each of the above elements, with the possible exception of the third (time horizon), could be part of a number of other monetary policy frameworks. As discussed in chapter 3, price stability is part of the mandate of most inflation-targeting central banks; numerical targets are set by or for each of them; and the authorities have adopted a variety of approaches for evaluating whether the target is likely to be or has been met. Most of the inflation-targeting central banks have a reasonably precisely specified

---

8. The early experience of Israel with inflation targeting is subject to a similar interpretation. For example, David Elkayam, Ofer Klein, and Edward Offenbacher (2002) estimate reaction functions for the Bank of Israel, and the unemployment gap is not significant. Their finding can be attributed to the bank's effort to establish inflation targeting credibility, to the volatility of the real economy in the early and mid-1990s, or a combination of the two factors.

time horizon over which the target or targets are to be met. However, most of their frameworks can be described as vague, at best, with respect to the specification of a time horizon for returning to the target in case of a departure from it. Finally, all inflation-targeting frameworks in practice include a number of elements to assist in evaluating whether the country's monetary policy objectives have been met. Again, no uniform approach to evaluation has emerged, and most such elements are not unique to inflation-targeting countries. Nevertheless, for some proponents, transparency to facilitate the accountability of monetary policy is central to and the principal contribution of inflation targeting.

Despite differences in construction and implementation, this study uses the criterion of self-description to identify inflation-targeting countries and their central banks. This criterion means that contrary to the practice of other investigators (for example, Bernanke et al. 1999, Schmidt-Hebbel and Tapia 2002), Switzerland is not classified in this study as either a de facto or a de jure inflation targeter (see box 2.1 for a discussion of the Swiss situation). The variations found in the frameworks of inflation-targeting central banks raise some methodological awkwardness. However, that awkwardness does not diminish the potential significance of inflation targeting as a framework for the conduct and evaluation of monetary policy in practice. In addition, for purposes of this study, inflation targeting differs from the technical economic literature on monetary policy regimes (see appendix 1.1 to this chapter for a summary of the principal differences).

Murray Sherwin (2000, 16), then deputy governor of the path-breaking Reserve Bank of New Zealand, stressed that an inflation-targeting framework for monetary policy involves political will and a constructive frame of mind more than technical preparations with respect to either the content of the framework or the condition of an economy when it adopts the framework. He articulated three principal requirements for an inflation-targeting country: "decide what level of inflation is appropriate to the economy; ensure that there is political acceptance of that objective, however defined; set monetary policy with the intention of meeting that inflation target and keeping inflation low thereafter."[9] In their guide to the practical issues associated with inflation targeting for emerging-market economies, Andrea Schaechter, Mark Stone, and Mark Zelmer (2000, 5) provide a slightly more operational definition of the approach: "Essentially

---

9. Sherwin's relatively loose definition of inflation targeting may, in part, reflect his laid-back Kiwi nature, but it also reflects New Zealand's unique experience, first, in adopting inflation targeting—an experience driven by political support for wide-ranging reforms of economic policy and public-sector management—and, second, in reviewing and substantially refining its inflation-targeting framework since its initial construction in the late 1980s. For more background, see Archer (1997 and 2000), Brash (1998 and 2002), Drew (2002), Scott (1996), Svensson (2001a), and Reserve Bank of New Zealand (2000 and 2002).

use an inflation forecast as an intermediate guide to monetary policy, and operate policy in a transparent framework that fosters accountability."[10]

What Are the Issues?

The primary focus of this study is the implications of inflation targeting for the structure, functioning, and evolution of the international financial system and the performance of the world economy. What challenges and opportunities does inflation targeting offer to the world economy? The term "international financial system" encompasses both the international monetary system with its official understandings, agreements, conventions, and institutions and private-sector processes, institutions, and conventions. The success or failure of an inflation-targeting framework, if widely adopted, is likely to have profound implications for many of the issues that have been the focus of international debate over the three decades since the end of the Bretton Woods system in 1971 and the de facto advent of generalized floating among the currencies of the major industrialized countries in 1973.[11]

The failure of governments and their central banks to deliver macroeconomic and financial stability has been the major cause of most international crises over the past three decades, though of course not all the blame can be laid at the doorsteps of their central banks. It follows that if the widespread adoption of inflation targeting by national authorities delivers better overall performance of the international financial system, the performance of the global economy as a whole will also improve. Moreover, if inflation targeting can produce increased macroeconomic stability, it will result in greater financial stability. However, in this context, the interesting question is whether a large number of economies are in a position to benefit from the adoption of such a framework.

---

10. Definitions of inflation targeting range from the general to the detailed. For example, Hans Genberg (2001) defines the framework as a statement of objectives about monetary policy and nothing more. On the other hand, Klaus Schmidt-Hebbel and Matías Tapia (2002) argue that the framework rests on four cornerstones: (1) an inflation target as an anchor to policy, (2) operational independence for the inflation-targeting central bank, (3) the capacity to forecast and react to inflation, and (4) a high degree of transparency and accountability about monetary policy. Takatoshi Ito and Tomoko Hayashi (2003) list a set of necessary conditions for inflation targeting combining institutional and conduct elements: (1) a publicly announced inflation target, (2) an institutional commitment to price stability, (3) the conduct of monetary policy using inflation forecasts as an operational target, (4) transparent explanations of monetary policy, and (5) the imposition of accountability on the central bank.

11. Kenneth Kuttner and Adam Posen (2001) emphasize that an economy's exchange rate regime might better be viewed as just one of a triad of dimensions of an overall monetary regime incorporating exchange rate arrangements, monetary policy framework, and institutionalization—for example, independence—of its central bank.

This study considers a number of aspects of inflation targeting under current conditions to address its potential. It answers four broad questions about inflation targeting and the challenges and opportunities for the global economy.

First, would the adoption of inflation targeting by the G3 economies improve the performance of the world economy? Through what channels or mechanisms?

The international financial system and the world economy would benefit if the G3 economies individually or, better still, collectively adopted inflation targeting as their monetary framework. The benefits would flow principally through two channels. The adoption of inflation targeting would contribute to better economic policies and performance in Japan, to a lesser extent in Euroland, and to a much lesser extent in the United States. Inflation targeting would not be a panacea for what ails those economies, but it would improve overall global economic performance. In addition, the adoption of inflation targeting by the G3 would improve the quality of the dialogue about economic policies and prospects both within the G3 and between the G3 and the rest of the world, thereby reducing general policy uncertainty. This study proposes concrete steps for each of the G3 central banks to implement inflation targeting with minimum disruption to current legal arrangements in their economies.

Second, is inflation targeting broadly applicable to industrial economies, most emerging-market economies, and other developing economies? If inflation targeting is not for all economies, at least at this time, what are the realistic alternatives? What are the implications, if any, for the global financial system of a combination of monetary frameworks including inflation targeting?

Inflation targeting is broadly applicable to a wide range of countries. Little evidence exists to support the view that many economies are too small, vulnerable, or unprepared to implement an inflation-targeting framework successfully. On the other hand, beyond the G3 adopting inflation targeting and the contribution of inflation targeting combined with greater exchange rate flexibility to underlying stability, the case for inflation targeting to improve the functioning of the international financial system is limited. At the same time, the world is not greatly threatened by a combination of monetary policy frameworks. Inflation targeting may not be optimal for all countries because no framework for monetary policy can promise to be the best for all countries in all circumstances. The framework should be employed flexibly, and experimentation is appropriate. The evidence to date, including that presented in this study as well as that assembled by other researchers, does not support any concern that the widespread adoption of inflation targeting would distort policy priorities in the direction of fighting inflation excessively to the neglect of economic growth. Inflation targeting in many cases may improve overall economic performance—growth as well as inflation—but the evidence at this stage is not conclusive either on average or for all countries individually.

Third, what are the implications of widespread adoption of inflation targeting as a framework for monetary policy for the evolution, structure, and functioning of exchange rate regimes? What are the implications for exchange rate stability?

The adoption of inflation targeting as a monetary policy framework does not guarantee exchange rate stability. On the margin, if inflation targeting contributes to better economic performance, including reduced inflation variability, it should make a small contribution to enhanced exchange rate stability. In the context of wide bands, inflation targeting is compatible with a variety of exchange rate regimes—ranging from free floating to regimes envisaging more active concerns about exchange rate movements such as managed floating—as long as the exchange rate remains an important economic price and does not rise to the level of a competing economic policy objective. I argue that a fear of floating that will take over monetary policy to focus it narrowly on the exchange rate will not necessarily undermine inflation targeting as a monetary policy framework.

Fourth, what are the implications of inflation-targeting frameworks for the international financial architecture, including the adjustment process, crisis prevention, crisis management, and IMF programs?

The widespread adoption of inflation targeting will not free the international financial system from financial crises. Inflation targeting has some promise to be useful to countries emerging from crises. In addition, the increased transparency and more flexible exchange rate regimes associated with the framework are consistent with recent trends in crisis prevention. This study supports the view that the IMF should actively encourage the G3 central banks to adopt inflation targeting to improve the performance of their economies and the global economy in the process. It also concludes that the IMF should be less institutionally resistant to other members' choices to adopt inflation targeting. In brief, I do not support the view of some IMF officials and staff that the inflation-targeting framework is demanding and resource intensive and that its successful implementation requires years of preparation and institutional changes. On the other hand, the IMF has been constructive in seeking to adapt its policy conditionality apparatus to inflation-targeting members with IMF-supported adjustment programs, but further modifications and experimentation are desirable.

These conclusions about inflation targeting and the challenges and opportunities the framework offers the global economy leave me as an inflation-targeting sympathizer, not an enthusiast or proselytizer.

My five broad policy recommendations are summarized below:

■ The G3 economies should adopt inflation targeting, preferably collectively or, as a second best, individually, to improve their economic performance and reduce the risk of deflation. The IMF should actively encourage the G3 to do so because of the benefits to the global economy.

- With respect to other potential inflation targeters, the IMF should project a more benign and constructive attitude toward its members—whether receiving IMF financial support—that choose to adopt inflation targeting as their monetary policy framework.
- Countries like Argentina, Russia, and Turkey, classified in this study as potential inflation-targeting "squeezers" because their inflation rates exceed 10 percent, should seriously consider adopting the framework.
- Inflation targeting should not be rejected on the grounds that countries will be unable or unwilling to implement the framework because of a fear of floating.
- The IMF should further modify and experiment with the application of its policy conditionality to inflation targeters with IMF-supported adjustment programs applying criteria laid out in chapter 6.

Plan of the Book

Chapter 2 considers the attraction of inflation targeting. First it reviews the analytical and historical developments that have led a significant number of countries to embrace inflation targeting as their monetary policy framework. Second, it examines whether any economic and institutional conditions are systematically associated with a country's choice of inflation targeting as its monetary framework.

Chapter 3 looks at inflation targeting in practice. First, it considers whether specific economic and institutional preconditions need to be met before adopting such a framework. Second, it reviews the technical details of established inflation-targeting frameworks. Third, it describes a classification of four categories of the 22 actual and a larger number of potential inflation targeters.[12] Finally, it presents empirical results that provide some perspective on a number of arguments for and against inflation targeting, looking at whether inflation targeting is contraindicated for some countries on the basis of their structural characteristics as well as at some measures of the overall macroeconomic success of inflation targeting on average.

Chapter 4 focuses on inflation targeting by the central banks of the G3 economies (United States, Euroland and Japan). It considers whether the

---

12. Data were assembled on the 68 countries listed in appendix table A.1. The criterion was that the country had been important enough long enough for Consensus Economics to include it in its Consensus Forecasts for a significant number of years. Twenty-two of those countries are actual or former inflation targeters; the remaining 46 are "potential inflation targeters" of significance to the international financial system for the purposes of this study.

world economy would be better off if the G3 economies were individually or collectively to adopt inflation targeting as their preferred framework for the conduct of monetary policy. It also describes the practical steps each of the G3 economies could take to adopt inflation targeting.

Chapter 5 turns to the interaction of inflation targeting and exchange rate regimes and policies—the exchange rate experience of inflation targeters, the compatibility of different exchange rate regimes and exchange market policies with an inflation-targeting framework for monetary policy, and the relationship between these issues and any fear of floating.

Chapter 6 looks at inflation targeting and the international financial architecture, including crisis prevention, crisis management, and the interaction of IMF-supported adjustment programs and their associated conditionality requirements with inflation-targeting frameworks of countries with such programs.

The final chapter, in addition to summarizing the study, expands on policy recommendations and the four broad issues sketched in this chapter.

Appendix 1.1 Monetary Policy Regimes

An extensive technical economic literature comparing the performance of monetary policy regimes has developed during the past 20 years. The recent emergence of inflation targeting as a framework for the conduct and evaluation of monetary policy has further developed that literature.[13]

The extensive and diverse literature on the performance of monetary policy regimes lacks a universally accepted nomenclature. However, much of the literature follows or can be translated into the structure exploited in Bryant, Hooper, and Mann (1993). Their structure contains four basic elements:

- **ultimate target variables**—the final goals of monetary policy.
- **instruments**—the tools used to achieve those goals including both the choice of *instrument* and the choice of the extent of *variation* of that instrument.
- **operating regime**—a description of how policymakers address the issues of *instrument choice* and *instrument variation* in order to reach the targeted variable, which may be the *ultimate target* (in a single-stage procedure) or an *intermediate target* (in a two-stage procedure); in short, the "monetary policy regime."
- **reaction function**—the mapping of the *operating regime* into an equation or policy rule linking the policy instrument with the intermediate or ultimate target or, more broadly, with its determinants.[14]

What is the relationship between inflation targeting as a framework for the conduct and evaluation of monetary policy, and, for the purposes of this study, the formal structures common to the literature on the performance of monetary policy regimes in terms of various economic variables that may be important to the policymakers and the public?

First, inflation targeting involves more than the choice of *price stability* as the policy goal. It is, of course, reasonable to expect under an inflation-targeting framework that inflation—at least some concept of it—will be included as a policy goal of the country and its central bank. (Some—Edward Gramlich [2003], for example—say that inflation anchors monetary policy even without the adoption of a numerical target.) However, inflation may not be the central bank's exclusive goal, and its legal mandate may include that goal with more or less precision and with or without mentioning other goals.

---

13. See, among other works, Ball (1999a and 1999b); Ball, Mankiw, and Reis (2002); Clarida, Galí, and Gertler (1998, 1999, and 2000); Jensen (2002); Kim and Henderson (2002); Isard, Laxton, and Eliasson (2001); Levin and Williams (2002); Levin, Wieland, and Williams (1999 and 2002); Rudebusch and Svensson (1999); Svensson (1999, 2002b, 2003a, and 2003b); Svensson and Woodford (2003); Taylor (1993, 1999a, 1999b, and 2001); and Woodford (2000).

14. Lars Svensson (1999) argues strongly that the latter formulation is technically preferred.

Second, the *inflation target*—a specific number or a range—is the principal operational element in the framework. However, it may be an intermediate target as part of a two-stage process or the ultimate target as part of a single-stage process. The direct connection between the numerical target and the mandate of the central bank may be vague or part of an array of objectives.

Third, an inflation-targeting central bank normally chooses a short-term interest rate as its *policy instrument*, but this is not true in all cases. The leading exception is the Bank of Mexico, which currently uses announced changes in the so-called corto—the level of nonborrowed reserves—to implement its policy.

Fourth, the *time horizon* element of inflation-targeting frameworks in effect places some restrictions on the central bank in terms of instrument variation, in the sense that changes in the relevant instrument, at least in principle, should be commensurate with the achievement of the target. However, this implicit restriction both in the abstract and in practice stops well short of a fully specified reaction function.

Fifth, inflation targeting in practice involves both more and less than a *reaction function* characterizing a monetary policy regime. Given that no central bank's inflation-targeting framework today involves strict inflation targeting, inflation targeting in practice is more than a reaction function characterizing a monetary policy regime because the framework can and normally does include other elements; some of those elements may be contained in the formal mandate of the central bank, and others may be part of only the operating practices of the institution. Inflation targeting in practice is less than a reaction function fully characterizing a monetary policy regime because it may be impossible to characterize the central bank's behavior in these terms.[15] The central bank either may not use any formal reaction function in developing its policy options or may use multiple reaction functions in doing so, or it may be impossible to capture its behavior ex post with any precision by trying to estimate a reaction function.[16] In this sense, inflation targeting in practice does not qualify as

---

15. One of the big issues in the technical literature on central bank reaction functions is the problem of model uncertainty. Does a particular reaction function perform equally well with different models? Alternatively, how can the central bank using a particular reaction function be confident that the model in which a particular reaction function performs well is the right model of the economy? These issues are highly relevant to the formalization of flexible inflation targeting and, in particular, strict inflation targeting, but they are not central to the concerns addressed in this study.

16. For example, the error bands around most estimates of Taylor rules designed to characterize the behavior of central banks are normally sufficiently wide to preclude much in the way of inferences about whether the central bank has or has not altered the weights (coefficients) in its implicit objective function for inflation and output. See Alan Blinder's comment to this effect in Frankel and Orzag (2002, 57) and Sharon Kozicki's (1999) analysis of the usefulness of Taylor rules for monetary policy.

a formal monetary policy regime—it is a *framework* to guide the *conduct* of policy, which may involve elements other than the past, present, or projected inflation rate.

Sixth, inflation targeting involves an active approach to *evaluate* whether the central bank has hit or is likely to hit its inflation target. This feature reflects the increased emphasis in recent years on transparency in monetary policy, as well as other economic policies. Increased transparency is not unique to central banks adopting inflation targeting as their framework for the conduct and evaluation of monetary policy, but transparency is an integral element of such inflation-targeting frameworks in practice. For this reason, I often refer not just to "inflation targeting" or an "inflation-targeting framework" or "inflation targeting for the conduct of monetary policy" but to an "inflation-targeting framework for the conduct and *evaluation* of monetary policy."

Thus, *inflation targeting as a framework for the conduct and evaluation of monetary policy* is more than the choice of inflation as the ultimate goal of policy; it also includes a specific numerical target, some sense of the time horizon over which that target is to be met, and an approach to evaluate the central bank's performance in meeting it. On the other hand, it is less than a fully articulated monetary policy regime such as can be found in the technical literature. However, that literature helps inform, in part via deliberate simplification, monetary policymaking in practice, including inflation targeting. The practice of inflation targeting, on the other hand, seeks to exploit a framework, a skeleton on which many somewhat diverse elements can be hung. One potential weakness of inflation targeting as a framework for monetary policy is that it can mean different things for different practitioners. Moreover, some have argued that the identification of the 22 inflation targeters in this study involves a degree of selection bias. To be selected into the sample, a central bank only has to adopt a numerical target for inflation and declare itself an inflation targeter. Such a criticism may not be entirely unjustified, but I would argue that inflation targeting as a framework for the conduct and evaluation of monetary policy also implies seriousness about the enterprise and a means (via evaluation) to test that seriousness, which substantially mitigates such a critique.

In short, this study is not about inflation targeting as a theoretical monetary policy regime. It is about inflation targeting in practice as a framework for the conduct and evaluation of monetary policy.

2

Attraction of Inflation Targeting

Inflation targeting as a framework for the conduct and evaluation of monetary policy has a short history of less than 15 years. However, its antecedents can be traced to the 19th-century debates about gold, silver, and other national monetary standards as well as to post–World War II developments in monetary history.

This chapter first sketches out the analytical and historical developments that have contributed to the decisions of a significant number of countries to adopt inflation targeting as their framework for monetary policy. It then presents the results of an empirical investigation of the economic and institutional conditions associated with countries choosing an inflation-targeting framework.

Intellectual Origins

The intellectual origins of inflation targeting as an applied monetary policy framework comprise six principal strands of thought and evidence:

- economists' traditional arguments about the economic costs of inflation,
- statistical demonstration and political recognition that higher inflation is associated with lower rather than higher growth in the medium term,
- a search for a new "anchor" for monetary policy when the chains on other anchors have failed,
- research on alternative monetary policy regimes,

- a favorable global macroeconomic environment, and
- increased awareness of the usefulness of inflation targeting as a defense against the growing risk of deflation.

Some of these strands—for example, the costs of inflation and the relationship between inflation and growth in the medium term—are germane to choices of other monetary frameworks; many of the strands are interconnected.

Costs of Inflation

Probably the oldest, but least influential, strand is the economists' traditional arguments about the microeconomic costs of inflation that, in turn, affect the macroeconomic performance of an economy. Economists agree that inflation, certainly high inflation, imposes microeconomic and macroeconomic costs. Their disagreements relate to the significance of those costs and the rate of inflation or amount of inflation variability at which they may kick in.[1]

The anticipated and unanticipated economic costs of inflation normally include negative effects on the allocative efficiency of individual economic agents—for example, higher information or "shoe-leather" costs for economic agents, blurred or distorted incentives with respect to production and consumption, reduced efficiency in the use of money, diversion of resources from the real economy to defensive financial-sector activities, and increased uncertainty about or misperceptions of inflation. Also often cited are distortions in the tax system, though some analysts point out that inflation is a tax on money and that the optimal tax on money, given that there are other tax distortions in the system, may not be zero. Other analysts point out that inflation is a source of government revenue in the form of seigniorage.

In addition to the economic costs—and in a few cases benefits—of inflation, economists cite social costs, including distortions to the distribution of income, adverse effects on poverty rates, reduced support for "good economic development," the interaction between financial market development and inflation, and the simple fact that high inflation is politically unpopular.

It is often noted that the problem of inflation lies not with central bankers—most of whom fully appreciate, and some observers would say overappreciate, the economic costs of inflation—but with the political process. For example, Lawrence B. Lindsey argued at the January 31, 1995, meeting of the Federal Reserve's Federal Open Market Committee

1. Among the contributors to the literature in the context of this study are Burger and Warnock (2003), Easterly and Fischer (2001), Fischer (1996), Heikensten and Vredin (1998), Khan, Senhadji, and Smith (2001), and King (2002).

(FOMC 1995) that "the right way to improve the loss function or gain function [via price stability] is not in this [FOMC meeting] room; but it is up there on Capitol Hill" where lawmakers were seeking to raise the minimum wage. Lindsey was echoing former Federal Reserve Chairman Arthur F. Burns (1979), who in his Per Jacobsson lecture in Belgrade on September 30, 1979 (the eve of the adoption by the Paul Volcker–chaired Federal Reserve of a new monetary policy operating procedure to reduce US inflation sharply), argued implicitly with Volcker in the audience that the fault for high US inflation (11.3 percent in 1979) lay not primarily with central bank behavior but in policy decisions made elsewhere that limited the central bank's capacity to bring down inflation, especially once it had increased.[2]

In 1979, Arthur Burns's four-part proposal for how the government should deal with US inflation included revision of the budget process, a comprehensive plan for dismantling regulations impeding the competitive process and modifications where regulations were driving up prices and costs, scheduled reductions in business taxes to stimulate the supply side of the economy, as well as "a binding endorsement of restrictive monetary policies until the rate of inflation has become substantially lower." Volcker returned from Belgrade and put the finishing touches on the Federal Reserve's new operating procedures, which the FOMC approved and announced within days. Key people in the executive branch had been informed in advance about Federal Reserve thinking, but their approval or endorsement was not requested or required. Moreover, the focus of the Volcker approach was squarely on what the Federal Reserve could and should do to deal with the inflation problem.

Inflation and Growth

Popular disillusion with the apparent negative association between inflation and growth has inspired a significant literature that principally has succeeded in demonstrating that the public is correct to be concerned about inflation at least up to a point. Looking at data from the 1960s to the early or mid-1990s, various researchers found that the simple correlation between inflation and growth is negative, but the statistical results were not very strong; they were sensitive to the inflation range considered, and researchers were unable to uncover strong evidence of the precise nature of the linkage—that is, through what channels higher inflation impedes growth. Thus, a well-established link not exist between the microeconomic costs—many of which presumably show up in lower growth via a less

---

2. One of Arthur Burns's favorite examples in this area was the Davis-Bacon Act, which mandates the payment of prevailing wage rates (often heavily influenced by rates in unionized sectors) on construction projects receiving federal financing. That act, along with the minimum wage, remains a hotly contested US economic and political issue to this day.

dynamic economy—and the macroeconomic costs of inflation measured by lower growth rates in the total economy. For this reason these two strands of the literature have been separated in this brief review.[3]

Agreement is widespread that sustained inflation above 40 percent per annum is disadvantageous to growth. Most researchers also agree that sustained double-digit inflation is bad for growth, but one finds more questions and qualifications about such results, and the lack of statistically established mechanisms to buttress them weakens their impact.[4] Ruth Judson and Athanasios Orphanides (1999) find breakpoints or knots at 40 and 10 percent. Michael Sarel (1996) finds one at 8 percent. Atish Ghosh and Steven Phillips (1998) find a change in the relationship between inflation and growth at 2.5 percent. Mohsin Khan and Abdelhak Senhadji (2001) find thresholds for the negative impact of inflation on growth in industrial countries at 1 to 3 percent and in developing countries at 11 to 12 percent, but their rationale for splitting the sample this way is not particularly convincing given the wide difference in the indicated thresholds for the two groups of countries.[5]

Notwithstanding recent findings of breakpoints at rates below double digits, Stanley Fischer's (1996, 15) earlier summary of economists' contribution to this subject probably still captures what consensus there is on this subject: "These results leave little doubt that double-digit inflation is bad for growth. However, they leave the nature of the relationship at lower inflation rates uncertain. . . . The overall conclusion is that it is not possible at this stage to draw any firm conclusion on the relationship between inflation and growth at the very low inflation rates current [1996] in the G-7, though there is little evidence for a significant positive association between inflation and growth even at very low inflation rates." Moreover, the economists' consensus may have only confirmed what the men and women in the street had learned by the mid-1990s about the negative relationship between growth and inflation over the previous 30 years (King 1999a, 2002).

The summary data presented in table 2.1 illustrate another strand of the debate on this issue. They show average consumer price index (CPI) inflation rates and average growth rates of real GDP for the 1990–2002 period for two groups of countries: the 22 countries that were or became inflation targeters during the period and 46 countries that might be con-

---

3. Among the more important contributors to the literature on the relationship between inflation and growth, in addition to those cited in the text, are Barro (1991, 1995), Barro and Sala-i-Martin (1990), Bruno and Easterly (1996), Feldstein (1997), Golob (1994), Jones and Manuelli (1993), Levine and Renelt (1992), Levine and Zervous (1993), and Smyth (1994).

4. For a detailed analysis of very high inflation and hyperinflation, see Fischer, Sahay, and Végh (2002).

5. Similarly, Peter F. Christoffersen and Peter Doyle (1998) find a threshold for transition economies at 13 percent.

Table 2.1 Average rates of CPI inflation and growth rates of real GDP, 1990–2002 (percent)

Inflation average (percent)	Inflation targeters			Potential inflation targeters		
	Number	Inflation	Growth	Number	Inflation	Growth
Less than 5	10	3.1	2.8	19	2.5	3.4
5 to 10	6	8.2	3.7	8	7.9	4.3
10 to 20	3	18.2	2.3	8	14.0	4.2
More than 20	3	396.9	2.7	11	140.8	0.3
Total/average	**22**	**60.3**	**3.0**	**46**	**38.5**	**3.0**

CPI = consumer price index

Source: IMF, International Financial Statistics.

sidered potential inflation targeters.[6] For both groups, the average growth rate for real GDP is generally lower the further average inflation is into double digits. However, the peak average growth rates are for countries with average inflation rates between 5 and 10 percent. For potential inflation targeters in particular, the average growth rate for those with average inflation rates below 5 percent is lower than for those with somewhat higher average inflation rates.

Economists on the other side of the debate about the relationship between growth and inflation generally do not dispute the negative effects on growth of very high average inflation rates, but they do contend that at low rates of inflation, the relationship between growth and inflation may be positive rather than negative. In the US case, George Akerlof, William Dickens, and George Perry (1996 and 2000) have argued and demonstrated statistically that some, but low, inflation in the United States contributes to lower unemployment and higher rates of economic activity and, presumably, growth.[7] They argue on the basis of theory and observation and conclude that "macroeconomic policy [in the United States] should aim for a rate of inflation in the range of 1.5 to 4 percent. Either higher or lower rates seem likely to result in lower output and employment" (Akerlof, Dickens, and Perry 2000, 39). They agree that they have not necessarily identified the right range for the "optimal rate of inflation" because they do not take account of other economic factors—for example, productivity—which may vary with inflation.

---

6. The list of countries and the data for the individual countries can be found in appendix tables A.2 and A.3. For purposes of this study, any economy significant enough for Consensus Economics to include it in its Consensus Forecasts for about six years, if it is not already an inflation targeter, is treated as a potential inflation targeter.

7. The literature does not always distinguish between the effects of inflation on economic activity in the short term and the effects on the growth rate or the sustained level of economic activity in the medium term. As with the debate about the slope of the Phillips Curve in the short run versus the longer run, this leaves room for those with differing views to talk past each other.

The work of Akerlof, Dickens, and Perry has its own historical roots in the debate about the nature of the Phillips Curve in the long run. Accepting, as most do, that in the short run there is a negative relationship between inflation and unemployment, is the long-run effect of higher inflation on employment zero, as argued by Milton Friedman (1968) and Edmund Phelps (1968), or might the long-run relationship also be negative, at least at low levels of inflation, say, less than 5 or 10 percent?

More recent debates have focused on what have come to be called sand and grease effects of inflation on economic activity. The grease (positive) effects of moderate inflation on growth generally are associated with fairness, efficiency wages, reducing nominal wage rigidity, and lowering information costs. Lower information costs mean inflation is sufficiently low for economic agents to ignore it and thereby save on the costs of collecting information. The sand (negative) effects of higher inflation on growth generally are associated with the dissipation of money illusion, higher information costs, the increased burden of uncertainty, increased real-wage rigidity, and less economic dynamism.

There is no consensus whether sand and grease effects operate at the same time or in sequence. One might like to think that the two effects may operate in sequence or that on balance one effect dominates the other at different rates of inflation. Erica Groshen and Mark Schweitzer (1999, 2000) suggest that inflation may have both effects on labor markets at the same time: inflation acts positively by relaxing nominal wage rigidity (grease) at the same time that it acts negatively by increasing real wage rigidity (sand) through the degradation of price signals.

One possible sequence of the net influence of sand and grease effects might be the following: at very low rates, slightly above zero, inflation on balance improves the long-run trade-off between inflation and growth (employment); the relationship between inflation and growth is positive. At somewhat higher rates, inflation on balance leads to a deterioration in growth; the relationship between inflation and growth becomes negative. After some point, as inflation increases, the relationship becomes vertical as postulated by Friedman (1968) and Phelps (1968). Perhaps, at even higher rates, inflation is associated with lower employment and lower growth; the relationship between inflation and growth is again negative.

One might reasonably expect that a different balance or sequence of sand and grease effects may prevail in different economies under different economic conditions as well as at different times. Most of the initial statistical analysis of the grease-sand issue has exploited US experience and data, but statistical relationships that hold in the context of US economic practices and institutions may not hold in other countries. Moreover, for purposes of this study, which takes an international perspective, one should not assume that US phenomena can be generalized to the rest of the world.

Charles Wyplosz (2001) has looked at the evidence for countries other than the United States. He finds evidence of both grease and sand effects in France, Germany, the Netherlands, and Switzerland, suggesting that the sand effect is initially dominant, contrary to the sequence outlined above. Starting from zero, higher inflation initially has a negative effect on growth, but as inflation increases further it has a positive effect on growth. Anja Decressin and Jörg Decressin (2002) have also looked at evidence on the behavior of wage rates in Germany compared with those in the United States and the United Kingdom, and they are unable to find significant differences, suggesting that whatever grease-sand or sand-grease patterns there are in the United States and the United Kingdom, despite their reputations for having more flexible labor markets than Germany, should also be found in Germany. Ana Maria Loboguerrero and Ugo Panizza (2003) find that the dominance of grease and sand effects of inflation differs between industrial and nonindustrial countries. Under the leadership of Erica Groshen at the Federal Reserve Bank of New York and William Dickens at the Brookings Institution, an impressive cooperative global research effort—the International Wage Flexibility Project—is under way to systematically investigate some of these issues at the micro level. Preliminary results suggest much greater heterogeneity among countries than many analysts expected.

Abstracting from statistical debates about technical issues, arguments against central banks targeting inflation rates that are too low come down to the three summarized by Lawrence Summers (1996) at a central bankers' meeting at Jackson Hole, Wyoming, under the auspices of the Federal Reserve Bank of Kansas City: (1) nominal wage rigidities, which inhibit the adjustment of labor markets and lead to higher unemployment at lower rates of growth; (2) nominal interest rate floors, which inhibit the capacity of central banks to offset negative shocks at low levels of inflation;[8] and (3) undermining the credibility of central bankers. On the last, his argument was that the general public is not likely to believe a target that is perceived to be "too low." Summers also cautioned against the adoption of targets that lead to forecasts of nominal growth of less than 3 to 4 percent because the implied real growth rate is likely to be associated with a rise in unemployment. In this he was anticipating more recent concerns about the specter of deflation, which is discussed later.

Some researchers have postulated two channels through which inflation affects growth: the level (or rate) of inflation and the variability of inflation. Judson and Orphanides (1999) examine this issue using a sample of 119 countries for the 1959–92 period. They find that for rates below 10 percent, inflation does not have a statistical effect on growth, but the negative effect of inflation variability remains significant throughout. If inflation variability increases with the level of inflation, as is commonly thought to

---

8. Lawrence Summers (1991) had previously issued a similar warning.

Table 2.2 Inflation variability and inflation in industrial countries over three decades

Scope of regression	All observations	Excluding observations with inflation mean greater than 10 percent
Independent variables		
Inflation mean	0.4849***	0.3642***
	(0.027)	(0.059)
Dummy (1980s)	1.0928***	0.8766***
	(0.3647)	(0.314)
Dummy (1990s)	1.4003***	0.6025
	(0.423)	(0.405)
Constant	−1.3178	−0.1842
Number of observations	69	55
Adjusted R-squared	0.85	0.56

*** represents rejecting the null hypothesis of no significance at a level of 1 percent. Standard errors in parentheses.

Notes: The dependent variable is the standard deviation of inflation. Inflation means and standard deviations are calculated for three 10-year periods, the first starting in 1971 and the last ending in 2000.

The countries included in the regression are all 22 industrial countries in our sample (see appendix table A.4) plus Luxembourg. The observations excluded in the second regression are: Australia 1970s, Finland 1970s, Greece 1970s and 1980s, Iceland 1970s and 1980s, Ireland 1970s, Italy 1970s, New Zealand 1970s and 1980s, Portugal 1970s and 1980s, Spain 1970s, and United Kingdom 1970s.

be the case, then the Judson-Orphanides result would tend to support an inflation target below 10 percent. As long as higher rates of inflation in the range of 0 to 10 percent are associated with increases in inflation variability, the inflation target should be in the lower part of that range.

To study this issue further, the statistical relationship was examined between the standard deviation of inflation and mean CPI inflation in the 23 industrial countries—based on the classification in the International Monetary Fund's (IMF) *International Financial Statistics*—from 1971 to 2000.[9] The results are presented in table 2.2. Using the full sample of countries, a significant positive statistical relationship was found.[10] To test whether countries with high average inflation rates unduly influenced these results, the observations where the average inflation rate for a 10-year period was more than 10 percent were dropped. The level of inflation continues to have a significant effect on inflation variability.

---

9. Frank Gaenssmantel, former research assistant at the Institute, conducted the statistical analysis.

10. The IMF (2002b) reports similar results on the relationship between the standard deviation of inflation and the level of inflation in the G7 countries, but the correlation coefficient is only 0.40.

The analysis of the statistical relationship in industrial countries between inflation rates and inflation variability, coupled with the Judson-Orphanides result about the continued adverse influence of inflation variability on growth at low levels of inflation, tends to support the view that a country's target inflation rate should be less than 5 percent per annum. In fact, few observers argue for a higher number.

A final argument with respect to the level of inflation and its interaction with macroeconomic performance is the often-presented "slippery slope" view. Allowing inflation to edge higher, on the grounds that there is little evidence that an inflation rate of, say, 5 percent has adverse economic effects, may tip the actual inflation rate down the slippery slope toward the range where adverse effects can be expected, especially in light of the inherent volatility of the inflation series and the inertia that can build into inflation (Friedman 2003). US experience in the late 1970s illustrates both viewpoints. In the mid-1970s, there was support for the view that there would be little harm if inflation rose a bit, as long as lower unemployment and faster growth accompanied it. Ultimately, by the end of the 1970s, inflation got out of hand. It became apparent that the economy had started down the slippery slope several years earlier.

The inertia that can build into inflation, combined with a view that at low levels of inflation the grease effects of inflation on growth may dominate the sand effects—thus increasing the sacrifice ratio (normally measured as the cumulative percentage points of growth lost to reduce inflation by one percentage point)—also may provide one rationale for the so-called opportunistic approach to disinflation: "When inflation is moderate, the central bank should not take deliberate action to reduce it further. Instead, the central bank should wait for exogenous circumstances—e.g., favorable supply shocks and unforeseen recessions—to deliver the additional reductions in inflation" (Orphanides and Wilcox 2002, 48).

Chapter 3 reviews briefly the choices by inflation-targeting countries of target points or ranges. No country has adopted a range with an upper limit of more than 6.5 percent as its longer-term or ultimate target, and the tops of most ranges are 3 percent. The above discussion about the negative statistical macroeconomic relationship between inflation and growth and the grease versus sand effects on that relationship helps explain why such choices have been made.

Search for a Better Anchor

The intellectual history of monetary economics can be depicted as the search for the holy grail of the right nominal anchor. An "anchor" can be a different concept for different people. At its simplest level, a nominal anchor for monetary policy is a single variable, for example the price of gold. At a complex level, an anchor is a device to pin down expectations of private agents about the nominal price level or its path and about what the authorities might do with respect to achieving that path, for example, the money supply. At a more complex, if not confusing, level, the anchor refers to the entire monetary regime.[11]

Whatever concept of a monetary anchor one prefers, the price of gold under a gold standard regime is the best-known anchor in the past 200 years of monetary history. Some might consider the price of gold to be a nonpolicy anchor, or at least an anchor for a policy of nonactivism, since in theory it is seen as part of a regime in which discretion is sharply limited. In practice, the limitation was much less binding especially with the increasingly widespread use of fiat money. In recent years, monetary policy anchors have progressed, if that is the right word, through reliance on a rough sequence of monetary aggregates from the monetary base to narrow definitions of money, to broader definitions of money, and most recently to credit aggregates. At each step, many practitioners found that the chosen monetary aggregate abandoned the central bank that was using it as an anchor for monetary policy; the relationship between the monetary aggregate—an intermediate objective—and the authorities' ultimate objective—usually inflation—broke down.

The past three decades or so have also seen a flirtation off and on, at least by academic economists, with nominal income (GDP or GNP) as an anchor for monetary policy.[12] However, no central bank has elevated nominal income to the level of an operational anchor for monetary policy. Central banks frequently use the concept of stabilizing nominal income in their analysis, forecasting, and formulation of policy alternatives. For example, in the case of a supply shock like an increase in petroleum prices, looking at the implications for nominal GDP helps in choosing whether to focus policy on the rise in prices or the decline in economic activity. However, use of nominal GDP as an analytical tool is not the same thing as elevating it to the level of an anchor to guide policy.

Two fundamental reasons are frequently given for not adopting nominal income targeting as a framework for the conduct and evaluation of policy. First, it would be very difficult to communicate the target; the general public, government officials, and market participants do not generally focus on the growth rate of nominal GDP as an important indicator of economic performance. Second, some observers, including politicians,

---

11. A useful summary of monetary policy frameworks and associated anchors in the post–Bretton Woods era can be found in Cottarelli and Giannini (1997). See also Flood and Mussa (1994), Jonas and Mishkin (2003), Khan (2003), Mishkin (1998), chapter 1 appendix, and the discussion later in this book on alternative monetary policy regimes.

12. Jeffrey Frankel and Menzie Chinn (1995) argue the empirical case for targeting nominal GNP; Henrik Jensen (2002) and Jinill Kim and Dale W. Henderson (2002) offer opposing views on the approach from slightly different theoretical perspectives compared with inflation targeting.

might easily confuse targeting nominal income with targeting real GDP. Most central bankers believe that to *target* real GDP would be at best unwise and at worst impossible because they are convinced that monetary policy has little or no influence over the long run on the level or growth rate of real GDP. Nevertheless, many central banks today publish near-term *forecasts* of real GDP, but these are not targets. Two more-technical reasons for rejecting nominal income targeting as a framework for monetary policy are that the data are available with long lags and are subject to considerable later revision. For all these reasons, central banks have resisted embracing nominal income targeting as an anchor for monetary policy in practice.

On the other hand, exchange rates have been frequently used as an anchor for monetary policy. The anchor may take the form of a hard peg—a fixed exchange rate, a currency board, or in the extreme the adoption of another country's currency as one's own. Less frequently the anchor may be embedded in a more flexible regime such as a basket, band, or crawl.

After World War II, under the Bretton Woods system, most countries in principle operated with adjustable-peg exchange rates as their monetary policy focus. A few countries opted for harder pegs in the form of narrower bands. Some outliers like the Canadians moved early on to a floating exchange rate regime. Carmen Reinhart and Kenneth Rogoff (2002) present persuasive evidence that de facto floating was more common in the Bretton Woods period than is normally acknowledged. Moreover, critics argue that under the Bretton Woods system, conflicts between domestic macroeconomic objectives and exchange rate fixity often were resolved in favor of the former.

Since the de facto advent of the generalized floating of the major currencies in 1973, exchange rate pegs have been used as disinflation devices. Until recently, exchange rate–based stabilization strategies were quite popular as devices to help impart monetary discipline and overcome inflation inertia. They were widely used to bring down inflation rates in Latin America, establish stability in transition economies such as Poland, and force policy convergence among the countries participating in the European Monetary System (EMS) and its exchange rate mechanism (ERM).

These devices have fallen out of favor, starting with the ERM crises of 1992 and 1993 (Truman 2002b). The most recent failures of monetary policy frameworks constructed with exchange rate anchors were Turkey's exchange rate–based stabilization program that started in December 1999 and came to a spectacular end in early 2001 and the abandonment in late 2001 of Argentina's so-called currency board arrangement.[13] One can de-

---

13. The actual anchor in Argentina was the Convertibility Law that promised that pesos would be freely convertible into dollars on a one-to-one basis; the Argentine system did not operate according to the rules of a currency board in which the money supply expands and contracts in lock step with increases and decreases in international reserves.

bate the underlying causes of those failures. A nice evaluation of the many factors contributing to failed disinflations can be found in Hamann and Prati (2002), but as a practical matter, hard pegs as disinflation devices are currently in substantial disrepute. As Maurice Obstfeld and Kenneth Rogoff (1995, 74) wrote, "Efforts to reform monetary institutions should focus directly on restraining domestic inflation. The exchange rate should be used as an indicator but virtually never as the central target for monetary policy."

Partly as a consequence of these developments, many countries and their central banks in recent years have questioned what should replace monetary aggregates or exchange rates as anchors for monetary policy. In many cases, the response has been to adopt inflation targeting as a framework or anchor for monetary policy. New Zealand was not forced by an economic or financial crisis to adopt inflation targeting in 1989; it came to this decision as the result of widespread dissatisfaction with the deterioration in its economic performance in the 1970s and 1980s and as part of a fundamental reform of economic policy and public-sector management.[14] Canada's and Australia's adoptions of inflation targeting were associated with similar, if not quite as intense, motives. On the other hand, the British, the Swedes, the Finns, and the Spanish adopted inflation targeting as their new anchor or framework for monetary policy in the wake of the 1992–93 ERM crises. Chile, Israel, Mexico, the Czech Republic, Poland, Brazil, Korea, South Africa, and Thailand; more recently Colombia, Hungary, Iceland, Peru, the Philippines, and Norway; and prospectively Turkey, Russia, and Argentina all have adopted, or have proposed to adopt, inflation targeting under a variety of circumstances, in some cases initially supported by special devices, for example, exchange rate bands in the cases of Chile and Israel and a monetary aggregate in the case of Mexico.

Table 2.3 lists the 22 countries that have adopted inflation targeting as their framework for monetary policy along with the date of adoption and the CPI inflation rate and growth rate of real GDP in the year of adoption as well as in 2002. Given the range of inflation-targeting approaches, as discussed in chapter 3, I have adopted the convention of considering a country and its central bank as an inflation targeter if it has a published inflation target and it describes its monetary framework as inflation targeting.[15] In the case of Switzerland, its central bank has explicitly declined to describe itself as an inflation targeter (see box 2.1).

---

14. See the references in chapter 1, footnote 9.

15. Alina Carare and Mark Stone (2003) and Stone (2003b) include 18 of these countries in their category of "full-fledged inflation targeting," which they associate with public description and communication of an inflation target and a transparent institutional framework to contribute to accountability. Because their data stop in 2001, they do not include Peru and the Philippines as inflation targeters, and they do not include Finland and Spain

Table 2.3   Countries with inflation-targeting monetary policy frameworks

		Economic conditions			
		CPI inflation (percent)		Real GDP growth (percent)	
Country	Date of adoption	Year of adoption[a]	2002	Year of adoption[a]	2002
Australia	June 1993	1.0	3.0	2.1	3.8
Brazil	June 1999	3.2	12.6	0.8	1.6
Canada	February 1991	4.8	2.3	−0.2	3.4
Chile	Early: September 1990	26.0	2.8	3.7	2.1
	Later: September 1999	3.3		−1.0	
Colombia	October 1999	11.2	7.0	−4.2	1.5
Czech Republic	December 1997	8.6	1.8	−0.8	2.0
Finland	February 1993	2.6	1.6	−3.3	1.6
Hungary	June 2001	9.8	5.7	5.2	3.3
Iceland	March 2001	5.2	5.2	5.5	−1.9
Israel	Early: December 1991	19.0	5.7	6.2	−1.0
	Later: June 1997	11.3		4.5	
Korea	April 1998	4.4	2.8	5.0	6.4
Mexico	Early: January 1995	7.0	5.7	4.4	0.8
	Later: January 2001	9.5		6.6	
New Zealand	December 1989	7.5	2.7	0.2	2.4
Norway	March 2001	3.1	1.3	2.7	1.0
Peru	January 2002	2.0	1.5	0.2	5.2
Philippines	January 2002	6.1	3.1	3.4	6.0
Poland	September 1998	11.7	1.9	4.8	1.3
South Africa	February 2000	5.2	10.6	2.1	3.1
Spain	January 1995	4.7	3.1	2.3	2.0
Sweden	January 1993	2.3	2.2	−1.4	1.9
Thailand	May 2000	0.3	0.6	4.4	5.2
United Kingdom	October 1992	3.7	2.2	0.2	1.4

a. Inflation and growth rates are for the year of adoption when adoption was in the second half of the year, and for the year before adoption when adoption was in the first half of the year. Inflation rates based on annual average CPI; growth based on annual average real GDP.

Source: IMF, *International Financial Statistics.*

Thus, an inflation target embedded in an inflation-targeting framework can be viewed as the newest anchor for monetary policy. The question is whether inflation targeting is merely another monetary fad or a framework for monetary policy that has more staying power because it can serve reasonably well the objectives of both the monetary and the political authorities in bad as well as good times.

because they are now part of the European System of Central Banks. In effect, their classification of full-fledged inflation targeters is dressed up self-description. They also introduce the category of "eclectic inflation targeting"—central banks of economies (Euroland, Japan, Singapore, Switzerland, and the United States) with so much credibility with respect to low and stable inflation that they do not have to announce targets. Finally, they introduce the category of "inflation targeting lite," which includes 19 other relatively large (emerging-market) economies with floating exchange rates. They presume that all economies with floating exchange rates fall in one of their three categories of inflation targeters.

Box 2.1 The Swiss situation

The Swiss National Bank (SNB) is not a self-declared inflation-targeting central bank but a self-declared noninflation-targeting central bank, a characteristic it shares with the European Central Bank (ECB), which has a similar numerical definition of price stability—0 to 2 percent.[1]

The SNB has a long history of successfully pursuing price stability. Bernanke et al. (1999) as well as a number of other observers (e.g., Schmidt-Hebbel and Tapia 2002)—who also note the SNB's official position—treat it as a de facto inflation-targeting central bank; for them the distinction is one of semantics. However, I have chosen to be guided by SNB officials who have repeatedly and firmly stated that the bank is not and never was an inflation targeter (Rich 2000, 2001; and Baltensperger, Fischer, and Jordan 2002).

By way of background, in December 1999 the SNB announced an evolution in its monetary policy framework (SNB 1999) that included (1) an explicit definition of price stability as inflation of less than 2 percent per year, as measured by the national consumer price index (CPI),[2] (2) the use of three-year inflation forecasts issued every quarter taking into account all relevant indicators including money growth, and (3) a target range for the three-month Swiss franc London Interbank Offered Rate (LIBOR) of one percentage point as an operational target that in general is reassessed every quarter. Thus, the SNB adopted some of the elements in the "toolkit" of inflation-targeting central banks, but it has not in my view adopted an inflation-targeting framework for the conduct and evaluation of monetary policy—in effect it has a published inflation target without the inflation-targeting framework. The Bank for International Settlements in its 71st Annual Report (2001, 70) described the SNB framework thus: "Switzerland does not target inflation but instead uses a broad-based inflation forecasting strategy primarily focused on a numerical target for price stability."

SNB officials have argued that the bank's framework differs from inflation targeting in that the emphasis is on a medium-term horizon without any elements of a contingency strategy—which some associate with inflation targets—that either contains escape clauses or may otherwise be adjusted. Ernst Baltensperger, Andreas M. Fischer, and Thomas J. Jordan (2002) identify the SNB's position on this matter with what they favorably describe as its "strong" goal independence, wherein the bank is left to interpret and implement flexibly—using its own judgment—its constitutional and legal mandate rather than having that interpretation come from the government (which they characterize as "weak" goal independence) or in collaboration with the government ("medium" goal independence).[3]

---

1. The ECB in May 2003 clarified that in pursuing price stability it would aim to maintain inflation rates close to 2 percent over the medium term. In mid-2003, the three-month Swiss franc LIBOR was 0.25 percent, the Swiss economy was experiencing year-over-year CPI inflation of around zero, and some members of the IMF Executive Board urged the SNB to follow ECB's example and target inflation close to the top of its definition of price stability.

2. Statements by SNB officials (Rich 2000) imply that the floor for price stability is an annual increase in the CPI slightly exceeding zero because the bank has made it clear that, in principle, it is unwilling to tolerate deflation.

3. This terminology draws upon Debelle and Fischer (1994).

Alternative Monetary Policy Regimes

The extensive literature on the macroeconomic performance of alternative monetary policy regimes is closely linked to, some would say conflated with, the search for a better anchor for monetary policy. Such regimes are normally characterized by an assumption about the ultimate goal or goals of monetary policy, an ultimate target variable (see the chapter 1 appendix for references to the extensive literature on monetary policy regimes). At the same time, the techniques and lessons from that literature have aided central banks in establishing, implementing, and refining inflation targeting as their framework for the conduct and evaluation of monetary policy. An important example is John Taylor's rule (Taylor 1993) that was originally put forward as an empirical description of the behavior of the Federal Reserve in setting its interest rate policy based on deviations of inflation and output from the central bank's stated or imputed objectives for those variables. The approach has been subsequently applied to many other countries, and the rule has been proposed as a guide for policy or to calibrate policy (see Taylor 1999a).

The formal structure of a monetary policy regime as frequently found in the technical literature includes ultimate targets, policy instruments, and operating regimes, which translate into policy reaction functions that are compared in the context of alternative representations of the economy in empirical models. Such structures and their analysis have clarified the choice of monetary policy frameworks for some countries. Studies of alternative monetary policy regimes have also warned against adopting—and also recommended modifying—frameworks that are, or turn out to be, excessively rigid, such as strict inflation targeting (SIT). These studies are also used to refine and contribute to decision making within many inflation-targeting as well as other central banks.

Finally, and perhaps most important, many formal studies of alternative monetary policy regimes have focused on expectation formation and the influence of expectations on monetary policy, and vice versa. This work has contributed to two features of inflation-targeting frameworks: first, it has reinforced the tendency to choose a framework that focuses on ultimate target variables (inflation) as opposed to intermediate target variables (exchange rates or a monetary aggregate). Second, it has reinforced the importance of transparency as an integral part of an inflation-targeting framework.

However, as discussed in the appendix to chapter 1, inflation targeting as a framework for the conduct and evaluation of monetary policy is both less and more than just another monetary policy regime, as it is normally interpreted in the technical literature.

Figure 2.1 CPI inflation, 1970–2002

percent

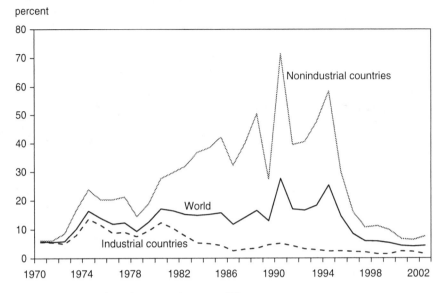

Note: Inflation rates based on annual average CPI.

Source: IMF, *International Financial Statistics.*

Favorable Environment

New Zealand was the first country formally to adopt inflation targeting as a framework for the conduct and evaluation of monetary policy in 1989, and most accounts of how the adoption occurred focus on the political economy of New Zealand rather than on any of the intellectual strands outlined earlier, with the possible exception of the abandonment of a fixed exchange rate regime.

New Zealand had one thing going for it that also assisted other countries as they adopted inflation targeting: the 1990s were a good decade to be an inflation fighter. Average inflation in the industrial countries in 1989 was 4.6 percent, down from 12.3 percent in 1980, and the same as in 1970 (4.6 percent). World inflation was 12.9 percent in 1989, down from 17.2 percent in 1980, reflecting the still-high level of inflation in developing countries on average, 27.4 percent in 1989 compared with 27.6 percent in 1980. By 2002, average world inflation was 4.2 percent; inflation in industrial countries was 1.4 percent on average, a level to which it had been close since 1994. Inflation in nonindustrial countries was 7.6 percent on average in 2002, about 10 percentage points below the average rate in 1996 and more than 50 percentage points below the average rate in 1994 (figure 2.1).

These favorable trends provided a positive backdrop for the adoption of inflation targeting; they also supported strategies favoring so-called opportunistic disinflation. However, it cannot be discounted that inflation targeting and, more generally, what the IMF (2002b) has described as "a more focused attitude toward inflation compared with the 1970s" contributed to this result, including the muted effects on overall inflation rates of the run-up in petroleum prices in 1999 and 2000. The IMF makes the case that this more focused attitude along with various supporting institutional changes have contributed to the establishment of a virtuous circle where increased concern about inflation has led to more forward-looking behavior by private agents, which has enhanced the ability of central banks to control inflation via both the traditional real interest rate channel and the less traditional expectations channel.

Against this background of improved inflation performance, Lars Svensson (2001a, 8) wrote in his review of the conduct of monetary policy in New Zealand under inflation targeting, "There is overwhelming international support, based on theory, empirical results and practical experience, for the general view that an optimal monetary policy framework is characterized by (1) a goal of price stability, (2) operational independence of the central bank, and (3) clear accountability of the central bank for achieving the goal." Chapter 3 presents a detailed review of the elements of inflation-targeting frameworks for monetary policy and addresses whether certain initial conditions are necessary or desirable if the framework is to be reasonably successful. At the moment it is appropriate to note that the favorable global macroeconomic environment during the 1990s, at least with respect to inflation, gave inflation targeting a good name and a good start, and inflation targeting appears to have contributed to the overall trend toward sustained lower inflation.[16] But how well will inflation targeting as a framework for monetary policy stand up to economic and political pressures when times are not so good?

Specter of Deflation

The 1990s also saw the surprising reemergence of the specter of deflation as a macroeconomic policy problem. Notwithstanding this renewed concern, there is no universally agreed definition of deflation. The simplest definition is a decline in some aggregate index of prices, but one should distinguish between a transient month-to-month decline, a decline over a 12-month period, and a more sustained decline that lasts for several years. The IMF (2003b, 6) defines deflation as "a sustained decline in an aggregate measure of prices such as the consumer price index or the GDP deflator."

However, for deflation to become a serious economic problem, more is required than price statistics. Aggregate indices of nominal wages should also record declines. Impacts on balance sheets are also relevant

---

16. See the statistical evidence presented in chapter 3.

because deflation raises the real value of nominal debt, and the process can lead to defaults and bankruptcies with negative feedbacks on the real economy. Serious deflation involves sustained declines in real spending, especially consumption, accompanying declines in prices and wages on average. If real output continues to increase at a substantial rate at the same time that the aggregate price level is declining—as has been the case in China recently—then nominal income and output will be rising, and statistical deflation is not indicative of a serious economic problem. Finally, an operational definition of deflation links the phenomenon to a zero (nominal) interest rate floor at which conventional monetary policy indexed by declines in real short-term interest rates is exhausted.

Some have argued (e.g., Bernanke 2000) that the dangers of deflation have been underappreciated. According to Ben S. Bernanke, what is relevant in terms of the burden of deflation on the debtor is the cumulative gap between the actual and expected price levels.[17] A second argument is that the effects of deflation are magnified today, compared with those in the 19th century, because financial assets have longer maturities. It is also possible that with rapidly changing economies, the upward bias in measuring inflation rates is higher today than it was decades ago. On the other hand, the increase in securitization of financial obligations, greater sophistication of consumers, and development of a variety of insurance mechanisms mean that deflation may be less damaging to the economy than it was a century or even half a century ago.

IMF (2002b) simulations illustrate that as target inflation rates decline below 2 percent, the probability rises that the central bank will hit the zero interest rate floor, confront a deflationary spiral, and experience increased output variability, largely as a consequence of the reduced effectiveness of monetary policy. Two industrial countries (Japan and France) had average annual rates of year-over-year CPI inflation during 1990–2002 of less than or equal to 2 percent (see appendix table A.2). Twenty-one of 23 industrial countries recorded at least one year of CPI inflation between 1990 and 2002 of less than or equal to 2 percent.[18] Annual CPI inflation was less than 2 percent 35 percent of the time, and inflation was less than or equal to 1 percent 13 percent of the time.[19] Among emerging-market economies, Argentina, China, Hong Kong, Singapore, and Taiwan have recorded negative annual CPI inflation rates over the past several years. Taking account of measurement biases in CPIs, which are generally estimated in the range

17. A similar focus on the price level in the same country that Bernanke was writing about (Japan) can be found in Krugman (1998) and Svensson (2001b).

18. Greece and Portugal were the exceptions. The 23 industrial countries include Luxembourg, although Consensus Economics does not include this country in its publications.

19. Twelve of the countries recorded annual CPI inflation rates of less than or equal to 1 percent. Three countries recorded six years of inflation less than zero; Japan accounted for four years, and New Zealand and Sweden accounted for the other two.

of half to one percentage point per year (IMF 2003b, 7), it can be said that in recent years there was a substantial amount of statistical deflation.[20]

Data from Consensus Economics provide an impressive picture of the shortfalls in inflation expectations in recent years, a factor relevant to the adverse effects of deflation on balance sheets and the ability of debtors to repay their obligations. For the 20 industrial countries with average CPI inflation rates of less than 5 percent during the 1990–2001 period, recorded inflation rates fall short of one-year-ahead forecasts of inflation by about a quarter of a percentage point on average.[21] The average forecast error was negative 0.4 of a percentage point or more for five countries not including Japan.[22] Looking at two-year-ahead inflation forecasts, the picture is even more dramatic. For all countries with average annual inflation rates of less than 5 percent, the average shortfall of actual inflation from expected inflation was 0.7 of a percentage point, and in four countries actual inflation fell short of expected inflation by more than one percentage point on average over the 12 years.[23]

This phenomenon of actual inflation falling short of expected inflation for countries with low average inflation rates during the 1990–2001 period was not confined to the industrial countries. Nine emerging-market economies had average annual inflation rates of less than 5 percent for the period, and the average shortfall of one-year-ahead forecasts was 1.1 percentage points and the average shortfall of two-year-ahead forecasts was 1.3 percentage points.[24]

To put these data in perspective, on a cumulative basis a sustained deviation between expected and actual inflation of half a percentage point

---

20. See Lebow and Rudd (2003) for an updated estimate of the measurement bias in the US CPI of 0.9 percent with an error band of 0.3 to 1.4 percent despite recent changes in the index.

21. The forecasts for inflation and growth from *Consensus Forecasts* were for February of each year, and the forecasts for that year were treated as one-year-ahead forecasts, and the forecasts for the following year as two-year-ahead forecasts. Among the industrial countries, the list of countries with average inflation rates below 5 percent excludes Greece and Portugal, whose average inflation rates for the period were above 5 percent, and Luxembourg.

22. The five are Australia, Denmark, Finland, Norway, and Sweden. The average forecast error for Japan was plus 0.2. See appendix table A.4.

23. The four were Australia, Finland, Norway, and Sweden. The shortfall for Japan was 0.5 percent. With respect to the growth forecasts, the average error in the one-year-ahead forecasts was 0.24 for the industrial countries and negative 0.03 percent for the two-year-ahead forecasts. See appendix table A.6.

24. The nine are Bangladesh, Hong Kong, Malaysia, Morocco, Panama, Saudi Arabia, Singapore, Taiwan, and Thailand. *Consensus Forecasts* does not have inflation forecasts for some countries for the entire period, and none are available for Morocco, which is excluded from the average. See appendix table A.5. With respect to the growth forecasts, the average error in the one-year-ahead forecasts was negative 0.27 and negative 0.78 in the two-year-ahead forecasts. See appendix table A.7. See Schellekens (2003) for an analysis of the origins of Hong Kong's deflation and the limited policy instruments it has to address the phenomenon, given its rigid monetary policy regime.

implies an unexpected increase in real interest and principal payments of 6 percent over 12 years.

The recent experience of Japan and a few other countries, reinforced by the data just presented, suggests that deflation is potentially a much bigger economic policy problem than many thought a decade ago. There is an active debate in many countries about whether central banks can combat deflation. In the case of the United States, the official answer from the Federal Reserve is positive (Bernanke 2002b, Greenspan 2002b, and Ferguson 2003), but that has not meant that the issue has not come up at FOMC meetings (FOMC 2002).[25]

However, it is also generally accepted that the power of the conventional monetary policy operating through the real interest rate channel is greatly reduced not only when the nominal short-term interest rate reaches zero and inflation is negative but also as the nominal short-term interest rate approaches zero and inflation is very low.[26] Moreover, the effectiveness of monetary policy operating through the expectations channel is also reduced; economic agents have less confidence in nonconventional approaches being fully effective in implementing policy because of the lack of experience with such approaches. Thus, monetary policy has asymmetrical effects at low levels of inflation—it is better able to limit or bring down increases in the price level than to contain or reverse decreases in the price level.[27]

Such concerns support the adoption of inflation targeting as a framework for the conduct of monetary policy, although no central bank to date has adopted inflation targeting when its economy was recording negative inflation. Inflation targeting as a framework for monetary policy involves setting either a target point or range for inflation. In choosing that target, and operating with it, the authorities can reasonably be expected to consider the possibility of deflation as well as inflation.[28] Moreover, inflation

---

25. See Clouse et al. (2000) for a discussion of the tools available to central banks facing a zero interest rate constraint. See also Johnson, Small, and Tryon (1999) on the role of monetary policy in achieving and sustaining price stability. See Bryant (2000) for a broader treatment of the challenge to monetary policy of the zero interest rate constraint.

26. Some of these issues are also addressed, in the context of tools to conduct open-market operations without outstanding government debt, in Federal Reserve System (2002).

27. These issues are discussed in greater detail in chapter 4 in the context of inflation targeting for Japan.

28. The Bank of Canada has been a strong and early supporter of this view. Governor Gordon Thiessen (1998, 11), speaking well before the recent upsurge of attention to deflation about the Canadian experience with inflation targeting, said, "I would contend that inflation and deflation are equally to be avoided. Both imply increased uncertainty for economic agents, and both have negative implications for economic performance. That is why the Bank [of Canada] treats the risk of moving above the top or below the bottom of the [1 to 3 percent] range with equal concern." On the other hand, I have heard one prominent European central banker ask Thiessen if inflation can really be too low!

targeting as a monetary policy framework encourages, even if it does not require, a forward-looking orientation to the implementation of monetary policy leading to a more proactive rather than reactive policy posture, consistent with the asymmetric demands on policy at low levels of inflation.

Summary

The intellectual origins of inflation targeting as a framework for the conduct and evaluation of monetary policy can be found in a number of strands of experience, analysis, and debate over the past several decades. The most important strand has been the search for a better anchor for monetary policy under conditions in which intermediate targets have proved unreliable, exchange rate–based regimes have proved to be brittle, and increased transparency about policy intentions has received growing analytical and political support.

The choice of inflation as a target or anchor for policy, in turn, has received substantial support from the vast literature on the negative influence of high inflation on growth, despite the fact that there is less than full agreement on the channels of that influence, on whether some inflation is better than no inflation, and on the level of inflation at which the negative effects of inflation on growth kick in. The empirical literature of the 1980s and 1990s on inflation and growth derives, in part, from an older literature on the costs of inflation as well as from political dissatisfaction with inflation, which surfaced first in the industrial countries in the late 1970s and early 1980s.

The emergence of inflation targeting as an attractive framework for monetary policy has also been supported by analytical work on the performance of alternative monetary policy regimes and explorations of the implications of different rules to guide monetary policies; this work has provided some of the theoretical underpinnings to inflation targeting and has guided the practical implementation of the framework. The apparent successful implementation of inflation targeting by a growing number of countries was also aided over the past decade by a general decline in inflation not only among industrial countries—where the decline began two decades ago—but also among nonindustrial countries where average inflation has been close to or in single digits for more than five years.

The most recent development that has increased the attraction of inflation targeting has been the emergence of the specter of deflation, particularly in Japan but also in debates about macroeconomic policies, performance, and prospects in many other countries. As discussed in chapter 3, increased recognition of the higher probability and challenges of deflation has recently led to greater attention to the lower bound associated with inflation-targeting frameworks, replacing—and to some extent relaxing—the traditional focus on the upper bound.

Choosing an Inflation-Targeting Framework

The preceding discussion focused rather abstractly on the major strands of analysis and experience over the past 50 years that have contributed to the emergence of inflation targeting as a framework for the conduct and evaluation of monetary policy and its adoption by more than a score of countries. The actual choice of inflation targeting as a framework by the authorities of each of the 22 countries that have done so, of course, was itself a policy decision. In making their choices, policymakers were influenced at least in part and, no doubt, in differing degrees by the six strands of analysis and experience.

Other factors such as recent economic performance, conditions, structure, and institutions also influenced the choice. For example, authorities in a country experiencing rapid economic growth might be very satisfied with the economy's performance and, therefore, less inclined to switch to inflation targeting as its monetary policy framework, but in a country experiencing rapid inflation, the authorities might be more likely to do so, as Manfred Neumann and Jürgen von Hagen (2002) assert. In a relatively open economy or one with a history of fiscal imbalances, the authorities might be less likely to choose inflation targeting because they might be concerned that they would be unable to meet the inflation target. In an economy with a floating exchange rate or in which the central bank is already substantially autonomous, the authorities might think their economy would be better positioned institutionally to adopt inflation targeting.

Yifan Hu has investigated these issues empirically.[29] She asked three principal questions: first, are there factors (conditions, structures, institutions) that have been systematically related to decisions by individual countries to switch to inflation targeting as their framework for monetary policy? Second, what is the direction or sign of any such influences? Third, are any of the factors particularly prominent? Given the relatively small number of choices of inflation targeting as a monetary framework, including the fact that several occurred after the end of the period for which data were collected—1980 to 2000—it would be unreasonable to expect very robust results from this analysis.[30]

For the reader who would prefer to skip the more comprehensive discussion of the analysis that follows, the results are summarized here. A number of factors were found to be systematically associated with the choice of inflation targeting. The influence of real growth has been nega-

---

29. Yifan Hu began this analysis when she was working with me as a research assistant. To a degree it was a collaborative effort. She completed the work as part of her Ph.D. dissertation with my support and close cooperation. See Hu (2003a and 2003b) for a detailed description of her work, including the sources and definitions for the various data series.

30. Two countries—Peru and the Philippines—adopted inflation targeting after mid-2001, and their decisions to adopt inflation targeting were not captured in this analysis.

tive, which is consistent with the view that one motivation for the adoption of inflation targeting is to improve overall economic performance; in other words, the better a country's growth rate, the less likely it is to adopt inflation targeting to further improve its performance. A similar interpretation, with the opposite sign, can be made about the (positive) influence of high real short-term interest rates on the choice of inflation targeting. However, higher inflation was negatively associated with that choice, contrary to the general view of inflation targeting as a mechanism to achieve disinflation rather than to maintain low inflation.

An expected result was that external financial crises, or exchange rate pressures, were positively associated with the choice of inflation targeting. The only structural factor that stood out in the results was the absence of fiscal pressures, which was interpreted as a factor contributing to the potential success of inflation targeting. The lack of significance of openness to trade or terms-of-trade variability is informative in light of the view of some, but not all, analysts that economies with these structural features should avoid inflation targeting because they are likely to undermine the capacity of the authorities to control inflation with any precision.

To conduct the analysis, a dataset was assembled for 68 countries on various aspects of their economic performance, structural characteristics, and economic institutions.[31] To investigate the factors related to the choice of inflation targeting, the larger dataset was reduced in size and coverage to the 17 independent variables listed in table 2.4: seven variables for economic conditions or recent performance (C), eight variables for each economy's economic structure (S), and two variables for its economic institutions (I).[32] Logit regressions were run with a 1–0 variable as the dependent variable taking on the value 1 in the year in which inflation targeting was adopted.[33]

---

31. Data were collected for each of the 68 economies listed in appendix table A.1, with the exception of Hong Kong and Taiwan. The 68 economies included 22 inflation targeters (9 industrial and 13 nonindustrial) and 46 nontargeters (13 industrial and 33 nonindustrial) and included 22 industrial and 46 nonindustrial economies.

32. The classification of some of the variables is somewhat arbitrary because several of them—for example, a country's fiscal position—could be placed in more than one category. The categories were most useful in thinking about the expected signs of the coefficients.

33. See table 2.3 for the list of inflation-targeting countries and the dates of their adoption of inflation targeting. Note that for three countries (Chile, Israel, and Mexico) two dates appear; the implications of both the dates were explored. (For some other countries—Colombia, Peru, and the Philippines—one can find earlier dates for the adoption of inflation targeting than those shown in table 2.3. However, it was judged that not enough of the framework was in place to justify the use of those earlier dates.) When inflation targeting was adopted in the second half of a year, that year was taken as the year of adoption; when inflation targeting was adopted in the first half of a year, the year before was taken as the relevant year. Once a country adopted inflation targeting, it was dropped out of the sample. Note that our procedure captured in the regressions the choice of inflation targeting by Hungary, Iceland, and Norway in the first half of 2001, but not for the choices of Peru and the Philippines in early 2002.

Table 2.4 Factors associated with a country's choice of inflation targeting

Independent variable	Type of variable	Expected sign	Moving average data			Annual data		
			Full	Partial	Final	Full	Partial	Final
Real GDP growth	C	–	-0.1882 (0.129)	-0.2064* (0.108)	-0.1978** (0.089)	-0.0988 (0.09)	-0.1066** (0.052)	-0.0987** (0.042)
Real GDP growth variability	C	+	-0.0967 (0.075)			-0.1411 (0.124)		
Real GDP gap	C	–	-0.0705 (0.065)			-0.0584 (0.07)		
Inflation rate	C	+	-0.0269 (0.033)	-0.0477* (0.025)	-0.0482*** (0.018)	0.0136** (0.007)	-0.0628 (0.039)	-0.0634** (0.031)
Nominal interest rate	C	+	-0.0100 (0.007)			-0.0501 (0.041)		
Real interest rate	C	+	0.1609*** (0.059)	0.0009* (0.001)	0.0009** (0.0004)	0.1777*** (0.061)	0.0011 (0.001)	0.0011** (0.001)
Foreign exchange pressure	C	+	1.0283* (0.573)	0.8818* (0.492)	0.9077** (0.492)	0.8382 (0.549)	0.8542* (0.492)	0.9138* (0.49)
REER variability	S	?	-0.0028 (0.015)			0.0046 (0.016)		
NEER variability	S	?	-0.0132 (0.014)			-0.0123 (0.012)		
Fiscal position	S	+	0.185** (0.091)	0.1048** (0.043)	0.0987** (0.042)	0.0232 (0.075)	0.0019 (0.058)	

		Sign should be	(1)	(2)	(3)	(4)	(5)	(6)
Current account position	S	+	−0.1271 (0.079)			−0.0383 (0.095)		
Trade openness	S	−	0.0020 (0.005)			0.0017 (0.005)		
Terms-of-trade variability	S	−	−0.0171 (0.063)			−0.0393 (0.073)		
External debt	S	?	−0.0235* (0.012)			−0.0156** (0.008)		
Financial depth	S	+	0.0087 (0.009)			0.0052 (0.008)		
Central bank autonomy	I	+	0.4811 (0.886)	0.1274 (0.705)		0.2770 (0.85)	0.1615 (0.701)	
Floating exchange rate (de facto)	I	+	0.2497 (0.538)	0.6713 (0.505)		0.4498 (0.569)	0.6145 (0.502)	
Constant			−2.5533	−2.9416	−2.7046	−3.0927	−3.4298	−3.2248
Number of observations			1008	1015	1017	994	999	1022
Pseudo R-squared			0.19	0.10	0.09	0.15	0.08	0.07

? = uncertain what sign should be
NEER = nominal effective exchange rate
REER = real effective exchange rate

Notes: The dependent variable is inflation targeting (1 = IT; 0 = non-IT).
*, **, and *** represent rejecting the null hypothesis of no significance at levels of 10 percent, 5 percent, and 1 percent, respectively. Standard errors in parentheses.

The regression results are presented in table 2.4. The use of three-year moving averages of the data on some of the independent variables for economic conditions and structure generated a better overall fit than the exclusive use of annual data. This finding is consistent with the view that the authorities in general did not lurch into adopting inflation targeting, but rather the decision was based on experience as well as, perhaps, certain pressures for change.

In the results using moving-average data, nine of the 14 coefficients had the expected signs. (For three of the 17 variables, Hu and I could not convince ourselves what the expected sign should be.) In the results using annual data, 10 of the 14 coefficients had the expected signs, but the overall fit was less good, based on the pseudo R-squared. Moreover, the final regressions, which included only those variables whose coefficients were statistically significant, involved five independent variables in the regression using moving-average data and only four in the regression using annual data. These results support the view that one can identify factors that are systematically associated with the choice of inflation targeting as a monetary policy framework.

A number of interesting points emerge from the results presented in table 2.4. Although the coefficient on real GDP growth had the expected sign (negative), and it was significant in the final regression, the coefficient on the variability of real GDP growth did not have the expected sign (positive). Our prior was that more growth variability would have been associated with dissatisfaction with macroeconomic performance, which would contribute positively to the choice of inflation targeting.

Higher inflation was also expected to be associated positively with the choice of inflation targeting; the coefficient on that variable had the expected sign in the full regression using annual data, but the sign was negative for the full regression using moving-average data. Moreover, in the final regressions the coefficient was not only negative but also statistically significant. It would appear that the adoption of inflation targeting has not been associated with high levels of inflation but quite the reverse.[34]

Higher levels of short-term nominal and real interest rates again were anticipated to be associated with dissatisfaction with economic performance and, therefore, might contribute positively to the choice of inflation targeting. This was not the case for nominal interest rates, where the coef-

---

34. This is contrary to the assertion of Neumann and von Hagen (2002) that the motivation to adopt inflation targeting is to reduce inflation and also to the finding of Mishkin and Schmidt-Hebbel (2002) that the adoption of inflation targeting is more likely when a country initially has a high level of inflation. The difference in our results, from those of Mishkin and Schmidt-Hebbel, may reflect our larger sample of both inflation targeters and nontargeters.

ficients in the full regressions had negative signs. But it was the case for real interest rates, and the coefficients were significant in the final regressions.[35]

The dummy variable that was employed for periods of foreign exchange pressure or crisis was expected to be associated positively with the choice of inflation targeting; that turned out to be the case.[36] The coefficient has the right sign and was marginally significant in the final regressions. The sensitivity of the results to the use of the later dates for the choice of inflation targeting by Chile, Israel, and Mexico was tested, and this coefficient became insignificant.[37]

With respect to the variables classified as structural, it was hypothesized that countries with strong fiscal positions might be more inclined to adopt inflation targeting because their authorities might reason that they would be better placed to achieve their inflation objective in the absence of fiscal dominance. (See the discussion in chapter 3 of initial conditions for successful inflation targeting.) Regression results supported this association, and the coefficient was significant in the case of the regression using moving-average data.[38]

The same reasoning was expected to apply to countries with strong current account positions. However, the coefficient on this variable had the wrong sign in the full regressions and was never statistically significant.

Both greater trade openness (indexed by the ratio of exports plus imports to GDP) and terms-of-trade variability were expected to be associated negatively with the adoption of inflation targeting.[39] But the coefficients on the first variable had a positive sign, and those on the second had a negative sign, but neither was significant.

Hu and I were uncertain what to expect with respect to the coefficients on the variability of nominal or real effective exchange rates and the ratio

---

35. Carare and Stone (2003) examine the choice of inflation targeting from the standpoint of distinguishing among their categories of full-fledged, eclectic, and lite targeters (see footnote 15). They argue that higher real interest rates would be negatively associated with inflation targeting.

36. The variable was based on the approach found in Kamin, Schindler, and Samuel (2001) that combines information on changes in international reserves with changes in exchange rates. However, their approach was applied to a larger group of countries.

37. A similar robustness test in which observations were eliminated for countries when their annual inflation rates were above 50 percent did not affect the results, except that the coefficient on the variable for fiscal position retained the correct sign but was no longer (but narrowly not) significantly different from zero at the 10 percent level.

38. This is broadly consistent with the Mishkin and Schmidt-Hebbel (2002) results for a much smaller sample of countries.

39. A different interpretation can be found in Calvo and Mishkin (2003). They argue that greater openness to trade reduces the vulnerability of emerging-market economies to external disturbances. Consequently such countries are better situated to successfully adopt inflation targeting along with a floating exchange rate regime.

of external debt to GDP. For the first two variables, the coefficients took on different signs depending on whether annual or moving-average data were used, but they were not statistically significant. In the case of external debt, the coefficient was negative and significant in the full regression. The variable for external debt was not included in the final regressions because of the absence of support from the coefficient on this variable for the external balance, because we did not have a good story for how this variable might affect the decision, and because the quality of the data used to measure external debt for both industrial and nonindustrial countries was questionable.

Financial depth, proxied by the ratio of M2 to GDP, turned out to have the anticipated (positive) sign, reflecting, as hypothesized, a greater capacity to implement effectively a more proactive monetary policy, but it was not statistically significant.

Turning to the two institutional variables, the coefficient on the dummy variable for countries with central banks with greater autonomy had the expected positive signs, consistent with the view that such a central bank would be better able to implement inflation targeting successfully, but it was not statistically significant.[40] The coefficient on the dummy variable for a floating exchange rate regime (using an index of the de facto regime) also had the expected positive signs, consistent with the view that inflation targeting is more compatible with a floating exchange rate, but it was not significant.[41]

Summary

Taken as a whole, the above analysis of the factors contributing to the choice of inflation targeting as a monetary policy framework is informative. It suggests that a number of economic, structural, and institutional factors are systematically and generally sensibly associated with such

---

40. The proxy dummy variable was used for central bank autonomy—drawing upon the work of Kuttner and Posen (2001)—not central bank independence, either instrument or goal independence. See the debate on the role of these two conceptually different variables in choosing a monetary framework in Baltensperger, Fischer, and Jordan (2002), Gerlach (1999), and Mishkin and Schmidt-Hebbel (2002). See also Cukierman, Miller, and Neyapti (2001) on the effect of central bank independence interacting with other variables on the liberalization of transition economies and inflation control.

41. When Yifan Hu (2003a and 2003b) ran the regressions using a dummy variable derived from an index of countries' de jure exchange rate regimes, floating had the wrong sign but was still insignificant. Moreover, when the later dates for the choice of inflation targeting were used, which eliminated the significance of the coefficient on exchange rate pressure (crisis), the coefficient on the variable for floating (de facto) became significant, consistent with the longer-run compatibility of inflation targeting with floating. Otherwise the results were unaffected by the use of the later dates of adoption of inflation targeting.

choices. Most of the coefficients had the expected signs, including most of the significant coefficients.[42]

The major exception was the coefficient on inflation, which had an unexpected (negative) sign that was quite significant. However, this result does tell us something: most countries have not adopted inflation targeting principally to produce substantial disinflation; they have done so either to maintain low inflation rates or, in some cases, to bring about further convergence of inflation to low rates. This point is discussed further in chapter 3.

Among the other factors that appear to have been strongly and systematically related to the choice of inflation targeting are high real growth rates; the negative coefficient on this variable is consistent with the view that one motivation for the adoption of inflation targeting was to improve overall economic performance. The same can be said about the (positive) influence of high short-term real interest rates.

An expected result was that foreign exchange pressures or crises were positively associated with the choice of inflation targeting. Similarly it was no surprise that the significance of the coefficient on this variable was sensitive to the date used for the adoption of inflation targeting. The result that de facto floating was positively and significantly related to the choice of inflation targeting when the later adoption dates were used is also broadly consistent with the finding of a reduced influence of exchange rate crises; by the later dates, the three countries with alternative dates had all adopted floating exchange rates.

The only structural factor that stands out in these results is the absence of fiscal pressures, which we view as a factor contributing to the success of inflation targeting. The lack of significance of trade openness or terms-of-trade variability is informative in light of the view of some, but not all, analysts that economies with such structural features should avoid inflation targeting because they are unlikely to be successful in controlling inflation.

---

42. Comparing these results with those in Carare and Stone (2003), which are not strictly comparable, a stronger positive relationship was found with a country's fiscal position and level of real interest rates (not included in the Carare and Stone empirical tests) and less of a relationship with financial depth, which is associated with the level of actual inflation, and government financing of the central bank. Government financing of the central bank is one element of central bank autonomy that was not found to be significant in the choice of inflation targeting, though the coefficient had the expected sign.

3

Inflation Targeting in Practice

Inflation targeting is an evolving framework for the conduct and evaluation of monetary policy. So far, inflation-targeting countries have been applying the framework differently, based on their central banks' mandate,
macroeconomic and financial conditions, and institutional capacity. There
is no agreed set of necessary preconditions that countries must satisfy to
ensure success when adopting the framework. There is considerable experimentation, and countries are learning by doing. One consequence is
that the list of potential targeters is either very long or very short. In addition, the effects of inflation targeting on economic performance—not
only inflation but also growth and their variability—are under dispute.
This chapter evaluates inflation targeting as it has been, is being, and
might be practiced in the world economy.

The first section considers whether and to what extent countries need
to satisfy certain preconditions before adopting inflation targeting, and in
that context, arguments of skeptics are summarized. I conclude that
inflation-targeting countries should be serious about wanting to achieve
and maintain low inflation rates, and their fiscal position should not
threaten macroeconomic stability. Beyond this, the institutional and environmental elements that are often identified as preconditions for inflation
targeting—financial system stability, central bank independence, and deep
knowledge about the monetary transmission mechanism—should be
viewed as desirable, not essential.

The next section reviews the inflation-targeting frameworks of the 22
practitioners. An inflation targeter's mandate may be somewhat vague.
The numerical target sometimes is fuzzy as well. More often than not, the

time frame for returning to the target is unspecified, and transparency and accountability devices are both varied and not unique to inflation-targeting frameworks.

Four categories of actual or potential inflation-targeting countries are distinguished in the third section, and the inflation and growth experience of the 22 practicing inflation targeters and 46 potential inflation targeters is briefly reviewed. There are many more realistic potential inflation targeters than some might think, even based on a strict interpretation of favorable conditions for inflation targeting—an inflation rate of less than 10 percent.

The last section presents the results of investigations that offer a perspective on a number of the arguments both for and against inflation targeting. The results provide only limited support for the view of those skeptics who argue that the circumstances of developing countries—more open to trade and more vulnerable to external financial disturbances, buffeted by more hostile external environments—dictate that they are less likely to be able to implement inflation targeting successfully because they are less likely to be able or willing to control inflation or its variability. The results also provide some support for the view that on average, inflation targeting has been associated with an improvement in overall economic performance.

Necessary Preconditions

The emergence of inflation targeting as a framework for the conduct and evaluation of monetary policy has been accompanied by considerable doctrinal debate about preconditions that a country should satisfy before adopting inflation targeting. It is easy to set out a long list of elements that are desirable, if not required, for an inflation-targeting framework to be reasonably successful.[1] Such a list often includes:

---

1. A lot of this work has come directly or indirectly from the staff of the International Monetary Fund (IMF) and is broadly indicative of the evolving position of that institution toward inflation targeting. See, for example, Schaechter et al. (2000), IMF (2001)—which draws in part on Schaechter et al. (2000)—and more recent syntheses by Carare et al. (2002) and Khan (2003). Alina Carare and Mark Stone (2003) and Stone (2003b) stress the need for potential inflation targeters that already have floating exchange rates and, on their terms, are practicing "inflation targeting lite" to lay the institutional groundwork carefully before becoming full-fledged inflation targeters. They ignore the fact that a number of industrial countries (including Australia and Canada) moved from "eclectic inflation targeting" to full-fledged inflation targeting. They undervalue the potential for countries (for example, Brazil) to move simultaneously from a fixed exchange rate to floating and (full-fledged) inflation targeting. (See also Berg et al. 2003.) The IMF's conference volume on the statistical implications of in-

- the central bank's mandate, its instrument autonomy, and mechanisms for ensuring its accountability;
- macroeconomic stability comprising the country's fiscal and external positions and low inflation;
- financial system stability and a well-developed financial market; and
- institutional elements such as an understanding of the monetary transmission process, a capacity to forecast inflation, the subordination of exchange rate objectives, and adequate support from and coordination with fiscal and debt management policies.

No doubt, an inflation-targeting framework supported to a high degree by all these elements is likely to be more successful than one without them. A few of these factors (or proxies for them)—in particular, a country's fiscal position—showed up in the Hu (2003a, 2003b) results on countries' choice of inflation targeting as a monetary policy framework. However, others were not significant—financial depth, terms-of-trade variability, central bank autonomy, and floating exchange rates—or had the wrong signs as with trade openness. To be sure, some observers stress that their lists of "preconditions" are not requirements and can be thought of as part of "full-fledged" inflation targeting that follows a transitional period. Moreover, generally these preconditions are equally desirable for the successful implementation of any monetary policy framework. Nevertheless, tension exists between any list of desirable preconditions for inflation targeting and a more pragmatic approach that embraces a good deal of learning by doing.

Such a pragmatic approach is implied by Alejandro Werner (2002, 3), "Inflation targeting does not presuppose anything new given that in a world of floating exchange rates and unstable relationships between monetary aggregates and prices, the only alternative is forward looking monetary policy, which is the way policy is conducted by inflation targeters and non-inflation targeters alike. Therefore, the strengths of inflation targeting as a monetary policy rest on establishing a transparent framework for the conduct of monetary policy that is useful as a marketing device, a communication tool and a mechanism of accountability to the public at large." Werner considers the experience of Mexico and other Latin Amer-

---

flation targeting—including the transparency elements of the framework—was premised on the view that inflation targeting imposes a high degree of discipline on central banks and national statistical offices (Carson, Enoch, and Dziobek 2002). See also Mishkin (1999) and (2000a), Mishkin and Savastano (2001), Eichengreen (2001), and Eichengreen et al. (1999) who tend to share the view that inflation targeting is a demanding framework for monetary policy. Christopher Sims (2003) provides a theoretical argument why high-inflation countries that might benefit most from inflation targeting, via reduced inflation, should not adopt the framework because they lack the supporting fiscal discipline and central bank independence.

ican countries that have adopted inflation targeting. He points to the past failed policies that generated high inflation and hyperinflation in an environment of fiscal mismanagement, to balance-of-payment and financial crises, and to failed attempts to maintain fixed exchange rates while fully participating in the global capital markets, all of which provide incentives to adopt resilient supporting elements. Let's consider next the four desirable elements identified earlier.

Central Bank Mandate

By definition, as illustrated in Werner's quotation, if a country chooses inflation targeting as its framework of monetary policy, that choice involves a number or a numerical range as the target for inflation. Both the government and the central bank should publicize the reasons for choosing both framework and target. It is helpful but far from essential that the central bank's mandate be either explicitly or exclusively focused on price stability. The central bank should have the technical capacity to achieve its objective without substantial outside interference, which normally translates into a substantial degree of instrument autonomy, or insulation, if not full independence, but may also imply something about macroeconomic stability. Finally, the framework should include an approach for ongoing review of whether the inflation target will be or has been met.

It is unnecessary and undesirable to be narrowly prescriptive about the precise content of any of these aspects of an inflation-targeting framework. It is unnecessary because the choice of the framework implies that each of these aspects somehow will be covered. It is undesirable because one of the strengths of inflation targeting as a framework for the conduct and evaluation of policy is that it can be flexibly applied.

Macroeconomic Stability

The success of any monetary policy framework is likely to be adversely affected if the country in question has an unsustainable fiscal situation, is vulnerable to external financial crises, or has a high initial inflation rate. The question is the extent to which a country should address such areas before adopting inflation targeting as its monetary framework, in particular compared with any other framework.

With respect to a country's fiscal position—the most important area— the argument is that if the government cannot finance its operations in the market and requires uncertain but substantial amounts of direct central bank financing, including revenues from seigniorage, to meet its domestic obligations, then it is risky for the country to adopt inflation targeting as its monetary policy framework.[2] The reason is that in such an environment—often referred to as fiscal dominance—a country's fiscal requirements rather than other objectives are likely to determine and dominate the central bank's monetary operations. If those needs force too expansionary a monetary policy on the central bank, because the central bank is constrained to finance an excessively large fiscal deficit, the inflation target will be more difficult to achieve.

More accurately, the fiscal policy or the framework for fiscal policy, and not monetary policy or the framework for monetary policy, would be the cause for missing the inflation target. Moreover, any monetary policy framework, or at least any framework that is intended to achieve a reasonable degree of macroeconomic stability, is not likely to deliver under such circumstances. Thus, if any country expects monetary policy to contribute to macroeconomic stability, it should first make sure that the fiscal situation is reasonably under control. Once that has been achieved on a sustained basis, nothing in inflation targeting as a monetary policy framework would dictate greater fiscal discipline than any other monetary policy framework.[3]

It also can be argued that the discretionary element in the constrained discretion of inflation targeting on the margin means that the monetary framework exerts less fiscal discipline than a more rigid framework. However, Argentina's recent fiscal failures under a rigid monetary framework offer a real-world counterexample. In practice, as Jeffrey Amato and Stefan Gerlach (2002) point out, many countries had rather weak fiscal positions on the eve of their adoption of inflation targeting. Nevertheless, as found in chapter 2 using moving-average data, a strong fiscal position was significant to the choice of inflation targeting.

When it comes to the country's external position and its vulnerability to external financial crises, any requirement that a country should be crisis-proof before adopting inflation targeting is much more debatable. A number of countries have adopted inflation targeting during or in the aftermath of a financial crisis, including those in Western Europe (Finland, Spain, Sweden, and the United Kingdom), Central Europe (the Czech Republic), East Asia (Korea and Thailand), and Latin America (Brazil and, arguably, Mexico). To the extent that inflation targeting, accompanied by a reasonably responsible fiscal policy, contributes to macroeconomic sta-

---

2. Eichengreen and Taylor (2003) extend the argument with respect to the fiscal preconditions for inflation targeting to an absence of "fiscal dominance mark II" with respect to the maturity structure of the stock of government debt, that is, lowering rollover risks and potential crises.

3. Yan Sun (2003) debunks the related notion that more fiscal discipline is induced by fixed than by floating exchange rates. Since the latter type of regime is generally associated with inflation targeting, her finding supports the proposition in the text.

bility, a country's vulnerability to external or internal financial crises already would be reduced. If that vulnerability is to be reduced in advance, the question is what type of monetary policy framework is more likely to achieve that result during the transition period.[4] An alternative view of inflation targeting is that it is an element that can improve economic performance including through stimulating ongoing institutional reform.

The potential requirement that a country have low inflation before adopting an inflation-targeting framework would again appear to put the cart before the horse. In fairness, those who have advanced this view (Carare et al. 2002) define low inflation as less than 25 percent per year and point out correctly that no country has adopted inflation targeting when its inflation at the time was above that rate.[5] Confirming this bias in practice, as seen in chapter 2, high inflation to date is negatively associated with the choice of inflation targeting as a monetary framework. However, the question remains whether it would be a mistake for a country to adopt inflation targeting when the current rate is above, say, 30 percent. If so, why, what is the alternative, and why might it be expected to produce better overall macroeconomic results?

Financial System Stability

With respect to financial system stability, the argument is that if the banking system is unsound or fragile, financial institutions have to turn frequently and on a large scale to the central bank for liquidity injections, and the institutions are likely to be so weak that their borrowers and their balance sheets cannot withstand the increases in interest rates that would be associated with the central bank mopping up in the market the liquidity that has been provided at the discount window, assuming the central bank has the technical capacity to do so. According to this argument, in such circumstances, the central bank will find it difficult to achieve its inflation objective, and its credibility will be undermined (Khan 2003). A related argument is that if the cost of bailing out a weak banking system becomes a large fiscal burden, it may lead to fiscal dominance.

---

4. The results presented in chapter 2 suggest a significant negative association between a country's external debt as a percentage of nominal GDP and the choice of inflation targeting as its monetary policy regime. This result may be viewed as supportive of the position that external stability should be a precondition for the adoption of inflation targeting. However, external debt ratios taken alone are notoriously unreliable in predicting external financial crises because they are endogenous to the circumstances and policies of many countries. Countries with weak or strong policies may have low debt ratios for supply and demand reasons, respectively. On the other hand, high ratios of external debt may signal strong policies (the United States) or weak policies (Argentina), depending on the circumstances.

5. If one says Chile adopted inflation targeting in 1990 when its inflation rate was 26 percent, it is a marginal exception (see table 2.3).

Again, however, it is not clear why inflation targeting as a framework for the conduct of a monetary policy that is directed at achieving or maintaining macroeconomic stability is any more vulnerable than any other monetary framework to being undermined by actual or potential financial system instability. With reasonably effective monetary policy instruments, the central bank should be able to mop up through its other operations liquidity that has been advanced through its discount window operations. With these qualifications, one can insist too strongly that financial stability and a well-developed financial system are necessary preconditions for successful inflation targeting. Accidents happen. Any country can have a banking crisis—inflation targeters, like Australia, the Czech Republic, Korea, Sweden, and Spain, and nontargeters, like Japan, Indonesia, and the United States. A potential tension will remain between price stability and financial stability (Corrigan 2001), but that potential should not itself bar a country's adoption of inflation targeting. Perhaps for this reason, the argument about inflation targeting and financial system stability is often reversed and used against inflation targeting. Stone (2003a) and Borio and Lowe (2002) suggest that a narrow focus on inflation may prevent an inflation-targeting central bank from paying appropriate attention to financial system stability.

Similarly a well-developed financial market is a tremendous advantage in the execution of any monetary policy, especially one that is implemented via market-related operating targets, such as overnight interest rates, and instruments, such as open-market operations. This positive contribution is not unique to inflation targeting. Moreover, measures of the extent of financial market development are imprecise. In empirical work, one is forced to rely upon proxy indices of financial depth, such as the ratio of M2 to nominal GDP. As reported in chapter 2, a positive association exists between financial depth and the choice of inflation targeting, but it is not significant.

Supporting Institutions

With respect to the need for strong supporting institutions, the argument is that if the central bank does not have the institutional capacity to implement inflation targeting, it would be better off not trying. However, this statement holds for any respectable framework for monetary policy and is not necessary to demonstrate that inflation targeting is a superior framework. To the extent that this argument is a code for the need for operational independence of the central bank, at least de facto and preferably de jure, then the argument is that short-run political considerations or a lack of fiscal discipline or the condition of the financial system could constrain the central bank from using its policy instruments to achieve its inflation objective.

A slightly different institutional argument is that a monetary policy framework that embodies a simple guide for monetary policy—for example, a monetary aggregate or an exchange rate objective—is not as demanding to implement. Again, this proposition can be debated. On the one hand, if the central bank has a reasonably accurate understanding of the mechanisms by which its policy instruments affect inflation and the economy, such an "operation framework" (Khan 2003) helps in the successful achievement of an inflation target. On the other hand, the guidance such knowledge offers is not unique to inflation targeting. If the central bank has a monetary target, other than a narrow target for the rate of expansion of the liability side of its balance sheet, then the bank's achievement of that target is also enhanced if it understands how its policy instruments affect the demand and supply of money. Moreover, if the monetary target is a means to an end (i.e., only an intermediate target), and if its policy is to be successful, then, even in the case of targeting a narrow monetary aggregate, the central bank needs to have a reasonably accurate understanding of the mechanism that links the monetary target to its ultimate objectives. A similar argument would apply to an exchange rate target, with the added qualification that with an exchange rate target, the central bank runs the risk of running out of reserves or sacrificing growth for too long as a result of an external financial crisis, or both.[6]

Thus, greater knowledge of the economy or substantial institutional capacity (experience, organization, and human resources) to acquire that knowledge will help a central bank implement its policy and achieve its objective, in particular its ultimate objective, as long as it is technically and politically feasible, regardless of the framework the central bank employs. It also follows that the institution's skill at articulating its policy through various devices, such as inflation reports, enhances understanding of its policy, increases transparency, assists in accountability, and thereby contributes to the overall success of the policy. Moreover, the adoption of inflation targeting may help focus or refocus the central bank's priorities in the allocation of its financial and human resources, but that is one potential consequence or implication of the adoption of such a framework and not the same as a precondition for its successful adoption.

If a central bank targets future inflation, it is likely to be more effective if it has the tools to forecast inflation with some precision. On the other

---

6. A related argument is that inflation targeting is incompatible with a country's also having a rigid exchange rate target; it must subordinate its exchange rate objectives to its inflation objective. This view is supported by the observation that all inflation-targeting countries have either moderately flexible or floating exchange rates. In a few cases, they have or have had mixed regimes, but the rules of engagement or disengagement were reasonably clear. This is not the same as saying that an inflation-targeting country cannot or should not pay attention to the foreign exchange value of its currency and take account or even seek to anticipate movements in it. These issues are discussed in detail in chapter 5.

hand, a central bank could use actual inflation or surveys of expected inflation to guide its policy instruments and still have a reasonable chance of achieving its objective as long as it is able to formulate a procedure, essentially through trial and error, to calibrate changes in its instrument with progress toward achieving its inflation objective. In effect it would construct a reduced-form model through experience.[7] Given that inflation is a lagging indicator, it is certainly possible that output would be more volatile, at least initially, under inflation targeting and assuming the central bank is reasonably successful in achieving its inflation target. However, the more relevant question is whether output and inflation would be more volatile than under an alternative monetary policy framework. This is largely an empirical issue and is discussed later in this chapter.

What the Skeptics Say

Inflation targeting as a framework for the conduct and evaluation of monetary policy is not without its skeptics. Many but not all the arguments of the skeptics are based on a view that many countries that some might consider to be candidates for inflation targeting either do not or cannot meet what those skeptics see as the "stringent technical and institutional requirements for inflation targeting" (Eichengreen et al. 1999).[8] Some arguments focus on the potential unintended consequences of inflation targeting for the performance of the economy or for the policy process. Some other arguments can be viewed as philosophical. The views of the skeptics fall into three broad categories: inflation targeting is too soft, too hard, or won't work. "If [the targets were] handled flexibly, little would change, while stringent interpretation would imply an ability to fine-tune, with dubious results for credibility" (Michael Heise, "The Seductive Charm of Inflation Targets," *Financial Times*, July 1, 2003).

---

7. Several inflation-targeting central banks use inflation surveys, which is attractive in this connection, but the danger is that expectations may not be independent of the central bank's performance and reputation. For example, those surveyed may believe that the central bank will do whatever is necessary to hit its target and may project inflation accordingly. Once those expectations are disappointed, there is the opposite risk, as was Brazil's experience in the second half of 2002. For much of the year, inflation expectations were quite supportive of the view that the Banco Central do Brasil would be able to reach its inflation target for 2003—despite the substantial depreciation of the real in 2002—with only a cautious tightening of policy. When inflation expectations turned more bearish later in the year, the central bank found itself behind the expectations curve and was forced to raise the short-term (Selic) interest rate by 700 basis points in the fall of 2002.

8. A similar view can be found in Agénor (2002), who argues that nonindustrial countries may not have the institutions, the technical capacity, or the necessary data to have a reasonable chance of implementing inflation targeting successfully.

Inflation Targeting Is Too Soft

This view emphasizes the discretionary aspects of inflation targeting as a monetary policy framework (Kumhof 2002, Genberg 2001, Rich 2000 and 2001, and Swiss National Bank 1999). Not only does the inflation-targeting central bank have discretion about how close to come to the target, or where to aim within the target range, but also the underlying political economy provides scope for changes in targets, as has happened in many countries.[9] As a result, the strength of the target as an anchor for policy or for expectations about policy is weakened, either potentially or in practice.

A related argument is that the distaste for high inflation that now supports inflation targeting will eventually give way to a greater tolerance of inflation—the target will be raised, or repeated misses will be tolerated, and any credibility gains deriving from the conditioning of inflation expectations will be dissipated. Holders of these views—for example, the Swiss National Bank (see box 2.1)—tend to favor a monetary policy framework that is anchored in medium-term price stability, preferably with a numerical definition of the concept.

Inflation Targeting Is Too Rigid

This view emphasizes the constraining aspects of inflation targeting as a monetary policy framework. Some exponents of this viewpoint (e.g., Baltensperger, Fischer, and Jordan 2002) stress that a central bank that enjoys not only instrument independence but also goal independence—in the sense that the central bank can choose how best to satisfy its mandate (Debelle and Fischer 1994), which is expressed in words, not figures—should not welcome the restrictions associated with the articulation, with or without the cooperation and support of the rest of the government, of an inflation target.

From this perspective, monetary policy via the commitment to an inflation target risks becoming inappropriately and unnecessarily constrained by other economic considerations—for example, allowing inflation to depart for a time from a level that normally would be associated with price stability. A similar perspective has been advanced by those who argue that the authorities may say they have an inflation anchor but other objectives (exchange rates, wage rates, or financial system stability) will come into play and, in practice, override the achievement of the inflation objective.

---

9. New Zealand has had three target ranges since 1989—0 to 2, 0 to 3, and 1 to 3 percent, in that order.

Some of the arguments that have been advanced by Federal Reserve officials (FOMC 1995, Greenspan 2001, and Meyer 2001) fall in this category: an inflation-targeting framework would in practice constrain discretion inappropriately—technology or economic changes could make a particular statistical measure of inflation obsolete—or inflation targeting is too confining in terms of a need to make an ex ante commitment about the time horizon for returning to the target once it has been missed. Alice Rivlin (2002, 54) is a strong proponent of this view:

> I think an inflation target for the Federal Reserve is a bad idea, whose time has passed. Inflation targets may be useful for small open economies or developing countries in danger of hyperinflation, but not for big industrial economies such as our own. Keeping inflation under control should not be the only objective of the central bank. The ultimate objective is a higher standard of living for average people. Hence, the central bank ought to be trying to keep the economy on the highest sustainable growth path. Inflation matters only if it is high enough to threaten the sustainability of growth.

Some of the arguments that inflation targeting is too rigid rest on views about likely economic performance under such a framework. Growth would be unnecessarily restrained by efforts to hit the target, which some would argue is an issue about the level or breadth of the target, or the variability of growth would increase inappropriately and unnecessarily. Olivier Blanchard (2003) argues that the alignment of inflation and output objectives in the standard representation of a central bank's objective function is more a function of the "divine coincidence" embedded in the assumed theoretical structure than a reflection of economic reality. In economic reality, he argues, not all price disturbances (departures from an inflation target) should be treated the same. Blanchard's (straw?) man is clearly a strict inflation targeter pursuing an inflation target at the expense of the rate or variability of economic growth.

The final set of arguments concerns the semantics of the inflation-targeting regime. For example, Ben Friedman's (2001) view is that the description of the framework—mentioning only inflation and not real economic activity—may over time lead to an atrophy of concerns with growth and employment within the practicing central bank, even as it successfully strengthens the effectiveness of monetary policy via the expectations channel. He also points out the irony in such a situation—the way a central bank lowers inflation in the short run lowers growth, although the amount of growth sacrificed to achieve lower inflation may vary over time as well as depend on the monetary policy framework and its implementation. Thus, an inflation-targeting central bank creates a tension between what it says and what it does, undermining its valuable transparency. His viewpoint has a number of points in common with Rivlin's. Frederic Mishkin (2002a) argues that inflation targeting assists central banks in placing its concerns with output fluctuations in a more appropriate longer-term context. Moreover, inflation targeting does not prevent a central bank from presenting an output forecast, even if it is not a target (see also Mishkin 1998).

Inflation Targeting Won't Work

This view rests primarily on arguments sketched out earlier that the institutional and technical preconditions for many countries and their central banks to successfully implement an inflation-targeting framework are too demanding and not likely to be in place in very many countries today.

The proponents of this view also tend to stress that industrial and nonindustrial countries are fundamentally different. The latter group of countries, proponents argue, have histories of high inflation and macroeconomic instability, are more vulnerable to speculative attack, and are unable to view movements in exchange rates with the necessary degree of detachment to permit the attainment of an inflation target that has been set in advance; in other words, the inflation process is fundamentally different in these countries.

For these countries, or any countries where the demanding preconditions have not been or cannot be met, the argument is that the benefits of inflation targeting are limited. The framework is either too difficult to implement, or the institutional conditions are not in place; as a result, the central bank is unable to perform adequately, and the credibility bonus from inflation targeting via its influence on expectations cannot be achieved. The country might just as well wait until its inflation somehow is brought down to the low double digits, until it has the necessary supporting institutions in place, and until the central bank has acquired the necessary technical capabilities.

Summary of Preconditions

The goal of a country's inflation-targeting framework should be well defined and broadly supported, which may or may not involve a precise or narrow central bank mandate. The country's fiscal position should not be one of fiscal dominance; financial stability is certainly desirable but can be overstressed; and the central bank should be reasonably equipped and motivated to achieve its objective. The country should be serious about controlling inflation, but beyond that it is unwise and unjustified to be very prescriptive. I am not sympathetic to the view that there is a long list of preconditions that countries must satisfy before they consider adopting inflation targeting as their framework for the conduct and evaluation of monetary policy.

Jiri Jonas and Frederic Mishkin (2003, 5) argue sensibly with respect to the transition economies in Eastern Europe that have adopted inflation targeting that the appropriate test should not be perfect compliance with a set of preconditions but whether potential inflation targeters have "met these requirements to a sufficient degree to make inflation targeting feasible and useful." Once a country has adopted inflation targeting, it can work toward other supporting institutional improvements, and the transparency element of the framework can assist in this process. Gordon Thiessen (1998) stresses the positive contribution inflation targeting has made to decision making in the Bank of Canada after it adopted the framework.

In particular, the importance of institutional and technical preconditions for the success of inflation targeting is frequently exaggerated. To argue that industrial countries can successfully implement inflation targeting by drawing upon their histories, institutions, and technical know-how and that nonindustrial countries cannot is both arbitrary and arrogant.

Such arguments are arbitrary because no bright line separates the two groups of countries. One piece of evidence supporting such a view is that no two lists of industrial countries are identical. At a more fundamental level, institutions and histories of countries range continuously and intricately along many spectrums; establishing thresholds or cut-off points to separate the potential inflation-targeting sheep from the unqualified nontargeting goats is not a fruitful activity. Some who have attempted to do so can reasonably be criticized as being arrogant.[10]

Institutions, such as the International Monetary Fund (IMF)—whose staff has put forward many, but not all, such precautionary judgments—may be reasonably criticized as elitist, placing too much emphasis on credibility and too little on performance (Schaechter et al. 2000, IMF 2001, Carare et al. 2002, and Khan 2003). Such criticism is doubly justified when the institutions have nothing better to offer.[11] Having no framework for monetary policy or a framework that has little or nothing to contribute to overall economic performance does not enhance the credibility of the authorities. Exchange rate targets have been demonstrated to be dangerous to economic prosperity, monetary targets have been demonstrated to be unreliable, and monetary frameworks that involve multiple objectives do not offer much in the way of guidance for policymakers or the general public.

It may well be that for many countries and their central banks, there is no realistic alternative to an eclectic approach to monetary policy—in some cases such approaches have produced reasonable results—but the critics of inflation targeting need to be more honest in their criticisms and state more clearly what they are for as well as against. Moreover, there is

---

10. For a more balanced (and positive) view on the relevance of some of these preconditions, see Debelle (2001) and Amato and Gerlach (2002).

11. For example, Berg et al. (2003, 42) argue that in post-crisis situations, despite the counterexample of Brazil, "Investing the credibility of post-crisis institutions and policymakers in achievement of an inflation target was therefore seen as risky." The preference was to fall back on the old standby, a monetary target!

scant support for the view that countries that have adopted inflation targeting on average have fallen short in their overall macroeconomic performance (an issue addressed in the last section of this chapter), and none to date has abandoned the framework.

The Framework in Practice: Four Principal Elements

The four principal elements in the framework of inflation targeting for the conduct and evaluation of monetary policy (already identified in chapter 1) are (1) the goal of price stability, (2) a numerical inflation target or sequence of targets, (3) a time horizon to reach or return to the target in case of departure, and (4) mechanisms to evaluate whether the target has been or will be met.[12] Table 3.1 summarizes the first three elements as they are found in the frameworks of the 22 inflation-targeting countries.

Price Stability and Other Goals

With respect to the central bank's mandate (the first column in table 3.1), only six of the 22 inflation-targeting countries have price stability as the sole element. Two have or had (Chile and Finland) currency stability as their principal objective. Twelve central banks operate under a hierarchical mandate in which price stability in some formulation is at the top. Thus, for almost all the inflation-targeting central banks, price stability is the focus of their mandates.

However, two of the inflation targeters (Canada and Israel) have mandates with multiple objectives and have found that they can successfully operate within an inflation-targeting framework under those mandates. In several cases, the establishment of price stability as the central bank's primary goal has relied upon a further agreement on or interpretation of the legal mandate. In general, the precise wording of the inflation-targeting central bank's mandate is less important than a clear understanding of the orientation of the central bank's policy. In this connection, the central bank's mandate plays a useful but not necessarily a central role.

---

12. This section is not intended to present a comprehensive compendium of the many technical aspects of inflation-targeting regimes in practice. My focus is on the four principal elements of an inflation-targeting framework that I have identified. Frank Gaenssmantel compiled information on these elements using primary and secondary sources. Each of the 22 inflation-targeting central banks were communicated with directly, and their assistance is gratefully acknowledged. The complete compilation of the information that was assembled, as of the end of 2002, is available on request. See Carare et al. (2002) and Schmidt-Hebbel and Tapia (2002) for compendiums of other more technical aspects of inflation targeting.

Table 3.1 Overview of inflation-targeting frameworks

Country	Mandate[a]	Target[b] Transitional	Ultimate	Transition	Time horizon[c]
Australia	H[d]		R (2–3)	None	D
Brazil	P	P (5.5, +/–2.5)[e]	P (3.75, +/–2.5)	Ongoing	R
Canada	M		P (2, +/–1)	Concluded	Y (6–8)
Chile	C		P (3, +/–1)	Concluded	Y (8)
Colombia	H	R (3.5–5.5)	P (3)	Ongoing	D
Czech Republic	H	R (2–4)[f]	R (1–3)	Ongoing	D
Finland[g]	C		P (2)	None	D
Hungary	H	P (3.5, +/–1)		Ongoing	D
Iceland	H		P (2.5, +/–1.5)	Concluded	R
Israel	M		R (1–3)	Concluded	R
Korea	H		R (2.5–3.5)	Concluded	D
Mexico	P		P (3, +/–1)	Ongoing	D
New Zealand	P		R (1–3)	Concluded	R
Norway	H[h]		P (2.5)	None	D
Peru	P[i]		P (2.5, +/–1)	None	D
Philippines	H	R (4.5–5.5)		Ongoing	R
Poland	H	P (3, +/–1)	P (2.5, +/–1)	Ongoing	D
South Africa	P	R (3–6)[j]		Ongoing	D
Spain[g]	H		P (2)	Concluded	D
Sweden	P		P (2, +/–1)	Concluded	Y (4–8)
Thailand	H[k]		R (0–3.5)	None	D
United Kingdom	H		P (2.5)	None	R

a. Classification of mandates: C = currency stability as principal objective; H = hierarchy with price stability first; M = multiple objectives, no hierarchy; P = price stability as sole objective. Based on legal mandate as supplemented by decrees, regulations, or formal agreements between governments and central banks.

b. P = point; R = range; targets in percent; last available transitional target listed when relevant, ultimate target when available.

c. Time horizon for return to target: Y = yes, explicit ex ante commitment (time horizon in quarters in parentheses); R = central bank required or committed to report time horizon after departure occurs; D = discretion, no explicit recognition of issue.

d. Australia's legislation mentions multiple objectives, namely currency stability, full employment, and general economic prosperity. The Statement on the Conduct of Monetary Policy that formalized the inflation-targeting regime in 1996 interprets currency stability as price stability and as a precondition to all other aims, making it the primary focus of monetary policy.

e. The National Monetary Council in June 2003 set a new transitional target, due to current economic conditions, for 2004.

f. Target for 2003.

g. Finland and Spain dropped their inflation-targeting frameworks when they joined the European System of Central Banks in January 1999.

h. Norway's relevant regulation cites in a first part internal and external currency stability, as well as support for fiscal policy, as aims; in a second part it emphasizes that implementation of monetary policy should be oriented toward low and stable inflation. In the interpretation of the central bank, the second part indicates what it is concretely required to do, which puts price stability at the top of the hierarchy of its aims.

i. In Peru the legal mandate is to preserve monetary stability. In the interpretation of the central bank this means price stability. The central bank has goal independence.

j. In February 2003 the transitional target for 2005 was raised to 3 to 6 percent.

k. In Thailand the legal mandate, based on a law from 1942, is very unclear. The central bank itself has set out the current hierarchy of aims in its first inflation report of July 2000. The central bank law is currently under review.

Source: See description in footnote 12.

Numerical Target Point or Range

As shown in the second and third columns of table 3.1, the inflation target for 14 central banks is defined as a point, and for eight it is a range.[13] However, among the 14, in only five is the point a single figure standing alone; in the remaining nine there is also a range.[14]

In almost three-quarters (16) of the 22 countries, the inflation-targeting framework was part of a transition to price stability (fourth column). Many of those transitions were very short, but eight of them are ongoing. Once a central bank achieves its long-run target, it may be redefined. For example, the September 2002 Policy Targets Agreement in New Zealand between Minister of Finance Michael Cullen and Central Bank Governor Designate Alan Bollard resulted in the adjustment of the inflation target range from 0 to 3 percent to 1 to 3 percent. In 1996, the target range was expanded from the original 0 to 2 percent to 0 to 3 percent.[15]

Most (11 of 18) of the targets that are associated with ranges have a width of two percentage points, but the widest is five percentage points (Brazil in transition) and the narrowest is one percentage point (Australia, whose range is often described as a thick point, Korea, and the Philippines).[16]

For the 10 *actual* inflation-targeting countries with mean inflation rates of less than 5 percent for the 1990–2002 period, the average standard deviation was two percentage points, and the average standard deviation was 4.5 percentage points for the six inflation-targeting countries with mean inflation rates of 5 to 10 percent (appendix table A.2). The corresponding standard deviations for the *potential* inflation targeters in the

---

13. Carare et al. (2002) stress that in most cases (out of their 20), the choice of the numerical inflation target involves the government. It is more remarkable that in eight cases the choice involves the central bank alone, and in only five cases is the central bank not formally involved at all. Note that as of the late 1990s, the Bank of England compiled a list of 54 central banks with inflation targets, out of 93 central banks that were surveyed, but only 16 were inflation targeters at that time (Fry et al. 2000).

14. In the United Kingdom, the target is a point, but if UK inflation is outside a range of plus or minus 1 percent around that point, it triggers an obligation for the Bank of England to write an open letter about its monetary policy explaining the deviation and the policy it has adopted to return inflation to target.

15. Canada has gone through several rounds of debates about both whether and how to set its inflation target. For some of the officially sanctioned debates, see Bank of Canada (2000). See Thiessen (1998) and Longworth (2000) on inflation targeting in Canada.

16. Note that a central bank may have price stability as its formal mandate (Mahadeva and Sterne 2000) or an inflation target (for example, Switzerland) and not be an inflation-targeting central bank, at least for purposes of this study. Given the range of approaches to inflation targeting, I have adopted the convention of considering a country and its central bank as an inflation targeter if it describes itself as one. In the case of Switzerland, it has explicitly declined to describe itself as an inflation-targeting central bank. The Swiss National Bank has a quantitative definition of price stability that it does not consider to be an inflation target (box 2.1).

two groups of 19 and eight countries with average 1990–2000 inflation rates of less than 5 percent and 5 to 10 percent, respectively, averaged 1.5 percentage points and five percentage points, respectively.

Given this historical pattern of actual inflation rates and their standard deviations, one might reasonably ask why countries choose such narrow ranges for their inflation targets.[17] One answer is that they believe that anything wider would lack credibility, notwithstanding the fact that the narrower the range, the higher the probability of missing the target in either direction. Another answer is that the authorities are relying upon the narrow bands to influence inflation expectations and thereby actual inflation (Tetlow 2000). A third answer, which supports the choice of a point rather than a range, is that a narrow range increases the discipline within the central bank just as a personal trainer contributes to more effective workouts. The results presented in the last section of this chapter shed some light on these issues.

It is noteworthy that only one inflation-targeting country has a target that includes zero (Thailand).[18] Moreover, many countries have raised their targets to exclude zero out of concern about deflation or to increase the midpoints of the range, or both. The average of all points or midpoints of the ranges for ultimate targets of the 19 countries not in transition or with defined ultimate targets for their transitions is 2.4 percent.

Time Horizon

With respect to the time horizon for achieving inflation targets, the revealed preferences of inflation targeters, not surprisingly, given the diversity of countries and their experiences, demonstrate great variety. The evidence of this is impressive.

The 22 inflation-targeting countries provide 31 examples of time horizon choices for the achievement of their inflation targets.[19] Those exam-

---

17. Christopher Erceg (2002) argues that inflation targeters should base their choices of target ranges on alternative models as well as judgment about actual experience. He bases this view on some illustrative examples of stylized economies with different parameters—for example, with respect to openness—and concludes that the case for an empirically based choice rather than an a priori choice (for example, "country X chose such a range so we should too") of a target-range width rests on three arguments: (1) it would provide a coherent assessment of the possible implications of a particular choice of a band for other economic variables of potential interest, (2) it helps build the case for a particular band compared with other alternatives, and (3) it helps clarify the linkage between the band and structural features of the inflation-targeting economy. It would appear from the data presented here that few inflation targeters have viewed their choices in this manner.

18. Switzerland's quantitative definition of price stability, 0 to 2 percent, also includes zero.

19. Three countries (Chile, Israel, and Mexico) are treated as having two dates for their adoption of inflation targeting, raising the number of examples to 25; eight other countries changed their approaches significantly, raising the number of examples to 31.

ples are classified into three categories: twelve cases of countries where inflation was already within the range when inflation targeting was adopted; eight cases of countries with a defined transition to a target or via a sequence of targets of choice, including a time horizon for reaching a range that the country declared to be its ultimate objective; and 11 cases of countries with an undefined transition, where the ultimate objective was not initially or has not yet been set.

For the first group, most (nine cases) involve a commitment to achieve the objective on an annual basis or continuously. For the second group with a defined transition to an ultimate target or range, the time horizons to reach that target ranged from 18 to 58 months, with a mean of 34 months. For the final group with transitions to an as yet undefined final target, the time horizon for hitting the transitional goals range from 12 to 60 months; the mean is 22 months—17 months excluding the cases with time horizons of 38 and 60 months.

Some observers quite reasonably consider the time horizon for returning to the target or the target range once inflation has departed from the target to be the essence of an inflation-targeting framework for monetary policy. As shown in the last column in table 3.1, only three central banks (Canada, Chile, and Sweden) have a formal time horizon that has been established in advance for returning to the target or range, if there is a departure. In six cases (Brazil and the Philippines, which are still transitioning to their ultimate goals, Iceland, Israel, New Zealand, and the United Kingdom), missing the target by a certain predefined amount triggers a reporting or review process; part of that process involves the articulation of a plan including a timetable to return to the long-run target.

However, more than half (13) of the 22 inflation-targeting frameworks in place (including Finland and Spain as inflation targeters for these purposes) do not involve any type of formal provision governing the return of inflation to target if there is a departure, including seven countries that have defined their ultimate or long-term objective for inflation and have concluded any transition. Some observers may consider that such an omission is a defect of the inflation-targeting framework or that it even disqualifies the country from being classified as an inflation targeter.[20] In this view, the omission reduces the rigor of the regime, adding a further undesirable element of discretion.

In practice, inflation-targeting central banks often follow an ad hoc procedure, indicating in each case what their intentions are with respect to the period for bringing inflation back within the range or close to the point target once it has departed. For the same reason, about a third of the

---

20. Laurence Meyer (2001) argues that the Federal Reserve should adopt an inflation target, but he also argues that it should not become an inflation-targeting central bank, his definition of which includes a rule or guideline for the period over which inflation is to be returned to target if there is a departure.

inflation-targeting central banks employ escape clauses that specify in advance circumstances in which the central bank should not be expected to achieve its target.[21]

Evaluation

Finally, with respect to evaluation—through transparency and accountability mechanisms—of central bank performance in achieving its objective, the 22 countries have adopted a variety of approaches.

The primary objective is to respond to the imperative of accountability in a democratic society. Transparency, often defined in terms of the extent of disclosure by the central bank, assists in holding the central bank accountable for its actions. A more theoretical objective is to communicate clearly the central bank's objectives and intentions and thereby to reduce uncertainty about the central bank's actions and favorably influence expectations in order to improve monetary policy efficiency and macroeconomic performance. These objectives are not, by any means, unique to the inflation-targeting countries and their central banks; however, some advocates or supporters of inflation targeting (Bernanke et al. 1999) stress that this transparency element is the central and most desirable feature of the framework.[22]

Over the past decade, in particular, there has been a sea change in the attitudes of governments as well as central banks toward the uses and misuses of transparency.[23] Nevertheless, the strong positive attitude toward transparency among many inflation-targeting countries and the

---

21. The countries are (or were) the Czech Republic, New Zealand, Norway, the Philippines, South Africa, Spain, and Sweden.

22. If a central bank has an inflation target and makes it public, the bank increases its transparency. Hence, the tight link that is sometimes made between transparency and inflation targeting. On the other hand, one should be careful about what one means by transparency; Adam Posen (2002) argues that the two aspects of central bank transparency for which there is empirical support of the economic benefits are announcing a nominal target and providing specific information about policy moves. Posen also distinguishes between central bank transparency and accountability—a central bank can be very transparent about what it is doing (define price stability, issue forecasts, and publish minutes and reports), but there may be no mechanism to hold it accountable for its actions. It is for this reason that Posen and some others argue that central banks, such as the Bank of Japan, Federal Reserve, and European Central Bank, should not enjoy as much goal independence (capacity to freely interpret their mandates) as they now do.

23. The literature on this topic is vast. A small sample that touches upon, but does not always reach the same conclusions about, transparency and inflation-targeting or noninflation-targeting central banks (or their practices) includes Blinder et al. (2001); Bomfim and Rudebusch (2000); Chortareas, Stasavage, and Sterne (2002); Eijffinger and Geraats (2003); Eijffinger and Hoeberichts (2002); Faust and Svensson (1998); Ferguson (2002); Geraats (2002); Green (2001); Kohn (2000 and 2002); and Posen (2002). See also Schmidt-Hebbel and Tapia (2002) on practices of inflation-targeting central banks in this area.

central banks is reflected in a statement by Klaus Schmidt-Hebbel and Matías Tapia (2002, 11), "The strength of inflation targeting *vis a vis* other monetary regimes lies precisely in how transparency enhances monetary credibility and anchors private expectations."

Central bank transparency in general, and certainly in the context of an inflation-targeting framework for monetary policy, can be viewed as an effort to resolve the time inconsistency problem identified by Kenneth Rogoff (1985). On the other hand, Ralph Bryant (1996, 27), commenting on the early days of inflation targeting in New Zealand, observed, "The tradeoff between credibility and time-consistency advantages on the one hand and the potential gains from stabilization flexibility on the other deserves more careful attention than it typically receives in New Zealand."[24] Moreover, in the inevitable presence of uncertainty about the central bank's implicit or explicit model of the economy, it is important to recognize that transparency can be misleading in the sense that the central bank may make a public statement about an expected outcome that turns out to be wrong (Geraats 2002). Therefore, some forms of transparency may be suboptimal (Eijffinger and Geraats 2003).

Table 3.2 identifies six potential elements for the evaluation of policy in inflation-targeting frameworks: inflation reports, inflation forecasts, other regular reports or statements of policy, publication of the minutes of the central bank's decision-making body, testimony before parliament, and letters or similar communications in case of a substantial breach of a target. None of the central banks employs all six elements, and only three employ as many as five of them. Five use only two elements.

Twenty-one of the 22 central banks issue inflation reports or the equivalent, but only 14 publish forecasts of inflation in those reports or elsewhere. Thirteen central banks also issue other types of reports or regular policy statements. Only 16 central banks indicate that they routinely appear before their parliaments, but the number is probably higher. Six central banks produce formal letters when they miss targets. In those cases, as discussed earlier, the letters contain proposals or recommendations about the time frame for returning to the target. Only seven of the central banks publish minutes of their meetings.

Thus, transparency and accountability are very much a part of most inflation-targeting frameworks, but there is no uniform pattern. Moreover, as with the other three elements normally associated with inflation-targeting frameworks, most of these evaluation devices may be at least as relevant to, and present in, other frameworks for the conduct of monetary policy. Consider, for example, a central bank that uses a monetary or an

---

24. Recall that New Zealand raised the midpoint of its target range at the end of 1996 by widening the range from 0 to 2 percent to 0 to 3 percent, thus allowing more attention to be paid to stabilization considerations. Subsequently, in 2001 New Zealand narrowed its range to 1 to 3 percent, further raising the midpoint in the process.

Table 3.2 Evaluation in inflation-targeting frameworks

	Elements of policy evaluation					
Country	Inflation report[a]	Inflation forecast[b]	Other reports[c]	Minutes[d]	Parliament[e]	Letter[f]
Australia	X				X	
Brazil	X	X	X	X		X
Canada	X		X		X	
Chile	X	X		X	X	
Colombia	X	X	X		X	
Czech Republic	X	X		X	X	
Finland[g]			X		X	
Hungary	X	X	X		X	
Iceland	X	X	X			X
Israel	X		X		X	X
Korea	X	X	X	X	X	
Mexico	X		X		X	
New Zealand	X	X			X	X
Norway	X	X	X			
Peru	X	X	X			
Philippines	X		X		X	X
Poland	X		X	X	X	
South Africa	X	X				
Spain[g]	X				X	
Sweden	X	X		X	X	
Thailand	X	X				
United Kingdom	X	X		X	X	X

a. Inflation report or equivalent publication.
b. Published official quantitative inflation forecast or projection.
c. Additional regular publications (reports, evaluations, and programs) on monetary policy.
d. Published minutes of monetary policy decision-making body's meetings.
e. Regular testimony before parliament.
f. Open letter or report that the central bank is required to produce in case of a breach of the target, explaining causes, and establishing measures and time frame to return to target.
g. Finland and Spain dropped their inflation-targeting frameworks when they joined the European System of Central Banks in January 1999.

Source: See description in footnote 12.

exchange rate target as its framework for the conduct of monetary policy. If the central bank misses its target, the miss is certainly transparent. Moreover, the central banker certainly can be held accountable for his or her miss!

In summary, countries considering the adoption of inflation targeting as the framework for their monetary policy have found the four principal elements useful, at a minimum, to organize their thinking about the design of their frameworks, but there is no one dominant pattern.

Actual and Potential Inflation Targeters

Before examining in the next section some empirical aspects of inflation targeting and economic performance, it is useful to lay out additional information on the 22 inflation-targeting countries and their inflation and growth experiences in recent years in comparison with those of 46 other countries that might be considered potential inflation targeters.

In this study, actual and potential inflation-targeting countries are grouped in four categories:

- "Maintainers" have essentially achieved whatever they have decided is an appropriately low level of inflation, sometimes referred to as stationary inflation; for maintainers one would normally expect inflation to average less than 5 percent per year, but more than zero, and expect that result to be achieved without artificial suppression of inflation, for example, through the manipulation (e.g., freezing) of administered prices.

- "Convergers" are well on their way to achieving stationary inflation, for example, with inflation rates of more than 5 percent (or if less than 5 percent, then only as the result of suppressed inflation) but less than double digits.

- "Squeezers" may have embarked on larger projects to bring down inflation rates that may be 20 percent per annum, or higher, to low single-digit rates.

- "Reversers" have inflation rates of less than zero, and are seeking to raise inflation to a low positive rate on a sustained basis.

Considering the 22 countries identified earlier as inflation targeters, and the rate of inflation of consumer prices in the year prior to their choice of inflation targeting as their framework for the conduct of monetary policy, one learns the following from tables 2.3 and 3.3—the majority of the countries (11) were maintainers at the time of adopting inflation targeting, seven were convergers, and only four were squeezers.[25] None were reversers. If China, Hong Kong, Japan, Saudi Arabia, Singapore, or Taiwan had adopted inflation targeting in early 2003 on the basis of their inflation performances in 2002, they would have been reversers.

The average inflation rates for the 1990–2002 period of these 22 countries give a different perspective on their inflation experience. Of course, some of the countries were inflation targeters for most of the period and others were inflation targeters for only a small part of the period. From this perspective, ten of the 22 countries were maintainers on average for the 13 years, and six each were convergers and squeezers.

A third perspective is provided by recent inflation experience. In 2000, 15 of the 22 countries had achieved the status of maintainers, six were

---

25. With respect to squeezers, Chile initially employed a mixed monetary policy framework in 1990, and by 1999, when it fully embraced inflation targeting, it was a maintainer; Israel also had a mixed framework in 1991, and by 1997, when it fully embraced inflation targeting, it was a converger. Moreover, Poland was only marginally a squeezer in 1998 when it adopted inflation targeting—that is, its inflation rate was more than 10 percent but substantially less than 20 percent—and Colombia was in a similar position in 1999.

Table 3.3 **Categorization of inflation targeters, based on inflation rates**

Country	Year before adoption[a]	Average (1990–2002)	2000	2002
Australia	M	M	M	M
Canada	M	M	M	M
Finland	M	M	M	M
Spain	M	M	M	M
Sweden	M	M	M	M
Thailand	M	M	M	M
United Kingdom	M	M	M	M
Norway	M	M	M	M
Korea	M	C	M	M
Peru	M	S	M	M
Brazil	M	S	C	S
Czech Republic	C	C	M	M
Hungary	C	S	C	C
Iceland	C	M	C	C
Mexico	C[b]	S	C	C
New Zealand	C	M	M	M
Philippines	C	C	M	M
South Africa	C	C	C	S
Chile	S[c]	C	M	M
Colombia	S	S	C	C
Israel	S[d]	C	M	C
Poland	S	S	S	M

a. For Chile (both adoption dates), Colombia, Czech Republic, Israel (first adoption date), New Zealand, Poland, and the United Kingdom, which adopted inflation targeting in the second half of the respective year, the inflation rate of that year was used.
b. Mexico was a converger (C) in both 1994, the year before it first introduced an inflation target, and 2000, the year before inflation targeting became the principal policy framework.
c. Chile was a squeezer (S) in 1990 when it first introduced an inflation target, and maintainer (M) in 1999 when inflation targeting became the principal policy framework.
d. Israel was a squeezer in both 1991, when it first introduced an inflation target, and 1996, the year before inflation targeting became the principal policy framework.

Note: Inflation rate calculated from annual average CPI.

Source: IMF, *International Financial Statistics.*

convergers, and only one was a squeezer.[26] In 2002, the number of maintainers was the same (Israel had become a converger, but Poland had joined the maintainers). Poland no longer was a squeezer, but Brazil and South Africa had moved into that category. The number of convergers had shrunk to five.

Two points emerge from the data presented in table 3.3 and this discussion:[27] first, countries do move among categories. Second, the direc-

26. Poland was a squeezer in 2000 but only by a small margin; its inflation rate was 10.1 percent.

27. The Philippines and Peru are excluded from this analysis because they did not adopt inflation targeting until 2002, as are Hungry, Iceland, and Norway, which only adopted the framework in 2001.

tion of movement is not all one way—that is, toward becoming a maintainer. Eleven countries were maintainers when they adopted inflation targeting, and ten of them were still in that category in 2002. Seven countries were convergers when they adopted inflation targeting, and three remained there in 2002. Three countries moved from the converger to the maintainer category (the Czech Republic, New Zealand, and the Philippines). Two countries moved the other direction—South Africa moved from the convergers to the squeezers, and Brazil moved from being a maintainer to becoming a squeezer.

As a prelude to the results presented in the next section, the data on inflation in appendix table A.2 shed some light on the issue of potential inflation targeters and the view that countries should not think about inflation targeting until their inflation rates reach the low double digits.[28] Recall the discussion on inflation forecasting and the preconditions for inflation targeting.

With respect to the 22 industrial countries, nine are or have been inflation targeters. Of the remaining 13, nine are already in the euro area, which also includes Luxembourg; Denmark's monetary policy is tightly aligned with that of the European Central Bank because of its exchange rate link to the euro.[29] Thus, with respect to industrial countries, there are four potential inflation targeters: the G3 economies (discussed in detail in chapter 4) and Switzerland, whose situation is summarized in box 2.1.

Turning to the 46 nonindustrial countries, 13 are already inflation targeters. Of the remaining 33, 11 had average inflation rates for 1990–2002 of 20 percent per year or more, which some might think implies that they should not consider adopting inflation targeting. However, only four (Argentina, Romania, Turkey, and Venezuela) had inflation rates of more than 20 percent in 2002; the other seven countries might be potential squeezers with inflation rates of less than 20 percent (Bulgaria, Ecuador, Nigeria, Russia, Slovenia, Ukraine, and Uruguay).

---

28. The interested reader will find in the appendix six tables with data on inflation and growth for 68 countries—22 inflation targeters and 46 potential inflation targeters. On the basis of the classification used in IMF's International Financial Statistics, there are 22 industrial countries and 46 nonindustrial countries. Appendix table A.2 shows CPI inflation rates for 2002, mean inflation rates for 1990–2002, and the standard deviations of inflation rates for the same period. Appendix table A.3 presents similar data for growth rates of real GDP. Based on data from Consensus Economics, appendix table A.4 presents data on the accuracy of inflation forecasts for 1990–2001 for the industrial countries; appendix table A.5 presents similar data for the nonindustrial countries. Appendix tables A.6 and A.7 similarly look at the accuracy of growth forecasts for 1990–2001.

29. Luxembourg is not included in the appendix tables or in Hu's (2003a, 2003b) exercises because of a lack of data from Consensus Economics.

In addition, eight countries had average annual inflation rates between 10 and 20 percent for the 1990–2002 period. Of those, six had 2002 inflation rates less than 10 percent, qualifying them as convergers (Costa Rica, Dominican Republic, Guatemala, Honduras, Sri Lanka, and Vietnam). Two did not (Indonesia and Paraguay).

Fourteen nonindustrial countries that were not already inflation targeters had average inflation rates of less than 10 percent per year in 1990–2002. Finally, only 10 of the 33 nontargeting, nonindustrial countries had inflation rates in 2002 of more than 10 percent.

Thus, under a strict interpretation of favorable conditions for economies to consider inflation targeting—an inflation rate of less than 10 percent, putting them among the convergers or maintainers—there appear to have been 27 potential candidates as of the end of 2002: the four industrial economies and 23 nonindustrial economies. This is not to say that each of them was a realistic candidate, because many of them may not have attached much importance to low inflation even if they had or were on the verge of achieving it. Nor is it to say that any of the remaining 10 nonindustrial economies were not candidates for inflation targeting, just because their inflation rates were above 10 or 20 or 30 percent in 2002; at least four of them (Argentina, Indonesia, Russia, and Turkey) were actively considering the option.

Empirical Investigations

The discussion about the necessary preconditions for inflation targeting and the views of skeptics suggest a number of issues that are susceptible to empirical investigation. Over the past dozen years or so, a substantial literature has developed on many of these issues.[30] The empirical literature has been handicapped by the relatively small number of countries, mostly industrial countries, that have been inflation targeters for an extended period and by the need to control for the performance of nontargeters during a period of generalized global disinflation. Many of the studies have adopted a case-study approach rather than a cross-section approach. Consequently, results may hold generally—that is, for many inflation targeters but not for all inflation targeters. Therefore, one is left with

---

30. Among the contributors are Ammer and Freeman (1995); Cecchetti and Ehrmann (2002); Chortareas, Stasavage, and Sterne (2002); Corbo, Landerretche, and Schmidt-Hebbel (2002); Debelle (1997); Eichengreen and Taylor (2003); Freeman and Willis (1995); Johnson (2002); Jonas and Mishkin (2003); Kahn and Parrish (1998); King (2002); Kuttner and Posen (1999); Laubach and Posen (1997); Laxton and N'Diaye (2002); Mishkin and Posen (1997); Sabbán, Rozada, and Powell (2003); and Siklos (1999). Ball and Sheridan (2003) and Neumann and von Hagen (2002) provide recent summaries of this literature.

the question of why inflation targeting is not more uniform in its effects on economic performance.

With these qualifications, the principal conclusions to date in the literature are that generally inflation targeting

- has had a favorable effect on inflation, inflation variability, inflation expectations, and the persistence of inflation.
- has not had a negative effect on growth, the variability of growth, and unemployment.
- has had mixed effects on interest rates, real, nominal, short-term, long-term, their level, and their variability.
- has had positive effects on exchange rate stability.
- has affected the reaction functions of the central banks that have adopted the framework. But this raises the question whether the favorable effects that have been found could have been produced by a change in behavior that did not include an adoption of the new framework or whether adoption of the new framework, as suggested by Mishkin (2002a), has been a mechanism for achieving a convergence to best practice.

The focus of this study is inflation targeting in the world economy and how applicable the monetary policy framework is to a broad range of countries. From this perspective, the principal question is the role inflation targeting plays on average in overall economic performance including the trade-offs between inflation and growth and between the variability of inflation and the variability of growth. Also of interest is the question of whether one can identify structural features associated with the economies of some potential inflation targeters—for example, their external environments—that suggest inflation targeting in general is contraindicated as a framework for monetary policy. Specifically, the following questions are examined:

1. What factors are strongly associated with the level and variability of inflation?
2. Can one detect an influence of inflation targeting in general on the level or variability of inflation?
3. Can one detect an influence of inflation targeting in general on the level or variability of growth?
4. What light can be shed on the question of the external circumstances or vulnerability of countries that suggest inflation targeting may be more or less successful for them in general as their framework for monetary policy?
5. Is there evidence that countries that have adopted inflation targeting on average have achieved lower inflation at the expense of lower growth (moved along the Phillips Curve) and lower inflation variabil-

ity at the expense of higher growth variability (moved along the Taylor Curve relating those two variables), as skeptics have suggested?

6. Is there evidence that countries that have adopted inflation targeting on average have improved the overall trade-off between inflation and growth or inflation and growth variability, that is, shifted the Phillips and Taylor Curves toward the origin, as has been implicit in the arguments of some advocates of inflation targeting?

Much of the empirical work was done in collaboration with Yifan Hu.[31] She assembled a dataset for 68 countries on aspects of their economic performance, structural characteristics, and economic institutions, including whether they are inflation targeters.

For readers who would prefer to skip the analysis, our conclusions on these questions were as follows: a number of factors were identified that are associated with either the level or variability of inflation, more successfully for the level. Little support was found for the proposition that nonindustrial countries with open economies and otherwise greater vulnerability to external influences have higher or more variable inflation rates and, therefore, are less likely to be successful with an inflation-targeting framework for their monetary policies. The empirical exercises provide no support for the view that inflation targeting involves the choice by a country of a different point on a stationary Phillips Curve. They provide some support for the view that following the adoption of inflation targeting, the targeters' Phillips Curves shift toward the origin. At the same time, the results provide little or no support for the view that inflation targeting involves the choice by a country of a different point on a stationary Taylor Curve and some support for the view that following the adoption of inflation targeting, the targeters' Taylor Curves shift toward the origin. Thus, some evidence was found of overall improvement in macroeconomic performance on average for those countries that have adopted inflation targeting.

Level and Variability of Inflation and Growth

To help address the first four questions, the factors associated with the level and variability of inflation were first identified. Initially the level of inflation was considered, and those results were used to inform the analysis of factors associated with the variability of inflation. Table 3.4 summarizes the results for both exercises. A parallel analysis of growth and its variability was conducted next.

---

31. See Hu (2003a, 2003b) for a more detailed description of her work including the sources and definitions for the various data series.

Table 3.4 Factors affecting the level and variability of inflation

Independent variable	Level of inflation Expected sign	Full	Final	Variability of inflation Expected sign	Full	Final
M2 growth (lagged)	+	0.0963*** (0.026)	0.1029*** (0.024)	+	0.0692*** (0.022)	0.0690*** (0.023)
Real GDP gap	+	−0.2280* (0.129)	−0.2203* (0.129)	+	−0.3254 (0.198)	−0.3120* (0.185)
GDP growth variability	+	0.1019 (0.165)	0.1083 (0.151)	−	0.2019 (0.276)	0.2109 (0.244)
Nonfuel commodity prices	+	−0.0024 (0.040)	−0.0098 (0.038)	+	−0.0903* (0.054)	−0.0931 (0.058)
Fiscal position	−	−0.0652 (0.067)		−	0.0276 (0.074)	
Financial depth	−	−0.0296*** (0.005)	−0.0270*** (0.005)	−	−0.0091*** (0.003)	−0.0110*** (0.003)
Inflation targeting	−	−2.4268*** (0.569)	−2.4208*** (0.611)	−	−0.6336 (0.418)	−0.6132 (0.508)
Central bank autonomy	−	−1.2693** (0.506)	−1.9134*** (0.504)	−	−0.089 (0.483)	−0.3099 (0.350)
Trade openness	+	−0.0104*** (0.004)	−0.0187*** (0.003)	+	−0.0040 (0.003)	−0.0062* (0.004)
Terms-of-trade variability	+	0.1197*** (0.046)	−0.0160 (0.038)	+	0.0180 (0.025)	−0.0076 (0.019)
Floating exchange rate regime (de facto)	+	1.1352* (0.597)	1.055* (0.572)	+	−0.6382* (0.383)	−0.5840* (0.334)
Foreign exchange pressure	+	0.0739 (0.800)		+	0.9566 (0.851)	
REER variability	+	0.0526** (0.022)	0.0068 (0.021)	+	0.0080 (0.025)	
NEER variability	+	0.1118*** (0.028)	0.1128*** (0.028)	+	0.0584*** (0.016)	0.0598*** (0.016)
Current account	?	−0.1207 (0.074)		?	−0.0645 (0.045)	
External debt	?	0.0076 (0.006)		?	−0.0004 (0.006)	
Constant		4.4105	6.6749		2.0397	2.5341
Number of observations		884	908		879	903
Adjusted R-squared		0.45	0.43		0.27	0.26

? = uncertain what sign should be
NEER = nominal effective exchange rate
REER = real effective exchange rate

Notes: *, **, and *** represent rejecting the null hypothesis of no significance at levels of 10, 5, and 1 percent, respectively. Standard errors in parentheses.
Regressions are based on the entire sample, excluding 15 countries with average 1980–2000 inflation above 25 percent.
Regressions include annual dummy variables that are not reported.

A somewhat larger set of independent variables than that presented in table 3.4 was first used, including those used to examine the choice of inflation targeting as reported in chapter 2. That list was refined on the basis of a few preliminary runs. This is one reason why some of the variables found in the left column titled "full" in table 3.4 differ from those found in table 2.4.[32] The other reason is that on an a priori basis, some variables, such as lagged money growth, were known to belong in these equations and were not appropriate to a country's decision to adopt inflation targeting. Most of the variables whose coefficients either had unexpected signs or were not significant were progressively eliminated; those variables whose coefficients were significant, had the expected signs, or were of particular interest regardless of the sign or the significance of their coefficients were retained. The result is displayed in the left column titled "final." The same exercise was repeated using the variability of inflation as the dependent variable. Variability was measured by the standard deviation of inflation over rolling five-year periods.[33]

With respect to the level of inflation, the results shown in table 3.4 were gratifying in terms of the overall fit and the number of coefficients that were significant, given the diversity of the countries in the sample.

Six independent variables (first six in table 3.4) were employed to capture traditional macroeconomic determinants of inflation. The coefficient on lagged money growth, the traditional proxy for the basic cause of rapid inflation, was strongly significant.[34] On the other hand, the sign of the coefficient on our estimate of the real GDP gap was negative, contrary to our expectation, and significant at the 10 percent level. If the regression were picking up a short-run Phillips Curve type of relationship, one would ex-

---

32. On the basis of the preliminary runs, countries that had average inflation rates of more than 25 percent for the 1980–2000 period were also eliminated along with economies without sufficient economic data, leaving 51 countries (22 industrial and 29 nonindustrial)—thirteen became inflation targeters within the sample period and 38 were potential inflation targeters, including three that later became inflation targeters. The 17 that were eliminated from the sample were inflation targeters Brazil, Israel, Mexico, Peru (a targeter after 2000), and Poland as well as potential inflation targeters Argentina, Bolivia, Bulgaria, Ecuador, Hong Kong, Nigeria, Romania, Taiwan, Turkey, Ukraine, Uruguay, and Venezuela. See appendix table A.1 for the list of countries excluded from the analysis.

33. In the regressions with the level or variability of inflation as the dependent variable, as well as regressions for the level or variability of growth reported in table 3.5, annual dummy variables (not reported) were included to capture any tendency for high or low inflation or its variability to return to a more normal level, in other words possible regression toward the mean. Although the dummy variables in general were not significant, their inclusion improved the overall fit of the regressions and affected the significance of some of the coefficients.

34. One of the distortions introduced by the use of the larger sample of countries is that the influence on inflation of money growth was positive but not significant in some of the preliminary regressions.

pect a positive sign on the gap; a smaller or more positive gap would be associated with higher inflation.[35]

Neither the variability of real GDP growth nor the percentage change in nonfuel commodity prices was associated significantly with the level of inflation; the coefficient on the former variable had the expected (positive) sign, but the latter variable did not.[36] Nevertheless, those variables were retained in the final regression in order to be sure to capture the basic inflation process.

The coefficient on a country's fiscal position had the expected sign (negative), but it was far from significant, and the variable was not included in the final regression.[37] On the other hand, the coefficient on the proxy for financial depth (the ratio of M2 to GDP) had the expected sign and was highly significant. The coefficient in the final regression implies that at the mean value for this variable (58 percent), inflation would be reduced by about 1.5 percentage points. At one standard deviation away from the mean, inflation would be reduced or increased by a bit more than one percentage point.[38]

With respect to the two economic institution variables, a gratifying result was the significant, negative association between the dummy variable for inflation targeting and inflation. We did not anticipate that inflation targeting would stand out as prominently in the results as it did.[39] On

---

35. One possible explanation is that even though money growth with a lag was included, the regression is picking up a "classical" relationship: faster money growth that does not show up in faster output growth (a smaller output gap) shows up in higher inflation.

36. Contrary to the results presented in table 2.4, the variability of real GDP growth was measured by the standard deviation over rolling five-year periods. The percentage change in petroleum prices was also tried in the equation and the coefficient estimates were even less precise than those for nonfuel commodity prices. One reason the percentage change in nonfuel commodity prices did not show up as significant for inflation for this group of countries may be that the influence of a rise in those prices has a positive influence on commodity-importing countries and a negative influence on commodity-exporting countries.

37. This finding is broadly consistent with the careful analysis by Luis Catão and Marco Terrones (2003), who find that fiscal deficits are positively associated with inflation among high-inflation countries and countries with underdeveloped financial markets. This estimation excludes most of their high-inflation countries and includes most of the countries whose financial markets are in the advanced or emerging categories used by Catão and Terrones.

38. Mohsin Khan, Abdelhak Senhadji, and Bruce Smith (2001) have carefully examined the relationship between inflation and financial depth. They point out that the relationship may run from inflation to financial depth as well as the reverse; they also find that at above low levels of inflation (3 to 6 percent), inflation may have a positive effect on financial depth. (John Burger and Francis Warnock (2003) come to a similar conclusion in the context of their examination of the development of domestic bond markets in emerging-market economies.) The results reported in table 3.4 confirm the view that inflation and inflation variability are negatively associated with financial depth regardless of the nature of the causation.

39. Laurence Ball and Niamh Sheridan (2003) examine the influence of inflation targeting on a longer list of measures of economic performance. However, their examination only covers

average, as shown by the constant term in the final regression, inflation was about 6.5 percent in the sample, excluding the influence of all the dummy variables in the regression. The mean value of the inflation variable was about 8.75 percent. Inflation targeting reduced it by about 2.5 percentage points. When the final regression was rerun using the later date for the adoption by Chile, the influence of inflation targeting was even stronger, close to three percentage points.[40] In the same vein, consistent with the expectation, the coefficient on the dummy variable for central bank autonomy was significant and negative, with an impact on inflation of almost two percentage points, on average.[41]

The last eight independent variables listed in table 3.4 can be viewed as representing the external environment for each country. The results do not offer much support for the view that external factors have a strong adverse influence on inflation performance and that, therefore, countries vulnerable to external influences should avoid inflation targeting as a framework for their monetary policies. Contrary to expectation, it was found that greater trade openness was significantly but negatively associated with inflation.[42] On the other hand, the coefficient on terms-of-trade

---

industrial countries and uses a very different statistical approach, comparing the pretargeting with the posttargeting period. Without controlling for any other variables, they also find that inflation targeting is associated with a reduction in inflation that is statistically significant; however, they argue that this result reflects regression to the mean inflation rate for all industrial countries. When they control for the rate of inflation in the pretargeting period, the beneficial effect of inflation targeting on inflation is no longer significant. We are not convinced that our results are subject to a similar bias, and the bias itself is open to debate since inflation targeting could have encouraged a faster regression toward the mean. Recall as well from the results reported in chapter 2 that the choice of inflation targeting appears to be negatively associated with inflation. Nevertheless, at the suggestion of Laurence Ball, annual dummy variables were introduced into the regressions to control for this possible bias. Their introduction was associated with a small—on the order of 15 to 20 percent—reduction in the size of the coefficient on the dummy variable for inflation targeting and essentially had no effect on its significance. (There was some impact on the size and significance of the other coefficients.) Moreover, in our experimentation with variables to better capture the basic inflation relationship and in the process reduce the number of independent variables from those in the full regression to those in the final regression, the size and significance of the coefficient on the dummy variable for inflation targeting was very robust.

40. Israel and Mexico—the two other inflation targeters where alternative dates for adoption were considered—were excluded from the regression because their average annual inflation rates in 1980–2000 were more than 25 percent.

41. Eva Gutiérrez (2003) obtains a similar result for the connection between inflation performance and constitutional central bank independence in a sample of Latin American and Caribbean countries.

42. Our expectation with respect to the sign of the coefficient on this variable was based on the view that the more open an economy, the more susceptible it is to external shocks, including inflation shocks. An alternative view associated with David Romer (1993) and Philip Lane (1995) is that in a more open economy, monetary policy is constrained to follow a time-

variability had the expected positive sign and was significant in the full regression but not in the final regression, where the sign was reversed but the coefficient was not significant.[43]

The coefficient on the dummy variable for a (de facto) floating exchange rate regime was positive, as was expected, and marginally significant (at the 10 percent level) in both the full and final regressions.[44] In contrast, the coefficient on the dummy variable for foreign exchange pressure, although positive as expected, was far from significant, and the variable was dropped from the final regression.

The coefficients on the variables for real and nominal exchange rate variability were positive and significant in the full regression, but the behavior of these variables is at least in part—and some would say largely—a function of the policies of the country in question rather than the external environment. In particular, in the case of the variability of the nominal effective exchange rate, the causality may run from the behavior of inflation to the behavior of the exchange rate index. Moreover, the significance of the coefficient on real exchange rate variability, which should be the most relevant in terms of the transmission of external disturbances, was not significant in the final regression.

The coefficient on the countries' current account positions was negative but not significant in the full regression—a stronger current account position was associated with lower inflation. This variable was omitted from the final regression because we were not sure what the sign should be. The same problem arose with respect to the sign of the coefficient on external debt, but since it was also insignificant in the full regression, we felt more comfortable dropping it from the final regression.

The results for the variability of inflation, shown in the right-hand columns of table 3.4, are arguably more relevant than the results for the level of inflation to the issue of whether inflation targeting as a monetary policy framework suits a country's economic characteristics. If inflation is more volatile and more difficult to predict or control, these circum-

---

consistent monetary policy with a lower inflation rate. Another argument that runs in the same direction is that a more open economy provides greater scope for the export of policy and nonpolicy disturbances to the rest of the world, limiting their adverse effects on the domestic economy, including inflation.

43. For terms-of-trade variability to impact inflation adversely, an economy would have to have internal nominal rigidities, as many do, so that improvements and deteriorations in the terms of trade would have asymmetrical effects on inflation.

44. When the regression was run with the dummy variable for a (de jure) floating exchange rate regime, the coefficient had the opposite sign in the full, but not the final, regression but in neither case was significant. This illustrates the sensitivity of results from this type of exercise to the specification of this variable.

stances might argue for a wider target range or, perhaps, against inflation targeting.[45]

The overall fit was lower and the number of significant coefficients was substantially smaller in the regressions with inflation variability as the dependent variable than for those with the level of inflation as the dependent variable. The results do not provide much support for the view that more open economies, which are normally also smaller, are more susceptible to external influences and, therefore, will have greater difficulty predicting and controlling inflation, suggesting that they should not try to use inflation targeting as their monetary policy framework.

With respect to macroeconomic determinants of inflation variability, only lagged money growth and financial depth had coefficients that had the expected signs and were significant. The coefficient on nonfuel commodity price inflation was negative, contrary to our expectation, and marginally significant in the full regression, but it lost significance in the final regression. The coefficient on the real GDP gap was (again, unexpectedly) negative and significant (at the 10 percent level) in the final regression. With respect to the variability of growth, a negative relationship with the variability of inflation was expected, consistent with the Taylor Curve trade-off, but that was not borne out in the results; the coefficient was positive but not significant.[46]

The association of inflation targeting with inflation variability was negative (as expected) but not significant, in both the full and final regressions.[47] The results for the dummy variable for central bank autonomy were similar.

With respect to the eight variables representing the external environment, only the variability of nominal effective exchange rates stands out as having a significant positive influence on the variability of domestic inflation. As noted in connection with the regressions for the level of infla-

45. This type of argument lies behind the recommendation of Takatoshi Ito and Tomoko Hayashi (2003) that emerging-market economies in Asia should adopt inflation targets with higher midpoints and wider ranges. A similar argument can be found in Erceg (2002) and Jonas and Mishkin (2003), although the latter, in particular, are not inclined to see such circumstances as disqualifying emerging-market or transition economies from adopting inflation targeting.

46. To be fair, a Taylor Curve was not being fit for one country or for a group of countries with similar economic structures and policies; to the extent that there are stable Taylor Curves with downward slopes—lower inflation variability associated with higher output variability—what the regression is picking up is the choice by different countries of points on their individual curves that have different shapes and locations.

47. For the comparable period starting in 1985, Ball and Sheridan (2003) obtain similar (insignificant) results for industrial countries, but the limited effect is washed out when they control for regression to the mean, which we have done by introducing annual dummy variables. See footnotes 33 and 39.

tion, this may be an instance of reverse causality. The coefficient for the dummy variable for (de facto) floating is significant but negative in both the full and final regressions.[48] Trade openness is associated with lower inflation variability, significantly so in the final regression. Terms-of-trade variability is positively associated with inflation variability in the full regression but negatively in the final regression, and in both cases not significantly. The other external variables contribute little to the general story. The overall results for the variability of inflation lend essentially no support to the view that countries should be wary about adopting inflation targeting if they face a hostile external environment.[49]

An investigation was then conducted to see how consistent these results were across the two groups of countries in our sample: industrial and non-industrial. Full and final regressions were run for both the level and variability of inflation in the form summarized in table 3.4 and also with interactive dummies for the industrial countries for all of the variables except the annual dummy variables. In each of the four relationships, the hypothesis that the two groups of countries were the same was rejected. However, the differences between the two groups, as indicated by the significance of the coefficients on the interactive dummies, were only in small part due to the influence of the eight variables loosely associated with the external environment. The interactive dummy variables on inflation targeting and central bank autonomy were not significant in any of the regressions.

As would be expected, in the case of the two regressions (full and final) for the level of inflation, the constant term for the industrial countries was significantly different from that for the developing countries (less than half), even though 15 countries with average inflation rates of more than 25 percent in the 1980–2000 period were eliminated from the sample. The other variables whose coefficients were significantly different for the two groups of countries included the real GDP gap, where the sign of the coefficient was positive for the industrial countries, consistent with the Phillips Curve story, and financial depth, where the sign of the coefficient was also positive.[50]

With respect to the variables reflecting the external environment, the interactive dummy variables for the industrial countries had significant coefficients in the cases of trade openness (but with the same negative sign

---

48. When the regression was run with the dummy variable for a (de jure) floating exchange rate regime, the coefficient was not significant, but it did have the expected (positive) sign in both the full and final regressions.

49. This result tends to contradict those who argue that developing countries are more likely to experience financial crises because they face more hostile external environments or that external pressures add significantly to inflation variability. Our proxy for financial depth does have a significant favorable (negative) influence on inflation variability, but this is a characteristic of the internal not the external environment.

50. This latter result is loosely consistent with the Khan et al. (2001) view of a positive relationship between inflation and financial depth at low levels of inflation.

as in the basic regression), de facto floating (but with a positive sign, which tends somewhat to strengthen the negative empirical link between floating and inflation variability for nonindustrial countries), and the variability of the nominal effective exchange rate (but with a negative sign, providing further evidence that the positive sign in the basic regression reflects the influence of the behavior of inflation on the behavior of the exchange rate index rather than the other way around).

In the regressions (full and final) for the variability of inflation, the differences in the constant terms for the two groups were not significant. In the final regressions, the association of the real GDP gap, financial depth, and nonfuel commodity prices with inflation variability was significantly different for the industrial countries, and for all three variables the sign was the reverse (positive), contrary to the basic regression.

In the case of the variables for external economic factors, the coefficient on the interactive dummy variable for trade openness was significant (but with the same negative sign) in the final regression; the coefficient for terms-of-trade variability was also significant (with a different [negative] sign) though only in the full regression; the coefficient for (de facto) floating was significant (with a different [positive] sign) though only in the full regression; and the coefficient for the variability of the nominal effective exchange rate was significant in both regressions, again with the opposite (negative) sign, reinforcing the view of the direction of causation with respect to inflation and this variable.

In summary, these results on differences between industrial and nonindustrial countries offer little additional support for the view that the external environment plays a substantially different role in determining the ability of nonindustrial countries to target inflation, thereby reducing the probability that they will be successful with such a monetary policy framework. It is possible that nonindustrial countries are subject to larger external disturbances, but the effects on the inflation per unit of external disturbance are in general similar to the effects for industrial countries. Moreover, to the extent that nonindustrial countries are subject to larger external disturbances, it is unlikely that this should shape their choice of monetary policy frameworks. Instead, they should focus on other institutional reforms, for example, in their financial sectors. Some of these issues are further discussed in chapter 5.

In light of the finding, presented in table 3.4, of the favorable influence of inflation targeting on reducing inflation, though not significantly its variability, and as a bridge to the results presented next on the trade-off between inflation and growth variability, a parallel set of equations were run where the dependent variable was growth or its variability. The results are presented in table 3.5.[51] Our expectations about the signs of coefficients

51. Again, the actual regressions included annual dummy variables, but their coefficients are not reported.

Table 3.5 Factors affecting the level and variability of growth

Independent variable	Growth of real GDP			Variability of growth		
	Expected sign	Full	Final	Expected sign	Full	Final
M2 growth (lagged)	–	–0.0064 (0.015)		+	0.0171 (0.011)	
Real GDP growth				+	0.4172*** (0.063)	0.4278*** (0.069)
GDP growth variability	+	0.8085*** (0.269)	0.7613*** (0.236)			
Inflation variability	–	–0.1730*** (0.067)	–0.0400 (0.037)	–	0.0806 (0.068)	0.0189 (0.031)
Fiscal position	–	–0.0208 (.057)		?	0.1654*** (.023)	
Financial depth	+	0.0006 (0.002)		–	–0.0003 (0.002)	
Inflation targeting	–	0.7460* (0.423)	0.6217* (0.329)	+	–0.9154** (0.385)	–0.7772* (0.416)
Central bank autonomy	+	0.2584 (0.489)	0.1753 (0.478)	–	–1.4736*** (0.276)	–1.4930*** (0.266)
Trade openness	–	0.0050 (.004)	0.0033 (.003)	+	–0.0001 (.003)	0.0030 (.002)
Terms-of-trade variability	–	0.0188 (0.021)	–0.0124 (0.020)	+	–0.0183 (0.020)	
Floating exchange rate regime (de facto)	–	–0.2811 (0.387)		+	0.0267 (0.246)	–0.0723 (0.218)
Foreign exchange pressure	–	–0.1955 (0.620)	–0.4403 (0.604)	+	–0.0216 (0.303)	
REER variability	?	–0.0036 (0.015)		?	0.0280** (0.012)	
NEER variability	?	0.0112 (0.012)		?	–0.0041 (0.005)	0.0032 (0.004)
Current account	?	0.0059 (0.066)		?	–0.0467 (0.031)	
External debt	?	–0.0078* (0.004)		?	0.0048 (0.004)	
Constant		–1.5351	0.3214		6.4459	2.9642
Number of observations		878	951		878	948
Adjusted R-squared		0.42	0.37		0.54	0.47

? = uncertain what sign should be

Notes: *, **, and *** represent rejecting the null hypothesis of no significance at levels of 10, 5, and 1 percent, respectively. Standard errors in parentheses.

Regressions are based on the entire sample, excluding 15 countries with average 1980–2000 inflation above 25 percent.

Regressions include annual dummy variables that are not reported.

were not as strong for most of the signs, and the move from the full to the final regressions was much less systematic because of the principal interest in the coefficients on the dummy variables for inflation targeting.

In the regressions for the level of growth, shown in the first half of table 3.5, inflation targeting is associated significantly (at the 10 percent level) with higher growth in both the full and the final regressions, adding more than half a percentage point to growth.[52] Output variability has a positive and significant association with growth in both regressions, and inflation variability has a negative association, but it is only significant in the full regression. The only external factor with a significant (negative) influence is the variable for external debt.

In the regression for the variability of growth (table 3.5), inflation targeting is associated significantly with lower growth variability in both the full and final regressions, at the 5 percent level in the former and the 10 percent level in the latter. Central bank autonomy has a much larger and more significant negative association. Higher growth and (inexplicably) a stronger fiscal position are associated with higher growth variability.[53] Higher variability in real effective exchange rates was also associated with higher growth variability in the full regression, but that variable was dropped in the final regression to see if nominal effective exchange rate variability would become significant as in the regressions with inflation variability, but it did not, though the sign of the coefficient did change from negative in the full regression to positive.

Finally, the growth regressions were run with interactive dummies on the independent variables for industrial countries. Again, the hypothesis that the two groups of countries were the same could be rejected, but the differences did not provide much in the way of additional insights except that for industrial countries increased trade openness was significantly associated with growth variability.

How do the results reported in tables 3.4 and 3.5 answer the first four questions posed earlier? The empirical exercise helped isolate a number of factors whose association with the level and variability of inflation was significant and in the expected direction, more so for the level of inflation than for its variability. Thus, we felt justified to look at questions two through four.

Inflation targeting was found to be associated significantly with lower inflation and with a remarkably large—some might say unrealistically large—coefficient. There is a similar favorable influence on inflation vari-

---

52. Ball and Sheridan (2003) obtain a positive but insignificant result for industrial countries for the comparable period starting in 1985, and that limited effect is washed out when they control for regression to the mean, as we did using our annual dummy variables. See footnotes 33 and 39.

53. The fiscal position was dropped from the final regression because the interpretation of its sign in the full regression was ambiguous.

ability, but it is not significant.[54] Inflation targeting had a significant positive effect on growth and a significant negative effect on the variability of growth.

On the issue of the economic circumstances of countries and the extent to which those circumstances suggest they may be better or less well suited to adopt inflation targeting as their framework for monetary policy, the results provide only limited support—once one has controlled for internal macroeconomic conditions—for the skeptical view that the circumstances of developing countries—more open to trade, more vulnerable to external financial disturbances, buffeted by more hostile external environments—dictate that they are less likely to be able successfully to implement inflation targeting because they are less likely to be able or willing to control inflation or its variability.

In the regressions for the level of inflation, coefficients on five of the eight variables that one might loosely associate with such adverse circumstances were significant, but one of those coefficients (on trade openness) had the wrong sign. Moreover, a couple of the other significant coefficients are on variables of less direct relevance—those for the variability of real and nominal effective exchange rates. The interpretation of the coefficient on floating also is somewhat questionable because it is not clear that floating per se captures the issue of vulnerability, and the results with the alternative dummy variable for (de jure) floating were different.

In the regressions for the variability of inflation, which provide a better indication of the potential for successful inflation control, only one of the coefficients on the external environment variables was significant with the expected sign—the coefficient on the variability of the nominal effective exchange rates. The coefficient on the dummy variable for (de facto) floating was significant, but its sign implied that floating reduces inflation variability.[55]

On the other hand, there do appear to be significant differences between industrial and nonindustrial countries in the factors affecting the level and variability of inflation. However, the factors identified with the external environment do not figure prominently in explaining those differences.

A related piece of evidence on this issue—which can be reduced to the question of whether industrial countries with their more-developed financial markets and larger central bank staffs are better able to achieve

---

54. The constant term in the regression with inflation variability as the dependent variable is two-thirds the size of the term in the regression with the level of inflation as the dependent variable, and the mean value of the variable is about half as large. The coefficients on the inflation-targeting dummies in the inflation variability regressions are about 25 percent of those in the inflation level regressions.

55. Michael Papaioannou (2003) examines the somewhat related question of the relationship between terms-of-trade fluctuations or capital openness and exchange rate regimes in Central American countries and finds no significant association.

their macroeconomic objectives—comes from tests of central bank reaction functions. It is well known that countries differ in their macroeconomic structures and those differences show up in the coefficients in estimated Taylor rules for countries (see, for example, Cecchetti and Ehrmann 2002 and Corbo, Landerretche, and Schmidt-Hebbel 2002). However, it is instructive that the differences among industrial countries are as pronounced as those between industrial and nonindustrial countries.

Another piece of evidence to support the view that differences among industrial and nonindustrial countries are no less pronounced than differences among industrial countries can be found in Schmidt-Hebbel and Tapia (2002); the dispersion of their results on the dynamic output and inflation effects of a uniform policy move (100 basis points) in each inflation-targeting country is as great among the seven industrial countries as for the six nonindustrial countries. One is hard-pressed to discern any systematic differences between the two groups of countries.

Trade-offs Between Inflation and Growth

Some of the skeptics have argued that the inflation-targeting policy framework is excessively rigid and that, if successful, it would produce lower inflation and/or lower inflation variability at the expense of lower growth and/or higher growth variability (see, for example, Bryant 1996, Rivlin 2002, and FOMC 1995). In this view, the choice of inflation targeting as a country's framework for monetary policy in effect implies the choice of a different point on the frontiers representing the trade-off for an economy between inflation and growth (on the Phillips Curve) and the trade-off between inflation and output variability. This latter trade-off is sometimes referred to as a Taylor Curve because it is linked to the loss function associated with the arguments in the Taylor rule—deviations from an inflation target and deviations from potential output.[56]

Alternatively it has been suggested, often implicitly, that inflation targeting as a framework for monetary policy can contribute to lower inflation outcomes and a reduction in the variability of inflation, and that such improved performance with respect to inflation is likely to be matched by an improved performance with respect to growth and its variability. In effect, the Phillips Curve may shift toward the origin, or the Taylor Curve—representing the trade-off between the variability of inflation and growth—may shift toward the origin.

---

56. The results of research on monetary policy rules often are presented in terms of the location and shape of the Taylor Curve associated with different monetary policy rules or reaction functions or with the interactions of different rules with different representations of the structure and behavior of individual economies; see, for example, Laxton and Pesenti (2002) and the literature cited in their paper.

An empirical examination was conducted in collaboration with Yifan Hu (2003a, 2003b) to shed some light on these issues. The analysis, however, was hampered by the fact that there are no long time series for a large number of inflation targeters and by the recognition that the period since 1989—during which 22 countries adopted an inflation-targeting framework—was one of generally declining inflation, lower inflation variability, and somewhat higher growth and lower growth variability. In other words, as researchers such as Mishkin and Schmidt-Hebbel (2002) and Corbo et al. (2002) have recognized, one needs to look at the contemporaneous performance of a control group of countries.

Thirty-seven countries were included in the sample—eight inflation targeters and 29 nontargeters.[57] For the inflation targeters, the standard deviation of inflation and output from 1985 until the year before they became inflation targeters and for the years after they became inflation targeters until 2000 was calculated. For the nontargeters (the control group), the standard deviation of their inflation rates between 1985 and 1994 and between 1995 and 2000 was calculated.[58]

Considering inflation targeting and its possible influence on a country's choice of a point on its Phillips Curve or on the location of that curve, recall the results from the left-hand sides of tables 3.4 and 3.5. Inflation targeting is associated on average with a significant lowering of inflation rates and a significant boost to growth rates.

Table 3.6 summarizes the data on average inflation and growth rates before and after the adoption of inflation targeting for the 37 inflation targeters and nontargeters included in the analysis. Average inflation rates declined for both the inflation targeters and the nontargeters for the full sample of 37 countries as well as for just the 20 industrial countries. The reductions were larger for the inflation targeters and statistically significant.[59] Average growth rates also rose for both the inflation targeters and the nontargeters in both samples, and again by more for the targeters. However, the difference is only significant for the larger sample, which includes Chile as an inflation targeter along with 16 other nonindustrial countries.

---

57. The criteria for the selection of countries excluded all inflation targeters with less than four years of experience by the end of 2000 and excluded all countries with average inflation rates of more than 50 percent from 1985 to 2000 and countries with any years with inflation of more than 50 percent from 1989–94. The eight inflation targeters who passed through this grid were Australia, Canada, Chile, Finland, New Zealand, Spain, Sweden, and the United Kingdom. See appendix table A.1 for a list of the countries excluded from the analysis.

58. The rationale was that by 1995 all of the inflation targeters in the sample had adopted the framework (table 2.3).

59. The significance test is applied to a small sample and requires that the distributions are approximately normal and distributed with equal population variances. Because these assumptions may not hold, the results of the significance tests should be taken with a grain of salt.

Table 3.6   Average inflation and growth rates pre- and post-inflation targeting

	Inflation			Growth		
Inflation targeter	Pre-targeting	Post-targeting	Difference between post- and pre-targeting	Pre-targeting	Post-targeting	Difference between post- and pre-targeting
Australia	6.33	2.25	−4.08	3.03	4.46	1.43
Canada	4.38	2.00	−2.38	3.24	2.70	−0.54
Chile	21.33	9.58	−11.75	6.21	6.65	0.45
Finland	4.68	1.23	−3.45	1.27	3.71	2.44
New Zealand	11.32	2.25	−9.07	2.72	2.39	−0.32
Spain	6.24	3.01	−3.23	2.91	3.11	0.20
Sweden	6.27	1.46	−4.81	1.33	2.40	1.07
United Kingdom	5.68	2.62	−3.06	2.38	3.01	0.63
Average						
All countries						
Inflation targeters	8.28	3.05	−5.23	2.89	3.56	0.67
Nontargeters[a]	7.48	4.68	−2.79***	3.81	3.83	0.02***
Industrial countries						
Inflation targeters	6.41	2.12	−4.30	2.41	3.11	0.70
Nontargeters[a]	4.65	2.15	−2.51***	2.65	3.17	0.52

a. For nontargeters, the average between 1985 and 1994 and the average between 1995 and 2000 are compared.

Note: *** represents rejecting the null hypothesis of no significance at the level of 1 percent.

In a final look at the possible influence of the choice of inflation targeting on a country's choice of a point on its Phillips Curve or the location of that curve, a different set of data (from Consensus Economics) was analyzed, which are presented in appendix tables A.2 to A.7 for 44 countries, including 13 inflation targeters.[60] Data from 2001, and for some countries from 2002, were added to Yifan Hu's dataset, and the number of post-adoption years was reduced from four to three.[61] A control group was created for each inflation targeter.[62] The average forecast errors (AFE) were calculated as the difference between the realized values for inflation and

---

60. In conducting this portion of the analysis, I was ably assisted by Frank Gaenssmantel.

61. This had the effect of increasing the number of nonindustrial countries in the dataset while at the same time reducing the number of industrial countries because data for New Zealand and Canada (early inflation targeters) were not available from Consensus Economics. See appendix table A.1 for a list of the countries excluded from this analysis.

62. For each inflation-targeting industrial country, its control group consisted of the other (nontargeting) industrial countries or, on a more restricted basis, the other industrial countries with average inflation rates for 1990–2001 of less than 5 percent, that is, excluding Greece and Portugal. The average variability of inflation and growth was calculated for each country within that control group for the three years before and the three years after the adoption of inflation targeting by the particular country. (In general, the year of adoption of inflation targeting was allocated to the period after adoption; however, when the month of adoption was in the second half of the year, the year of adoption was treated as the follow-

growth and the one-year-ahead forecasts reported by Consensus Economics. If after the adoption of inflation targeting, inflation declined (growth rose) more rapidly than forecast, the AFE would be more negative (positive).

The results of this analysis are presented in table 3.7. With respect to inflation, the AFE was more negative for the industrial-country inflation targeters after their adoption of inflation targeting than for either of the control groups, but the differences were not significant. For the nonindustrial targeters, the AFE actually rose, but the rise was not significant.[63] The inclusion of the nonindustrial countries pulled up the AFE for the entire group of inflation targeters relative to their two control groups, but again the differences are not significant.[64] With respect to growth, the inflation targeters exhibited positive post-targeting AFE for the entire group and the two subgroups, and the differences with the respective control groups were significant.

On balance, the results of the three investigations[65] do not support the view that inflation targeting involves the choice by a country of a different point on a stationary Phillips Curve. Inflation rates decline, often significantly, after the adoption of the framework, but rather than falling, growth rates increase, more often significantly. These results, in turn, provide some support for the view that following the adoption of inflation targeting, the targeters' Phillips Curves shift toward the origin. In other words, there is an overall improvement in macroeconomic performance and the effectiveness of monetary policy.[66]

Turning to the possible influence of inflation targeting on a country's choice of a point on its Taylor Curve—representing the trade-off between

---

ing year.) The average variability for the control group was used to deflate the variability calculated for the inflation targeter. For the inflation-targeting nonindustrial countries, similar procedures were followed, except membership in the control group was limited to nonindustrial countries with average 1990–2001 inflation rates of less than 20 percent or, on a more restricted basis, less than 10 percent.

63. Mexico's experience heavily influenced the average, but the overall results were unchanged using the later date for Mexico's adoption of inflation targeting.

64. These results on inflation are broadly consistent with those of David Johnson (2002), who conducted a more extensive analysis using a similar set of data derived from Consensus Economics for a smaller number of industrial-country inflation targeters and a smaller associated control group. He found that for the inflation targeters, actual and expected inflation fall relative to the control group, but the variability of expected inflation and the average absolute forecast error do not. Johnson does not examine the behavior of actual growth relative to forecasts of growth.

65. See tables 3.4 and 3.5 (left-hand sides) and tables 3.6 and 3.7.

66. Douglas Laxton and Papa N'Diaye (2002) examine a similar question and find that low inflation improves the unemployment-inflation trade-off in a sample of industrial countries.

Table 3.7 Analysis of average forecast errors

Inflation targeter	Inflation			Growth		
	Pre-targeting	Post-targeting	Post- minus pre-targeting	Pre-targeting	Post-targeting	Post- minus pre-targeting
Industrial						
Australia	−1.55	−0.51	1.04	−0.81	0.43	1.23
Finland	−1.01	−1.74	−0.73	−4.75	−0.33	4.42
Spain	−0.06	−0.30	−0.24	−1.04	0.02	1.06
Sweden	0.31	−0.27	−0.58	−0.96	2.18	3.15
United Kingdom	0.66	−0.48	−1.14	−0.92	1.15	2.07
Average						
Targeters	−0.33	−0.66	−0.33	−1.70	0.69	2.39
Restricted control group	−0.09	−0.32	−0.23	0.21	0.10	−0.11***
Broader control group	−0.06	−0.35	−0.29	0.15	0.03	−0.12***
Nonindustrial						
Brazil	−3.42	−1.55	1.87	−0.71	2.01	2.72
Colombia	0.64	−0.06	−0.70	−3.03	−0.66	2.38
Czech Republic	0.31	−0.91	−1.21	−1.35	−0.61	0.74
Korea	−0.54	−1.76	−1.22	−0.07	1.91	1.98
Mexico	−1.66	8.36	10.02	−0.54	0.15	0.69
Poland	−1.12	−0.22	0.90	0.57	−1.52	−2.09
South Africa	−0.60	1.36	1.96	−0.37	−0.13	0.24
Thailand	−1.30	−0.70	0.60	−5.56	0.11	5.67
Average						
Targeters	−0.96	0.57	1.53	−1.38	0.16	1.54
Restricted control group	−1.61	−1.64	−0.03	0.02	−0.25	−0.26*
Broader control group	−1.24	−1.15	0.10	0.07	−0.27	−0.34**
All targeters (average)						
Targeters	−0.72	0.09	0.81	−1.50	0.36	1.87
Restricted control group	−1.03	−1.13	−0.11	0.09	−0.11	−0.20***
Broader control group	−0.79	−0.84	−0.05	0.10	−0.15	−0.26***

Notes: *, **, and *** represent rejecting the null hypothesis of no significance at levels of 10, 5, and 1 percent, respectively.
The average forecast error (AFE) is the mean of realized minus forecast values. The AFE is over three-year periods before and directly after adoption of inflation targeting.

Sources: For realized values: IMF, *International Financial Statistics*; Consensus Economics, *Consensus Forecasts*; and selected government statistics. For forecasts: Consensus Economics, *Consensus Forecasts*.

the variability of inflation and growth—or on the location of that curve, recall the results from the right-hand sides of tables 3.4 and 3.5. Inflation targeting is associated with lower inflation variability—but the influence is not significant—and with lower growth variability that is statistically significant.

A regression analysis of the 37-country subset of Hu's data was again conducted. It was not possible to include a large number of control variables in the regressions because of the limited number of observations; the

Table 3.8 Trade-off between inflation and growth variability

Independent variable	Dependent variable				
	Pre-/post-inflation targeting				
	Inflation variability	Growth variability	Growth/inflation variability	Growth/inflation variability[a]	Inflation variability[a]
Growth rate	−0.29*** (0.14)	0.001 (0.18)	0.29 (0.23)	0.20 (0.14)	
Growth variability					0.34*** (0.16)
Inflation rate	0.20 (0.13)	−0.09 (0.17)	−0.30 (0.22)	−0.61*** (0.08)	
Inflation targeting	0.17*** (0.09)	−0.04 (0.11)	−0.21 (0.14)	−0.11 (0.10)	−0.07 (0.12)
Constant	−0.20	−0.13	0.07	0.17	0.24
Number of observations	37.00	37.00	37.00	74.00	74.00
Adjusted R-squared	0.17	0.01	0.09	0.47	0.06

a. Includes observations from pre- and postadoption periods separately.

Notes: *** represents rejecting the null hypothesis of no significance at the level of 1 percent.
Standard errors in parentheses.
Variability measured by at least four-year standard deviation.
All variables except "inflation-targeting" dummy in logarithms.

average inflation rates and the average growth rates in the two subperiods were used.[67] Table 3.8 presents the results.

Considering the first three columns, where the dependent and independent variables are in the form of the ratio of the observations pre- and post-adoption of inflation targeting, the coefficient on the dummy variable for inflation targeting is significant only in the regression with inflation variability as the dependent variable. The coefficient is positive, which would not be expected if one held the view that inflation targeting would contribute to lower inflation variability at the expense of higher growth variability. Moreover, the coefficient on the dummy variable for inflation targeting has a negative sign in the regression where growth variability is the dependent variable and in the regression where the ratio of growth variability to inflation variability is the dependent variable. However, in both cases it is not significant. With respect to the control variables, only the coefficient on growth in the regression with inflation variability as the dependent variable is significant, and the now-familiar result that higher growth is associated with lower inflation variability is found.

The results presented in the last two columns of table 3.8 increase the sample size by including the observations from the pre- and post-

---

67. The regressions were run in logarithms, except for the dummy for inflation targeting, because that representation did a somewhat better job in capturing any relationship than linear regressions. The results were similar for the linear regressions.

Table 3.9 Output and inflation variability pre- and post-inflation targeting

	Inflation			Growth		
Inflation targeters	Pre-targeting	Post-targeting	Difference between post- and pre-targeting	Pre-targeting	Post-targeting	Difference between post- and pre-targeting
Australia	1.80	1.71	−0.09	1.70	1.04	−0.66
Canada	1.16	1.16	0.00	1.59	1.55	−0.03
Chile	6.16	3.88	−2.28	2.11	3.03	0.92
Finland	1.92	1.28	−0.63	3.03	2.22	−0.81
New Zealand	4.74	2.00	−2.74	2.50	1.89	−0.61
Spain	1.68	1.30	−0.38	1.58	0.56	−1.03
Sweden	2.52	1.71	−0.81	1.30	1.76	0.46
United Kingdom	2.00	1.23	−0.77	1.93	0.78	−1.15
Average						
All countries						
Inflation targeters	3.52	2.12	−1.41	1.97	1.61	−0.36
Nontargeters[a]	2.75	1.78	−0.96**	2.03	1.69	−0.34
Industrial countries						
Inflation targeters	2.26	1.49	−0.78	1.95	1.40	−0.55
Nontargeters[a]	1.91	1.05	−0.86	1.46	1.34	−0.12***

a. For nontargeters, the average between 1985 and 1994 and the average between 1995 and 2000 are compared.

Notes: ** and *** represent rejecting the null hypothesis of no significance at levels of 5 and 1 percent, respectively.
Variability measured by at least four-year standard deviation.

adoption periods separately. The dummy variable on inflation targeting suggests again a negative but not significant effect on the ratio of growth variability to inflation variability (shown in the fourth column). In this regression, higher inflation significantly depresses the ratio, presumably via the denominator—that is, higher inflation variability.

The last column displays a regression with inflation variability as the dependent variable and output variability and the inflation-targeting dummy as the independent variables, with double the number of observations, except for inflation targeting. Here, inflation targeting is negatively associated, but not significantly, with lower inflation variability, and a significant positive relationship was found between the variability of inflation and the variability of growth.

Table 3.9 summarizes the data used in the analysis on inflation and growth variability before and after the adoption of inflation targeting. Inflation variability declined for both the inflation targeters and nontargeters for the full sample of 37 countries and for just the 20 industrial countries. The reductions were larger for the inflation targeters and statistically significant for the full sample, which included Chile as an inflation targeter and 16 other nonindustrial countries. Growth variability also declined for both targeters and nontargeters, but in this case the declines relative to the nontargeters are significant only for the industrial countries.

A somewhat different approach was used, again by exploiting Consensus Economics data, to shed some additional light on the question of the influence of inflation targeting on the trade-off between the variability of inflation and growth. Data only for 2001 were added this time to Hu's data set, and again the number of postadoption years was reduced from four to three. This permitted an increase in the number of inflation targeters to 14 by including six more nonindustrial countries, compared with Hu's analysis. A control group was again created for each inflation targeter.

The results are summarized in figure 3.1. Panel A shows the basic data unadjusted for the average performance of each country's control group. In nine out of 14 cases (70 percent), inflation variability declined, but output variability declined as well in eight cases. In five cases, inflation and growth variability both declined, and in six cases growth variability rose. As shown in panel B, when the basic data are adjusted for the performance of each country's restricted control group, the results are less favorable to inflation targeting.[68] Inflation variability declined in eight cases, growth variability declined in five cases, but in only three cases did both decline.

As is shown in the top portion of panel C in figure 3.1, on average, using the basic data, inflation variability declined by 15 percent, and growth variability rose by 38 percent. In the industrial countries on average, inflation variability declined and growth variability differed little from prior to the adoption of inflation targeting. The variability of both inflation and growth rose on average in nonindustrial countries, and the rise in growth variability was substantially more. Relative to their respective restricted control groups, the results again do differ somewhat; the mean percentage changes in inflation variability are essentially the same, but the mean percentage changes in growth variability are boosted for the industrial countries.[69]

Finally, the root mean squared errors (RMSE) of Consensus Economics forecasts were examined. The results are shown in figure 3.2. They are broadly comparable to the results presented in figure 3.1. However, for the 10 countries included in both analyses, the results differ for four countries on the basic data, and for three countries relative to the restricted

---

68. The results shown are for the restricted control groups because they are least favorable to the hypothesis that inflation targeting is benign. Using the broader control group, Canada remains a case where inflation variability increased and growth variability decreased.

69. Using the later dates for the adoption of inflation targeting by Chile, Israel, and Mexico leaves only Israel in the sample. The results for the smaller group of 5 nonindustrial countries are a bit more favorable to inflation targeting. In the basic data, the variability of both inflation and growth still rise after adoption, but by less. Adjusted by the control group, inflation variability rises more on average than in the basic data.

Figure 3.1 Changes in variability of GDP growth and inflation with adoption of inflation targeting

a. Basic data

		Growth variability	
		Increased	**Decreased**
Inflation variability	**Increased**	Korea (1,213; 397) Mexico (87; 463)	Canada (350; −19) Czech Republic (1,330; −38) Spain (83; −66)
	Decreased	New Zealand (−53; 164) Poland (−43; 68) Sweden (−70; 97) United Kingdom (−68; 1)	Australia (−50; −53) Brazil (−81; −56) Chile (−22; −18) Finland (−65; −8) Israel (−54; −26)

Notes: The figures in parentheses show the percentage changes in the standard deviation from before adoption of inflation targeting to after for inflation (left) and growth (right) over three years.

b. Relative to restricted control group

		Growth variability	
		Increased	**Decreased**
Inflation variability	**Increased**	Canada (371; 4) Korea (1,934; 177) Mexico (32; 570) Poland (15; 65)	Czech Republic (1,898; −65) Spain (120; −41)
	Decreased	Chile (−39; 6) Finland (−33; 78) New Zealand (−43; 53) Sweden (−43; 280) United Kingdom (−39; 96)	Australia (−4; −9) Brazil (−63; −57) Israel (−40; −8)

Notes: The figures in parentheses show the percentage changes in the standard deviation from before adoption of inflation targeting to after for inflation (left) and growth (right) over three years. The restricted control group includes for industrial inflation-targeting countries all other industrial countries in the sample with inflation means for 1990–2001 of less than 5 percent, and for nonindustrial inflation-targeting countries all other nonindustrial countries in the sample with inflation means for 1990–2001 of less than 10 percent.

(figure continues next page)

Figure 3.1 *(continued)*

c. Mean percentage changes from before inflation targeting to after

	Inflation variability	Growth variability
Basic data		
Total	−15	38
Industrial countries	−43	−2
Nonindustrial countries	9	69
Relative to restricted control group[a]		
Total	−2	62
Industrial countries	−11	63
Nonindustrial countries	16	60
Relative to broader control group[b]		
Total	−22	28
Industrial countries	−39	−6
Nonindustrial countries	28	61

a. Includes for industrial inflation-targeting countries all other industrial countries in the sample with inflation means for 1990–2001 of less than 5 percent, and for nonindustrial inflation-targeting countries all other nonindustrial countries in the sample with inflation means for 1990–2001 of less than 10 percent.
b. Includes for industrial inflation-targeting countries all other industrial countries and for nonindustrial inflation-targeting countries all other nonindustrial countries in the sample with inflation means for 1990–2001 of less than 20 percent.

Note: Inflation rates based on annual average CPI. Growth rates based on annual average real GDP.

Sources: IMF, *International Financial Statistics*; and Consensus Economics, *Consensus Forecasts*.

control group. For the mean percentage changes shown in panel C of figure 3.2, compared with those in figure 3.1, they are somewhat less favorable to inflation targeting with respect to lower inflation variability and somewhat more favorable to inflation targeting with respect to lower growth variability.

On balance, the results of the four investigations[70] provide little or no support for the view that inflation targeting involves the choice by a country of a different point on its stationary Taylor Curve. Inflation variability declines, sometimes significantly, after the adoption of the framework, but growth variability also tends to decline, sometimes significantly. These results, in turn, provide some support for the view that following the adoption of inflation targeting, the targeters' Taylor Curves shift toward the origin. In other words, there is some overall improvement in macroeconomic performance.[71]

---

70. See tables 3.4 and 3.5 (right-hand sides), tables 3.8 and 3.9, and figures 3.1 and 3.2.

71. Francisco Nadal-De Simone (2001) looked at the same question and obtained more mixed results.

Figure 3.2 Changes in root mean squared errors (RMSE) of GDP growth and inflation forecasts with adoption of inflation targeting

a. Basic data

		RMSE of growth forecasts	
		Increased	Decreased
RMSE of inflation forecasts	Increased	Brazil (17; 269) Korea (123; 505) Mexico (627; 154) Poland (35; 84)	Czech Republic (375; –38) Finland (45; –52) South Africa (92; –34)
	Decreased	Sweden (–50; 65) United Kingdom (–60; 57)	Australia (–56; –13) Colombia (–89; –70) Spain (–641 –74) Thailand (–63; –71)

Note: The figures in parentheses are the percentage changes from before adoption of inflation targeting to after of the three-year average RMSE of inflation forecasts (left) and growth forecasts (right).

b. Relative to restricted control group

		RMSE of growth forecasts	
		Increased	Decreased
RMSE of inflation forecasts	Increased	Brazil (20; 130) Korea (107; 150) Mexico (577; 406) Poland (38; 15)	Czech Republic (341; –74) Finland (78; –50) South Africa (137; –28)
	Decreased	Sweden (–38; 74) United Kingdom (–50; 65)	Australia (–46; –8) Colombia (–86; –68) Spain (–37 –71) Thailand (–54; –69)

Notes: The figures in parentheses are the percentage changes from before adoption of inflation targeting to after of the three-year average RMSE of inflation forecasts (left) and growth forecasts (right). The restricted control group includes for industrial inflation-targeting countries all other industrial countries in the sample with inflation means for 1990–2001 of less than 5 percent, and for nonindustrial inflation-targeting countries all other nonindustrial countries in the sample with inflation means for 1990–2001 of less than 10 percent.

(figure continues next page)

Figure 3.2 *(continued)*

c. Mean percentage changes from before inflation targeting to after

	Inflation variability	Growth variability
Basic data		
Total	−19	−4
Industrial countries	−38	−27
Nonindustrial countries	40	8
Relative to restricted control group[a]		
Total	44	−11
Industrial countries	−26	−24
Nonindustrial countries	128	−3
Relative to broader control group[b]		
Total	75	−8
Industrial countries	−20	−27
Nonindustrial countries	216	5

a. Includes for industrial inflation-targeting countries all other industrial countries in the sample with inflation means for 1990–2001 of less than 5 percent, and for nonindustrial inflation-targeting countries all other nonindustrial countries in the sample with inflation means for 1990–2001 of less than 10 percent.

b. Includes for industrial inflation-targeting countries all other industrial countries and for nonindustrial inflation-targeting countries all other nonindustrial countries in the sample with inflation means for 1990–2001 of less than 20 percent.

Note: Inflation rates based on annual average CPI. Growth rates based on annual average real GDP.

Sources: IMF, *International Financial Statistics*; and Consensus Economics, *Consensus Forecasts*.

Conclusion

Based on the material presented in this chapter, five broad conclusions can be drawn about inflation targeting in practice.

First, the preconditions for the successful adoption of inflation targeting should not be regarded as particularly demanding. It is important that countries are serious about wanting to achieve and maintain low inflation rates, and the country's fiscal position should not pose a threat to macroeconomic stability. Beyond this, the various institutional and environmental elements that are often identified as necessary preconditions for inflation targeting—financial system stability, central bank independence, and deep knowledge about the monetary transmission mechanism—should be viewed as desirable not essential.

One implication of this conclusion is that some observers and advisers—for example, from the IMF—may be inclined to place too high a hurdle in front of potential inflation targeters. Although no countries with very high inflation rates (above 30 percent) have to date adopted the framework, it has yet to be demonstrated that doing so would be a mistake for such countries. Moreover, with the general decline in inflation rates in recent years, by the strict criterion of current inflation of less than 10 percent in 2002, more than 25 countries were potential candidates for the adoption of inflation targeting.

Second, comparing the frameworks of inflation-targeting practitioners, based on the four principal elements discussed earlier, one sees much variety and considerable experimentation. With respect to the time horizon to return to a target or range once an inflation target is missed, practices are particularly wide-ranging. There are a few cases of ex ante commitment to what would be done, but a majority of cases involve complete discretion.

Third, based on their inflation rates at the time of adopting inflation targeting, four categories of inflation targeters have been distinguished: maintainers, convergers, squeezers, and reversers. Most countries were either convergers or maintainers; there are no examples to date of reversers—those adopting inflation targeting as part of an effort to raise their inflation rates above zero.

Fourth, looking at the experience of inflation targeters and other countries, a number of factors were identified that are associated with either the level or variability of inflation, more successfully for the level. Little support was found for the proposition that nonindustrial countries with open economies and otherwise greater vulnerability to external influences have higher or more variable inflation rates and, therefore, are less likely to be successful with an inflation-targeting framework for their monetary policies.

Fifth, our empirical investigations provide no support for the view that inflation targeting involves the choice by a country of a different point on a stationary Phillips Curve—less inflation at the expense of less growth. They provide some support for the view that following the adoption of inflation targeting, the targeters' Phillips Curves shift toward the origin. At the same time, the results provide little or no support for the view that inflation targeting involves the choice by a country of a different point on a stationary Taylor Curve—less inflation volatility at the expense of more growth volatility—and some support for the view that following the adoption of inflation targeting, the targeters' Taylor Curves shift toward the origin. In other words, there is some evidence of overall improvement in macroeconomic performance on average for those countries that have adopted inflation targeting.

An important qualification to these results is that the economic performance of inflation targeters does not uniformly improve after their adoption of the framework. Among the possible explanations for divergence in the results are: first, each country faced different internal and external economic and financial conditions both before and in the wake of its adoption of inflation targeting; at best, statistical analysis can only employ proxies to try to capture those differences. Second, some countries may have adopted other institutional or policy changes at the same time that they embraced inflation targeting as their monetary policy framework, and those frameworks themselves differ across countries. It is also possible that the favorable overall results for inflation and growth reflect a more general pattern that sound monetary and fiscal policies are generally associated both with lower inflation and better overall growth performance.[72] Thus, experimentation with inflation targeting has been imprecise.

Finally, the theoretical case for inflation targeting is grounded in the New Keynesian economics with its combination of forward-looking (or model-consistent) expectations and the incomplete nominal adjustment of prices. In this context, inflation targeting is viewed as informing the forward-looking behavior of economic agents and favorably conditioning the economic adjustment process, producing positive effects on overall economic performance. The assumptions underlying such theoretical models may fit some countries embarking on inflation targeting better than others. Alternatively, economic agents may have forward-looking expectations, but those expectations may be based on a diverse set of models of the economy—model uncertainty. The less forward-looking the expectations, the more diverse the implicit models, and the more extrapolative the behavior of economic agents, the less likely inflation targeting is to be associated with immediate favorable impacts on economic performance because the expectations of economic agents are influenced more by what the central bank does and less by what the central bank says it will do.[73]

---

72. The evidence presented in Truman (2002a) for a dozen emerging-market economies for the 1980–2000 period supports this interpretation.

73. Athanasios Orphanides and John Williams (2003) recently explored at a theoretical level some of the implications for the behavior of the economy associated with imperfect knowledge about both structural model parameters and policymaker preferences.

4

Inflation Targeting and the Group of Three

Only four industrial economies or groups of economies—the G3 (Euroland, Japan, and the United States) and Switzerland—have meaningfully held out from the adoption of an inflation-targeting framework for the conduct and evaluation of their monetary policy. Nevertheless, their commitment to low inflation or price stability has been deeply embedded in their monetary policies for at least the past two decades. Moreover, each of their respective central banks currently releases forecasts—though in some cases only staff forecasts or projections—for inflation and often other variables, and the Swiss National Bank uses a three-year forecast of inflation as the main indicator to guide monetary policy decisions (box 2.1).

Thus, all four could be called de facto inflation targeters. However, to date, each has resisted that sobriquet despite considerable criticism and argumentation urging them formally to embrace inflation targeting. Resistance in each case is based on different considerations but involves more than a semantic argument that the existing focus on price stability should be enough, though some have suggested that the term "target" has discouraged some central banks from adopting inflation targeting. In other words, the consideration of inflation targeting for these four economies is not an academic exercise. Moreover, if the central bank of any one of the G3 economies were to adopt inflation targeting, it would be consequential for the international financial system,[1] and the consequences would be larger if all three were to do so.

---

1. The Swiss National Bank's decision to adopt inflation targeting would be influential, but it is more difficult to argue that the adoption would be consequential for the international financial system. For that reason, the Swiss case is not dealt with in any detail.

This chapter first considers the implications for the world economy of the individual adoption of inflation targeting by the G3 central banks and later considers the implications if they were to do so as a group, for example, on the eve of the G7/8 Summit in June 2004 at Sea Island, Georgia. The case for each of the G3 central banks to adopt inflation targeting rests on somewhat different arguments at present. It is stronger for the Bank of Japan (BOJ) than for the European Central Bank (ECB) and stronger for the ECB than for the Federal Reserve. However, if all three central banks adopted an inflation-targeting framework, it would improve economic performance in each case, reduce uncertainties about G3 economic policies, and as a result enhance the stability of the international financial system.

Individual Adoption

If the G3 central banks were to adopt inflation targeting today, the Federal Reserve and the ECB would be maintainers (having achieved a substantial degree of price stability with inflation less than 5 percent), and the BOJ would be a reverser (with its inflation rate not only below 5 percent but also less than zero). Figure 4.1 presents data on consumer price index (CPI) inflation rates in Germany, Japan, and the United States for the 1990–2002 period, and appendix table A.4 presents data on inflation and forecasts of inflation for the individual G3 economies for 1990–2001, with Germany treated as a proxy for Euroland. The table also shows the average inflation rates for the nine current and former inflation targeters among the industrial countries as well as for the 13 potential inflation targeters, including each of the economies of the European Union separately (excluding Luxembourg).

On the basis of the level, variability, and predictability of inflation in the inflation-targeting industrial countries, the G3 economies are well positioned to adopt inflation targeting. Mark Stone (2003a, 1) classifies the G3 central banks as eclectic inflation targeters. They "have so much credibility that they can maintain low and stable inflation without full transparency and accountability with respect to an inflation target and with the flexibility to pursue other objectives." On average, for the 1990–2001 period US CPI inflation (3 percent) exceeded German inflation (2.3 percent) by about three-quarters of a percentage point, German inflation exceeded Japanese inflation (0.9 percent for the period as a whole) by almost one-and-a-half percentage points. The G3 average was about a percentage point less than the average for all the inflation targeters among the industrial countries.[2] Inflation variability (standard deviation) has been

---

2. The consumer price indices of the G3 economies are not strictly comparable. For example, although US CPI inflation has been higher than inflation in the euro area on average by half to one percentage point in recent years, the difference is roughly cut in half, and some-

Figure 4.1 Inflation in Germany, Japan, and the United States, 1990–2002

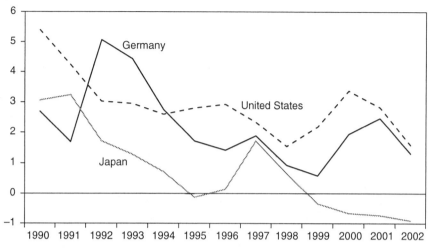

CPI = consumer price index

Note: Rates calculated from annual average CPI.

Source: IMF, *International Financial Statistics.*

about the same in Germany as in Japan, somewhat higher than in the United States, but the average for the G3 was about three-quarters of a percentage point less than the average of the industrial-country inflation targeters.

The one-year-ahead average forecast errors shown in appendix table A.4 have been remarkably small for each of the G3 economies and slightly negative on average. The root mean squared errors of these forecasts were also relatively small but on average were about double the average standard deviation reported in connection with the one-year-ahead forecasts. All three measures of accuracy on average were smaller in absolute size than the average of inflation-targeting industrial economies. The same absolute and relative relationships hold in the two-year-ahead forecasts.

The G3 economies are relatively homogeneous in their economic structures, compared with the range found in countries that are already inflation targeters. Several of the economies—or constituent national econo-

---

times is reversed, if the weights in the euro-area harmonized index of consumer prices (HICP) are used to estimate US inflation. The US CPI has higher weights on housing and the HICP has higher weights on food, apparel, and recreation. The HICP weights correspond more closely to those in the US chain-type price index for personal consumption expenditures (PCE). See Federal Reserve Bank of Cleveland (2000 and 2001).

mies in the European Union—face entrenched fiscal problems, but they have not reached the point where fiscal dominance affects the capacity of their central banks to implement monetary policy without being overwhelmed by a need to finance the government.[3] In the past decade or two, each of the G3 economies has dealt with instability in its domestic banking and financial system, and Japan continues to grapple with very deep-seated problems. The problems in Japan's financial system impair, at least to some degree, the effectiveness of monetary policy, but the BOJ does not face a monetary policy conflict—it is not constrained to focus on those problems and ignore inflation. On the contrary, the same expansionary monetary policy could help achieve both the objectives. Each of the central banks has more than enough institutional and technical capacity to implement an inflation-targeting framework for monetary policy.

The mandate of each central bank is compatible with the adoption of inflation targeting. In the case of the ECB and the BOJ, the mandates are hierarchical, placing price stability on top; in the case of the Federal Reserve, the mandate is dual, giving weight to both price stability and full employment.[4] Each of the central banks enjoys instrument independence; each has the authority to use the monetary policy instruments available to it to achieve its objectives without substantial interference from the rest of the government—executive branch (cabinet) or legislature (parliament).

In addition, each of the G3 central banks enjoys a substantial degree of goal independence, in the terminology of Guy Debelle and Stanley Fischer (1994). Subject to the constraints the central bank's legal mandate imposes, including the possibility that the mandate may be revised, goal-independent central banks are free to decide how to frame as well as implement monetary policy.

Debelle and Fischer along with Bernanke et al. (1999), Mishkin (2000b), Posen (2002), and many others argue that central banks should not enjoy goal independence because it undermines their accountability in a democratic society. Ernst Baltensperger, Andreas Fischer, and Thomas Jordan (2002), on the other hand, argue that goal independence is good because it permits the central bank to respond flexibly to changing and unknown circumstances and that this fact explains why central banks with strong

---

3. Some may argue that Japan is an exception to this generalization. However, in Japan the present issue is not loss of monetary control—that is, pressure on the BOJ to purchase directly the government's debt because the government is having difficulty placing it in the market. Rather, the issue is whether an even easier monetary policy in Japan would inappropriately or appropriately encourage the government to run even larger fiscal deficits.

4. Some might argue that a central bank with a dual mandate cannot or should not adopt inflation targeting, but the evidence presented in table 3.1 suggests that it is technically possible, and the argument of this study is that flexible inflation targeting is fully compatible with a dual mandate involving maximum sustainable employment and price stability.

goal independence have not chosen inflation targeting—to do so would be unnecessarily constraining.[5]

Alina Carare and Mark Stone (2003) argue similarly that countries in their category of flexible inflation targeting, such as the G3, Switzerland, and Singapore, should not practice full-fledged inflation targeting because it would provide no benefit with respect to low inflation since these countries appear to be less prone to time-inconsistency problems in their policies and to a possible cost with respect to reduced discretion in output stabilization. This issue is further discussed later in this chapter when I consider the best transition to inflation targeting of each of the G3 central banks by drawing upon, but not fundamentally altering the nature of, their goal independence. At this point, it is sufficient to observe that in a democratic society, the case for inflation targeting may be stronger for a central bank with substantial goal independence because it helps pin down the bank's policies. The goal independence of the Federal Reserve in the 1970s was associated historically with high US inflation rates!

The United States

In recent years, most advocates of inflation targeting for the United States have not based their arguments on the perception that the Federal Reserve has been doing a poor job in achieving a reasonable degree of price stability in the context of its existing mandate to conduct policy "commensurate with the economy's long run potential to increase production, so as to promote effectively the goals of *maximum employment, stable prices, and moderate long-run interest rates*" (emphasis added). This language was first introduced into the Federal Reserve Act in the Full Employment and Balanced Growth (Humphrey-Hawkins) Act of 1978, and Chairman Arthur F. Burns heavily influenced its crafting. He sought to avoid in the legislation specific numerical goals for the economy—although in the end, near-term numerical goals for inflation and unemployment were included for the government as a whole—to ensure that the three goals for

---

5. Baltensperger, Fischer, and Jordan base their classification of 21 industrial countries (excluding Iceland) on the data reported in Mahadeva and Sterne (2000) and find that only one of the five central banks that had "strong" goal independence as of 1999 (the Swedish Riksbank) had adopted inflation targeting; the other central banks with strong goal independence are in the United States, Japan, Germany (now ECB), and Switzerland. Carare et al. (2002) note that the central bank of Spain—classified by Baltensperger, Fischer, and Jordan as a central bank with "medium" goal independence (setting its objectives in consultation with the government)—was solely responsible for setting its inflation target in 1995, although there were, no doubt, informal consultations with the government. They also identify the central banks of six nonindustrial countries as setting their targets without the formal involvement of their governments—Chile, Colombia, Finland, Mexico, Poland, and Thailand. They do not include Peru in their analysis, but its central bank would also fall in this category.

the Federal Reserve were reasonably consistent and to avoid imposing on the Federal Reserve a monetary policy framework narrowly based on targeting a monetary aggregate.[6]

The Federal Reserve's mandate—often called a dual, though really a tripartite, mandate—conveys upon the Federal Reserve substantial goal independence in addition to its instrument independence; its mandate is expressed in words, and it is free, subject to the ex post review by Congress, to interpret those words as it sees best. In recent years, Federal Reserve officials have frequently interpreted the mandate as a dual mandate calling for "full employment and price stability" over the medium term (Meyer 2001). This interpretation recognizes no fundamental conflict between the two objectives, but it also provides no hint about how the Federal Reserve would or should handle the short-run trade-off, or any short-run conflict, between the two goals.

Inflation in the United States has declined steadily over the past 20 years and is now at a historically low level (figure 4.2).[7] One has to go back before 1967 to find a five-year period with lower average inflation (total CPI or core CPI) than over the past five years. Yet, apparently there are those who believe that the United States can and should do better on inflation to improve the performance of the real economy. The US inflation record of the past decade falls within any implicit or explicit band associated with a target of, say, 2 percent, but the bias in US inflation performance, by this standard, has been toward more than 2 percent. The increase in the CPI has averaged less than 3 percent with only one year (2000) with a larger annual change, 3.4 percent. The smallest annual

---

6. The Full Employment and Balanced Growth Act of 1978 did require the Federal Reserve to "maintain the growth of monetary and credit aggregates" at rates the Federal Reserve chose in order to achieve the goals listed. The Federal Reserve was required to announce objectives for the growth or diminution of one or more money and credit aggregates from the mid-1970s until July 2000, when the Federal Reserve Board stated in its *Monetary Policy Report to the US Congress,* "The legal requirement to establish and to announce such ranges had expired, and owing to uncertainties about the behavior of the velocities of debt and money, these ranges for many years have not provided useful benchmarks for the conduct of monetary policy." The Federal Open Market Committee (FOMC) had been chafing under this requirement since at least the mid-1990s. A new law, passed in 2000, dropped the requirement that the Federal Reserve announce such objectives.

7. Figure 4.2 presents data for the United States from 1983 to 2002 on the total (or headline) CPI, the chain-type price index for personal consumption expenditures (PCE), and the core (excluding food and energy) PCE index. The latter two indices are included, rather than the more conventional core CPI, because they are currently the preferred measures of inflation that the Federal Reserve Board presents in its semiannual *Monetary Policy Report to the US Congress.* The Full Employment and Balanced Growth Act of 1978 and the successive legislation of 2000 require the Federal Reserve to present its outlook for the economy. This outlook currently includes numerical forecasts by the board of governors and federal reserve bank presidents of nominal GDP, real GDP, PCE inflation, and unemployment presented as ranges, including all forecasts, and central tendencies, excluding outliers.

Figure 4.2 US inflation: CPI, PCE deflator, and core PCE deflator, 1983–2002

percent

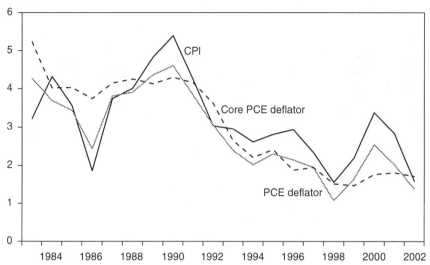

CPI = consumer price index

PCE = price index for personal consumption expenditures

Note: Rates calculated from annual averages of CPI, PCE, and core PCE. Core PCE excludes food and energy prices

Sources: CPI inflation: IMF, *International Financial Statistics;* PCE deflator and core PCE deflator: US Bureau of Economic Analysis.

change in the core price index for the personal consumption expenditures (PCE) deflator over the past 10 years was 1.5 percent in 1999; the total CPI increased 1.6 percent in 1998, aided by the collapse in oil and other commodity prices associated with the Asian financial crisis.[8]

The recent more favorable US inflation performance may or may not be due to less volatility in output, may or may not be sustainable, and may or may not have been due to good luck or good policy. Olivier Blanchard and John Simon (2001) tend to favor the first interpretation with respect to output and implicitly with respect to inflation, while Shaghil Ahmed, Andrew Levin, and Beth Anne Wilson (2002) tend to favor the second, at least with respect to inflation performance.

The active, global, intellectual debate about inflation targeting as a framework for the conduct and evaluation of monetary policy has touched US shores. Former Federal Reserve Chairman Paul A. Volcker

---

8. One can make too much of the differences between various measures of inflation, but the gap between the headline CPI and the core PCE deflator, which was about 35 basis points on average from 1990 to 1995, widened to 68 basis points between 1996 and 2002.

(1983) is on record with a definition of price stability: "A workable definition of reasonable 'price stability' would seem to me to be a situation in which expectations of generally rising (or falling) prices over a considerable period are not a pervasive influence on economic and financial behavior. Stated more positively, 'stability' would imply that decision making should be able to proceed on the basis that 'real' and 'nominal' values are substantially the same over the planning horizon—and that planning horizon should be suitably long." This definition of price stability is not unlike the one offered six years later by his successor Alan Greenspan (1989), "Price levels sufficiently stable so that expectations of change do not become a major factor in key economic decisions."[9]

The Federal Open Market Committee (FOMC) received a report on the achievement of price stability in 1989 and debated targeting inflation in 1995 and 1996. In 1999 the board of governors and seven federal reserve banks sponsored a conference on "Monetary Policy in a Low Inflation Environment" (Fuhrer and Sniderman 2000). The principal focus of this conference was on how to conduct monetary policy in a low-inflation environment, but it was inspired by one of the major issues in the debate about price stability and the desirability of the Federal Reserve's adopting an inflation target—whether an inflation target can be set too low.

More recently, Edward Gramlich (2000), Laurence Meyer (2001), Ben Bernanke (2003a), and Anthony Santomero (2003) have spoken about inflation targeting. Marvin Goodfriend (2000) of the Federal Reserve Bank of Richmond argues that the Federal Reserve is a quasi-inflation targeter but would like it to become a full-fledged member of the club (Goodfriend 2003). Frederic Mishkin and Adam Posen (1997) initiated their project with Bernanke and Thomas Laubach when the former were director of research and economist, respectively, at the Federal Reserve Bank of New York.[10] The Federal Reserve Bank of San Francisco sponsored a conference on inflation targeting in 1998 (Rudebusch and Walsh 1998).

Former Congressman Steve Neal as far back as 1989 introduced a joint resolution that would have instructed the Federal Reserve to achieve price stability.[11] Former Senator Connie Mack and Congressman James Saxton more recently have regularly introduced similar legislation. These

---

9. Greenspan (1994) used very similar words: "We will be at price stability when households and businesses need not factor expectations of changes in the average level of prices into their decisions."

10. Mishkin and Posen (1997) wrote favorably about international experience with inflation targeting. Bernanke et al. (1999) advocate inflation targeting for the United States. Bernanke has continued to promote the debate on inflation targeting for the United States since he became a member of the board of governors in 2002.

11. Federal Reserve Chairman Alan Greenspan testified at that time, "the Federal Reserve Board fully supports the thrust of the current resolution, because price stability is in the best interest of the nation, and because it is achievable."

proposed amendments to the Federal Reserve Act uniformly adopted some version of the Volcker-Greenspan language to define price stability and left it to the Federal Reserve to decide how to make that language operational, in effect leaving substantial goal independence with the Federal Reserve under a revised mandate with a single objective of price stability. They differed in the stringency of the requirements, including the time period over which "price stability"—so defined and made operational—was to be achieved and what was to follow after that point. The 2003 version of the legislation Saxton proposed calls upon the Federal Reserve Board and the FOMC to establish a definition of price stability, implement it through inflation targeting, and determine the action to be taken in case the target is missed—superflexible inflation targeting. None of this proposed legislation has yet made it out of a committee of the Senate or the House.

Notwithstanding this academic and, to a far lesser extent, political support for inflation targeting—or something closer to it than is now practiced in the United States—suspicions remain, including within the Federal Reserve, that the framework, if formally adopted, would or could be inappropriately constraining. The FOMC's discussion on January 31, 1995, in the expectation that the Federal Reserve would soon have to testify on the Mack legislation, is illustrative of the tensions (FOMC 1995, 38–59).

President Al Broaddus of the Federal Reserve Bank of Richmond argued in favor of a nonquantitative target using the Volcker-Greenspan-Neal formulation to characterize price stability. He used the terminology of inflation targeting to defend his position: "The credible objective would allow the Committee to pursue a more activist policy more freely in the short run . . . a credible long-term objective arguably would increase our flexibility in dealing with such shocks because we would not be worried about losing credibility in that situation" (FOMC 1995). Some of the supporters of Broaddus's position were a bit more doctrinaire, speaking against fine-tuning monetary policy in light of developments in the real economy and in favor of an increased focus on what central banks can achieve over the long run, which in this view does not include faster sustained real growth.

Then-Governor Janet Yellen made the case against Broaddus's position, focusing on the issue of inflation as the "sole objective of policy . . . with no weight being placed on achieving competing, ultimate goals for real variables . . . actions of this Committee affect not just the level and the variability of inflation but also at a minimum the variability of output and employment" (FOMC 1995). Supporters of her position, inter alia, argued "if it ain't broke, don't fix it."

I would score that FOMC debate more than eight years ago as 11 to 7 in favor of Yellen's position, or alternatively as 8 to 4 with 6 in the middle.

Greenspan summed up the discussion: "A general long-term view of price stability of the Neal form is a very useful conceptual anchor for us to do basically what we have been doing . . . I think we ought to have an inflation goal that is qualitative, as Al Broaddus says, one that is defined in operational terms, not in terms of numerical targets" (FOMC 1995). He also said,"We would always be moving in the direction of price stability, recognizing that we would not do so in a straight line because I do not think we have the philosophical, cultural, or political support in this society for that. There is still a short-term Phillips curve. People respond to it; they are aware of these trade-offs, and to deny them, I think, is a misunderstanding of how our political system works." During the discussion, he had commented,"My own judgment is that if we do not announce any specific inflation targets, our policy can actually be similar to what Al Broaddus was suggesting [a nonnumerical inflation objective]. If we do announce explicit inflation targets, they become in effect a statutory obligation for this Committee to adhere to; and I am not sure that by any reading of the Humphrey-Hawkins statute inflation targeting is consistent with it."

The FOMC returned to this issue twice in 1996, in January and July, in the context of the deliberations associated with the Federal Reserve Board's semiannual *Monetary Policy Report to the US Congress*. In July, they had before them a comprehensive summary of the literature as of that date prepared by David Stockton (1996) on the benefits and costs of establishing an inflation or price stability target for US monetary policy.

In the January discussion (FOMC 1996a, 37–50), Broaddus proposed that the Federal Reserve should declare that its objective was to keep inflation below 3 percent in 1996 and 1997 and "to take steps to bring the inflation rate down further over time."[12] His proposal did not carry; it was not put to a vote, but about half the participants sympathized with it. The judgment was made that it would be desirable and appropriate first to learn how much support Senator Mack had for his legislation. The substance of the discussion touched on issues such as the possible credibility bonus from having a numerical target and the usefulness of having a bit of inflation grease to help ease nominal wage rigidities.

The July discussion (FOMC 1996b, 41–68) featured a more formal "debate" between Janet Yellen and Al Broaddus. Yellen gave an articulate assessment of the pros and cons of low inflation as a target for monetary policy and concluded that the evidence at the time did not support an objective of less than 2 percent. Broaddus again made a specific proposal that the Federal Reserve should announce its intention to hold the line at 3 percent inflation and press the rate down further over time; as in the January meeting, about half the participants supported his position. The discussion touched on such issues as the need for an anchor for monetary policy, the definition of price stability and associated measurement issues,

---

12. The CPI inflation rate was 2.8 (2.5) percent in 1995, 3 (3.3) percent in 1996, and 2.3 (1.7) percent in 1997 (numbers in parentheses are December-to-December rates; the others are for the years on average).

the desirability of institutionalizing good performance on inflation, the usefulness of an inflation target in guarding against deflation, and the appropriate role of the central bank in a democracy.

On the last point, Chairman Greenspan concluded and effectively shut down the discussion: "I think the type of choice [of whether the central bank should proceed to try to achieve price stability given the progress that had been made] is so fundamental to a society that in a democratic society we as unelected officials do not have the right to make that decision. Indeed, if we tried to, we would find that our mandate would get remarkably altered." On the one hand, Greenspan did not think that the Federal Reserve should define its goals with any further precision than does its mandate; on the other, as long as Congress does not do so, the Federal Reserve retains its substantial goal independence to proceed as it sees best.

The remarks of the participants in the 1995 and 1996 FOMC discussions reflected the crosscurrents of opinion on monetary policy and the public relations challenge in establishing an inflation-targeting framework for monetary policy in the United States. In the ensuing period, US performance on inflation has come even closer to what one might expect of an inflation-targeting US central bank. As a consequence, some argue there is even less pressure to tamper with the status quo. The Federal Reserve has essentially achieved price stability, certainly on the Volcker-Greenspan definition; all that is lacking is an explicit target and a time horizon or procedure governing the return to that target if there is a significant departure. Moreover, policymakers tend to be concerned with avoiding failure; once they have an explicit target (for inflation), they have an opportunity to fail.

On the other hand, some are concerned that the Federal Reserve would err too much in the direction of ensuring success in achieving any inflation target, but one would expect more sophistication. As Lars Svensson (2001a), in his independent review of New Zealand's monetary policy, reminded New Zealand Minister of Finance Michael Cullen, when it comes to monetary policy, "mistakes in retrospect are unavoidable." It goes with the territory, but that does not mean that central bankers, anymore than anyone else, are comfortable inviting criticism.

Meanwhile, the debates continue about the pros and cons of inflation targeting for the United States. Within the Federal Reserve "family," Governor Edward Gramlich concluded (2000, 8), "For the United States, given the strong aversion to inflation already apparent in policy responses, there are pros and cons, but it is not obvious that a more formal regime of inflation targeting will lead to very great differences in actual monetary policies." Laurence Meyer (2001), then on the Federal Reserve Board of Governors, proposed a halfway house: adoption of an explicit inflation target, retention of the Federal Reserve's dual mandate, but rejection of inflation targeting. The staff of the International Monetary Fund (IMF

2003d) endorsed the Meyer view, advocating that the Federal Reserve should adopt a quantified statement of its longer-term inflation objective in the range of 2 percent to anchor inflation expectations and help guard against the risk of deflation while maintaining the Federal Reserve's dual mandate. A number of IMF executive directors subsequently supported the IMF staff view, but a few others argued that a numerical inflation objective is unnecessary and might erode the central bank's credibility in the absence of instruments to hit an inflation target with precision.

Greenspan (2001, 3), in remarks widely viewed as a response to Meyer, commented several months later, "The Federal Reserve can be quite explicit about its ultimate objective—price stability and the maximum sustainable growth in output that is fostered when prices are stable. By price stability, however, I do not refer to a single number as measured by a particular price index. In fact, it has become increasingly difficult to pin down the notion of what constitutes a stable general price level. . . . For all these conceptual uncertainties and measurement problems, a specific numerical inflation target would represent an unhelpful and false precision. Rather, price stability is best thought of as an environment in which inflation is so low and stable over time that it does not materially enter into the decisions of households and firms."

At his confirmation hearings in July (2002c, 3–4), Ben Bernanke said, "The main operational change under inflation targeting would be that the Fed, in consultation with the executive and legislative branches, would announce an explicit objective for core inflation over the medium term, say one to two years. . . . Although I am favorably disposed toward these incremental changes in the current framework of U.S. monetary policy, I know that not everyone agrees with this view, and that there are important, substantive arguments to be made on both sides of the issue."

Gramlich (2003, 2) more recently stated that the most important point is that monetary policy should be anchored in price stability. He could imagine achieving that objective through flexible inflation targeting (FIT), but he appears to favor a "flexible anchoring approach," in effect using a Taylor rule as an internal operational guide but without an announced inflation target: "The Fed, for example, does not follow FIT and has never announced a formal inflation target. But it has told the world many times that of all the available measures, it regards the price index for core personal consumption expenditures as the most realistic indicator of actual inflation. The time series for this preferred indicator shows that, over the past seven years, inflation has averaged 1.7 percent per year, not much above what many consider to be an inevitable quality-change bias in the index, implying a true inflation rate of close to zero. The standard deviation is only 0.12 percent per year. Pretty stable prices, and a pretty reasonable indication of an inflation target for a central bank that has never announced one."

Finally, Bernanke (2003a, 9) concluded a speech at a Washington conference in March saying,

> Inflation targeting, at least in its best-practice form, consists of two parts: a policy framework of constrained discretion and a communication strategy that attempts to focus expectations and explain the policy framework to the public. Together, these two elements promote both price stability and well-anchored inflation expectations; the latter in turn facilitates more effective stabilization of output and employment. Thus, a well-conceived and well-executed strategy of inflation targeting can deliver good results with respect to output and employment as well as inflation.

In the August 10, 2001, Blue Chip Economic Indicators report, 78 percent of an undisclosed number of those responding to a special survey answered "no" to the question: "Do you believe the conduct of U.S. monetary policy should be guided by FOMC's adoption of a specified inflation target?" A follow-up question was: "If the Fed utilized the consumer price index, excluding food and energy prices (core CPI), what should be its inflation target?" The consensus (average) was 1.92 percent; the average for the 10 respondents citing the highest figure was 2.5 percent, and the average for the 10 respondents citing the lowest figure was 1.25 percent. To benchmark the respondents' thinking, the year-over-year increase in the US CPI excluding food and energy averaged 2.4 percent over the previous five years (through 2000) and 3 percent over the previous 10 years. For the headline CPI, the average increases were 2.5 and 2.7 percent, respectively.

This report, presumably inspired in part by Meyer's paper (2001) on inflation targets, inflation targeting, and the Federal Reserve, delivered a month earlier, is interesting on several grounds. First, inflation targeting in the United States is not just a matter of academic or specialist interest, though the respondents to the Blue Chip survey hardly qualify as a representative sample of all Americans. Second, their choice of an inflation target for the FOMC is about half a percentage point below actual US experience over the previous decade but similar to Meyer's preference for 2 percent. This discrepancy tends to confirm the views of those who believe that if the United States were to have an inflation target, it would be set too low and would unduly constrain the growth of output. Third, notwithstanding the alleged biases of the respondents, they did not favor the FOMC's adoption of an inflation target to guide US monetary policy. Fourth, the questions did not ask whether the target should be expressed as a range or what time horizon should be associated with achieving any target. Finally, the questions did presume that the choice of a numerical target would be left to the FOMC—that is, without reliance on any political initiative or approval process.

Each of these elements bears on the issue of whether the United States should adopt an inflation-targeting framework for the conduct and evaluation of its monetary policy. The performance of the US economy over the past 20 years has been pretty good by US standards as well as from the vantage point of the stability of the international financial system, though some are critical of the asset price bubble, the wide swings in dollar exchange rates, or the US current account deficit. Growth has been sustained with only two, relatively mild, recessions. Against this background, why should the United States adopt inflation targeting?

Should the United States Adopt Inflation Targeting?

The case in favor of the United States adopting inflation targeting rests on six basic arguments. To review those arguments, I will assume that the US inflation-targeting framework would include the following basic elements:[13]

- A numerical target for inflation—headline CPI, core CPI, chain-type price index for PCE, or chain-type price index for core PCE—as a point, or a range with a midpoint of, around 2 percent.
- A time horizon for achieving that target if it has not already been achieved.
- Once the target has been achieved, a statement that the central bank will endeavor to achieve the target continuously.
- If there is a departure from the target, a statement in advance either about the time horizon for returning to the target (or range) or about the procedure to communicate such a time horizon to the central bank's publics—Congress, financial markets, and US citizens.
- Some enhancement of the Federal Reserve's semiannual *Monetary Policy Report to the US Congress* to make it look a bit more like an inflation report.[14]
- Inclusion in the reports of forecasts for inflation as well as the real economy (expected growth and unemployment), perhaps augmented with more detailed or longer-term forecasts and forecasts of other economic variables.

In this context, the first argument in favor of adopting inflation targeting as the Federal Reserve's framework for the conduct and evaluation of

---

13. These elements are presented not to spell out in detail what the Federal Reserve's inflation-targeting framework *should* look like but to provide some context for the discussion that follows. For these purposes, the devil is not in the details.

14. Some argue that the Federal Reserve's *Monetary Policy Reports* today are not "true" inflation reports. Those familiar with these reports over the past quarter century should recognize that their further evolution is not the biggest obstacle to the Federal Reserve's adopting inflation targeting as its framework for the conduct and evaluation of monetary policy. The addition of other bells and whistles with respect to evaluation is not excluded if the Federal Reserve were to adopt an inflation-targeting framework—for example, quarterly rather than semiannual monetary policy reports.

US monetary policy is that doing so would increase the transparency of its policy. Politicians, market participants, and the general public on Main Street as well as Wall Street would better understand the Federal Reserve's objectives. On the margin, this would reinforce the effectiveness of Federal Reserve policy because its actions would be more easily understood and implemented. In more pragmatic terms, if the Federal Reserve today is, as Greg Mankiw (2002) argues, a "covert inflation targeter," there is a strong case that it should "come clean," although Mankiw is ambiguous on this point. Goodfriend (2003) agrees with Mankiw that Federal Reserve policy has evolved over the past two decades to include many elements of inflation targeting and argues that the time has come to codify qualitative behavior in the form of a quantitative target.[15]

Second, the adoption of such a framework would enhance the consistency, continuity, and, therefore, credibility of Federal Reserve policy. In one form, this is the institutionalization argument for a stability-oriented US monetary policy—Volcker was not around forever and neither will be Greenspan. This familiar argument is insulting to the Federal Reserve and the serious women and men who serve on the FOMC. None of them, chairperson or member, is determinative in the conduct of US monetary policy; this is the strength of the Federal Reserve's collegial culture. What is more important, in my view, is to establish a basis for consistency in policy because the memories of central bankers are not infinitely long—a different perspective on the time-inconsistency problem. They are only longer than those of the average participant in financial markets because of their older average age. Throughout the Volcker and Greenspan eras at the Federal Reserve, the wrenching experience of the high US inflation in the late 1970s has served as a reminder of the consequences of carelessness when it comes to inflation. Inflation targeting would help institutionalize these memories in the Federal Reserve.

Third, the adoption of such a framework would increase the Federal Reserve's accountability. The central bank would have a well-defined, though far from precise, objective. More often than is now the case, the Federal Reserve would be obligated to explain both why it did or did not achieve that objective and what other considerations influenced its thinking, including the level of economic activity—the other principal element in the Federal Reserve's mandate. Greater transparency in the Federal Reserve's implicit objectives would interact with increased accountability

---

15. His preferred target is a range of 1 to 2 percent for the core PCE index over an 18–24-month period in the form of "strict inflation targeting," despite the narrowness of his preferred range. I suspect that he exaggerates the capacity of the Federal Reserve to anticipate movements in the core PCE, despite the fact that the core PCE has been within that range on an annual basis since 1995. Donald Kohn (2003), now a member of the Federal Reserve Board and a long-time member of the staff, rejects the view that the Federal Reserve's policy framework has evolved into implicit inflation targeting and therefore would only need to make its target explicit to become an inflation targeter.

with respect to their achievement, which would be fully consistent with other trends in public-sector management, including the Federal Reserve's discharging its responsibilities.

Fourth, as a consequence of the first three arguments, uncertainty about Federal Reserve policy would be somewhat reduced, contributing on the margin to reduced volatility in the economy.[16] The results presented in chapter 3 support placing some weight on this argument. As a consequence, the overall performance of the US economy would improve. The international financial system would also benefit not only from improved US economic performance but also from greater clarity about Federal Reserve policy.

Fifth, also on the international side, if the United States were to adopt inflation targeting, its North American Free Trade Agreement (NAFTA) partners—Canada and Mexico, both of whom are inflation targeters— would be better positioned to take account of US economic policies, improving the quality of their assumptions about those polices and, in the process, contributing to better policies in their own countries.[17] In effect, the adoption of inflation targeting by the United States would facilitate policy cooperation. Without going so far as explicit macroeconomic policy coordination among NAFTA partners, the Federal Reserve's inflation target would provide Canadian and Mexican authorities with an improved guide to US policy intentions. This in turn would facilitate policy dialogue, which is an important part of the coordination process (Truman 2003a).

Sixth, if the Federal Reserve were to adopt inflation targeting unilaterally, it would set a good example for the other two G3 central banks—the probability of the adoption of inflation targeting in Japan and Euroland would be increased. One's evaluation of this argument depends on one's evaluation of the benefits of the adoption of inflation targeting by the BOJ and the ECB.

The case against US adoption of inflation targeting also rests on six basic arguments. First, it is argued that by doing so, the Federal Reserve would be giving up flexibility that is inherent in its high degree of goal independence to respond differentially to disturbances that produce different effects on inflation rates or to different disturbances that produce sim-

---

16. It has been argued that the performance of the US economy in recent years has been good compared with industrial-country inflation targeters. Donald Kohn (2003) offers comparisons with Canada, the United Kingdom, and Sweden. However, the issue is not relative or good performance but better performance, and athletes, for example, know that they can always perform better.

17. Barry Eichengreen and Alan Taylor (2003) present statistical evidence in support of participants in a Free Trade Area of the Americas (FTAA) combining the adoption of floating exchange rates with inflation targeting to achieve a greater degree of exchange rate stability than is possible with alternative monetary frameworks.

ilar effects—for example, demand and supply shocks, shocks from financial-market tensions or widespread pressures on financial institutions, or asset price bubbles.[18] According to this argument, in seeking a balance between the two objectives specified in its dual mandate, the Federal Reserve under inflation targeting would tend to tip the balance always in favor of less inflation and more unemployment. This type of case can be made against strict inflation targeting (SIT), where the central bank is committed to reaching its target or the midpoint of its target range no matter what the circumstances. However, the practice of no inflation-targeting central bank today fits that description; all practice flexible inflation targeting (FIT). The possibility that some inflation-targeting central banks may come close to a SIT-type situation in their early days is not ruled out, but one of the strengths of inflation targeting is that it need not be a rigid formulaic approach to monetary policy that focuses exclusively on inflation in all circumstances.

The second common argument is "if it ain't broke, it don't need to be fixed." The common response to this argument can be found in some combination of, or variation upon, the first four arguments in favor of inflation targeting by the United States. More generally, this argument is most effective when it is anticipated that there are large unintended and unknown consequences associated with a decision. By definition, unknown consequences must remain unknown, but enough experience with inflation targeting as a framework for monetary policy in other countries leads one to conclude with reasonable confidence that the downside risks in the United States are likely to be small.

Third, if the United States adopts inflation targeting, the Federal Reserve may fail to reach its objectives, and its credibility will be undermined. This argument suffers from two weaknesses. One, mistakes are part of central banking as well as other human activities. The Federal Reserve could equally fail, or be considered to have failed, if it did not practice inflation targeting. Increased precision about one's objective does not normally lower the true probability of achieving them. Two, the chances of significant failure are limited because the United States, as a potential inflation targeter, is already classified as a maintainer.

---

18. This is the argument found in Carare and Stone (2003) for why countries in their category of flexible inflation targeting do not favor moving to the Carare-Stone category of full-fledged inflation targeters. On the other hand, Svensson (2003a) argues that inflation-targeting central banks should deal with the issue of the short-run trade-off between output and inflation objectives—which is particularly relevant to the US situation with the Federal Reserve's dual mandate—by announcing the parameter of the policymakers' objective function encapsulating the relative weights they place on missing their inflation target versus a deviation of actual from potential output. My view of this proposal is, "May work in theory, but can't see it working in practice." Mishkin (2003) reaches a similar conclusion; Svensson's proposal violates Mishkin's KISS (Keep It Simple, Stupid) principle.

Fourth, the Federal Reserve would be required to introduce a false sense of precision about what it is trying to accomplish, including with respect to price stability. In this view, the numerical definition of price stability may change as the nature of the economy and the statistical measurement of its progress change. The contrary view is that this happens today, and the Federal Reserve has to explain why, for example, it reduced its focus on the monetary aggregates or shifted its focus from the CPI to the PCE price index. There is nothing stopping an inflation-targeting central bank from modifying its framework for monetary policy, and many have done so, some several times. For some advocates of inflation targeting, such modifications of the framework may undermine inflation targeting's usefulness, but that is an extreme view and should not be associated with inflation targeting in general.

Fifth, some argue, or might argue, that inflation targeting would distract the Federal Reserve from other important issues in addition to the trade-off between inflation and output or employment—for example, the foreign exchange value of the dollar. According to this argument—which is somewhat hypothetical but nonetheless illustrative—the dollar became grossly overvalued in recent years, or may still be overvalued, and this is a serious blot on the overall US economic performance, contributing to an ever-widening US current account deficit, an ever-expanding net international debt position, and a distorted pattern of US production favoring nontraded over traded goods and services. I find it difficult to defend the view that the dollar's strength has on balance been a sustained negative factor for US economic performance since the mid-1990s. The US current account deficit has widened considerably, the US net international investment position is significantly more negative, and the production pattern of the US economy is more distorted than optimal, but these are not evidence of fundamental weakness of the US economy or a deep failure of national economic policy.

Exchange rates are endogenous variables, and policymakers are well advised to treat them as such, which is not the same as saying that they should ignore actual or expected (to the extent that they can be expected) movements in exchange rates. At times it may be appropriate for monetary or fiscal policy to be adjusted in light of exchange rate considerations—for example, imbalances in patterns of production of traded and nontraded goods and services or between overall production of goods and services in the economy and the absorption or demand for goods and services. On this basis, US policymakers have made reasonable judgments over the past decade, at least until the 2001 and 2003 tax legislation, which severely cut into the prospects for US saving and, all else equal, would be expected to contribute to further dollar appreciation, rather than depreciation, by putting upward pressure on long-term dollar interest rates and attracting more funds into dollar assets. Moreover, it is misguided to think that policymakers can or should seek to permanently alter or micromanage exchange rates through words or (sterilized) intervention (for an extensive discussion of this topic, see Truman 2003b).

Nevertheless, in the context of inflation targeting, it is reasonable to ask whether exchange rate considerations—in the narrow sense in which they may be relevant to large, mature industrial economies—strengthen or weaken the case for inflation targeting.[19] In the US case, if the Federal Reserve, say, in 1995 had adopted an inflation target of 2 percent (plus or minus 1 percentage point) for the core CPI, Federal Reserve policy would presumably have been marginally tighter, the expansion of economic activity would have been slightly dampened, which would have contributed to smaller current account deficits, and conventional macroeconomic models would predict that the foreign exchange value of the dollar in both nominal and real terms would have been slightly higher, which would have contributed to a larger US current account deficit.[20] Of course, conventional models have been quite mistaken in their predictions or assumptions about the behavior of dollar exchange rates in recent years. On balance, however, most empirical macroeconomic models imply that there will be little or no net impact on US external balances in nominal or real terms from changes in US monetary policy.[21]

Sixth, a related argument is that inflation targeting would distract the Federal Reserve from focusing on matters such as trends in prices of assets other than foreign currencies.[22] This argument is treated separately here because the literature on asset prices and inflation targeting is extensive.[23] The debate boils down to two related questions: should monetary

---

19. Chapter 5 considers this issue more broadly in the context of emerging-market and smaller industrial economies.

20. In the late 1990s, if the Federal Reserve had been more concerned about the dollar's strength than it was and had followed an easier policy to weaken the dollar, the likely net effect on the current account balance would have been negligible, but the net effect on the US economy would have further fueled what is now seen as a period in which excesses built up in the real and financial sectors of the economy.

21. For example, see Bryant et al. (1988) and Bryant, Holtham, and Hooper (1988). It should be noted that if the impact of tighter monetary policy on the nominal balance were zero, then the impact on the real balance would normally be expected to be slightly negative because the direction of the price effect on the nominal balance is positive (appreciation has a larger negative impact on the price of imports than on the price of exports). Thus, the structure of production and employment would be tilted marginally further against nontraded goods.

22. Much of the debate about the appropriateness of Federal Reserve's policies in the late 1990s concerns this issue, and it is also relevant to Japanese monetary policy, addressed later in this chapter.

23. See, for example, Stephen Cecchetti, "The Perils of Ignoring Bubbles," *Financial Times*, September 4, 2002, 11; Bordo and Jeanne (2002); Cecchetti, Genberg, and Wadhwani (2002); Cecchetti et al. (2000); and King (2002). On the general issue of asset prices and monetary policy, see, as a small sample, Borio and Lowe (2002); and Borio, English, and Filardo (2003). And on the other side of the issue, see Greenspan (2002a), Bernanke and Gertler (1999 and 2001), and Bernanke (2002a).

policy take account of asset prices? How does the answer to this question affect one's assessment of inflation targeting as a framework for monetary policy in an industrial country such as the United States?

On the first question, while opinions do differ, the weight of those opinions is on the side of those who think that it is very challenging to identify with conviction bubbles or booms in asset prices. Even if one thinks the central bank can detect them, in a market-oriented economy, the central bank should think deeply before using monetary policy (interest rates) to deal with them. If the central bank decides to do so, whether or not it is right, it risks doing greater damage to the economy than if the boom had just run its course possibly, but not necessarily, leading to a bust. The IMF (2003f) finds that busts followed booms for only one quarter of all asset price booms from 1959 to 2002 in industrial countries.

If the central bank is correct in identifying an asset price boom and decides to do something about it, it could counteract the overshooting in one direction with an overshooting in the other direction. If it is wrong, it will have needlessly tanked the economy. Nothing in this line of reasoning says that central banks should not worry about asset prices or that they should not consider the possibility of price bubbles and their implications for economic performance; central banks should worry about everything. Nor does it say that central banks should never take account of trends in asset prices nor try to affect bubbles or booms. The key point is that the occasions on which any given central bank is likely to be in a position to act decisively are more like once every four business cycles rather than four times every business cycle.

On the second question—whether concern about asset price bubbles should affect a decision to adopt inflation targeting—the arguments are subtler. Once again, much depends not only on how frequently one might think that an inflation-targeting central bank might want or need to act to deal with the bubble but also on whether one envisages inflation targeting as strict or flexible. As a practical matter, flexible inflation targeting is relevant to any sensible discussion of this topic. Inflation targeting is not a monetary rule—as Michael Bordo and Olivier Jeanne (2002) characterize it—that prevents central banks from exercising judgment; it is also not fixated on a single horizon—as Claudio Borio and Philip Lowe (2002) characterize it—preventing the central bank from taking a longer-term view.[24] Inflation targeting is fully consistent with the view that monetary policy is and should be an art informed—not dictated—by science.

What is the bottom line? The reader will have noted that, as a well-trained former central banker, I have not only cleverly included the same number of arguments in favor of inflation targeting by the United States

---

24. Claudio Borio, William English, and Andrew Filardo (2003) arrive at a more balanced judgment on this issue.

as against that view but also offered more rebuttals to the latter than the former, thereby tipping my hand.

On balance, if the United States were to adopt inflation targeting as its framework for monetary policy, the evidence from theory and practice is that the benefits in terms of somewhat better US economic performance would outweigh the costs, which mostly take the form of remote downside risks that any sensible central banker should be able to avoid. Moreover, the direct neighborhood benefit to Canada and Mexico might be substantial, comparable to the direct benefit to the world economy if the G3 adopted inflation targeting. The world economy would benefit from somewhat better US economic performance. However, increased clarity about US monetary policy under inflation targeting could be a considerably larger benefit to the extent that the Federal Reserve is the de facto global central bank on which decisions of many other monetary and fiscal authorities depend. Moreover, the indirect benefit to the international financial system from US leadership in this area would be more substantial if US adoption of inflation targeting induced the ECB and BOJ to follow suit.

How to Get from Here to There?

How might the United States go about adopting inflation targeting? This is not a trivial issue. The US political system is complex, and the Federal Reserve's policies, status, methods, and legitimacy have been challenged in the past. Although the Federal Reserve has strong overall public support, it has often been criticized by those who think that its policies should be looser or tighter; should be guided by the price of gold, grain, the international value of the dollar, or other assets; or should be decided upon at public meetings by a body with a very different composition. As noted earlier, the Federal Reserve now has operational or instrument independence; it can set the federal funds rate without seeking any other body's or official's permission, subject to ex post review by Congress of the consistency of the Federal Reserve's actions with its statutory mandate.[25] Its dual or tripartite mandate conveys upon the Federal Reserve a large degree of goal independence, or "insulation"—which is my preferred term—in addition to its instrument independence.[26]

Recent historical experience has contributed to reluctance on the part of thoughtful observers to recommend that Congress write into law a specific target for inflation. The Full Employment and Balanced Growth

---

25. Bernanke (2003a) and Kohn (2003)—both members of the Federal Reserve Board but with different views on inflation targeting—recognize that this is a delicate issue with respect to the democratic balance governing the Federal Reserve's role in the United States.

26. Kohn (2003) argues, unconvincingly in my view, that the Federal Reserve's dual mandate severely restricts its goal independence.

(Humphrey-Hawkins) Act of 1978 did so on a one-time basis. The targets were missed by wide margins, and the exercise was never taken very seriously, in part because of increases in oil prices in the late 1970s. Moreover, Congress would be unlikely to cede such authority over the Federal Reserve to the executive branch. Thus, it might be a challenge for the United States to be able to get to the "there" of inflation targeting from the "here" of its current legal framework and the reality of recent good economic performance on inflation and, also, growth.[27]

It is conceivable that in an outpouring of international cooperation in the context of the adoption of inflation targeting by the other two G3 economies and by coincidence of the alignment of the political stars within the country, the United States could adopt a simple framework for inflation targeting through an act of Congress. Such coincidences do occur even in central banking.[28] The legislative route to inflation targeting would be a long shot, no matter how desirable it might be from the standpoint of democratic legitimacy or of solidifying the consensus for this type of minor adjustment in the Federal Reserve's monetary policy framework.

Bernanke et al. (1999) deal with the question of "how to get there" for the United States by proposing that the responsibility for setting a numerical long-run target that defines price stability might be assigned by an act of Congress to a standing commission, including the Federal Reserve. The commission would have the power to change the goal, for example, in the face of a change in the estimates of the measurement bias in the CPI.[29] They suggest that any actual transition path, which might not be needed today, should be left to the Federal Reserve.

The proposal by Bernanke et al. has three obvious weaknesses, if the principal aim is to accomplish the objective of having the United States become an inflation targeter: first, standing commissions to bring about changes in US policy have not been overwhelmingly successful in US po-

---

27. Recall the results presented in table 2.4: the choice of inflation targeting in practice has been negatively associated with both higher growth and higher inflation. US growth performance over the relevant period, 1980–2000, was slightly below the mean for the countries included in the regression, and US inflation performance was substantially below the mean, implying that both factors can be interpreted as consistent with US adoption of inflation targeting.

28. One example is that the Federal Reserve took up its seat on the board of the Bank for International Settlements in 1994, more than 60 years after that seat had been set aside for the US central bank. This change did not require an act of Congress, but it did involve extensive consultations with the executive branch and the chairpersons and ranking minority members of five congressional committees.

29. Their recommendation, as of the time of writing, was for a goal of 2 percent (one percentage point above a point estimate of the measurement bias in the CPI), and they declared themselves as "leaning toward" recommending targeting the core CPI, excluding food and energy prices.

litical history. Occasionally, ad hoc commissions have focused public opinion, but in general, commissions (standing or ad hoc) are a means to avoid—not resolve—issues. Second, this route would require legislation, which would certainly stretch out the process of adopting inflation targeting and could well lead to some unintended negative consequences for an institution—the Federal Reserve—that most observers agree has done admirably in recent years in fulfilling its mandate. Third, the proposal would create another layer of oversight of the Federal Reserve between the Congress and the institution itself, which would tend to undermine the very political legitimacy that the proposal was intended to establish. The proposal is designed to get around the Federal Reserve's high degree of goal independence. A better course would be to live with it and exploit other channels to ensure that the Federal Reserve's exercise of its goal independence does not go against the will of the people or that of the people's representatives.[30]

What is a better path toward the adoption of inflation targeting by the United States for the benefit of the United States and the world economy? Following is a proposal for the concrete steps the Federal Reserve could take:

- The Federal Reserve, having decided that inflation targeting would be an improved framework for the conduct and evaluation of US monetary policy, should consult informally with the administration and key members of Congress on its intention to adopt the framework under its existing mandate.
- The chairman of the board of governors, subsequently, should publicly announce the Federal Reserve's intention in one of the Federal Reserve's *Monetary Policy Reports to the US Congress*, providing a full rationale for the move, including how this move would be consistent with its current mandate.
- In his testimony, the chairman should specify a date six or more months ahead when the Federal Reserve would put forward the parameters of its implementation of the framework in its next *Monetary Policy Report*. This would allow public debate on the basic proposal and an opportunity for Congress, via its oversight role and, possibly, a congressional resolution, to advise the Federal Reserve not to proceed.

---

30. Goodfriend (2003) has a similar solution to the challenge faced by the Federal Reserve and the Congress with respect to short-run policy—that is, whether it is too tight given the long-run objective for inflation or too easy. His proposal is that the Federal Reserve should agree to the establishment of an independent "monetary policy forum" that would meet semiannually—a month before the regularly scheduled FOMC meetings—to debate the short-run outlook and what the Federal Reserve should do about it. Again, I fail to see how creating another layer between the Federal Reserve and the Congress serves the democratic objective.

- Assuming that this second phase ignites only mild criticism from those who want the Federal Reserve to target the level of a particular price or from those who want the Federal Reserve to target an unemployment or real growth rate, the Federal Reserve in its following *Monetary Policy Report* would put forward the parameters of the proposed inflation-targeting framework: (a) price index; (b) target figure and/or range; (c) time horizon in which it would expect to meet the target, including whether it would expect the target to be achieved continuously, as of a certain date (fourth quarter), or over the cycle; (d) any exceptions or escape clauses that it would propose to establish ex ante; (e) time horizon over which it would anticipate returning to the target if there were a departure or a process by which such a time horizon would be chosen following such an event; and (f) other changes in its policies and procedures that would enhance the Federal Reserve's transparency and accountability under the new framework.
- After a further discrete interval for comment and possible adjustments, the Federal Reserve would announce the formal adoption of its inflation-targeting framework, or perhaps abandon the effort.

Thus, the entire process might take a year from the announcement in, say, February 2004 until final adoption in February 2005. After the Federal Reserve completes the adoption of its inflation-targeting framework, it would be free to make adjustments in the framework—as other inflation targeters have—and would be expected to communicate those adjustments promptly to Congress and the public. Those adjustments might occur in response to reactions from Congress, or critiques by the market, academics, and think tanks, or merely in light of experience and changing conditions. The most important point is that Congress would retain the power to advise or require the Federal Reserve to modify or abandon the framework.

Three arguments support this proposed approach. First, it is pragmatic. Second, it is fully consistent with the existing institutions, the powers of the Congress, and the delegation through legislation of some of those powers to the Federal Reserve. Third, it recognizes that the adoption of inflation targeting would be an evolution not a revolution in the conduct and evaluation of US monetary policy: inflation targeting for the United States would be a minor improvement on the current monetary policy framework, but it would not require or bring about radical changes. The suggestion that the proposed step-by-step procedure would upset the democratic balance governing the Federal Reserve today is difficult to understand in light of historical experience, including the Federal Reserve's decision—without public consultation—in October 1979 to alter its implementation of monetary policy.

The two principal arguments against this proposed approach are: first, that the Federal Reserve would be taking unto itself power that belongs in the political arena; second, that there is no consensus in favor of inflation targeting in the United States. The answer to the first argument is that the Federal Reserve is exercising this power every day as it reaches judgments about how best to achieve its mandate and what precise figures to use to judge its success or failure; inflation targeting as outlined would help legitimize current practice. The answer to the second argument is that the process outlined should reveal whether there is sufficient consensus, including on the parameters of the inflation-targeting framework that the Federal Reserve would be using; the process should either strengthen the Federal Reserve in discharging its mandate or lead to adjustments in the way the Federal Reserve is doing so. Either way, it would be a healthy, open, and democratic process.[31]

In conclusion, the objective case for US adoption of an inflation-targeting framework for the conduct and evaluation of monetary policy is positive but not overwhelming. If the Federal Reserve were to adjust the framework under which it conducts its policy and under which that policy is evaluated, the transparency and accountability of its policy would be improved. This would, on the margin, benefit US economic performance, without any major downside risks. As a result, other countries, in particular, and the world economy in general, would also benefit from unilateral US action in this area. On the other hand, if the United States were to act in concert with the rest of the G3, the benefits might be more substantial.

Euroland

Europe is the only region where economies have stopped using an inflation-targeting framework for the conduct and evaluation of their monetary policies. Finland and Spain—having adopted inflation targeting in early 1993 and 1995, respectively, in the wake of the crises in the exchange rate mechanism (ERM) of the European Monetary System (EMS) in the fall of 1992 and the summer of 1993—joined nine other countries in stage three of the Economic and Monetary Union (EMU) on January 1, 1999, exiting from inflation targeting in the process.

One can fairly assume that the governors of their national central banks (NCBs) favored inflation targeting as a monetary policy framework for the ECB at the center of the European System of Central Banks (ESCB)

---

31. Some would argue that my proposed path to inflation targeting for the United States is deficient precisely because of a lack of formal endorsement by the executive or legislative branch. According to this argument, such an endorsement would inter alia serve to discipline the accompanying fiscal policy. This argument is an example of the perfect being the enemy of the good and of the error made in setting too many preconditions in the way of the adoption of inflation targeting.

when it began full-scale operations.[32] Two of the three members of the European Union that continue de jure to conduct independent monetary policies—Sweden and the United Kingdom—also are dedicated inflation targeters whose practices in this regard are held up to the world as sterling examples.[33] Although their governors have not formally opined on such a sensitive matter, no one doubts that the Riksbank and the Bank of England would be more supportive of fully joining the ESCB if the ECB adopted inflation targeting. The same goes for the central banks of the Czech Republic, Hungary, and Poland—three countries that will join the European Union in May 2004 but are now inflation targeters.

As shown in appendix table A.2, five of the 14 EU central banks covered in this study had average CPI inflation rates of more than 3 percent during the 1990–2002 period.[34] Three of them had standard deviations of more than two percentage points.[35] Inflation performance has been more subdued in recent years. Based on the European Union's harmonized index of consumer prices (HICP), inflation in the euro area averaged 1.8 percent during the 1998–2002 period.

Figure 4.3 presents data on the evolution of Euroland's annual average short-term interest rate, output gap (as estimated by the Organisation for Economic Cooperation and Development, OECD), and areawide HICP inflation rate along with the difference between the highest and lowest national CPI inflation rates and the standard deviation of those national rates from the areawide average for the 1998–2002 period. The first year, 1998, was a year of transition for 11 of the 12 euro area countries, as they qualified for and joined the ECB's common monetary policy.

It is instructive that since 1998 the standard deviation of the national inflation rates—excluding Greece, which only joined in 2001—has been higher than in 1998. The degree of monetary independence for the NCBs before 1999 was severely limited as they strove to qualify for the third stage of the EMU. Policy was directed at achieving convergence, including convergence of inflation to low rates.

Subsequently, under a common monetary policy, differences in national inflation rates have become the principal means of adjusting competitiveness. Thus, for faster-growing countries like the Netherlands, CPI inflation rose from 2 percent in 1998 to 4.5 percent in 2001, and for Ireland from

---

32. Many outside observers also urged the ECB to adopt inflation targeting, including Bernanke et al. (1999).

33. Denmark is the third EU country. It has not de jure turned over its monetary policy to the ECB, but its policy is linked to the ECB's as a consequence of Denmark's participation in the transitional ERM.

34. The five are Greece, Italy, Portugal, Spain, and the United Kingdom. Forecast data for Luxembourg were not available, and therefore that country is not included in the sample.

35. The exceptions were Italy and Spain.

Figure 4.3 Euro area: Short-term interest rate, output gap, and inflation, 1998–2002

percent

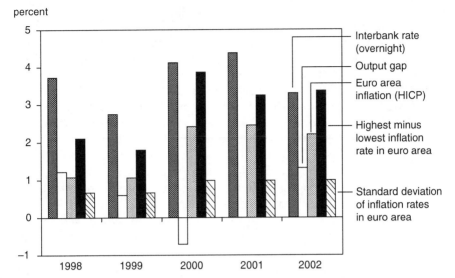

HICP = harmonized index of consumer prices

Notes: Output gap and euro area inflation include Greece. All other figures exclude Greece for all years. Interbank rate for 2002 is January to November average, as December data are not yet available. Output gap is shown with opposite sign compared with the standard presentation; a positive sign means actual output was below potential.

Sources: Interbank rate: IMF, *International Financial Statistics*; output gap: OECD, *Economic Outlook*; euro area inflation: ECB, *Monthly Bulletin*.

2.4 percent in 1998 to 5.6 percent in 2000. Meanwhile in slower-growing countries like France, inflation has been subdued at less than 2 percent for the past four years (1999–2002), and in Germany 12-month inflation for May 2003 reached a low of 0.7 percent, and the shortfall in output relative to potential widened to 2.6 percent.[36] The common monetary policy aids and abets this process of adjustment via differential inflation rates because in the first group of countries, real interest rates are lower than in the second group. Of course, ECB monetary policy is based on the actual and expected performance of the euro area as a whole, and a comparison

---

36. Senior ECB officials, for example, Otmar Issing (2001c), have acknowledged this issue of inflation disparities and the risk that a low average inflation for Euroland as a whole may push some constituent national economies into deflation. Their answer appears to be a combination of (a) "that is what a common monetary policy is all about" and (b) "get your internal act together so that you have a more flexible economy." The ECB (2003a) has published an analysis of the dispersion of inflation rates among euro area economies. Dispersion declined substantially from the early 1990s until 1999, but since has edged up by about half a percentage point.

of the evolution of short-term interest rates and output gaps in figure 4.3 suggests that ECB policy has been mildly countercyclical for Euroland as a whole.

As noted earlier, the ECB has been endowed with a high degree of goal independence, perhaps the most of any central bank in modern history, because its mandate is enshrined in a treaty. Under the Maastricht amendments to the Treaty establishing the European Community (Article 105(1)), "The primary objective of the ESCB shall be to maintain price stability. Without prejudice to the objective of price stability, ESCB shall support the general economic policies in the Community with a view to contributing to the objectives of the Community as laid down in Article 2." Article 2 states those objectives, "To promote throughout the Community a harmonious and balanced development of economic activities, sustainable and non-inflationary growth respecting the environment, a high degree of convergence of economic performance, a high level of employment and social protection, the raising of the standard of living and quality of life, and economic and social cohesion and solidarity among Member States."

A commonsense interpretation of this language would be that the ECB has a hierarchical mandate, with the price stability goal at the top but with full employment and growth as subsidiary objectives. All do not share that interpretation. Otmar Issing et al. (2001, 67), in writing about the monetary policy strategy of the ECB in its first years, argue that the language of Article 2 is of such a general nature that it is not a practical guide to policy. They state, "Uncertainties on the effectiveness of monetary policy as a means to stabilize output fluctuations are mirrored, instead, by the unwillingness [of the ECB] to take a specific stance in this respect." The medium-term view of the ECB is not unlike that of the Federal Reserve: "The maintenance of price stability represents the key contribution of monetary policy to 'support the general economic policies in the Community' and it is the best monetary policy can do to foster a high rate of growth." The difference between the views of the two central banks lies in their different views of their responsibilities in the short run.[37]

Not surprisingly, much of the discussion of the success or failure of the ECB over its first four years has focused on two issues: (1) the definition of price stability adopted by the ECB's governing council and (2) the extent to which the ECB has pulled its weight with respect to its subsidiary objective of supporting the general economic policies of the European Community.

---

37. It is indicative that the index of the book authored by Issing et al. (2001) on ECB monetary policy and strategy contains no entries for employment, unemployment, demand, supply, or potential output, although the text uses the concepts and occasionally the words. On the other hand, the index contains multiple entries for inflation, inflation bias, and, of course, price stability!

The ECB adopted as its operational definition of price stability the "year-on-year increase in the HICP for the euro area of below 2 percent." This "is to be maintained over the medium term." The ECB has argued (*Monthly Bulletin*, January 1999, 46), "The phrase 'below 2%' clearly delineates the upper bound for the rate of measured inflation in the HICP which is consistent with price stability. At the same time, the use of the word 'increase' in the definition clearly signals that deflation, i.e., prolonged declines in the level of the HICP index would not be deemed consistent with price stability." Thus, the ECB laid out a hard ceiling for inflation, did not specify what it meant by the medium term—other than saying that the phrase "reflects the need for monetary policy to have a forward-looking, medium-term orientation"—and indicated a soft floor for inflation. Eugenio Domingo Solans (2000) stated explicitly that the ECB has not adopted a symmetric definition of price stability in which rates of inflation below the floor are treated with the same amount of concern as rates of inflation above the ceiling.[38]

According to many critics, the ECB has confused financial markets and the public by operationally resting its "stability-oriented strategy" on two pillars: "a prominent role for money, as signaled by the announcement of a quantitative reference value for the growth rate of a broad monetary aggregate, and a broadly based assessment of the outlook for price developments and risks to price stability in the euro area as a whole" (ECB *Monthly Bulletin*, January 1999, 46). Solans (2000) states that this broadly based assessment is not the same as an inflation target. Moreover, he says that the ECB's definition of its price stability mandate is not the exclusive focus in this broadly based assessment; in other words, the definition is not the same as the second pillar. Commenting on the ECB's decision in December 2000 to issue to the public conditional staff "projections" (not "forecasts"), Issing (2000, 4) states, "Neither the ECB [overall] strategy nor, for that matter, its second pillar can be characterized as pursuing an inflation targeting policy." The ECB can be said to have an active aversion to being classified as an inflation-targeting central bank!

---

38. Solans' statement (2000, 4) leaves considerable ambiguity about whether the ECB would be more concerned about inflation above 2 percent or deflation below zero: "The idea of symmetry when targeting the objective, which characterizes inflation targeting, does not apply in any way to the definition of stability of the ECB. Avoiding deflation as well as inflation cannot be compared with the symmetric approach of inflation targeting, which implies not accepting inflation levels below the target as a policy to foster economic growth." Issing et al. (2001), however, argue that because the ECB has established a floor, price stability in the euro area excludes both inflation and deflation and is symmetric. Issing (2002) argued that the floor should be considered to be 1 percent. It also can be argued that the ECB's "reference value" for M3 growth of 4.5 percent, along with the midpoints of its range for potential growth (2 to 2.5 percent) and M3 income velocity (.5 to 1 percent), imply a midpoint for inflation of 1.5 percent; the ranges for potential and velocity imply a range of 1 to 2 percent. However, the ECB has not embraced either inference.

The ECB's critics sometimes argue that the central bank's stated policy is limited tolerance for inflation above 2 percent and concern if inflation is below zero for an extended period; in other words, the ECB can be described as having a point target of 1 percent, not very far from many estimates of the measurement bias in aggregate price indices.[39] In this sense, the range implies a willingness to tolerate de facto, though not statistical, deflation.[40] To date, one has only observed the ECB's behavior with respect to the upper end of the range, a short-term tolerance; neither actual nor projected inflation in the euro area has been less than 1 percent since January 1999.

On December 5, 2002, ECB President Wim Duisenberg announced the bank's intent to conduct a serious assessment and evaluation of its monetary strategy. On May 8, 2003, he announced the results of that evaluation: the definition of price stability was left unchanged at inflation less than 2 percent. However, the ECB's governing council agreed that in pursuit of that goal, "it will aim to maintain inflation rates close to 2 percent over the medium term, thus, in effect, raising the soft floor of its definition of price stability." The announcement and the background papers (ECB 2003b) give a nod in the direction of some concern about the potential problem of deflation but otherwise argue that the ECB found no convincing argument to change its strategy. The ECB did find arguments but judged that they were not convincing!

ECB critics argue that it has adopted a target that is too low for the good of the European economy (Wyplosz 2001), is insufficiently concerned about deflation, and is obsessively concerned about inflation above 2 percent. On the other hand, Anja Decressin and Jörg Decressin (2002) find no evidence from their comparison of German labor markets with those in the United States and the United Kingdom to support an ECB inflation target above 2 percent. However, they ignore the fact that the ECB's implicit target is not 2 percent but less than that.

More broadly, ECB critics argue that it has failed adequately to support the general economic policies in the European Community under its hierarchical mandate. Not only has it chosen too low a ceiling for inflation but it has also been obsessive, some would say, about not easing once it was

---

39. Paul de Grauwe (2002) gives the ECB higher marks on transparency than the Federal Reserve because at least the ECB uses numbers in its definition of price stability, which de Grauwe characterizes as an inflation "target" of 0 to 2 percent versus the Federal Reserve's creative ambiguity.

40. Giancarlo Corsetti et al. (2002, 55–56) conclude that the ECB's definition of price stability as inflation of less than 2 percent may be too tight: "Once measurement errors in prices due to quality improvements are taken into account, implementing Euro-area wide policies implying a 1 percent inflation rate in Germany could easily push this country to the verge of deflation."

breached, even though inflation was expected to decline to below 2 percent. Moreover, members of the ECB's governing council have consistently argued that monetary policy has no role in dealing with the euro area's challenging macroeconomic problems: high unemployment, low investment rates, modest increases in productivity, and—for a period until early 2001—a declining currency.

In response to such criticisms, one hears two arguments from ECB representatives: first, the ECB does not believe in fine-tuning the economy through monetary policy. For example, Issing et al. (2001) question whether it is wise for central banks to attempt to stabilize output in the short run. Second, ECB monetary policy has little or no role to play in dealing with the serious problems in the real economy of the euro area. The correct way to deal with these problems, it is argued, is through additional restraint and rationalization of the fiscal accounts of the euro area governments and fundamental structural reform through accelerated deregulation of markets for factors of production (labor and finance) and goods and services (lower barriers to competition and increased efficiency).

By way of illustration, Issing (2000, 2001a, and 2002) and more recently Wim Duisenberg and Lucas Papademos (2002) point to a lack of fiscal discipline and structural reforms as holding back euro area growth. The implicit argument is that all euro area unemployment may not be structural, but most of it is; therefore, it would be a mistake for monetary policy to be directed at dealing with the nonstructural component because politicians and policymakers—ever reluctant to make decisions that are painful to some groups in society—will get the mistaken impression that the ECB can do it all, and they will relax their own modest, plodding efforts at fundamental reform.

The ECB may be right about the political economy of structural reform, but critics may reasonably claim that the ECB has limited competence in political economy, and it is not fulfilling its own mandate. It could have been providing more support to the general economic policies of the European Community without prejudice to its primary objective of maintaining price stability. Laurence Ball (1996) has demonstrated, and the evidence in Blanchard and Wolfers (2000) also supports the view, that European macroeconomic policies, in their failure to adequately deal with shocks, have contributed not only to the nonstructural component of today's high level of unemployment in Europe but also, through sins of omission via "hysteresis" effects, to the structural component. At the less technical level, one needs only to look at OECD data on output gaps to infer that macroeconomic policy, in particular monetary policy with its greater room to maneuver, has played a role in sustaining a high level of unemployment in the euro area. For the 1994–2003 period, using projections for 2002 and 2003, the average output gap (shortfall of actual output relative to potential output) in the euro area has been 1.2 percent of potential GDP.[41] For the United Kingdom, a country that presumably was well situated to be affected by similar external shocks, the comparable figure was 0.5 percent, while for Canada and the United States the average gaps were 0.4 and negative 0.09 percent, respectively. (A negative output gap means that actual output exceeds potential.) Over the second half of the 1994–2003 period, 1999–2003, when the ECB was fully responsible for euro area monetary policy, the average output gap was 0.5 percent for the euro area, while for the United Kingdom it was 0.2 percent, for Canada a negative 0.7 percent (with average inflation through 2002 of less than 2.5 percent), and for the United States a negative 0.08 percent.

In retrospect, the ECB could have safely followed a more activist policy on growth starting in 1999. Some may argue that the euro's weakness until early 2001 prevented the ECB from doing so. Outside observers do not know how important the euro's value has been in ECB deliberations. As is well known, and often commented upon negatively, the ECB has chosen not to reveal much about the nature of its internal discussions of monetary policy.[42] Euroland is about as closed an economy as the United States, suggesting that the ECB should be quite safe in ignoring the first-round effects of any euro weakness.

Moreover, because the dollar was strong against most currencies through early 2002, the nominal effective decline of the euro from the fourth quarter of 1998 through the first quarter of 2002—when the dollar peaked—was only 15.1 percent, less than 5 percent per year, compared with its depreciation of 25.5 percent against the dollar (IMF *International Financial Statistics*). Finally, the evidence from around the world supports a view of reduced pass-through effects on inflation from exchange rate changes (Gagnon and Ihrig 2002 for industrial countries, and Kamin 1998, Goldfajn and Werlang 2000, and Choudhri and Hakura 2001 primarily for developing countries).

Thus, the ECB would have been more than justified to take a medium-term view of the euro's weakness. For relatively closed economies like the euro area and the United States, sustained movements in exchange rates in the first instance affect price levels (movements expected to be transitory can be safely ignored) and the allocation of production and resources between traded and nontraded goods and services, and not rates of price level changes over the medium term. Therefore, ECB policy should have ignored the decline in the euro except to the extent that it was expected to

---

41. These data are from annex table 11 in the OECD's *Economic Outlook* 72, published in December 2002. Mishkin (2003) argues caution in using estimates of potential output to help guide monetary policy; they are constructs that require constant attention but are useful constructs, and the constant attention is itself an analytical aid.

42. Issing (2000) and, one would presume, his colleagues are highly critical of any emphasis on core measures of inflation, other than for analytical purposes, for any stability-oriented central bank.

excessively stimulate demand for Euroland goods and services or to have direct or indirect spillover or second-round effects on prices. Given the closed nature of the euro area and the relatively modest decline of the euro on an effective basis, those effects should not have been particularly large.[43] However, I suspect, based on ECB statements about second-round effects and impacts on wages, that that was not the conclusion in Frankfurt.

One has the impression that over the past four years, ECB policy has been designed—much like the policy of the BOJ during the same period for Japan—to permit unemployment to rise in order to force governments to address more forcefully the structural problems of Euroland's economy, a policy that might be described as reverse fine-tuning.[44] On the general issue of fine-tuning and monetary policy, it is true that policymakers commit errors; particularly in the 1970s, those mistakes were often blamed on a fine-tuning of policies in light of short-term fluctuations in the real economy, which was felt to be in vogue at the time (see Siebert 2000 for the case in favor of rules and against fine-tuning). However, central banks do adjust their monetary policies in light of economic and financial developments (see Truman 2003a on the lessons of the 1970s). They are generally well paid to do so. They are also paid to make judgments about those developments.

The argument against fine-tuning is that the world is uncertain, and central bankers are better off waiting to see what actually happens—that is, don't assume that the projected decline in inflation will occur but wait until it materializes (Issing et al. 2001). Central bankers with those views would be more transparent if they just said that they continued to be more worried about inflation than growth in the short run!

It is instructive that following the September 11, 2001, tragedy, when the ECB was viewed as being proactive—albeit inelegantly with respect to the timing of the announcement of its action on September 17 following the Federal Reserve's action—Otmar Issing (2001b) was at pains to argue that the ECB's reduction in its refinancing rate was exceptional and did not represent fine-tuning because the ECB was getting ready to ease in any case. In the same speech (2001b, 5), he commented, "Asking monetary policy to do more or to serve other purposes [than the maintenance of price stability] risks creating illusions about what monetary policy can do." There are limits to what monetary policy can do, but it is irresponsi-

---

43. In real terms—which is more relevant to judging the effects of exchange rate changes on aggregate demand—the effective decline in the euro from the fourth quarter of 1998 to the first quarter of 2002 was 19 percent (about 6 percent per year). It is true that the OECD estimates a negative output gap for the euro area in 2000 (the year the euro weakened most sharply); subsequently a substantial positive gap emerged. It is also true that on the standardized basis, unemployment in the euro area averaged 8.8 percent that year.

44. Alternatively, the problem may be one of policy coordination or lack of it in the euro area. See Posen (2003) on this issue as it relates to the risk of Germany's following Japan into a period of deflation and stagnation.

ble for monetary policy not to perform up to those limits even in the presence of considerable uncertainty.

The jury is still out on the question of whether Euroland macroeconomic performance would be enhanced if the ECB were to adopt inflation targeting as its monetary policy framework. Perhaps for that reason, the proposal elicits as many different answers as the many voices that ask the question inside and outside Europe, within as well as outside the ECB. One voice from within the ECB is that of a member of the board, Eugenio Domingo Solans (2000, 5). He expressed a clear negative view in late 2000, "inflation targeting implies a degree of simplicity, automatism, mechanism and pre-commitment which makes it unsuitable to tackle a high degree of complexity and uncertainty as the one prevailing in today's world and especially in the euro area after the huge structural break produced by the introduction of the euro." He frankly states that the ECB does not have an (official) inflation target; the 0 to 2 percent range is only a definition of price stability.

He argues that inflation forecasts require models, and models cannot encompass all the relevant information.[45] He favors (2000, 6) "a more comprehensive, detailed, flexible and discretionary strategy" than he thinks inflation targeting has to offer. In this he seems to agree with Janet Yellen's view in the Federal Reserve's January 1995 discussion, but Yellen was inclined to come to quite different policy conclusions about the im-

---

45. Starting in December 2000, the ECB published staff projections, expressly not forecasts, of inflation and other major macroeconomic variables. Those projections, one assumes, have some influence on the council's discussions but clearly are not determinative in that process. However, Issing (2000) explained at great length how marginal those projections are to the policy process within the ECB, using much the same language as did Solans about how projections are an incomplete representation of the second (assessment) pillar of the ECB's monetary strategy, where the first pillar is monetary analysis. The ECB also published in June 2001 *A Guide to Eurosystem Staff Macroeconomic Projection Exercises*. This is a useful and interesting document because it illustrates the challenges the staff face in coming up with a coherent economic forecast for the euro area. It is also revealing in its discussion of the projections of inflation, stressing "the detailed analysis of short-term price developments" and the use of a range of models to project particular components. "Structural Phillips curve equations, relating inflation to excess demand, are used by some NCBs [national central banks]." Apparently such aggregate output gap relationships are not used, or not emphasized, by the staff of the ECB itself for the euro area as a whole. This is unfortunate. Aggregate relationships have their weaknesses, but they capture broad statistical regularities. Without them, staff forecasts risk getting lost in the forest examining the individual trees. For example, during a period of rising US inflation in the 1970s, much attention in Federal Reserve deliberations was paid to increases in prices of individual items, each of which had its own aberrations and therefore could be discounted as not indicative of the trend in the aggregate. It was as if inflation was caused by the statistical phenomenon of rising prices and had no connection with the overall condition of the macro economy or stance of monetary policy. One result was that US monetary policy failed for too long to deal with the fundamental problem. The risk for Euroland, particularly in the absence of consistency checks at the aggregate level, is that this type of bias also can introduce an unhealthy degree of inflation phobia: every price rise is caused by monetary policy that is too easy, and as a consequence monetary policy must be cautious in order to ensure that those individual price increases do not continue. The ECB

plications of this view for actual policy, favoring a more proactive approach. Duisenberg (2001) makes similar arguments, linking inflation targeting to inflation forecasts and denigrating forecasts as too narrow and too frequently inaccurate in that they do not take account of so-called monetary developments.[46]

Steve Roach (2001) and Joachim Fels (2001), both of Morgan Stanley Dean Witter, put forward in mid-2001 a more positive view of ECB policy, as of that date, to achieve price stability. Roach argued that the ECB had failed to do the one thing that was important to establish its "credibility": keep inflation within its target zone of 0 to 2 percent. Meanwhile, the Euroland economy as of early June 2001 was slipping into "the recession danger zone," and he points to the substantial decline of the euro against the dollar as evidence of the ECB's failure to establish its credibility. Fels argued that the ECB had done quite well during its teething phase and pointed out that inflation expectations—as measured by the difference between nominal and inflation-protected interest rates on French government bonds—were only 1.7 percent in June 2001 and had been less than 2 percent since the start of the ECB's operations in January 2000.[47] A jury of largely European investors voted 61 to 39 percent that Fels had the stronger case.

On the other hand, a Reuters poll of European economists published on November 2, 2001, found that 24 out of 28 (86 percent) agreed that the ECB had been focusing too much on inflation risks and not enough on the global reluctance to spend since the September 11, 2001, attack on the United States. Who knows which poll was more representative or closer to the truth? Real growth in 2002 and projected growth for 2003 in the euro area are below potential. The basic point is that the ECB's history has been short, and the evidence of the ECB's shortcomings to date is not all on one side.[48]

(2003b) does not include in its list of nine illustrative categories of information analyzed as part of the bank's second pillar either aggregate supply or aggregate demand. On economic projections, it notes (2003b, 17) "the ECB has taken the position that its policy-making should not rely exclusively on such tools."

46. Mads Kieler (2003) is sympathetic to Duisenberg's arguments.

47. The general view is that this measure of inflation expectations is biased downward because inflation-adjusted bonds are less liquid, which biases upward their implicit estimate of the real interest rate. The more important point, therefore, is that there had not been a rise in this measure of inflation expectations.

48. At a more technical level, Jean-Paul Fitoussi and Jérôme Creel (2002, 9) conclude that the ECB's policies "have been generally appropriate, given the prevailing economic circumstances." Kevin Ross (2002) concludes that the ECB is less predictable in its actions than the Federal Reserve and the Bank of England. Jon Faust, John Rogers, and Jonathan Wright (2001) conclude that ECB policy, taking account of euro area developments, has been more supportive of output and less concerned about inflation than Bundesbank policy would have been if similar conditions had prevailed in Germany alone when the Bundesbank was running monetary policy for much of the European Union.

IMF staff on May 28 (IMF 2003a, 5) concluded that Wim Duisenberg's May 8, 2003, announcement had removed any remaining problems with the ECB's monetary policy: "We strongly welcome the restatement of the ECB's monetary framework. It disposes of earlier communication problems and clarifies the objective of price stability. The objective of below but close to 2 percent provides a buffer against shocks that could threaten to lead to area-wide deflation, while also providing scope for inflation differentials across countries." However, views within the IMF are not unanimous—on April 9, 2003, Reuters quoted Kenneth Rogoff, chief economist of the IMF, as calling for a symmetrical inflation target for the ECB around 2.5 percent, which is not what was announced a month later and subsequently welcomed by other members of the IMF staff. Thus, the debate about inflation targeting by the ECB continues even within the IMF.

Should Euroland Adopt Inflation Targeting?

Would Euroland and the world economy be better served if the ECB adopted inflation targeting as its framework for the conduct and evaluation of its monetary policy? The short answer is yes, and it comes in three parts.

First, the ECB would have been well advised formally to adopt inflation targeting based on its recent review of its monetary policy strategy. Even if it were to implement that policy using a figure consistent with its revised monetary strategy—for example, a target range of 1 to 2 percent—the increased transparency associated with a tighter link between the ECB's primary objective—price stability—and the actual operation of policy would increase its policy effectiveness. The ECB tightened its definition of price stability, but what it really meant remains very ambiguous.

ECB policy is criticized on the grounds that it represents the policy of an institution with inflation phobia—even if this charge is incorrect—and on the grounds that, in implementing a policy oriented toward price stability, the means obscures the message. Under inflation targeting, the ECB would remain free to look at any aspect of the euro area's actual and prospective economic performance in setting its policy, including M3 behavior. Moreover, if the ECB adopted inflation targeting, it would increase the attractiveness of participating in the euro area for other important current (Sweden and the United Kingdom) and potential (the Czech Republic, Hungary, and Poland) inflation-targeting euro area members. Finally, given the ECB's high degree of goal independence, enshrined in a treaty, the case for an explicit inflation target would provide greater focus for ensuring the bank's accountability in a democratic society.[49]

Second, the ECB should adopt at least 2 percent—rather than close to but below 2 percent implied by its revised monetary strategy—as the tar-

---

49. Mishkin (1998) made a similar argument.

get or the midpoint of its target range. In doing so, the ECB would acknowledge that its de facto inflation range over the first five years has been 1 to 3 percent. Preferably, the bank should choose 2.5 percent as its midpoint because of the risk of deflation in some of the constituent countries of the euro area. Euro area inflation averaged 2 percent from 1999 to 2002 but only because inflation was 1.1 percent in 1999, the ECB's first year—since 1999, inflation was 2 percent or higher, averaging 2.2 percent (figure 4.3). Duisenberg (2001) set as a test for the ECB's monetary policy that actual inflation should remain within the definition of less than 2 percent when evaluated over an extended period. Fortunately for the real economy, the ECB has failed Duisenberg's own test in recent years. However, it would be well advised going forward to alter the test's parameters.[50]

As discussed earlier, in the absence of both an independent monetary policy and substantial labor migration, differential rates of inflation are the principal channel through which adjustments in national competitiveness are achieved. In order to accommodate those differences and at the same time avoid deflation in any part of the euro area, a higher target would be justified at little risk to long-run price stability in the sense of the Volcker-Greenspan definition.

Third, the ECB should modify its behavior and rhetoric in three respects. It should recognize more explicitly the risks of deflation and demonstrate that it understands that it is easier for monetary policy to reduce inflation from 4 to 2 percent than to raise inflation from minus 1 to plus 1 percent. Moreover, when the euro area's economy is operating below potential, the ECB should be more proactive in boosting demand with the knowledge that the short-run Phillips Curve is not vertical. This also will boost its credibility. Finally, the ECB should resist the temptation to criticize at every opportunity the performance of other policymakers in the euro area, in particular until its own countercyclical monetary policy receives higher marks. People who live in glass houses should not throw stones.

If the ECB were to adopt these three changes in its monetary strategy—inflation targeting, a target at 2.5 percent, and a more progrowth, antideflation, and focused policy orientation—the performance of the euro area economy would improve and the international financial system would benefit.

---

50. By way of comparison, UK inflation on the HICP basis averaged 1.1 percent in 2000–02 compared with 2.1 percent on the retail price index excluding mortgage interest payments (RIPX) that is the basis for the Bank of England's target. In contrast, UK growth averaged 2.2 percent over the period compared with 1.9 percent in the euro area, suggesting that the euro area might use a higher inflation target to accommodate more growth. Meanwhile, in preparation for sterling's joining the euro area, Chancellor of the Exchequer Gordon Brown has proposed shifting to the HICP as the basis for the Bank of England's target and lowering the target from its current 2.5 percent to make it more compatible with the ECB's definition of price stability.

What are the arguments against this agenda? Most of them are familiar from the discussion of the case for US adoption of inflation targeting. First, the ECB's flexibility in interpreting its mandate would be constrained and its goal independence compromised. On the other hand, it is difficult to believe that through the adoption of inflation targeting, the ECB would somehow become less zealous in its stability-oriented policy. Moreover, a more well-defined, balanced, and forward-looking policy framework would enhance its stature and its capacity to act flexibly if conditions warranted.

Second, the ECB's adoption of inflation targeting would involve not only too much narrowing of its policy focus but also introduce a false precision about what price stability really means. Again, the ECB would be able to both set its inflation target and modify it as conditions changed, all in the name of price stability.

Third, inflation targeting would risk undermining the ECB's credibility. On the one hand, the ECB might not be able to achieve the target it had set; on the other, the ECB and its publics (politicians, market participants, and citizens) might become too accustomed to the discretionary element in inflation targeting—flexible inflation targeting—and inflation would get out of control. Of course, the ECB's inflation target might well be missed but probably less frequently or by a smaller margin than the guideline for M3 growth has been missed. A realistic framework for inflation targeting would be more supportive of achieving long-run price stability than the current situation where the inflation rate has exceeded for some time the rather arbitrary definition of price stability (an inflation rate less than but close to 2 percent).

Finally, inflation targeting would distract the ECB from focusing on certain factors that potentially affect inflation, such as exchange rates. It is a challenge to appropriately take account of exchange rate movements in the formulation and implementation of monetary policy. However, if the ECB had been using a formal inflation-targeting framework, European public opinion or G7 discussions would have more likely compelled it to articulate a clearer answer to some of the questions posed by such movements than has been the case over the ECB's early years.

On balance, if the ECB were to adopt inflation targeting for Euroland, the evidence from theory and practice, while not overwhelming, is that the benefits in terms of better economic performance, on the terms of the ECB's mandate, would outweigh the costs by a good margin. The improved economic performance would have a positive economic and demonstration effect on its current EU partners and on prospective EU members. The broader international financial system would also benefit especially if the other two G3 economies joined the ECB in such a move or were inspired individually to follow the ECB's example of adopting inflation targeting.

How to Get from Here to There?

How might Euroland go about adopting inflation targeting? Because the ECB is the most independent central bank in history, any initiative toward inflation targeting, aside from public discussion and other forms of persuasion practiced in democratic societies, would have to come from the ECB itself. As was noted earlier, the ECB's goal independence as well as its more traditional instrument independence from direct political interference are enshrined not in a law that a legislative body can change but in a treaty, in effect in the constitution of the European Union—a constitution that requires unanimous consent to amend. Nevertheless, the ECB also is not immune from public and political comment or controversy. However, any transition to inflation targeting should be sensitive both to ECB's institutional origins and to the need to establish or strengthen supporting euro area institutions.

Fortunately, from the constitutional perspective, the adoption of inflation targeting as the framework for the conduct and evaluation of European monetary policy is fully consistent with the achievement of the ECB's price stability mandate. Writing before the ECB made its final decisions on its monetary policy framework, Bernanke et al. (1999) recommended that the ECB adopt inflation targeting and proposed how the ECB should proceed. The ECB made different choices and in May 2003 largely confirmed the monetary strategy that it had earlier put in place despite all the subsequent confusion about its ambiguity. Thus, the ECB's challenge in changing course is more complex.

It is hoped that the ECB under the leadership of Jean-Claude Trichet will embrace inflation targeting and embark on the following course of action:

- The ECB, having decided that it would contribute to improved performance of Euroland's economy and the fulfillment of the ECB's price stability mandate, would announce its intention to move to an inflation-targeting framework for the conduct and evaluation of its monetary policy.
- The ECB would establish a timetable for the transition, indicating that in six months it would propose the parameters for its implementation of the framework and in 12 months it would make a final decision.
- During the first six-month period, the ECB would collect the views of experts and sample public opinion about its proposal. It should openly solicit the views of the European Commission, the European Parliament, and the euro area finance ministers and governments.
- Assuming that this consultation period did not produce overwhelming opposition to the ECB's basic proposal, six months later it would announce the parameters for the inflation-targeting framework that it

proposed to follow: (a) the price index; (b) the target, which should be no lower than 2 percent, or the range, which should not have a figure lower than 2 percent as its midpoint; (c) the time horizon in which it would expect to meet the target, including whether it would expect the target to be achieved continuously (most likely), as of a certain date (for example, for the year as a whole as of the end of the year), or over the cycle or a period of years on average; (d) any exceptions or escape clauses that it would propose to establish ex ante, which would be expected to be none; (e) the time horizon over which it would anticipate returning to the target if there were a departure, or a process by which such a time horizon would be chosen and communicated; and, importantly, (f) other changes in its policies and procedures that would enhance the ECB's transparency and accountability under the new framework, such as inflation reports, a shift from staff projections to ECB forecasts for inflation, releasing appropriately worded minutes of ECB monetary meetings with a suitable lag, and less frequent meetings on monetary policy.

- During the second six-month period, the ECB would again seek comments from experts and the public as well as consult directly but informally with the European Commission and euro area finance ministers and governments. The ECB should also testify before the European Parliament about its proposals.[51]
- At the end of the second six-month period, assuming that comments on its proposals were generally supportive, the ECB would announce its formal adoption of parameters for the implementation of inflation targeting in the euro area.

The ECB would, of course, have the power to alter its inflation-targeting framework going forward. In the interests of promoting coherence and credibility in macroeconomic policy for the euro area as a whole, it would be desirable not only that the ECB consult with the euro area finance ministers on its initial proposals but also that it seek their views about any subsequent substantive changes and any restatement of parameters if this were, for example, an annual process. It would not be wise for the ECB to

---

51. Bernanke et al. favor regular testimony by members of the ECB governing council (normally NCB governors) before national parliaments to enhance the ECB's accountability, arguing that the European Parliament is insufficiently prominent. This would be a substantive mistake. It would inject national economic considerations more deeply into ECB policy making. For example, it would have been a mistake for the president of the Federal Reserve Bank of Dallas to testify before the Texas legislature in the mid-1980s when the Dallas Federal Reserve District was feeling the adverse effects of the oil market collapse. The president appropriately did make frequent speeches during the period in his district, which includes states other than Texas. The ECB is a creation of the European Union as a whole and, until supporting euro area institutions are further developed, it will be difficult to establish fully functioning channels for accountability, but the appropriate interim arrangement does not lie in pretending that it should be accountable to 12 to 15, and soon 25, national parliaments.

seek formal approval from the euro area finance ministers or governments of its adoption of inflation targeting or its inflation target. Although doing so would enhance the overall commitment under the EMU to the framework, it would be inconsistent with the ECB's institutional structure.

In conclusion, the case for the ECB's adoption of inflation targeting as its framework for the conduct and evaluation of euro area monetary policy is moderately strong. It would contribute to better performance of Euroland's economy. The technical quality of ECB policy should improve as a consequence of the ECB abandoning the monetary aggregates as one of its policy pillars.[52] The need to introduce into ECB internal policy deliberations public statements about monetary policy's forward-looking features more systematically and the subsidiary elements of its mandate more deliberately should also improve the policy's technical quality. Inflation targeting should enhance the ECB's transparency and accountability, thus improving Euroland's economic performance and benefiting the international financial system as well as the ECB's current and prospective EU partners.

Japan

Given the global interest in inflation targeting over the past dozen years or so, the serious problems besetting the Japanese economy for most of that period, and the controversies surrounding Japanese economic, financial, and monetary policies, it is no surprise that inflation targeting has featured prominently in policy debates outside as well as inside Japan, including at the BOJ.[53]

The new Bank of Japan Law, which became effective in April 1998 and established both goal and instrument independence for the BOJ, states in Article 2, "Currency and monetary control shall be aimed at, through the pursuit of price stability, contributing to the sound development of the national economy." Price stability is the principal goal but is embedded in a hierarchical mandate, that is, the bank is to contribute to the sound de-

---

52. I agree with Bernanke et al. that the monetary aggregates should be abandoned as a formal pillar of ECB monetary policy strategy. This would not prevent the examination of these and many other indicators in the implementation of inflation targeting as the ECB's framework. However, the ECB decided in May 2003 to retain its monetary pillar at least in part on the argument that it would help guide the bank in avoiding asset price bubbles, notwithstanding the fact that it provided little guidance in 1999–2000. Albert Jaeger (2003) supports the ECB's decision.

53. The extensive literature includes Bernanke (2000 and 2003b); Coenen and Wieland (2002); Eggertsson and Woodford (2003); Fujiki, Okina, and Shiratsuka (2001); Jinushi, Kuroki, and Miyao (2000); Krugman (1998); McCallum (2000 and 2002); Mikitani and Posen (2000); Okina, Shirakawa, and Shiratsuka (2001); Posen (1998); and Svensson (2001b and 2002a).

velopment of the national economy through its pursuit of price stability. The plain words of this mandate are fully consistent with the constrained discretion associated with an inflation-targeting framework for the conduct and evaluation of Japanese monetary policy.

The issue central to the debates in Japan is whether the adoption of inflation targeting would be wise in the short run, for the longer term, or ever. The BOJ has resisted the idea that inflation targeting would be beneficial to Japan in general or under current circumstances.

In an October 2000 BOJ report titled *On Price Stability*, the bank concluded that inflation in Japan was likely to be lower in the short term than in the longer term, that the adoption of a numerical target for inflation should be for a "very long period of time," that any numerical target for inflation would "not serve as a reliable guidepost in the conduct of monetary policy" under the then circumstances in Japan, and "therefore, it is not deemed appropriate to define price stability by numerical values," but the bank would continue to explore the issue (Fujiki et al. 2001, 123–24).

Immediately after Toshihiko Fukui became governor of the BOJ in March 2003, he called an ad hoc monetary policy meeting of the Bank of Japan Policy Board. At that meeting he initiated a discussion on two points (BOJ 2003a, 4): "First, it was necessary for the Bank to examine whether there was room for improvement in the current framework for the conduct of monetary policy, given the prevailing severe economic conditions and the effects of the military action against Iraq. And, second, enhancing monetary policy transparency and strengthening the monetary policy transmission mechanism were particularly important points for consideration." The policy board discussed inflation targeting in the context of the second issue and agreed to continue the discussion of the monetary policy framework and of measures to improve monetary policy transparency and the transmission mechanism.

At the next meeting of the policy board in April 2003, the discussion did continue. Some members expressed the view (BOJ 2003b, 11) that "it would be useful to express price stability in terms of numerical values, as, for example, a reference rate of inflation, even if it was not a strict target." One of these members explained that "a reference rate could serve to anchor the expected inflation rate and reduce time and costs required for price adjustments. . . . Moreover, it was worth considering taking a dynamic approach in conducting monetary policy in the following way: the Bank would divide the process up to the point where the ultimate goal would be achieved into several phases, and set different goals and adopt different measures in each phase."

These proposals did not carry the day. Concerns were expressed about the lack of tools to achieve a numerical target, the challenge in communicating the idea, and the need first to strengthen the transmission mechanism of monetary easing. At the same meeting, the policy board adopted a small change in the way its forecasts were released to include the median figure for projected inflation, but some members were at pains to make sure that the change not be presented as establishing a target or reference inflation rate.[54]

At the May 2003 meeting, members proposed an examination of inflation targeting and proposed changes in operating procedures. One member said (BOJ 2003c, 10), "[T]he Bank should start examining introduction of a numerical target for the inflation rate. To achieve such a target, this member suggested the following possible policy measures: an increase in outright purchases of JGBs [Japanese government bonds] with options, which enabled holders to convert their bonds into inflation-indexed JGBs, when the government started issuing such JGBs; or introduction of outright purchases of foreign bonds. A different member said that it would be worthwhile to examine issues related to a desirable rate of inflation consistent with sound economic growth, and how this rate should be employed as a tool in the conduct of monetary policy, although the Bank might not set a time frame for achieving it." The minutes of the policy board's meeting on June 10–11, 2003, report similar proposals (BOJ 2003d).

Earlier in June, Governor Toshihiko Fukui (2003) had commented extensively about inflation targeting in a speech at the spring meeting of the Japan Society of Monetary Economics. He noted the arguments in favor of adopting the framework but argued that the bank's commitment to maintain the current policy framework until the nationwide CPI (excluding fresh food) records a year-on-year increase of zero percent or more on a sustainable basis is more flexible because expected or projected inflation might exceed the inflation target before recorded inflation had satisfied the bank's criteria.[55] He also argued that the bank could not be confident about reaching an inflation target, discussed the various assets the bank might buy, and expressed considerable concern about not impairing the BOJ's capital as a result of losses on assets, including JGBs, that the bank might buy. These issues, which relate to the monetary transmission mechanism as well as inflation targeting per se, are discussed below.

It is noteworthy that in the end Fukui left open the possibility of the bank's adoption of some form of inflation targeting (Fukui 2003, 9): "I would like to examine, in the process of reviewing how to make full use of the monetary easing policy in the future, whether we can reorganize the policy framework of the Bank, and whether there will be any room for

---

54. The BOJ in October 2000 adopted a policy of releasing twice a year, in April and October, the range of individual forecasts of the policy board members of CPI inflation (excluding fresh food), wholesale price index or WPI (now corporate goods price index or CGPI) inflation, and real GDP growth for the current (April and October) and following (October) fiscal year.

55. Fukui's argument implicitly assumes that the bank would adopt a rather strict form of "inflation forecast targeting," which, as he notes, could be unnecessarily restrictive. However, this is a straw man argument because the bank would not be required to adopt such an approach.

introducing such a tool as inflation targeting within that framework. I cannot predict honestly what results will be produced by this wide-ranging discussion, or when."

The Japanese government, depending on the day of the week or who is speaking for the government or reporting on its views, either urges the BOJ to adopt inflation targeting or is cool to the idea. However, in the context of the BOJ's policy board discussions in the second quarter of 2003, Yuzo Kobayashi, representing the Cabinet Office, expressed the government's view at several meetings in words similar to the following (BOJ 2003c, 11): "In order to overcome deflation in fiscal 2005, the government hoped that the Bank would further deliberate on tools for monetary operations, in addition to reviewing the basic framework for the conduct of monetary policy, and implement monetary policy that were effective in overcoming deflation." This statement suggests more openness to inflation targeting in the Japanese government than in the BOJ.

Turning to international official views, the IMF staff (2002a) called for Japan's adoption of an inflation target, but only once has deflation been eliminated from the country. The IMF executive board, as of mid-2002 and mid-2003, was divided on the issue. However, IMF First Deputy Managing Director Anne Krueger (2003, 2), in a statement issued on June 4, 2003, appeared to be warmer to the immediate establishment of an inflation target than either the IMF staff or the executive board: "A medium-term inflation target combined with clear communication of the strengthened strategy [for the implementation of policy] would help convince the public that deflation will end, and encourage spending."

Before examining in more detail the issues that have been raised in the ongoing debate about inflation targeting in Japan, it is useful to review the performance of the Japanese economy since the mid-1980s. Figures 4.4a and 4.4b present background data on the CPI inflation rate, short-term interest rate, real GDP growth, and yen/dollar exchange rate for the 1985–2003 period. After five years of over-rapid expansion of the Japanese economy at an average annual rate of 4.9 percent in 1987–91, the economy has been in deep stagnation. Real GDP expanded at an average annual rate of only 1.1 percent over the following 10 years, with growth in only two years (1996 at 3.3 percent and 1997 at 1.9 percent) exceeding 1.8 percent, which is the potential growth rate estimated by the OECD for Japan for this period. By 2002, Japan's output gap, conservatively estimated by the OECD, had reached 2.9 percent. Unemployment rose from 2.1 percent on average in 1991 to a post–World War II peak of 5.5 percent in 2002 and remained at around that rate during the first half of 2003.[56]

---

56. A common rule of thumb is that the Japanese unemployment rate should be doubled to approximate the rate in other major industrial countries. Moreover, except for a brief period in 2001, employment growth has been negative for five years.

Figure 4.4a Japan: Inflation and short-term interest rate, 1985–2003

percent

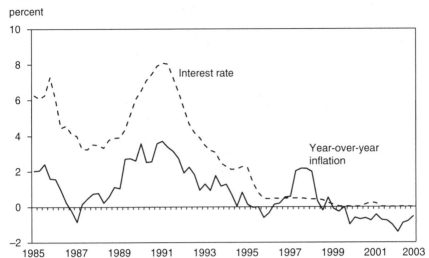

Notes: Inflation calculated as year-over-year rates based on quarterly average CPI. Interest rates are quarterly averages.

Source: IMF, *International Financial Statistics*.

Figure 4.4b Japan: Growth and yen/dollar exchange rate, 1985–2003

percent   yen/dollar

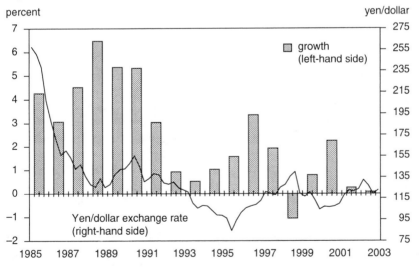

Notes: Growth rates calculated from annual average real GDP. Exchange rates are quarterly averages.

Source: IMF, *International Financial Statistics*.

Consumer price inflation, on the other hand, averaged 2.9 percent in 1989–91. In the following 10 years, the average was only 0.4 percent; in four years prices declined on average, and in no case did the increase in the CPI exceed 1.8 percent, including 1992 and 1997 when the increases were 1.7 percent; 1997 saw an increase in the value-added tax, which added to recorded inflation in that year. The average error in one-year-ahead forecasts of Japanese inflation from 1990 to 2001 was zero (appendix table A.4). However, the root mean squared error (RMSE) was half a percentage point, or more than half the actual average inflation rate, suggesting considerable volatility. The average error in the two-year-ahead forecasts over the past 12 years was negative by almost half a percentage point. Over 10 years, this represents an average additional repayment burden of roughly 5 percent on debtors with obligations as short as two years, and the shortfall of actual inflation below expected inflation was even larger for longer periods. In these longer forecasts, the RMSE is roughly the same as the actual inflation rate.

Over the past decade or so, the yen/dollar exchange rate has fluctuated over a wide range, appreciating from an annual average of ¥134 per dollar in 1991 to a high of ¥94 per dollar in 1995, depreciating back to ¥131 per dollar in 1998, almost hitting ¥100 per dollar again in late 1999 and early 2000, and hovering in the ¥115–130 range for much of the past two years.

This has not been a pretty picture. The causes for the sorry performance of the Japanese economy are many. Prominent on most observers' lists are the collapse of the equity price and land price bubbles in late 1989 and early 1990, the ensuing weakness of the banking and financial systems, an inability to muster the political and financial capital to address these problems decisively, procrastination in promoting corporate restructuring, fitful efforts to deal with bureaucratic and regulatory constraints on Japanese economic performance, and, last but not least, failures of macroeconomic—monetary and fiscal—policy.

The major consequence of failing to deal with the problems of the financial and business sectors is that vast amounts of Japan's economically viable land and capital stock either stand idle or are being employed unproductively. The major consequence of failing to develop a coherent macroeconomic strategy has been not only a feeble economy but also a net debt stock for the general government, which is expected to have increased by more than 50 percent between 1998 and 2003 as a share of nominal GDP (IMF 2002a, 37), while nominal GDP has declined by about 5 percent. An expansionary fiscal policy in 1996 produced 3.6 percent growth that year, but premature, excessive fiscal contraction in 1997 plunged the economy back into recession by 1998. A mild recovery to 2.2 percent growth in 2000 led the BOJ in August to abandon its zero interest rate policy (ZIP) that it had adopted in February 1999, contributing to another downturn in 2001.[57]

In October 1992, two years after the bursting of Japan's asset price bubbles, Federal Reserve Chairman Alan Greenspan visited Japan and gave a major speech to the Confederation of Bankers' Associations of Japan. He cautioned against expecting a surge in economic growth as the economy adjusted to the decline in real estate and financial-asset prices. He warned that standard models and recent experience had little to offer in dealing with large declines in asset prices. In Japan, even more so than in the United States in the late 1980s and early 1990s, balance sheet problems could be expected to persist and dampen growth prospects for some time to come. The *Financial Times* (October 15, 1992) report on his speech and his visits with Japanese officials—where Greenspan made the same points, which were out of character with his normal posture of offering few criticisms of policies of other countries in public or private—noted that Greenspan's views ran sharply against the consensus among Tokyo's financiers and economists who were expecting growth to pick up by mid-1993 to 3 percent from the then expected 1.5 percent in 1992. In the event, after several revisions, Japanese growth is now estimated to have been 0.9 percent in 1992 and 0.5 percent in 1993.[58]

On the burden of deflation, Bernanke (2000) presents a vivid example of a small borrower using land as collateral and borrowing in 1991. Using plausible estimates for expected inflation and increases in land prices, he shows that the borrower by 1999 would have experienced a 27 percent increase in the real value of his principal obligation and a 42 percent decline in the real value of his collateral. There is a strong presumption that by 1999 the borrower had long since defaulted, but the bank was still holding on to the collateral, which was either standing idle or being inefficiently employed.

What was monetary policy's contribution to this situation? The BOJ, and the Ministry of Finance (MOF) before the new Bank of Japan Law went into effect in April 1998, were not responsible for the entire mess. However, they must bear a large share of the responsibility. Research exploiting Taylor-rule methodology (Jinushi, Kuroki, and Miyao 2000) has

---

57. When the BOJ abandoned its ZIP on August 11, 2000, it declared that the Japanese economy had "substantially improved," was "showing clearer signs of recovery," and had "reached the stage where deflationary concern [had] been dispelled, the condition for lifting the zero-interest-rate policy." The annual average CPI proceeded to fall 0.7 percent in 2000 and 2001 and 0.9 percent in 2002.

58. The Consensus Economics forecasts to which the *Financial Times* may have been referring were for the respective fiscal years, but the point still holds. Growth in the 1994 calendar year was 1 percent.

shown that Japanese monetary policy after 1987 became increasingly anti-inflation oriented. In addition, the monetary authorities were determined not to repeat the bubble period of the late 1980s, which was, perhaps, understandable in 1990 and 1991, but became increasingly unfortunate as the decade unfolded. They learned too late the familiar lesson about not driving while looking in the rearview mirror.

With the benefit of hindsight and given that the United States, Australia, and several Scandinavian countries had gone through similar experiences in the late 1980s, the appropriate posture for Japanese monetary policy during this period—once the stock market and land market bubbles had burst in 1990—was to get real interest rates down, preferably into negative territory, and keep them there until balance sheet problems had been repaired and the real economy turned up. In the event, the estimated short-term real interest rate averaged 3.4 percent in 1987, 3 percent in 1988, and 2.6 percent in 1989.[59] The rate rose to 4.2 percent in 1990 and 1991, edged off to 2.9 percent in 1992, but did not decline below 2 percent until the third quarter of 1993. It stayed above 1 percent through the second quarter of 1995, a period during which CPI inflation on a lagging four-quarter basis averaged 0.7 percent. By mid-1995, the nominal interest rate and also the estimated real interest rate were less than 1 percent (figure 4.4a). By that time, the game was over as far as conventional monetary policy was concerned, and the game remained over as far as the BOJ was concerned for the following six years!

Toshiki Jinushi, Yoshihiro Kuroki, and Ryuko Miyao (2000) comment on BOJ policy in the early 1990s: "The BOJ did not recognize the prospect of debt deflation at this time and pursued an 'optimistic anti-inflation policy.' . . . The BOJ recognized the situation was more serious than it had expected and also used the expression 'the bursting of the bubble' in the *Monthly Bulletin* [of June 1992]. . . . The BOJ might have misjudged how serious the economic situation was, so that the pace of monetary loosening lagged events. . . . A further loosening in 1994 might have prevented the abnormal yen appreciation in March 1995 and might have accomplished stronger recovery afterward."

Some might argue, citing Alan Ahearne et al. (2002), that the descent of the Japanese economy into deflation was largely unanticipated. On the other hand, one lesson from this paper as well as other examinations of the Japanese situation is that "when inflation and interest rates have fallen close to zero, and the risk of deflation is high, such stimulus [monetary and fiscal] should go beyond the levels conventionally implied by baseline forecasts of future inflation and economic activity" (Ahearne et al. 2002, 7). By 1992, CPI inflation had already dipped below 1 percent

---

59. The estimates of short-term real interest rates are quarterly averages of the overnight call rate adjusted by CPI inflation over the preceding four quarters. The annual estimates are averages of the four quarters.

(12-month change), and by early 1994 it had dipped again to that level and continued downward.

A case could be made that a Japanese monetary policy that was forward-looking and had grasped the importance of this point could have and should have been more aggressive as of the first date and certainly as of the second date when, in fact, short-term rates remained significantly above zero for at least another year, until the second half of 1995. Instead BOJ policy in effect was then, and remains as of this writing, afflicted by doing too little until it is too late. Caution and partial adjustment are normally sound guides to policymaking under uncertainty. However, these guides for monetary policy need to be adjusted in light of the reality that it is easier for monetary policy to lower inflation from 4 to 2 percent than to raise it from minus 1 to plus 1 percent. At low levels of inflation, the risks are asymmetric.

Should Japan Adopt Inflation Targeting?

The question whether Japan should adopt inflation targeting can be asked and answered for the long and the short runs. In the long run, once Japan emerges from its deflation, successfully addresses the problems of its banking and financial system, and repairs its fiscal position, should it adopt inflation targeting? The IMF staff's (2002a) answer is affirmative; however, they do not advocate the adoption of inflation targeting in the short run, but, as noted earlier, Anne Krueger (2003) has expressed a more sympathetic view. The short-run question also has two parts: can monetary policy be effective in combating deflation and contributing to the solution of Japan's economic and financial problems? If yes, could inflation targeting play a role in assisting monetary policy?

Judging by both words and deeds, the BOJ's view on the short-run question appears to be: (1) deflation is not a problem because it is either caused by restructuring in the economy, which is a healthy supply-side phenomenon, or by a lack of needed restructuring, which would be further delayed by an even easier monetary policy; (2) an even easier monetary policy would not succeed in assisting the Japanese economy under current circumstances; and (3) even if an even easier monetary policy might succeed in assisting the Japanese economy under current circumstances, the BOJ would be making a mistake if it were to give in to national and international opinion and adopt such a policy.

The arguments of Jinushi, Kuroki, and Miyao (2000) explaining why the BOJ, as of early 2000, should not have adopted an inflation target or inflation targeting as its framework for the conduct of Japanese monetary policy are illustrative of BOJ views.[60] They argue that, first, with the

---

60. Fred Bergsten, Marcus Noland, and Takatoshi Ito (2001) review these arguments drawing on Jinushi, Kuroki, and Miyao (2000) as well as Okina, Shirakawa, and Shiratsuka (2001) and Fujiki, Okina, and Shiratsuka (2001).

overnight call rate at zero, the bank lacks the instruments of monetary policy to stimulate inflation or the economy; it is in unfamiliar territory. To this argument, the now standard reply is that at least the BOJ could have tried to stimulate the economy through the use of a quantity-oriented monetary policy—for example, increasing its outright purchases of JGBs.

In the event, in March 2001 the BOJ announced a new policy of quantitative easing and adopted a type of inflation target that is focused on the level of current account balances of banks and nonbanks at the BOJ until year-on-year core nationwide CPI inflation (excluding fresh food) is nonnegative on a sustained basis.

The bank's policy and its implementation can be criticized in several respects. First, if what the bank adopted were a target, instead of a guideline as the BOJ prefers to call it, it would be asymmetrical, providing a floor for inflation but not a ceiling. Second, the objective that the change in the CPI is no longer negative does not do away with the problem of deflation given measurement biases in consumer price indices. Third, the bank's efforts to implement its guideline have been overly cautious. It only gradually and grudgingly pushed up its guideline for current account balances at the bank from ¥4 trillion before March 2001 to ¥15–20 trillion as of December 2002 to around ¥27–30 trillion as of mid-2003, and similarly it raised the amount of JGBs it would purchase each month from ¥400 million before March 2001 to ¥1.2 trillion as of October 2002.[61] The bank also initiated programs to purchase equities from banks as well as asset-backed securities, but has deliberately described these actions as not affecting monetary policy; in other words, the purchases were sterilized and the bank purchased smaller amounts of other assets.

Surely the economic, financial, and psychological impact of BOJ policy would have been greater if it had been as aggressive in March 2001 as it was two years later, and surely the impact would be greater if the BOJ were even more aggressive two years later. Instead, the BOJ has adopted a defensive posture, stepping up the implementation of its quantitative easing only when forced to do so by external events, such as the war in Iraq and the failure of Resona Bank during the first half of 2003, and reserving the possibility of acting more forcefully if the Japanese economy should deteriorate further. One consequence is that the BOJ has blunted any positive effects of its actions on expectations about inflation and growth in the Japanese economy.

---

61. On March 25, the government requested that the bank raise its monthly purchases of JGBs to ¥2 trillion, but the policy board did not accept this proposal. When the policy board on May 20 approved an increase in the guideline for the outstanding balances of current accounts to around ¥27–30 trillion in the context of the government's rescue of Resona Bank, two members dissented on the grounds that the case had not been made for the need of additional liquidity.

Bernanke (2000) addresses the theoretical case that the BOJ is powerless to influence the economy because of a liquidity trap: if one thinks that monetary expansion has limited effects, then one should just print money (with indefinite maturity and a zero interest rate) and buy everything up. However, the effects of monetary policy in a deflationary environment may not be quite as straightforward as this comment suggests (see Bryant 2000 for a more skeptical view). Moreover, strong arguments have been made for why the effectiveness of monetary policy may be limited in the face of a weakened financial system (Morsink and Bayoumi 2001) or may require a strong belief in the neutrality of money in the context of a stylized model of the Japanese economy (Hori et al. 2002).

Therefore, it is legitimate to ask the strategic question whether monetary policy can be effective in a deflationary environment. What are the mechanisms through which a monetary policy of quantitative easing can be expected to work in a deflationary environment?[62]

One potential channel is the *banking system*—increased liquidity and reserves allow banks to make more loans to creditworthy borrowers. When the banking system is weak, and banks are husbanding their liquidity and repairing their balance sheets, monetary policy is less effective than normal operating through this channel, but it is not totally blocked. Japanese banks are not turning away all borrowers; they are making some profitable loans, and more aggressive quantitative monetary easing should assist them in doing so. The banking channel in Japan is weakened but not wholly inoperative.

What about the *expectations* channel? In order to obtain some monetary policy mileage via this channel, one does not have to believe—as Paul Krugman (1998) posited—that the central bank can declare that inflation will be higher, expected inflation will rise, and positive real interest rates will turn overnight into negative real interest rates and induce borrowers to borrow, banks to lend, and investors to invest. First, monetary policy today affects expectations about monetary policy tomorrow; an expansionary policy and a commitment to continue an expansionary policy place downward pressure on the term structure of nominal interest rates relative to any expected level of inflation in the future. Second, monetary policy encourages borrowers and investors to make longer-term plans safe in the knowledge that the central bank will not jerk up interest rates at the first hint that inflation may be edging above zero.

---

62. A related line of argumentation is that there is no precedent for a successful operation of this type. Some cite the Swedish experience of the 1930s (Berg and Jonung 1999), which may or may not be relevant; Taimur Baig (2003) and Masaaki Shirakawa (2002) also deal with the US experience after 1933. Sweden was and is a small economy operating in a very different economic environment with nominal short-term interest rates that were far from zero. However, the point is that no one knows for sure whether an aggressive strategy of quantitative easing is effective unless the BOJ actually implements one.

A monetary policy of quantitative easing can still operate through the *portfolio balance* channel, which is essentially what Bernanke was describing—driving up the prices of a wide array of assets indirectly through substitution effects or directly because the central bank is purchasing those assets. Masaaki Shirakawa (2002) argues that by purchasing a wide range of assets, the central bank is subsidizing the issuers of those assets and that it should not do so because subsidies should be covered by fiscal policy and recorded in the government's budget. This argument does not wash. Under conditions where there is no zero interest rate floor, monetary policy operates through the portfolio balance channel, though normally indirectly if the central bank only purchases government paper. The operation of this channel is not considered to be an inappropriate subsidy to the issuers of those assets, which includes issuers of corporate bonds.

An expansionary monetary policy putting downward pressure on interest rates and upward pressure on asset prices not only benefits the issuers of those assets and encourages them to issue more such assets but also benefits the holders of those assets and close substitutes, such as equities, and stimulates the economy through the *wealth* channel.

Finally, a monetary policy of quantitative easing can affect one other important set of asset prices, *exchange rates*, depreciating the yen and stimulating the economy as a result. Few would doubt that this channel exists and remains operational even with short-term yen interest rates near zero. Investors can borrow yen supplied directly or indirectly by the BOJ, buy assets denominated in foreign currencies with positive real returns, and generate profits. If those investors are Japanese, this will add to their incomes and spending power (McCallum 2000 and 2002, Svensson 2001b and 2002a).

A monetary policy of quantitative easing operating through these channels under conditions of deflation and a zero interest rate floor for a range of short-term obligations has less precise effects than one operating under conditions of low inflation and no floor on nominal short-term interest rates. The effects of monetary policy are more uncertain, but the emphasis should be on the "more" not on the "uncertain" because the effects of monetary policy in the real world are never precisely calibrated.[63] In addition, not only will the empirical relationships between monetary aggregates and nominal variables, such as nominal GDP, be less precise but also the average value of the coefficient linking them will be smaller; in effect, the zero interest rate floor has introduced a discontinuity. However, this is not the same as saying that the coefficient is zero.

---

63. The IMF (2003b, 36), in the context of discussing the instruments available to a central bank faced with deflation, comments, "Even during inflationary times, the lag structure and impact of change in the monetary policy stance may be unclear." However, that does not prevent central banks from seeking to reduce the inflation.

Taimur Baig (2003) supports the view that monetary policy can be effective with deflation and a zero interest rate floor on some short-term assets. His analysis, in turn, underpins the IMF staff recommendation in mid-2002 that the BOJ should make a public commitment to end deflation before the end of 2003! The Baig-IMF message is consistent with the views of Allan Meltzer (2002a) and Gauti Eggertsson and Michael Woodford (2003). Moreover, these views of the effectiveness of monetary policy in a deflationary environment are not fundamentally inconsistent with the views found in Shirakawa (2002) from the BOJ.

Shirakawa asks four questions: whether a central bank can increase reserves indefinitely? Whether an increase in reserves affects asset prices? Whether it affects the behavior of financial institutions? Whether it can activate economic activity? His answers are not 100 percent negative, therefore he implicitly leaves room for positive effects on the real economy and inflation from a more aggressive BOJ monetary policy of quantitative easing.[64] However, he offers a different interpretation (1): "When evaluating the effectiveness of current [BOJ] monetary policy, it is indispensable to make clear exactly what kind of transmission mechanism is assumed." Shirakawa's, and one can safely assume the Bank of Japan's, implicit conclusion is: unless the bank can be absolutely sure that a policy of further quantitative easing will be precisely effective, the institution would be unwise to embark on such a policy.[65]

Having dealt with the strategic arguments against the use of monetary policy in Japan to deal with deflation, what can be said about the tactical arguments against doing so? The tactical arguments can be classified under six headings: (1) use of the exchange rate channel is inappropriate or impossible, (2) more aggressive quantitative easing threatens to undermine the BOJ's balance sheet, (3) such a quantitative easing monetary policy strategy would undermine the BOJ's credibility and independence, (4) it would be inconsistent with a responsible fiscal policy, (5) it could or should only be part of a comprehensive policy to address the problems of the Japanese economy, and (6) it might ignite inflation, which would have a negative impact on growth.

First, on the exchange rate issue, the BOJ and the MOF would be better off treating the foreign exchange value of the yen as an endogenous variable and not a policy instrument that they can control through intervention operations. If the yen depreciates as the BOJ implements a more aggressive policy of quantitative easing, then so be it.

---

64. The somewhat discouraging results of Hori et al. (2002) can be characterized the same way. Their forward-looking model relies on the long-run neutrality of money to obtain its positive effects, which leads to their rather strange plea that economists should endeavor to explain the concept of neutrality to politicians and the general public.

65. This view is echoed in the minutes of the Bank of Japan Policy Board meetings (BOJ 2003a, 2000b, 2000c, and 2000d) as well as in Fukui (2003).

On the other hand, the BOJ is right, and critics such as Meltzer (2002a) are wrong when they call for unsterilized foreign exchange–market purchases of dollars. The BOJ is right because intervention operations in Japan are conducted under the aegis of the MOF and for its balance sheet. Consequently, they have no impact on the BOJ's balance sheet and by definition are sterilized. Meltzer is wrong to suggest that such operations should not be sterilized; he should separate the BOJ's decision to undertake expansionary monetary policy from the MOF's decision to make sterilized purchases of dollars. Monetary policy should be separated from intervention policy, in particular when different parts of the government are responsible for decisions about the two instruments. On the other hand, there is nothing stopping the BOJ from cooperating with the MOF in this area; it could expand liquidity by purchasing instruments issued by the MOF to finance the MOF's purchases of foreign currency bonds. However, Lars Svensson's (2001b and 2002a) suggestion of using exchange market sales of yen to guide the exchange rate and thereby the Japanese price level to lower and higher levels, respectively, smacks of gimmickry. Moreover, if the international financial community were to accept the suggestion as something other than a beggar-thy-neighbor policy, the Svensson approach would have to be accompanied by a comprehensive program, including banking reform, economic restructuring, and fiscal support as well as monetary easing.

Second, on the issue of the BOJ's balance sheet, the bank has repeatedly argued—only to decide later to do so—against increased outright purchases of JGBs, for example, because doing so would not only underwrite continuing large fiscal deficits but also potentially damage the bank's balance sheet if interest rates ever rose.[66] The consolidated balance sheet of the Japanese government, which is the relevant balance sheet since the BOJ is a government institution, would be unaffected by a subsequent rise in long-term interest rates, even if the BOJ decided it must mop up a substantial amount of the liquidity that it had created through its quantitative easing policy. Moreover, first, the BOJ should not and is not likely to have to move quickly. Second, central banks do not have to worry about or mark-to-market their balance sheets, as a first approximation, because they have the power to create money to meet their obligations.[67] Third, as Bernanke (2003b) suggests, the government could ex ante enter into a bond swap with the BOJ either now or for future delivery that would compensate the bank for any losses it might incur because of selling JGBs at a price lower than they were purchased.

---

66. Fujiki et al. (2001) present scary estimates of these impacts on the BOJ's balance sheet and on the government's future fiscal position. Shirakawa (2002) makes similar arguments.

67. Providing a fiscal transfer by buying low-quality assets at inflated prices is a different matter, but the accounting and balance sheet issues, even in that case, remain secondary compared with the incentive and political economy issues.

The third tactical argument against the BOJ's adoption of a more aggressive strategy of quantitative easing is that doing so risks undermining either the bank's credibility or its independence or both. The credibility argument is that the bank may try and fail. As the IMF (2002a, 27) reports, "The BoJ saw the cost of potential failure—if instruments [of such a policy] were ineffective as it believed—as very damaging to its credibility." The effectiveness issue was discussed earlier. Moreover, the BOJ now has put itself in a situation where it may be better to have tried and failed than not to have tried at all.

The independence argument is understandable in light of the fact that the bank struggled for years to gain its instrument and ultimately goal independence and gained it largely as a consequence of the failure of the MOF's stewardship in the monetary and, more importantly, the financial stability area. Jinushi, Kuroki, and Miyao (2000, 43) state, "It is highly likely that a failure by the BOJ to meet an announced target would lead to a media campaign calling for still further monetary loosening to achieve the target at all cost. . . . The setting of policy instruments would be determined as much by the public or media pressures as by the BOJ's own judgment. In this sense, then, instrument independence [under the new Bank of Japan Law of April 1998] would be seriously undermined." The counterargument is that central banks need to do what is right, and they need to be ahead of the curve, which means managing public opinion and the views of the rest of the government. The issue is whether a strategy of more aggressive quantitative easing would help the bank achieve better results, and the answer is yes.

The fourth tactical argument is based on the relationship between the BOJ's monetary strategy and Japan's fiscal policy. There are many reasons to be worried about the quality and effectiveness of Japanese fiscal policy and the build-up of government debt, but these worries should not inhibit the BOJ. It is not confronting a condition of fiscal dominance. It does not advocate immediate fiscal retrenchment. It should do what it can for the Japanese economy and not place artificial internal policy limits on its purchases of JGBs.[68] The IMF (2002a) has provided a useful analysis of how much adjustment in Japan's fiscal position (2.25 percent of GDP) over five years would be necessary to stabilize Japan's net debt (excluding social security assets) as of 2007 *if*—and it is an important "if"—monetary and other policies can get the Japanese economy expanding with real growth reaching its 2 percent potential by that year and with increases in the GDP deflator of 1 percent a year starting in 2003.[69] In other words, Japan's fis-

---

68. The BOJ has a limit set by policy not by law that its holdings of JGBs should not exceed the amount of banknotes in circulation.

69. The Japanese GDP deflator declined at an average annual rate of 1.25 percent from 1998 to 2002.

cal situation is a worry, but it will become worse if the BOJ does not do its part to get the economy moving and to end Japan's debilitating deflation.

Fifth, Japan's fiscal problems are linked to the problems in its banking and financial system and the need to restructure many businesses as well as their balance sheets. A comprehensive package of actions and reforms—financial-sector, structural, fiscal, and monetary—would be the first-best answer to Japan's problems.[70] However, it is foolish to reject easy money coupled with less than comprehensive measures in the other areas as a second-best approach. Easy money is not bad for the restructuring of the Japanese economy and balance sheets. The BOJ was mistaken in August 2000 to justify its slight tightening of policy on the opposite view; Japan lost valuable time, its situation deteriorated further, and the BOJ lost credibility.[71]

The final tactical argument against a more aggressive strategy of quantitative easing by the BOJ is that the risks may not be worth the potential limited benefits because the costs of deflation are smaller than the risk of a renewed outbreak of inflation. Such a strategy might prove to be too expansionary and destabilize the economy; once inflation is started again, it will be difficult to stop it. Many in the BOJ apparently subscribe to some variant of this argument; otherwise, the bank would have acted earlier, measurable by years and soon to be measurable by decades (Fujiki, Okina, and Shiratsuka 2001; Jinushi, Kuroki, and Miyao 2000; and Shirakawa 2001 and 2002). The evidence has been accumulating for more than a decade that the risk of renewed inflation in goods and services prices or asset prices is about as remote in Japan as it can be in an industrial economy at this point in the economic history of the world. In the interests of symmetry, perhaps, it is also argued that if the BOJ were to adopt inflation targeting, it might be used not as a framework to constrain discretion but as a rule that would limit the bank's flexibility—that is, it would become too focused on restraining inflation and create excessive volatility for the real economy.[72] The extreme version of this argument is that such a policy, if successful, might produce inflation without growth.[73]

---

70. Bernanke (2003b) suggests a temporary agreement (accord) between the BOJ and the MOF under which the bank would agree to purchase the JGBs issued by the MOF to finance a fiscal expansion.

71. Masaaki Shirakawa (2001) argues the case for why an easy money policy by the BOJ may delay economic recovery by slowing down structural reform.

72. A related argument is that measurement problems with price indices prevent the establishment of a credible inflation target. Alternatively, outsiders do not understand the Japanese economy, and they are wrong that there is deflation. Events in 2001 appear to have reduced the salience of this argument. As noted earlier, the BOJ appears to have accepted, at least as a guideline for policy, the achievement of nonnegative core inflation nationwide on a stable basis.

73. The *Financial Times* on January 29, 2003, interpreted Prime Minister Junichiro Koizumi's remarks to the Diet as reflecting his conversion to this view.

Of course, in this context, most advocates of inflation targeting for Japan under the current circumstances believe that higher inflation would induce growth because the BOJ would keep nominal interest rates low and thereby contribute to additional growth. On the other hand, skeptics such as Alice Rivlin (2002, 54) reject inflation targeting in Japan precisely because it focuses on the wrong target: "Nor is inflation targeting useful when the central bank faces a stagnant economy, such as the one facing the Bank of Japan, with falling prices and interest rates in the zero range. The central bank can say that inflation has fallen below its target range, and that it is trying to generate more inflation, but that is a tough case to make to the public. The real objective of the central bank is not more rapid price increase, but faster growth, and it would seem more honest to say so."

Where does this leave the debate about inflation targeting for Japan?

On the subsidiary short-run question of whether a more aggressive strategy of quantitative easing by the BOJ would benefit the Japanese economy, the evidence with respect to both the strategy and associated tactics is positive.

On the additional short-run question of whether the BOJ should now adopt an inflation-targeting framework for the conduct and evaluation of its monetary policy, the answer is also yes. It should do so not because it would be a panacea or because it would allow the bank to do nothing concrete to implement its new policy. The bank should adopt inflation targeting precisely because this framework would provide it with scope to act more flexibly and imaginatively in implementing its quantitative easing policy, and the inflation-targeting framework would protect the bank from the only real risk it faces at present: being too easy for too long. Of course, having adopted inflation targeting for the short run, the BOJ should retain it for the long run.[74]

Thus, inflation targeting could have helped Japan cope more effectively with the economic challenges of the past 10 years. It would have been in the interests of Japan as well as the world economy if the Japanese monetary authorities had adopted an inflation-targeting framework for Japan's monetary policy in the early 1990s. It also would have been preferable if Japan could have avoided its land and stock market bubbles of the 1980s, although it is debatable whether monetary policy alone could have done so. At the time, the MOF controlled monetary policy, and it was concerned about the impact on the Japanese economy of yen appreciation. Monetary policy was used to combat that appreciation and cushion its effects on the

---

74. The logic of the IMF staff's views (2002a) on the issue of the short run versus the long run is difficult to understand. They state that Japan can and should end deflation within 12 to 18 months, but the bank should only then adopt an inflation target and, by implication, inflation targeting as its framework for monetary policy. The IMF staff's views (2003g) modulated a year later into a call for a commitment to end deflation by a specific date and the establishment of a medium-term inflation target.

real economy, which fed the bubble, and the adverse implications for Japan's economic performance were appreciated too late.

It would have been reasonable to expect that if Japan had been employing an inflation-targeting framework starting in the early 1990s when other countries and their central banks were doing so, Japan's economic performance would have been better. The forward-looking feature of the framework should have aided the bank in anticipating the risks of deflation and in acting preemptively to deal with them; the transparency feature of the framework should have reinforced the effectiveness of the BOJ's policy actions. As a result, Japan should not have experienced as much deflation; its deflation was a risk that should have been well if not widely anticipated. The real economy might not have sunk so far; the fiscal imbalance might not have increased as much; the financial sector might now be in better shape; nominal interest rates might not have had to be at such low, unnatural levels for so long; and the yen might have been less volatile.

Each of these potential effects would have benefited both Japan and the world economy. These effects are equally applicable to the present and future. The world economy will benefit by the assurance that inflation targeting offers—that the BOJ is willing and able to follow a responsible domestic monetary policy.

How to Get from Here to There?

Having established that Japan should adopt inflation targeting as its framework for the conduct and evaluation of monetary policy, how should it go about the process? Fortunately, like the ECB, the BOJ has both substantial goal and instrument independence and a hierarchal mandate that places price stability as the bank's primary goal, though it has a subsidiary obligation to contribute to the sound development of the national economy. Thus, the BOJ, in principle, could act on its own without consultation. However, that would be unwise because, among other reasons, the bank is already suffering from a transparency deficit, and transparency is a key component of an inflation-targeting framework for monetary policy. The bank should not get off on the wrong foot once it decides to proceed down the right path.

What sort of parameters should Japan adopt as part of its inflation-targeting framework for monetary policy? This issue is of even greater relevance than in Europe, where the risk is that the inflation target would be set too low, or in the United States, where some might argue that the inflation target would be set too low. As a reverser, Japan would have to adopt a transition strategy. The BOJ's transition strategy should involve, first—in line with the IMF staff's recommendation—a commitment to end deflation in 12 to 18 months, by early 2005, if the inflation-targeting framework were adopted in late 2003.[75]

In 1998, Adam Posen proposed that Japan should target a rate of 3 percent for core inflation in the summer of 2000, with the possibility of later lowering the target to 2 percent; Posen wanted to reverse some of the deflation that had already occurred in the Japanese economy. For similar reasons, two years later, Bernanke (2000, 159) proposed that the BOJ's inflation target should be 3 to 4 percent "to make up some of the 'price-level gap' created by 8 years of zero or negative inflation."[76] Japan has now had two more years of deflation, and that would argue for an even higher target for a longer period and, realistically, for a longer transition to get to a positive inflation rate. Benjamin Hunt and Douglas Laxton (2001) favor a target of more than 2 percent in order to have some confidence that the zero interest rate floor does not become binding again in Japan, and the IMF staff (2002a) recommend a target of 2 to 3 percent.

While not being dogmatic about it, an ultimate goal for headline CPI inflation of 1.5 to 3.5 percent with a midpoint of 2.5 percent, which might be adjusted at some point in the future, to be achieved by the end of 2005 and sustained thereafter would be a realistic goal for the BOJ. The lower end would recognize that Japan has been a low-inflation economy since the early 1980s. With respect to the "price-level gap," closing it is all very good in theory and might well aid the recuperation of the Japanese economy, but in practice central banks tend to want to let bygones be bygones. However, all of this is just advice, at best, and idle speculation, at worst; the parameters·in the BOJ's longer-term inflation-targeting framework for monetary policy should emerge from its consultation process. A realistic course for that process would be the following:

- The BOJ would announce its intention formally to adopt in six months an inflation-targeting framework for the conduct and evaluation of its monetary policy and to propose parameters for its framework in three months. At the same time, it should announce steps to dramatically accelerate its monetary strategy of quantitative easing.

---

75. The deflation could be ended earlier if, while consulting about its inflation-targeting framework, the bank also embarked on a more aggressive implementation strategy of quantitative easing. Thus, it would create some leeway to overachieve in hitting its target to end deflation by the end of 2004.

76. Bernanke does not say whether the target he favored was for core inflation, but that is his normal inclination (Bernanke 2002c). Bernanke (2003b) renewed his proposal to focus on the price level gap (in CPI inflation excluding fresh food) between the deflation that has occurred over the past five years and a positive inflation rate of 1 percent to allow for measurement errors, augmented by each year that the shortfall continues; once that price level has been achieved, the Bank of Japan would adopt a normal inflation target. Eggertsson and Woodford (2003) advance the theoretical argument for this price level approach to restoring the stability of the Japanese economy.

- During the next three months, debate about the parameters of the framework and the desirability of its adoption should continue within and outside the BOJ.
- After three months, the BOJ should announce the proposed parameters that would be consistent with its hierarchical mandate: (a) the price index; (b) an ultimate target figure and/or range; (c) how it would propose in the interim, as part of a transitional process, to describe and deal with the challenge of not being able to establish with great confidence a time horizon in which it would hope to hit the ultimate target or range; (d) whether it would expect to achieve that ultimate target continuously, as of a certain date (for example, the fourth quarter of its fiscal year), or over the cycle or a period of years on average; (e) any exceptions or escape clauses that it would propose to establish ex ante with respect to the performance of prices; (f) the time horizon over which it would anticipate returning to the target if there were a departure, or a process by which such a time horizon would be chosen and communicated following such an event; and (f) any other changes to its policies and procedures that would enhance the bank's transparency and accountability. Discussions on these parameters would continue within and outside the bank.
- Assuming that a ground swell of opinion against the framework and its parameters had not developed in the meantime, after a further three months the Bank of Japan would announce the adoption of the inflation-targeting framework, perhaps adjusted in light of the comments it had received.

As already noted, debate about inflation targeting already has been extensive within and outside the BOJ, as well as within and outside Japan. Fukui (2003) implicitly called for a continuation of that debate. It would be preferable that the BOJ adopt inflation targeting as part of a package of measures and with the implicit endorsement, on the basis of informal prior consultations, of the Japanese government, which is likely.[77]

One might imagine a more accelerated process than in other countries in which the BOJ sets a good example for its other G3 partners and demonstrates its seriousness to the international financial system by moving more expeditiously than might be possible in the case of the other G3 monetary authorities. The entire process might be completed in six months, for example, by March 31, 2004. Of course, changes in the framework could be made later based on experience, as long as their rationale was clearly communicated to the public.

---

77. I do not rule out formal parliamentary endorsement of inflation targeting by the BOJ, which should be relatively easy to accomplish without too much risk of political damage to the BOJ, but I do not think that it is essential.

Joint Adoption

Non-G3 countries should support the G3's joint adoption of inflation-targeting frameworks for the conduct and evaluation of G3 monetary policies, if as a consequence the G3 economies in the aggregate could produce better outcomes in terms of growth, inflation, and overall macroeconomic stability. Their action would benefit the system as a whole. It would almost certainly be welcomed even if there were not a wide consensus outside the G3 on the precise definition or quantification of those better outcomes.

From the discussion of possible individual adoption of inflation targeting by G3 countries, their better economic performance would appear to be a reasonable expectation, perhaps to a greater extent in the case of Euroland than in the case of the United States and to the greatest extent in the case of Japan. It is possible that the particular G3 inflation-targeting frameworks might be too demanding, in that the inflation targets would be set too low, adversely affecting G3 growth, but this could happen without inflation targeting. It is also possible that the inflation-targeting frameworks could be operated in too rigid a manner, increasing the volatility of G3 output, but the empirical analysis presented in chapter 3 for actual inflation targeters suggests that it would be unlikely.

The central banks of the G3 economies might adopt either a common inflation target or inflation targets that differ. Most of the benefits would flow from either approach. The former might be seen as more elegant, coming closer to the hypothetical gold standard system. The latter might be seen to be more pragmatic; advocates of inflation targeting by the G3 should not want G3 adoption of the framework to be delayed by technical arguments about what type of price index to target and the comparability of those indices.

Some might favor the adoption of a common inflation target by the G3 because it would contribute to exchange rate stability. Allan Meltzer (2002b) for one has advocated that the G3 adopt a common inflation target and thereby supply a public good—contribute to global price stability through more stable G3 exchange rates. I do not attach a high probability to the G3 adopting a common inflation target, and I think the likely contribution of doing so to G3 exchange rate stability, and therefore to stability in effective exchange rates for other countries, no matter how desirable, would be minimal. On the other hand, a G3 inflation-targeting framework using a common target might facilitate the implementation of IMF's suggestion (2003b) that joint action by the G3 central banks to combat deflation might be desirable and appropriate to deal with a common deflationary shock. However, the common target would not be essential to implement this suggestion.

Therefore, the most reasonable assumption is that the parameterization and operations under the respective G3 inflation-targeting frameworks would reflect the revealed preferences of the respective authorities today: somewhat greater tolerance of inflation by the Federal Reserve along with somewhat greater willingness to experiment and take risks; less tolerance of inflation by the ECB and less willingness to experiment or take risks; and the least tolerance of inflation and the least willingness to experiment and take risks on the part of the BOJ. In the absence of action-forcing events, continuity and gradual evolution generally dominate abrupt change and revolution, especially when it comes to institutions like central banks. Thus, the rest of the world should expect de facto continuity if the G3 as a group were to adopt inflation targeting, but some might hope to be favorably surprised. However, it is possible that over time the G3 central banks find themselves under some pressure to conform their frameworks.

Although one cannot with certainty predict that the G3's adoption of inflation targeting would contribute to what the rest of the world would consider to be substantially better outcomes for the three economies—aside from some reduction in uncertainty about G3 policies—the thrust of the effect of their adoption should be in that direction; the sign would be positive. However, the rest of the world also has an interest in the "quality" of G3 cooperation, and one might reasonably expect that if the G3 were able to reach a collective decision to adopt inflation targeting, this step might improve the quality of G3 cooperation.

First and most obviously, a common framework, even if the parameters were different in the different economies, should improve communication, compared with the present less transparent and more eclectic approaches. The G3 central bankers and their finance ministry colleagues would all be speaking a common language.

Second, a common framework would force the central bankers in their discussions with each other and with their finance ministry colleagues to be more frank about the objectives of their policies and about how they intend to achieve those objectives. This judgment follows from the forward-looking focus embedded in the inflation-targeting framework itself, in which, as generally practiced, the use of output gaps (between aggregate demand and potential aggregate supply) as analytical devices is a central element in the assessment of potential inflation pressures.[78]

---

78. As was noted under the discussion of potential inflation targeting in Euroland, this framework is not entirely embraced in Europe. Vitor Gaspar and Frank Smets, perhaps not by coincidence working at the ECB, have written (2002) a detailed theoretical and empirical argument for why central banks should not use this framework under *strong* assumptions, which most observers would reject, about the endogeneity of inflation expectations; they also raise some practical objections. In a companion article, Frederic Mishkin (2002b) reaches a quite different conclusion, although in 2003 he emphasizes some of the potential pitfalls associated with the use of this type of analytical apparatus in implementing monetary policy. As a practical matter, central banks do and should (under realistic assumptions about the formation of inflation expectations) worry about output and output gaps. Indeed, critics of

However, more important than objectives is straightforward communication about current and prospective developments and great clarity about how each of the G3 authorities is likely to respond to departures from expected performance. The G3 central banks, each of which has price stability as its principal or joint goal, appear to have fundamentally different analytical frameworks when it comes to inflation. The Federal Reserve employs as a starting point a forward-looking apparatus based on estimates of actual and potential GDP and output gaps. The ECB, in the Bundesbank tradition, tends to downplay forward-looking indicators and the associated use of output gaps in favor of an emphasis on current and past inflation and the influence of special factors like oil prices, exchange rate movements, and wage settlements on prospective inflation. The BOJ until recently appears to have taken the view that the less inflation the better, even if that means deflation.[79]

The preceding sentences may be regarded as caricatures of what actually goes on in G3 central banks, but they are not that far removed from their revealed preferences. The information presented in figure 4.1 about actual inflation aversion in the United States, Euroland, and Japan is consistent with this view. If inflation targeting were adopted by each of the G3 monetary authorities, popular perceptions might become better informed even if the underlying behavior of the central banks did not change significantly.

If each G3 central bank employed an inflation-targeting framework in conducting and articulating its monetary policy, it would contribute to improved dialogue among them, and thereby, one would hope, contribute to improved cooperation because each party would have a better understanding about how the other party thinks about its challenges.[80] Quantification contributes to improved communication, and improved communication contributes to more effective policy cooperation and coordination as appropriate (Truman 2003a).

Of course, it is possible that if the G3 each adopted inflation-targeting frameworks for their monetary policies, the parameterization of those frameworks and a failure to articulate their rationales and their implications for policy could increase macroeconomic tensions among the G3 and

---

inflation targeting, such as Alice Rivlin (2002) and Ben Friedman (2001), worry precisely about the risk that the semantics of inflation targeting will at best undermine the reality of the framework and lead central banks to focus exclusively or excessively on inflation to the detriment of output and employment.

79. The BOJ (2003e) issued a paper on output gaps, potential growth rates, and inflation, which suggests qualified support for this type of an analytical framework.

80. The Bank for International Settlements (BIS) annually hosts conferences for central bank economists, and a conference in the fall of 2000 dealt with inflation forecasting. The BIS is to be commended for these efforts; they contribute to improved understanding among central banks and to the advancement of knowledge generally. However, they are no substitute for high-level discussions of inflation forecasts and their implications for central bank policy.

deliver a setback to international monetary cooperation. One would hope not! If each of the G3 were to adopt inflation targeting, high-level dialogue about inflation forecasts and their implications would be a natural result. A concern might be that the frameworks would become a straightjacket, focused too narrowly on achieving individual inflation targets and insufficiently on G3 growth, or that they might constrain G3 central banks from responding imaginatively to shocks to the global economic and financial system, such as stock market breaks or international financial crises.

For example, might there be the risk that the G3 central banks—the core source of monetary clout in the international financial system—turn inward in their policy perspectives? Would they come to care less than they do today about what is happening outside their borders? Would they become less preoccupied with domestic and international financial stability? Would they become less supportive of the international financial institutions (IFIs)? These are risks with any framework for monetary policy, and they cannot be ruled out a priori in the case of a collective G3 switch to inflation targeting. When one successfully advocates change in institutional arrangements, there may be unintended consequences for the functioning of the international financial system as whole. For example, the end of the Bretton Woods system of exchange rates and the advent of generalized floating among the major currencies in the early 1970s initiated a period in which national central banks became increasingly less involved and interested in IMF operations at least until the international financial crises of the latter half of the 1990s. Over time they retreated more to the Bank for International Settlements (BIS). As long as exchange rates were the main preoccupation of the central banks and the IMF, the former had to pay more attention to all aspects of IMF operations.

If the G3 were to adopt inflation targeting as the framework for their respective monetary policies, this would tend to refocus the attentions of their central banks, to liberate them from other concerns. Some central bankers and advocates of what might be called "narrow central banking"—by which I mean a focus only on the core competencies of the institutions (monetary policy and the payments system)—might favor such an evolution. If this were to happen, the international financial system as a whole would stand to lose. Central banks tend to be the locus of a large amount of technical expertise on a substantial range of economic issues; they tend to have long institutional memories; they act as the principal interface with private financial markets, for example, in the context of dealing with international financial crises. It would be unfortunate, from this perspective, if the G3's adoption of inflation targeting were to lead to a narrowing of the focus of their central banks. Put the other way around, the international financial system has an interest not only in the specific parameters of any inflation-targeting framework that might be adopted by the G3 authorities but also in preserving the active interest and involvement of the G3 central banks in other important international financial issues.

Turning to G3 exchange rates, a case could be made that if the G3 were to adopt inflation-targeting frameworks for their monetary policies, it would provide a useful guide for nominal exchange rates on purchasing power parity grounds. As noted earlier, Meltzer (2000b) makes this argument. If the point targets or midpoints of target ranges for each of the G3 economies were the same, nominal exchange rates might be expected not to be influenced by monetary policy over the longer run. If the targets or the midpoints of ranges differed, then nominal exchange rates might be expected to move over the very long run in the direction of the net difference.

One can point to three problems with this putative advantage associated with G3 inflation targeting. First, few observers think that nominal exchange rates do or should follow purchasing power parity paths, at least in the short run or when differences in inflation rates are small. From this perspective, inflation targets are unlikely to provide much of an anchor to short-run exchange rate expectations.

Second, if the authorities or the market were to take the implications of inflation targets for nominal exchange rates seriously, it might not improve the working of the international adjustment process or contribute to public or official discourse about it. Those who advocate more active management of G3 exchange rates might consider the introduction of this competing framework as a step backward. Crudely put, their perspective is that monetary policy should be directed principally at achieving exchange rate rather than price stability.

Some facts suggest that inflation targeting for the G3 economies would have been a mixed bag from the standpoint of guidance for exchange markets over the past decade. In 1990, the average dollar/yen rate was 141 and the average dollar/deutsche mark rate was 1.62. By December 2002, the dollar had depreciated 16 percent against the yen to ¥121, compared with the 22 percent depreciation to ¥112 that an average annual differential in CPI inflation of 2.1 percent would imply over 12 years; this was a move in the direction "predicted" by changes in consumer price levels, but it left a gap of about 7.5 percent. Over the same period, the dollar had appreciated by 24 percent against the deutsche mark, or its successor the euro, to an implied rate of DM2.00, instead of depreciating about 5.5 percent to an implied DM1.52 as would have been consistent by an average annual inflation differential of .5 percent in favor of Germany—a gap of 30 percentage points.

Third, it would be unlikely that as a result of G3 adoption of inflation targeting, their exchange rates would display the type of increased stability that some critics feel would provide much improvement in the exchange rate dimension of the functioning of the international financial system. The adoption of inflation targeting might contribute to greater underlying stability in the G3 economies, in particular Japan, but most critics of the medium-term swings in G3 exchange rates do not cite macro-economic instability in the G3 as the principal cause. However, one can infer from Kuttner and Posen (2000) that the increased monetary transparency associated with inflation targeting by each G3 member might provide the G3 as a group with an additional scope to address short-term exchange rate volatility through other means, for example, occasional exchange market intervention.

On the other hand, two risks can be identified if G3 inflation targeting, contrary to my presumption, would contribute to greater nominal exchange rate stability. The stability might be achieved around the wrong rate in real terms from the standpoint of a reasonable reallocation of the US current account deficit. In addition, most of that adjustment in real exchange rates would have to occur via nominal changes in the rate as long as G3 inflation rates are low and similar.

Conclusion

What is the bottom line on inflation targeting for the Group of Three? G3 inflation targeting would be a net plus for the world economy. The G3 economies as a group could be expected to produce better economic outcomes; the improvement in clarity and transparency of monetary policies would tend to outweigh any risk of excessive rigidity. More generally, the quality of G3 monetary cooperation could reasonably be expected to improve, which would be desirable.

Moreover, if as some think the world is going into a period where global deflation is a real risk, inflation targeting by the G3 in the form of *antideflation targeting*, in effect, would serve as a potentially valuable insurance policy for the global economy.

Implications of G3 inflation targeting for the behavior and management of G3 exchange rates might be a very small net plus.

On balance, the collective G3 adoption of inflation targeting is not essential to the improved functioning of the international financial system and the global economy, but it would make a positive contribution and improve its functioning. Moreover, the downside risks are minimal.

5

Exchange Rate Regimes, Policies, and Practices

The principal argument of skeptics is that inflation targeting as a framework for the conduct and evaluation of monetary policy suffers from too great an emphasis on inflation at the expense of other worthy policy objectives such as achieving and sustaining the highest possible level of employment and growth. This line of argumentation also includes views to the effect that inflation-targeting central banks will be distracted from other aspects of economic performance such as financial stability and bubbles or booms in asset prices, which should be the central banks' concern either in their own right or because they affect overall economic performance, including with respect to inflation or deflation.

Some argue that exchange rates will or should distract inflation-targeting central bankers because of their influence on the overall performance of the economy. If the behavior of exchange rates does distract an inflation-targeting central bank from focusing primarily on its inflation target, others would argue that its monetary framework is likely to come under pressure because a successful monetary framework cannot have two potentially conflicting targets. The basic question addressed in this chapter is how much can a successful inflation-targeting central bank afford to be distracted by exchange rate considerations.

What can be said about inflation targeting as a framework for the conduct of monetary policy and debates about exchange rate regimes? The issue for the most part has been settled for the industrial countries in favor of either floating or adoption of a collective currency, as in the case of most EU members.[1] However, for inflation-targeting industrial countries such as Australia, Canada, New Zealand, Sweden, and the United Kingdom, solid inflation performances over the past decade and reasonably strong growth performances have not been associated with either exchange rate stability or the avoidance of wide swings in exchange rates. The behavior of exchange rates is an economic and political challenge and raises important policy issues.

For emerging-market economies, the debate about the appropriate choice of an exchange rate regime continues to rage among economists and political economists in large part because of the less than accepted wisdom that no exchange rate regime is best for all countries at all times in all circumstances, or as Jeffrey A. Frankel (1999) stated in the title of his essay "No Single Currency Regime Is Right for all Countries or at All Times."[2] Vittorio Corbo and Klaus Schmidt-Hebbel (2001) argue with respect to the choice of inflation targeting in Latin America that economists and policymakers do not have an all-encompassing framework for choosing among exchange rate regimes; there is a lack of consensus on the empirical weight to be given to different costs and benefits, and those costs and benefits change over time as circumstances or conditions change. A related question, however, is whether a country by choosing inflation targeting is also choosing an exchange rate regime of (near) pure floating or whether it can reasonably choose another regime from a longer menu of options.

In the context of inflation targeting, the debate about exchange rates comes down to three questions: what types of exchange rate regimes are compatible with an inflation-targeting framework for monetary policy? What types of exchange market policies or approaches to exchange market operations are consistent with that framework? Is a "fear of floating" likely to undermine, for either rational or irrational reasons, the capacity, in particular of authorities in emerging-market economies, to implement inflation targeting reasonably effectively? These questions are addressed after a discussion of exchange rate experiences of five inflation targeters— New Zealand, the United Kingdom, Poland, Sweden, and Brazil. My basic

---

1. The birth of the euro can only partly be attributed to a coalescence of views within Europe about exchange rate regimes, contrary to the views expressed by Stanley Fischer (2001) and Paul A. Volcker (2001). The euro phenomenon is at least as much a consequence of the 50-year trend toward European economic and, importantly, political integration. That latter factor, of course, also figures in controversies about exchange rate regimes and national sovereignty, as is illustrated by the debate in the United Kingdom about joining the euro area and by debates in Ecuador and El Salvador about dollarization. Richard Cooper (1984), Rudiger Dornbusch (2001), and Kenneth Rogoff (2001) have also analyzed the Volcker view on the trend toward fewer currencies or a single global currency.

2. A similar thought can be found in Bryant (2003, 290): "Good exchange rate policy is context dependent. No single exchange regime will work well for all nations in all circumstances at all times." See also Calvo and Mishkin (2003).

conclusions are (1) inflation targeting does not guarantee exchange rate stability, and (2) inflation-targeting central banks can, and in some cases should, actively but consciously consider exchange rates without seriously undermining the rationale for or the usefulness of the framework.

Performance of Exchange Rates under Inflation Targeting

In the three years following New Zealand's formal adoption of inflation targeting at the end of 1989, consumer price index (CPI) inflation averaged 2.7 percent in New Zealand, 7.2 percentage points lower than during the three-year period ending in 1989 (table 5.1). Real GDP growth, which had been low in the three years ending in 1989 (3.5 percent), not only did not pick up but also was negative—minus 0.1 percent on average in 1990–92. Growth subsequently recovered; in 2001 and 2002, the increase in real GDP averaged more than 4 percent in the context of the global economic slowdown. Inflation has remained subdued, and New Zealand, which started inflation targeting as a converger with an inflation rate of 7.5 percent in 1989, has been an inflation maintainer for a decade.

However, on balance, New Zealand's growth performance has been disappointing, especially compared with Australia's, another inflation targeter but one that had less extensive accompanying economic reforms.[3] The Reserve Bank of New Zealand's policies under the previous Policy Targets Agreement (PTA) between the minister of finance and the governor of the reserve bank have been blamed for unduly constraining growth.[4] One result is that the most recent (September 17, 2002) PTA raises the midpoint of the target band from 1.5 to 2 percent by narrowing the band from 0 to 3 percent to 1 to 3 percent—an adjustment that also could be justified on the basis of concern about resistance to deflation. The new PTA also relaxes somewhat the interpretation of the target moving from "12-monthly increases in the CPI" to the "average over the medium term." It has also similarly adjusted the notification requirement—when annual inflation is outside or is projected to be outside the range.

A major puzzle about New Zealand's experience has been the performance of the Kiwi dollar, which on the IMF's real effective basis declined

3. Nils Bjorksten and Anne-Marie Brook (2002) provide a nice summary of New Zealand's relative economic performance and wide swings in the Kiwi dollar since the adoption of inflation targeting. For more on New Zealand's experience with inflation targeting, see Sherwin (2000) and the references in footnote 9 in chapter 1. On Australia's experience, see Debelle (2000) and Simes (2002); Simes argues that the Reserve Bank of Australia should abandon the "pretence of targeting inflation" and admit it is targeting financial stability.

4. See the Reserve Bank of New Zealand's Web site for more information on the PTA, www.rbnz.govt.nz/monpol/pta/.

Table 5.1 Average annual inflation and GDP growth rates before and after adoption of inflation targeting (percent)

Country	Date of adoption	Inflation		GDP growth	
		Before	After	Before	After
New Zealand	December 1989	9.9	2.7	3.5	−0.1
United Kingdom	October 1992	6.4	2.5	−0.1	3.4
Sweden	January 1993	7.4	3.1	−0.6	1.6
Poland	September 1998	15.5	7.7	5.9	3.1
Brazil	June 1999	8.6	7.4	2.1	3.4
Average					
(except New Zealand)		9.5	5.2	1.8	2.9

Note: Data are averages of the three years before and after adoption. For Brazil, the adoption year 1999 was omitted because the adoption was in the middle of the year.

Source: IMF, *International Financial Statistics.*

17 percent from 1989 to 1992, appreciated 30 percent by 1997, then backed off again 29 percent through the fourth quarter of 2001, and rose again by 20 percent through the end of 2002 (figure 5.1).[5] By way of comparison, since adoption of inflation targeting by Australia in early 1993, the low-to-high range of the Australian dollar has been 20 percent in real effective terms, while the range for the New Zealand dollar has been 35 percent.

Price stability and reasonably solid growth performance, though not as much growth as the New Zealand authorities hoped, have not been rewarded with exchange rate stability. Between 1997 and 1999, the Reserve Bank of New Zealand tried to address the problem through the use of a so-called monetary conditions index to guide the implementation of its policy. The index seeks to capture the joint influence of short-term interest rates and exchange rates on the behavior of the real economy. This experiment was much less successful than inflation targeting itself largely because the index involved a lethal combination of an endogenous (exchange rates) with an exogenous variable (the short-term interest rate set, or heavily influenced, by the central bank) in the context where expectations about the latter played havoc with the behavior of the former. The experiment was abandoned in 1999.

On the issue of inflation targeting and the behavior of exchange rates, it is also instructive to compare and contrast the experiences of the United Kingdom, Sweden, Poland, and Brazil. By way of background, the first two adopted inflation targeting in the early 1990s in the wake of the exchange rate mechanism (ERM) crisis in 1992 and still practice it because

---

5. Real effective exchange rates presented in this chapter are from IMF's *International Financial Statistics.* For Brazil—which does not allow the IMF to publish its calculations—the source is JPMorgan.

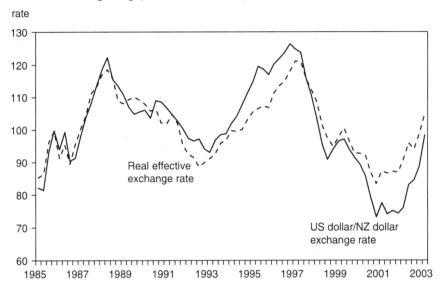

Figure 5.1 Performance of the New Zealand dollar under inflation targeting (1985Q1–2003Q1)

rate

Real effective exchange rate

US dollar/NZ dollar exchange rate

Note: Both rates indexed with average 1990Q1–2003Q1 = 100.

Source: IMF, *International Financial Statistics.*

they remain outside the euro area.[6] The last two adopted inflation targeting in the late 1990s—Poland did so as part of a further evolution away from an exchange rate–based disinflation strategy, and Brazil adopted inflation targeting following an external financial crisis and the forced abandonment of an exchange rate–based disinflation strategy.

On average, inflation declined 4.3 percentage points in these four countries in the three years following their adoption of inflation targeting compared with the three years before adoption (table 5.1).[7] On average, real GDP growth rose 1.1 percentage points in the four countries in the three years following their adoption of inflation targeting compared with the previous three years. However, this average gain was mostly accounted

---

6. See Truman (2002b) for a retrospective review of the 1992–93 exchange rate mechanism (ERM) crisis and its implications for the United Kingdom and the euro area. See Berg (2000) as well as Heikensten and Vredin (1998) on Sweden's experience with inflation targeting, and Andrew Haldane (2000), King (1997a, 1997b, 1999a, 1999b, and 2002), and Wadhwani (2000) on the UK experience.

7. The Brazilian calculations shown in table 5.1 exclude 1999 because the inflation target was adopted in the middle of the year. If that year were included in both three-year averages, inflation rose from 5 percent on average for 1997–99 to 6.3 percent for 1999–2001, which was still quite remarkable given the substantial depreciation of the real in 1999.

Figure 5.2 Performance of the pound sterling under inflation targeting (1992Q4–2003Q1)

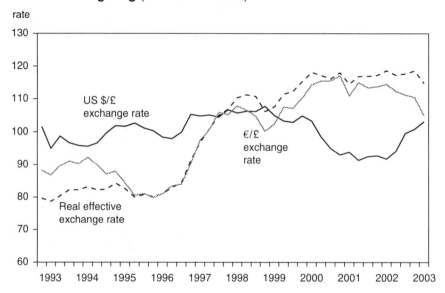

rate

US $/£
exchange rate

€/£
exchange
rate

Real effective
exchange rate

1993 1994 1995 1996 1997 1998 1999 2000 2001 2002 2003

Notes: Both rates indexed with average 1992Q4–2002Q3 = 100. Euro/pound exchange rate constructed for the 1993–99 from the deutsche mark/pound rate and the euro conversion rate: 1€ = DM1.95583.

Source: IMF, *International Financial Statistics.*

for by the two EU countries (United Kingdom and Sweden), whose economies were in recession before the 1992 ERM crisis; growth slowed substantially in Poland.

These overall favorable results on inflation and growth are only indicative of the macroeconomic success or failure of inflation targeting. The more extensive evidence on overall macroeconomic performance under inflation targeting presented in chapter 3 generally supports the view that on average the effects were positive.

What about the behavior of exchange rates in these four countries?

In the case of the United Kingdom, the pound sterling remained relatively steady against the dollar from early 1993 until 2000, declined somewhat through early 2002, before appreciating for the rest of that year (figure 5.2). However, in real effective terms, the pound was steady through 1996 but subsequently appreciated substantially along with the dollar until early 2002 and was essentially unchanged through the end of that year, before easing off in early 2003. Consequently, at the end of 2002, the pound was still 2 percent above its old ERM central rate with the deutsche mark (DM2.95 per pound) but had dipped to 7 percent below that sensitive rate by July 2003. The pound's strength on average against the euro in recent years represents one of the many real or imagined barriers to the United Kingdom joining Euroland.

As in the United States over the past several years, a relatively strong economy and currency have enlarged the UK current account deficit and tended to depress activity in sectors producing traded goods and services, while nontraded sectors have continued to do quite well. The Bank of England faces no real dilemma in its policy. The United Kingdom is a relatively large economy (population of almost 60 million) and not as open as some countries (imports of goods and services are about 25 percent of GDP). The Bank of England lowered interest rates 200 basis points in 2001 to help cushion the slowdown in the economy while not endangering its medium-term target for inflation and, possibly, hoping in the process to take a bit of air out of the pound.[8] Sterilized intervention is an option for the UK authorities as well as for the Bank of England acting alone; in mid-2000, Sushil Wadhwani (2000), then a member of the Monetary Policy Committee of the Bank of England, argued for the judicious use of sterilized intervention, but his argument did not carry the day.

In contrast, the Swedish krona appreciated against the US dollar from its low in early 1994 until 1996 but subsequently dropped sharply until late 2001 before recovering during 2002 and early 2003 (figure 5.3). In real effective terms and against the euro, the krona's performance was similar but more dampened.

Unlike the Bank of England, the Swedish Riksbank faced more of a dilemma as its currency weakened. How much should it worry about the risk of imported inflation? Sweden is a small (population of less than 9 million) and open (imports are about 40 percent of GDP) economy. The Riksbank has a much stronger case for not ignoring the first-round effects of a weaker currency on inflation than does the Bank of England and either the European Central Bank (ECB) or the Federal Reserve. On the other hand, the Riksbank has comfortably achieved its inflation objectives in recent years despite the krona's weakness.

A more difficult issue is the potential for distortions in the Swedish economy favoring the production of traded over nontraded goods and services, production patterns that pushed Sweden's current account surplus above 4 percent of GDP in 2002, a level that is unlikely to be sustainable and may be sharply reversed down the road. It may be best to live with the krona's weakness rather than to fight it with tighter monetary policy that further weakens the domestic economy, where growth has been less than 2 percent for the past two years. In fact, the Riksbank lowered its repurchase rate only by 25 basis points on balance over 2001 and 2002, a period during which the Bank of England and the ECB each cumulatively reduced their key rates by 200 basis points and the Federal

---

8. The Bank of England's repurchase rate was unchanged during 2002 but was dropped 50 basis points by early July 2003.

Figure 5.3 Performance of the Swedish krona under inflation targeting (1993Q1–2003Q1)

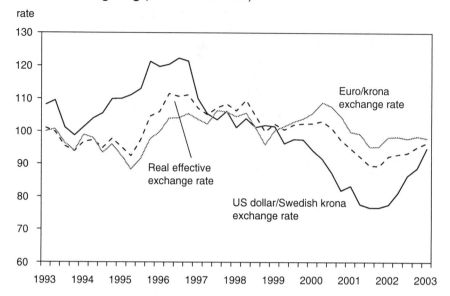

Notes: Rates indexed with average 1993Q1–2003Q1 = 100. Euro/krona exchange rate constructed for 1993–99 from the deutsche mark/krona rate and the euro conversion rate: 1€ = DM1.95583.

Source: IMF, *International Financial Statistics.*

Reserve dropped the federal funds rate 525 basis points.[9] Sterilized intervention is an option, which the Riksbank employed in the summer of 2001, and may help inform foreign exchange and financial markets of the authorities' views about the appropriateness of the exchange rate's movement, but it is not likely to be particularly effective in industrial economies especially beyond the very short run.[10]

This brief review of the British and Swedish experiences illustrates three points: first, the generally successful performance of these economies under inflation targeting; second, the different trends in their exchange rates, suggesting that successful inflation targeting does not map one for one into a particular type of exchange rate behavior; and third, inflation targeting does not remove the need for the authorities to think about movements in exchange rates and their impact on the economy, cer-

---

9. The Bank of Sweden reduced its rate a further 100 basis points over the first seven months of 2003 as the krona rose against the euro and by a larger amount against the dollar.

10. On the limits of the effectiveness of intervention by industrial countries, see Truman (2003b).

Figure 5.4 Performance of the Polish zloty under inflation targeting (1998Q4–2003Q1)

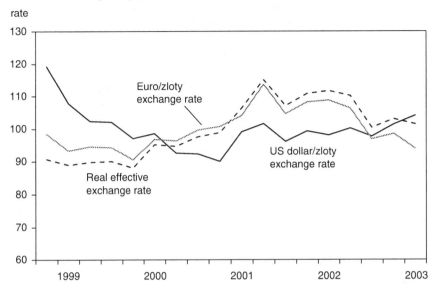

rate

Notes: Rates indexed with average 1998Q4–2001Q1 = 100. Euro/zloty exchange rate constructed for 1998Q4 from the deutsche mark/zloty rate and the euro/deutsche mark conversion rate: 1€ = DM1.95583.

Source: IMF, *International Financial Statistics.*

tainly on the structure of the economy and to some extent on inflation, though the impact on inflation is an unsettled question and may depend more on circumstances than many central bankers are willing to admit.

Turning to Poland, the zloty has been relatively strong—against the background of a large fiscal deficit and a widening current account deficit—since Poland adopted inflation targeting in September 1998 (figure 5.4). The currency depreciated about 20 percent against the US dollar from the fourth quarter of 1998 through the third quarter of 2000, but it appreciated against the euro in the process and had retraced more than half the depreciation against the dollar by early 2003. In real effective terms and in terms of the euro, the currency appreciated more than 20 percent through mid-2001, before backing off somewhat over the next two years.

From the end of 2000 to mid-2003, the National Bank of Poland reduced its 28-day intervention rate by more than 1,350 basis points to less than 5.5 percent, lowering short-term real rates significantly as inflation declined from above 9 percent in the fourth quarter of 2000 (year-over-year basis) to around 1 percent at the end of 2002, below the bank's band of 2 to 4 percent adopted to help Poland qualify for admission to the European Monetary Union (EMU). However, growth also slowed from 4 percent in 2000 to around 1 percent in 2001 and 2002. Nevertheless, with a relatively strong currency, large fiscal deficits of more than 5 percent of GDP in 2002 and 2003, and current account deficits of about 3.5 percent of GDP, the pressures on the Polish government in the context of their efforts to qualify for EU and EMU membership have been intense.[11]

Brazil adopted an inflation target in June 1999 in the wake of the devaluation of the real in January 1999, which terminated what was for a time a very successful exchange rate–based disinflation strategy adopted in the wake of the appreciation of the real at the start of the Real Plan. Inflation came down from quadruple digits in 1992–93, to 10 percent in 1996, 5.2 percent in 1996, and 1.7 percent in 1998, and growth averaged 3.5 percent during 1995–97 but was only 0.2 percent in 1998.[12] Aided by a substantial improvement in Brazil's fiscal situation in 1999 and the weakness in the real economy in advance of the devaluation of the real, Brazil experienced a much lower than expected pass-through of the real's depreciation into inflation. Inflation in 1999 was held to 8.9 percent, within the 2 percent band around Brazil's initial inflation target of 8 percent, and growth was positive.[13] In 2000, inflation was right on the target of 6 percent set by the National Monetary Council, based on the recommendation by the minister of finance, but growth did not pick up, and the current account deficit remained at more than 4 percent of GDP.

In 2001 and 2002, the performance of the Brazilian economy was adversely affected by the global economic slowdown, the trials and tribulations of neighboring Argentina, the continuing rise in the ratio of government debt to GDP to more than 60 percent by the end of 2002, and the uncertainties associated with a presidential election. Growth in 2001 and

---

11. At the end of 2002, Hungary faced a similar unattractive mix of a strong currency, a substantial current account deficit, a large fiscal deficit, accompanying faster growth than in Poland, but an inflation rate slightly above its band of 2.5 to 4.5 percent. See IMF (2003c) for a description of the dilemma for Hungarian monetary policy as of early 2003 when the Bank of Hungary chose to temporarily subordinate its inflation target to exchange rate considerations and eased monetary policy. The Czech Republic, the third inflation-targeting transition economy, was not much better situated with a strong currency, very low interest rates, inflation below its band of 3 to 5 percent in 2002 (declining to 2 to 4 percent in 2005), slow growth, and sizable fiscal and current account deficits. See Jonas and Mishkin (2003) and their positive assessment of inflation targeting for transition economies. See also Begg et al. (2002) on the challenges facing the EU accession countries and their choices of transitional exchange rate regimes.

12. The inflation data are December over December in contrast to those in table 5.1.

13. In addition to the inflation-targeting framework itself, the central bank credits the international financial community for supporting it to contain successfully inflation in 1999. See Bogdanski et al. (2002) and Goldfajn and Werlang (2000). For more background on the central bank's perspective on inflation targeting in Brazil, see Fraga (2000) and Banco Central do Brasil (2000 and 2002).

Figure 5.5 Performance of the Brazilian real under inflation targeting (1998Q4–2003Q1)

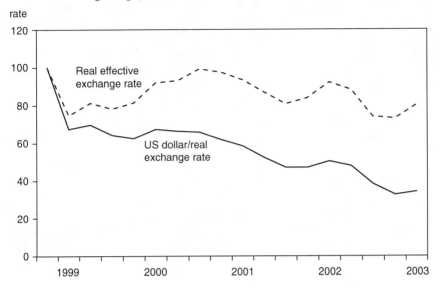

Note: Both rates indexed with 1998Q4 = 100.

Sources: IMF, *International Financial Statistics;* real effective exchange rate: JPMorgan.

2002 and that projected for 2003 was a meager 1.5 percent. As a consequence of these factors, and despite overachievement of the target of 3 percent of GDP for the primary surplus in 2001 and 3.75 percent in 2002, the overall fiscal deficit in nominal terms increased by 0.7 percentage points of GDP to 5.2 percent in 2001 and to more than 10 percent in 2002.

The real depreciated against the US dollar by about a third from the second quarter of 1999—at the end of which Brazil formally adopted inflation targeting—through the third quarter of 2001; after a brief recovery in early 2002, the depreciation continued until, at its low point, the currency had lost more than half its value against the dollar in less than three years (figure 5.5). In real effective terms, the real's initial depreciation in 1999 was largely eaten away by mid-2000, but in 2002 the depreciation again reached about 25 percent. Brazil's current account deficit widened in 2001 to 4.6 percent of GDP but narrowed sharply in 2002 and 2003 under the influence of slow growth and the substantial real effective depreciation of the real.

The Banco Central do Brasil pushed up the overnight (SELIC) interest rate by 325 basis points during 2001 to 19 percent, before lowering it 100 basis points in the first seven months of 2002 to 18 percent. When it became apparent in the fall of 2002 that the depreciation was feeding through to expected inflation, the SELIC rate was pushed up 700 basis points by the end of 2002 and a further 150 basis points in the first two months of 2003 to reach a peak of 26.5 percent. Around mid-2003, inflation and expected inflation eased off, and the central bank began to reduce the rate.

In mid-2001, the central bank initiated a program of daily foreign exchange sales, in part to cover the unexpected shortfall of inflows of foreign direct investment, and in 2002 it intervened on a larger scale and stepped up its issuance of dollar-linked domestic debt, in effect providing cover to Brazilians with foreign currency obligations. At the same time, this program tended to exacerbate the government's potential debt problem by transferring the currency mismatch from the balance sheet of the private sector to that of the public sector.

The National Monetary Council sets Brazil's annual December-over-December inflation targets by June 30, two years in advance of the target year. The target for 2003 was revised on June 27, 2002, to 4 percent from 3.25 percent, and the target for 2004 was set at 3.75 percent, in both cases with margins of 2.5 percent. However, with 12-month *índice de preços ao consumidor amplo* (ICPA) or extended consumer price index inflation at 12.5 percent in December 2002 and a sharp rise in expected inflation to 11.2 percent for the end of 2003 and 8 percent for the end of 2004 (as of early 2003), induced by the depreciation of the real, the central bank in January 2003 "adjusted" those targets for the end of 2003 and 2004 to 8.5 percent (plus or minus 2.5 percent) and 5.5 percent (plus or minus 2.5 percent), respectively. The National Monetary Council confirmed the 2004 target in June 2003.[14] Under inflation targeting Brazil moved from being a maintainer with an inflation rate of less than 5 percent to becoming a squeezer with an inflation rate above 10 percent in late 2002 and early 2003.

Some might argue that inflation targeting has failed in Brazil. I would argue that inflation targeting has been a dramatic success to date including during two transition periods—the economic transition following the abandonment of the exchange rate band in early 1999 and the political transition from President Fernando Henrique Cardoso to President Luiz Inácio Lula da Silva in 2002. The constrained discretion of the framework helped discipline monetary—and to some extent fiscal—policy while not being so rigid as to bring on either an economic or a financial crisis.

---

14. Brazil is not the only Latin American inflation-targeting country that faced tension at the end of 2002 between its inflation target and the depreciation of its currency. The Mexican peso depreciated against the US dollar by 15 percent from the first quarter of 2002 to early 2003. In Colombia, the peso lost more than 20 percent of its value against the dollar over the same period, prompting the IMF executive board in its review of Colombia's Article IV consultation in mid-January 2003 to comment that the continued skillful management of the inflation-targeting framework in the period ahead would need to balance carefully the risk that the recent peso depreciation may fuel higher inflation against the still largely unused capacity in the economy. See Gómez, Uribe, and Vargas (2002) on the implementation of inflation targeting in Colombia.

The review of the Polish and Brazilian cases, following the British and Swedish cases, reinforces the point that inflation targeting does not absolve the authorities from taking into account exchange rate considerations, including the possibility that exchange rate performance may be incompatible with the successful operation of an inflation-targeting framework for monetary policy in terms of hitting or coming close to the inflation targets.

Against this background, the questions that the exchange rate debate boils down to are discussed next. What types of exchange rate regimes are compatible with inflation targeting? This question can be divided into two issues: first, to what extent should monetary policy be directed at an exchange rate target or conditioned by exchange rate considerations? Second, to what extent should exchange market operations be undertaken either to achieve an exchange rate target or merely supplement monetary policy? The next two sections consider these two issues. The final section discusses whether a "fear of floating" is likely to undermine, for either rational or irrational reasons, the capacity, in particular by authorities in emerging-market economies, to implement inflation targeting reasonably effectively.

Inflation Targeting and Exchange Rate Regimes

Some advocates of inflation targeting take the position that the only exchange rate regime that is fully compatible with an inflation-targeting framework for the conduct of monetary policy is essentially free floating.[15] In this view, anything in the direction of the more rigid pole in the spectrum of exchange rate regimes is at best a distraction and at worst confusing to policymakers and economic agents (Blejer and Leone 2000). In this area virtue does not reside in being doctrinaire.

Some countries (Chile, Israel, and more recently Hungary) have combined an inflation-targeting framework for the conduct of monetary policy with crawling-peg or fixed-band exchange rate regimes.[16] These countries faced numerous challenges in successfully operating with their regimes, but on balance they succeeded in their overall policy objective, which was to bring down inflation gradually.[17] Meachem Brenner and

---

15. Alina Carare and Mark Stone (2003) classify any relatively large country with a floating exchange rate as some type of inflation targeter (see footnote 15 in chapter 2). They downplay the possibility that full-fledged inflation targeting, in their terminology, may be a realistic alternative to a fixed exchange rate. However, they are tolerant of mixed regimes and of some scope for exchange market intervention with inflation targeting.

16. Finland and Spain also operated with hybrid regimes combining inflation targeting with participation in the ERM before their joining the euro area.

17. See Mishkin (2000a) and his discussion of Chile's careful and successful execution of a dual approach. See also Morandé and Schmidt-Hebbel (2000) on Chile's experience.

Meir Sokoler (2003) argue that the hybrid regime of inflation targeting and an exchange rate band did not become credible in Israel until the government and the Bank of Israel agreed that inflation targeting should take precedence over the exchange rate band. They apply a narrow market test to investigate the credibility of Bank of Israel policy before June 1997 and find that when the exchange rate was near the appreciated edge of the exchange rate band, the response of inflation expectations to monetary policy differed in a less favorable direction compared with when the exchange rate was away from the edge of the band. They note the recent similar experience of Hungary in early 2003, when monetary policy was loosened in the face of an exchange rate appreciation that threatened to take the forint above its 15 percent exchange rate band with the euro.

In contrast, David Elkayam, Ofer Klein, and Edward Offenbacher (2002) offer a more nuanced perspective on the Israeli case. They point out that inflation targeting in Israel is the stepchild of the crawling-peg regime; the inflation target determined the rate of crawl. They also argue that Israel became a serious inflation targeter by early 1994. Their estimated Taylor Curves for Israel, in which the coefficient on unemployment is not significant, might even suggest that the Bank of Israel was a practitioner of strict inflation targeting.

The issue is neither inflation targeting nor exchange rate targeting. Rather, the issues are how much weight should be placed on the respective targets, under what circumstances, and whether a hybrid framework or incomplete inflation targeting, as in the case of Hungary, nevertheless serves the country well. In this connection, it is notable that in 2002, inflation in Israel soared to 5.7 percent, substantially above the Bank of Israel's target, suggesting that the bank did exercise discretion to allow inflation to exceed its target.[18] Jiri Jonas and Frederic Mishkin (2003) also offer a more sympathetic view of the Hungarian experience. Moreover, the IMF staff (2003e), who often share the doctrinaire view in Brenner and Sokoler (2003) of the viability of hybrid monetary frameworks, have argued in the case of Poland for flexibility and the importance of containing undue pressures for the appreciation of the zloty.

Only time will tell whether other countries—for example, Turkey or Argentina, if they choose to adopt inflation targeting—are likely to be equally successful with inflation targeting in reducing inflation or maintaining low inflation.[19]

Also, a country's choice of an exchange rate regime to accompany inflation targeting depends on the country's own prior experience. In this connection, Alejandro Werner (2002) makes two telling points about the Mexican case: given the failure of the previous relatively rigid exchange rate regime (a crawling peg in 1994), returning to a similar type of regime

---

18. On Israel, see also Leiderman and Bufman (2000).

19. See chapter 6 on inflation targeting and the international financial architecture.

was not advised even though the Mexican authorities were very uncomfortable when the floating peso strengthened against the dollar in nominal and, especially, real terms in 1999 and 2000 (see also Carstens and Werner 2000).

At the same time, the Mexican authorities had to be mindful of the fact that the collapse of the previous exchange rate regime and the associated rise in inflation to more than 30 percent in 1995 and 1996 meant that inflation expectations were very sensitive to exchange rate movements, and the Bank of Mexico had to take this into account in its policy. Werner might have added that the economic costs associated with abandoning rigid exchange rate regimes are normally high. From this perspective, a more flexible exchange rate regime combined with inflation targeting, even if it is a hybrid, may often offer substantial benefits at lower costs.

Two factors under the control of the authorities appear to be essential in combining an inflation-targeting framework for monetary policy with more rigid or more heavily managed exchange rate regimes.[20] The authorities need to be clear, preferably in advance, about which element of such a hybrid framework normally will be given priority in the case of a conflict—for example, downward pressure on a country's currency when inflation is running below target or vice versa. Preferably, they should communicate their thinking about the relevant considerations ex ante, and at a minimum should clearly explain their choices ex post. The authorities also need to be realistic. As Jeffrey Amato and Stefan Gerlach (2002) argue, there should be some flexibility in the exchange rate regime that accompanies inflation targeting, but it need not go all the way to a free float as long as the authorities are clear about their priority and objectives.

With respect to clarity, Mario Blejer and Alfredo Leone (2000) argue that the coexistence of "multiple anchors" sooner or later becomes a source of policy conflict; the issue is whether the conflict can be anticipated and thereby be largely defused in advance. In nonconflict cases, the issue is not one of strategy but of tactics. It is important, however, to be as precise as possible about what are and are not conflict cases. When the real economy is strong, for example, performing at around its potential, and inflation is on the high side of whatever figure the authorities have chosen as their objective, and the exchange rate appreciates, there is no conflict. Monetary policy need not react. Nor is intervention called for except possibly when the exchange rate appears to be moving too fast and there is the risk of substantial overshooting.

To take another hypothetical example, if the exchange rate depreciates under these macroeconomic circumstances, it is reasonable to expect monetary policy to react—that is, interest rates to rise—because the depreciation can be expected to put further upward pressure on both prices

---

20. The debate about the fear of floating, discussed later, is largely about external factors that are not under the control of the authorities.

and aggregate demand.[21] Similarly, when the real economy is weak and inflation is running below target, monetary policy does not need to respond to a depreciation of the currency, except possibly in the case of movement that is judged to be too rapid; an appreciation might suggest an easing of policy. These are not conflict situations.

Conflicts arise when economic activity is strong (weak), running above (below) potential, and inflation is low (high), running below (above) target, and the exchange rate appreciates (depreciates). The currency movement is analogous to a supply shock, and the central bank has to decide whether to worry about the impact on activity or the impact on prices analogous to the situation facing a net oil importer of an increase in imported petroleum prices, which raises inflation and dampens economic activity.

Inflation targeting does not offer an answer to this type of conflict. Monetary policy requires the exercise of judgment. However, inflation targeting is fully compatible with an approach to monetary policy under such situations where the first-round effect on prices is largely ignored but the second-round effects through aggregate demand channels are resisted. For example, in the case where the currency depreciates with aggregate demand around potential but inflation is under control, a modest tightening of policy, perhaps by enough to leave the projected real short-term interest rate unchanged, might well be appropriate.

This balanced conclusion is in the spirit of the advice found in Taylor (2001) that monetary policy should indirectly take account of the effect of exchange rate changes on prices and output rather than targeting the exchange rate directly. Richard Clarida, Jordi Galí, and Mark Gertler (2001) similarly argue within their analytical framework that openness, which includes openness to exchange rate movements, changes the parameters but not the fundamental nature of the monetary policy problem. On the issue of the different dimensions of openness and their effects on inflation and its variability, recall the results in chapter 3 that provide little support for the view that openness in general is associated with either higher or more variable inflation.

With respect to the second factor—realism about the exchange rate policy that accompanies inflation targeting—in light of the recent failures of exchange rate–based disinflation strategies and follow-on regimes, care needs to be paid to the design and operation of more rigid or directional exchange rate regimes than one of ad hoc managed floating.[22] Maurice

---

21. This analysis assumes that a tightening of monetary policy—that is, higher interest rates—will tend to appreciate the currency.

22. Javier Hamann and Alessandro Prati (2002) have found that there are many potential causes of failures of disinflations and that exchange rate–based stabilizations do better controlling some of those causes. However, their sample necessarily includes observations from more than 30 years ago and as a result their conclusion may not be relevant to economies operating in today's global financial markets.

Obstfeld and Kenneth Rogoff (1995, 74) advise, "Efforts to reform monetary institutions should focus directly on restraining domestic inflation. The exchange rate should be used as an indicator but virtually never as the central target for monetary policy." They point out that there may be secular changes in relationships that require secular changes in real exchange rates.

In this connection, the BBC (band, basket, and crawl) approach advocated by John Williamson (2000 and 2002a) in the most recent evolution of his thinking about more structured exchange rate regimes merits serious consideration as long as the band is sufficiently wide, for example, at least plus or minus 10 percent. This approach involves a band around some notion of an exchange rate norm. The exchange rate norm should be expressed in effective terms, as a basket of currencies, and it might crawl if the inflation rate in the country were higher than that of a weighted average of its trading partners. The BBC approach adds another layer of complexity, though some would say clarity, to the monetary policy decision because it implies that the central bank should consider not only the sign of the movement of its currency but also whether the movement is toward or away from an exchange rate norm, which may incorporate a view about a sustainable external balance as well as considerations of internal balance.

I see no particular danger in using a BBC type of approach, and there may well be advantages depending on a country's circumstances.[23] It is preferable that the BBC component of the overall monetary framework not be too rigid. It should provide a guide primarily with respect to exchange market operations.[24] The use of exchange market intervention as well as monetary policy to help deal with unwanted, or unwarranted, movements in exchange rates is addressed in the following section.

Inflation Targeting and Exchange Market Operations

Monetary authorities in industrial countries as well as emerging-market economies care about their exchange rates, and it is unrealistic to constrain them from doing so or to pretend that they do not.[25] They care about their exchange rates for many reasons, including the impact on inflation, on particular sectors of the economy, on social cohesion, and on fi-

---

23. Takatoshi Ito and Tomoko Hayashi (2003) reach a similar judgment.

24. In this connection, it is noteworthy that Eichengreen and Taylor (2003) and Sabbán, Rozada, and Powell (2003) provide some empirical evidence that inflation targeting contributes to exchange rate stability.

25. It is equally unrealistic and misleading to pretend that the authorities in fact worry about exchange rates more than they do, as suggested by some of the more extreme statements by proponents of the "fear of floating" view; see the next section.

nancial stability. The challenge is to channel these concerns in realistic and constructive directions and resist the construction of Maginot lines. What is pressure on a country's currency telling the authorities of that country about their macroeconomic and, possibly, other policies? What is the best way to respond to such pressures?

Morris Goldstein (2002) has recently put forward a mixed strategy that he calls "managed floating plus." The approach involves managed floating plus inflation targeting as a focus for macroeconomic policy discipline (more than just a guide to the central bank and an anchor for inflation expectations) plus aggressive measures (a) to reduce currency mismatching on the balance sheets, and with respect to their off-balance-sheet operations, of the authorities, financial institutions, and private borrowers; (b) to discourage short-term foreign borrowing; and (c) to enhance supervision of financial institutions because they are the most likely suspects with respect to such behavior.

In the Goldstein (2002, 43–44) world, the authorities could intervene in the exchange market to smooth "excessive short-term fluctuations in exchange rates or to maintain market liquidity," but they would not use sterilized intervention on a large scale to alter the course of the exchange rate. They would not intervene to dampen small-scale, short-term volatility of exchange rates because allowing those fluctuations helps enhance the market participants' perceptions of exchange rate risk. There would certainly not be a publicly announced exchange rate target.

Although Goldstein rejects it, his "lightly managed" floating plus could be further enhanced in the direction of somewhat greater management of exchange rates by combining his proposal with a "light" version of the Williamson (2000 and 2002a) BBC approach—for example, with bands of plus or minus 15 percent as were used in the ERM after 1993. It would have to be clear that the band was purely indicative of the authorities' thinking on the appropriate longer-term trend for their currency in terms of a basket of currencies. For some countries, the crawl might reinforce the inflation target; this was essentially how the Chilean system of inflation targeting and a band that crawled operated before the late 1990s and how Israel's system operated in the early 1990s. For an inflation-targeting maintainer, the crawl dimension of the BBC approach would be unnecessary.

Moving from concept to practice, when the authorities of an inflation-targeting economy become concerned about pressures on their currencies, they need to consider how best to respond under the circumstances.

One option open to the authorities, if they feel they have to resist exchange market pressures on their currency, is to adjust their monetary policy, as was discussed earlier.[26] The challenge, if the authorities choose

---

26. I am deliberately excluding the option of comprehensive capital controls. The recent revival of attention to the so-called impossible trinity—fixed exchange rate, capital mobility, and monetary policy dedicated to domestic objectives—as a framework to think about the

this course, is that in their desire to resist pressures on their currency, they may implement monetary policies that may be too tight or too easy, thus undermining the achievement of their inflation and stabilization objectives. It is human to seek to achieve, or to fool oneself into thinking that one can achieve, incompatible objectives. Under such circumstances, an inflation-targeting framework for the conduct of monetary policy may provide some discipline on the choices that are made, but inflation targeting offers no foolproof way of achieving incompatible objectives or of preventing foolish attempts to do so.

A second option is (sterilized) exchange market intervention. Not all policymakers or experts agree about the effectiveness of exchange market intervention, but there is reasonably broad consensus that the more open a country's capital market and financial system, the less likely intervention is to be effective, but also vice versa. It is quite possible that a $10 billion sale or purchase of yen or euro by the US monetary authorities, whether or not it is in coordination with the Japanese or European authorities, will be less effective—or whatever effect there is will be less sustained—than, say, a $250 million sale or purchase of reais or Mexican pesos by the authorities of those countries even though the United States is 20 times the economic size of Brazil or Mexico. Moreover, as long as central banks hold foreign exchange reserves, which normally entail a fiscal burden, it is reasonable that they should use them.[27]

If the country's monetary policy is being conducted using an inflation-targeting framework, in particular if the country has recently had negative experience with rigid exchange rate regimes, there is considerable

---

international financial system has contributed to the mistaken view that the first and third elements of that trinity can be achieved in practice on a sustained basis via capital controls. For example, Mohsin Khan (2003, 14) states, "It is possible to have *any* two of these policies, but not all three" (emphasis added). As with sterilized foreign exchange market intervention, comprehensive capital controls on either outflows or inflows are unlikely to be effective for very long in a country with well-developed financial markets; the more controls are strengthened and made more comprehensive in the name of sustaining or enhancing their effectiveness, the more costly are the distortions they introduce into the economy, including the administrative costs of the controls. It is a separate issue whether something less than full capital account convertibility, as Brazil practices, is a net benefit to an emerging-market economy as part of a transitional regime. I would also distinguish between comprehensive capital controls and prudential regulations, such as restrictions on currency mismatches that are designed to limit the negative externalities for the economy as a whole as a consequence of private institutions taking on large open positions.

27. The use of foreign exchange reserves is connected to IMF conditionality, discussed later. (For example, what is the rationale for IMF-imposed limits on a member country's net international reserve position?) It is also connected to the Greenspan-Guidotti rule or guideline that the ratio of foreign exchange reserves to short-term external obligations maturing in less than one year ideally should exceed one. (For example, should reserves only be used to pay off those short-term obligations or should they be potentially available for other purposes as well?)

merit in conducting any intervention operation with as much transparency as possible. The authorities of Brazil, Mexico, and Colombia have recently demonstrated such transparency by operating essentially at arm's length from the market, by responding to movements in rates rather than seeking to maintain or achieve a particular rate, and by announcing on a daily basis what has been done. Given that one potential channel through which exchange market intervention affects exchange rates is by altering expectations about the future course of monetary policy, the risk is that nontransparent operations will generate the wrong signals about those policies.[28]

To what extent might foreign exchange operations fit an inflation-targeting framework for monetary policy supplemented by a BBC view of a country's exchange rate regime? Again, conflicts among objectives and signals about policy are relevant considerations.

In a nonconflict situation—for example, where the economy looks as if it might be overheating—one might think that the authorities would be more aggressive with their monetary and (sterilized) intervention operations in the case of a depreciation, depending upon whether the movement of the exchange rate was away from or toward the center of the band.[29] They might choose to respond with monetary policy but not with intervention, if the rate were depreciating away from the center of the band, though such a situation could raise questions about either the consistency of the presumed trajectory for the exchange rate or about the consistency of other macro (fiscal) or structural policies with overall stability.

In a conflict situation, where the need to restrain or boost economic activity was not fully consistent with the need to boost or restrain inflation, it is possible that a BBC type of indicative regime might help the authorities to resolve their conflict. If activity were strong, but inflation were low, and the exchange rate were depreciating away from the center of the band, there might be a stronger case for intervention sales of foreign currency, and perhaps some tightening of policy, than if the exchange rate were moving toward the center of the band.

---

28. See Truman (2003b) on the limits placed on foreign exchange market intervention associated with potential collateral damage in terms of false signals about policy. Despite the reluctance of the IMF staff to endorse hybrid regimes, Berg et al. (2003, 43) make a similar point: "Relatively small-scale and intermittent [foreign exchange market] intervention can be a useful tool" when supported by higher interest rates in the case of exchange rate depreciation.

29. In the case of an appreciation, where the movement was away from the center of the band, there would be the risk of a confusing signal about monetary policy if the authorities tried to resist the movement through exchange market purchases of foreign currencies.

The "Fear of Floating"

What about a fundamental conflict between inflation targeting and floating? Detractors and skeptics about an inflation-targeting monetary policy framework when combined with a floating exchange rate regime, in particular for emerging-market economies, argue that the authorities may pretend to allow their currency to float as they target inflation, but their "fear of floating" will prevent them from doing so. To the extent that this fear is irrational, the economic psychiatrists should be called in to handle the condition. However, these critics argue that the fear is entirely rational because countries with floating exchange rate regimes, especially emerging-market economies, are prone to experiencing external financial crises, which involve severe economic contractions, because these economies have noncontinuous access to international capital markets and so experience "sudden stops" of capital inflows, and because their financial systems are more vulnerable as a result of extensive liability dollarization.[30]

The fundamental issue is whether the structure and condition of an economy and its institutions support a monetary policy that principally addresses achieving a substantial degree of price stability. This question does not have easy answers that apply uniformly to all economies. Eduardo Borensztein, Jeromin Zettelmeyer, and Thomas Philippon (2001) look at the issue from the standpoint of the *monetary* independence of the central bank, derived from a country's exchange rate regime, and how it responds to external disturbances such as changes in US interest rates. Their results are mixed, in the sense that there is no simple mapping between the degree of monetary independence and the influence of changes in US interest rates on domestic interest rates.

The IMF staff (2001) argue on both sides of the issue. First, to the extent that inflation targeting takes account of movements in exchange rates, as it should to some extent, it indirectly takes account of the "fear of floating" argument. On the other hand, if balance sheet considerations associated with a high degree of dollarization of the domestic economy are dominant in a country's monetary policy, this may limit the usefulness of inflation targeting as a framework within which to conduct monetary policy.

The IMF staff are right to argue that floating exchange rates offer no panacea. Advocates of floating exchange rates at best are justified in making the case that floating offers many countries in a wide range of circumstances a more attractive and more viable option than other alternatives. At the same time, advocates of the extreme alternative—the

---

30. The insightful and provocative writings of Guillermo Calvo and Carmen Reinhart (2000 and 2001) and Reinhart (2000) lay out this case. On the theme of dollarization as the appropriate response to this fear, see Hausmann et al. (1999) and Hausmann, Panizza, and Stein (2000).

abandonment of the country's currency in favor of the adoption of another country's currency, for example, the dollar via dollarization—also should be forthright about the risks. Economies that opt for dollarization may reduce the probability of experiencing a currency crisis, by construction. However, the probability of experiencing an international credit crisis may increase; see the experience of Panama, which experienced an external debt crisis in the early 1990s. The jury is still out on whether Ecuador's desperate embrace of dollarization in January 2000 or El Salvador's more deliberate adoption of dollarization in January 2001 will succeed in avoiding external financial crises. What one does know is that their adoption of such a monetary regime has not been a panacea.

It is not appropriate to focus on the incidence and severity of crises as the principal test for exchange rate and monetary policy regimes. Such a misplaced focus can be found in the analysis by Guillermo Calvo and Carmen Reinhart (2000), and in Hausmann et al. (1999 and 2000), who push the "fear of floating" view. There are more effective ways of preparing for winter blizzards than walking around all summer in heavy overcoats. If the nature of an economy lends itself to exchange rate crises that are associated with severe economic contractions, and the reason is that the government and private economic agents lose access to international capital markets after having taken on excessive dollar liabilities, then the authorities should consider other means of lessening those risks and protecting their domestic financial systems, namely via policies and regulations that reduce their vulnerability. Here, Goldstein (2002) and his recommendations about an aggressive approach toward currency mismatching and related issues deserve serious attention.

On the assertion that authorities of some countries nominally favor floating but behave as if they actually favor fixed exchange rates, one must be careful in the analysis. As argued earlier, taking account of exchange rate movements in an inflation-targeting framework for monetary policy is not the same as targeting the exchange rate. Calvo and Reinhart (2001) comment with respect to inflation targeting, "in countries where the pass-through from exchange rates to prices is high, inflation targeting often starts to resemble a soft peg, as swings in exchange rates are resisted."[31] This statement involves two separable issues: the extent of the pass-through from movements in exchange rates to prices and the authorities' response to it.

On the pass-through issue, if prices of most or all goods and services in an economy are linked, pari passu, to movements in the economy's currency both in terms of level and rate of change, then one can reasonably ask whether the economy will be well served by floating. However, this is usually not the case, unless the authorities in the economy follow a monetary policy that completely accommodates all nominal exchange rate

---

31. Barry Eichengreen (2001) appears to have some sympathy with this position.

movements. Research on various economies' experience with the pass-through of exchange rate movements to prices reveals a range of experience depending on various structural characteristics of the economies, their changing economic circumstances, and their histories.[32] A reasonable conclusion from this literature is that pass-through coefficients are not universal constants but endogenous variables and as such can be influenced by policy and the policy regime.

On the question of how the monetary authorities should respond to exchange rate movements, the appropriate answer is not that they should be ignored. However, the fact that the authorities do not ignore such movements should not be interpreted as evidence that they are closet advocates of fixed exchange rate regimes because of their fear of floating. In some cases, the better interpretation is that they are just manifesting a healthy bias in favor of stability.

Amato and Gerlach (2002) emphasize the need for clarity as well as balance in the central bank's response to exchange rate changes under inflation targeting. Ricardo Caballero and Arvind Krishnamurthy (2003) argue in the context of a very stylized model with rational expectations that exchange rate and financial pressures associated with sudden stops of capital inflows should not lead to an abandonment of the inflation target, rather the target should be "state contingent," adjusted in light of the availability of foreign capital, and more heavily weighted toward inflation in prices of nontraded goods and services.[33]

In practice, the central bank should consider whether movements in exchange rates are telling it something about the country's underlying policies, for example, whether the weakness of the currency is a reflection of a temporary phenomenon associated principally with external factors (a temporary supply shock), a more permanent phenomenon associated with either external or internal structural changes (a permanent supply shock), or something reflecting weaknesses in the country's macroeconomic policies (a demand shock). The weakness of the US dollar in the late 1970s initially was interpreted as falling in the first category, but ultimately the Federal Reserve under Paul Volcker concluded that monetary policy was and had been too easy for too long.[34]

---

32. On cross-country experiences, see Goldfajn and Werlang (2000), Kamin (1998), Gagnon and Ihrig (2002), and Choudhri and Hakura (2001); on the Mexican situation, see Werner (2002); on New Zealand's experience, see Hampton (2001); on Australia's, see Debelle and Wilkinson (2002); and on South Africa's, see Bhundia (2002).

33. In their model, sterilized intervention can also play a positive role.

34. One hypothesis for why US monetary policy and the monetary policies of a number of other industrial countries in the 1970s were too easy for too long is that it was believed that with floating exchange rates, monetary policy was liberated from the exchange rate and, therefore, inflation concerns. One still hears echoes of reactions to that view in the view that floating exchange rates are inflationary or contribute to inflation persistence. Michael

Even if a message about a pro-inflation bias in monetary policy such as the type the United States received from the markets in the late 1970s is not relevant to another country's circumstances, and the explanation for the exchange rate movement is entirely exogenous, the authorities should take account of such movements, perhaps with more vigor depending on judgments about the permanence of the shock and the overall condition of the economy. The fact that countries do so, for example, in the case of Canada, which Calvo and Reinhart (2001) cite as exhibiting a "fear of floating," should be taken as a measure of responsible policy, not a policy distortion.[35]

In a very open economy, where the authorities judge that the pass-through coefficient is large, they may choose to tighten monetary policy (raise interest rates) to resist their currency's depreciation, including the first-round effects of that depreciation. In the limit, the economy may, in fact, perform better under a regime with zero exchange rate flexibility. However, the results presented in chapter 3 provide little support for the view that openness is associated with higher or more variable inflation.

In a less open economy, where the pass-through coefficient is expected to be small, the authorities nevertheless have to take account of the impacts of movements in exchange rates on the economy (output gap and structural imbalances) and on inflation (sympathetic movements in prices of import-competing and export goods and second-round effects). To do so does not weaken the case for the adoption of inflation targeting as a framework for the conduct and evaluation of monetary policy, it merely illustrates that such a framework is not self-executing and requires the application of judgment and discretion.

Bleaney (2001) investigated this issue and found that inflation persistence, one measure of monetary accommodation to shocks, has increased in the post–Bretton Woods period, but there is no variation across exchange rate regimes. The results presented in chapter 3 lend some support to the view that de facto floating rates are associated with higher inflation though the direction of causation is unclear.

35. Calvo and Reinhart's work, as well as Reinhart and Rogoff's (2002), can be viewed as part of a challenging intellectual effort to disentangle de facto from de jure exchange rate regimes. (See also Eduardo Levy-Yeyati and Federico Sturzenegger [2001a and 2001b] whose work Yifan Hu and I drew upon to distinguish de facto from de jure regimes in her analysis of the choice of inflation targeting and other empirical issues examined in chapters 2 and 3 of this study.) In this context, the Reinhart-Rogoff critique of the results found in Ghosh et al. (1997) on the importance of the nominal exchange rate regime, where Ghosh et al. found—based on a de jure classification—that pegged exchange rates are associated with better economic performance, is illustrative of the pitfalls in the analysis of some of these issues. However, the deck should not be stacked against the finding that an exchange rate regime in practice is de facto floating by requiring, as do Reinhart and Rogoff, that a candidate regime pass a large battery of statistical tests in order to qualify as a floater. This type of procedure can yield equally anomalous findings, such as the Reinhart-Rogoff "result" that the US exchange rate regime from February 1973 to February 1978 was not floating but a de facto moving exchange rate band with the yen.

Nevertheless, some economies, perhaps emerging-market economies in particular, are more vulnerable to external disturbances, for example, capital outflows *and* inflows and exchange rate fluctuations. The data on the variability of real effective exchange rates that were employed in the empirical analysis reported in chapters 2 and 3 reveal that during the 1980–2000 period, the variability for industrial countries on average was half that for nonindustrial countries, excluding the observations from countries with average inflation rates of more than 25 percent. Moreover, Shaghil Ahmed et al. (2002) confirm the result that the phenomenon of contractionary devaluations (from a peg or rigid regime) in emerging-market economies does not seem to be related to the abrupt change in regime; for industrial countries both devaluations (abrupt changes in fixed rates) and depreciations (of floating rates) are generally expansionary.

One should note, however, that the behavior of nominal and real exchange rates is endogenous to other dimensions of policy and economic institutions. High inflation rates are associated with higher nominal and real exchange rate variability. Countries with fixed exchange rates may experience relatively high real exchange rate variability because their inflation rates are relatively high, and, largely as a consequence, the variability of their inflation rates is relatively high.

As Ahmed et al. (2002) note, the cause of the differential response of different economies to exchange rate movements may be found in the structure of the economies. In particular, as Calvo and Mishkin (2003) argue, the institutional structure of the economy may be what really matters. In this connection, the finding by John Burger and Francis Warnock (2003) that there appears to be a link between vigilance on the inflation front and the development of domestic bond markets, as well as a link between the development of domestic bond markets and vulnerability to external shocks, suggests that inflation targeting may be one, but only one, of those institutions that could over time contribute to reduced vulnerability.

Conclusions

The analysis in this chapter points to the following conclusions about the relationship between inflation targeting and exchange rate regimes, policies, and practices.[36]

First, an inflation-targeting framework for the conduct of monetary policy does not narrowly proscribe the type of exchange rate regime inflation targeters should adopt. The framework should condition that choice and would exclude hard pegs.

---

36. Ho and McCauley (2003), which came to my attention after I had completed this chapter, reaches broadly similar conclusions.

Second, inflation targeters should choose a compatible exchange rate regime; under some circumstances, a regime or policy that involves relatively heavy management of the exchange rate may be not only viable but also appropriate.

Third, the greater the clarity about the relationship between the inflation-targeting framework and exchange rate policy, the better. In particular, hybrid frameworks may be viable or desirable under some conditions, but it is preferable that the hierarchy of objectives be understood in advance and departures clearly explained.

Fourth, inflation targeting does not eliminate the potential for wide swings in exchange rates—sometimes up, sometimes down, and sometimes up followed by down over short periods of a few months or over years.

Fifth, inflation targeting also does not remove either the incentive or the need for the authorities to think about movements in exchange rates and their impacts on the economy.

Sixth, as with any monetary framework and exchange rate regime, these judgments are more difficult in conflict situations. The exception is when a country adopts another country's currency. In doing so, the country essentially hands over these decisions to another central bank and country but does not eliminate the potential for conflict.

Seventh, the fact that the authorities may react to and seek to transparently influence exchange rate movements is not necessarily equivalent to manifesting a "fear of floating;" it is equally likely to be consistent with good monetary policy.

Finally, both Williamson's BBC approach and Goldstein's "managed floating plus" approach offer some potentially useful guidance to the authorities of some inflation-targeting countries, subject to the third point.

6

International Financial Architecture

The international financial architecture—a term coined in the context of efforts to reform the international financial system and its institutions in the wake of the external financial crises of the late 1990s—consists of many distinct elements. The reform efforts include greater transparency, better data provision by international borrowers, and strengthening of domestic financial systems. The rubric also encompasses aspects such as the robustness of exchange rate regimes, the principal topic of the previous chapter.

This chapter addresses inflation targeting and three aspects of the international financial architecture: (1) crisis prevention (whether inflation targeters are more or less prone to international financial crises), (2) the management of crises after they occur, and (3) IMF-supported adjustment programs. The first two aspects are addressed immediately below and the third aspect, which overlaps to some degree with the second, in the following section.

I conclude that inflation targeting offers some benefits in the area of crisis prevention and management. I also conclude that the IMF policy toward programs with members that choose inflation targeting as their framework for monetary policy should continue to evolve so that the IMF is perceived to be more supportive of inflation targeting by nonindustrial countries than has been the case to date.

Prevention and Management of Crises

No economy using an inflation-targeting framework for its monetary policy has experienced an external financial crisis, with the possible exception of Brazil in 2001 and 2002, which already was receiving support from the IMF following its 1998–99 crisis and had been using an inflation-targeting framework for its monetary policy since mid-1999. Brazil received additional IMF support in the summer of 2001 linked to concerns about contagion from Argentina and, again, in the summer of 2002 linked to further contagion from Argentina, increasing concerns about Brazil's government- and external-debt situation, and about uncertainty surrounding the outcome of its presidential election. However, to date, experience with inflation-targeting frameworks has been limited among emerging-market economies; ten of the 13 nonindustrial countries that have adopted inflation targeting have done so since late 1997 (table 2.3). Moreover, the behavior of the global economy over the past decade generally has been conducive to the reduction of inflation rates, which may have limited the incidence of conflict situations.

Thus, it is too early to say whether economies with inflation-targeting frameworks will be particularly prone to international financial crises. Inflation targeting does offer three potential benefits with respect to crisis prevention. First, compared with the alternative of a rigid exchange rate regime, an inflation targeter should be less vulnerable to speculative attacks. Second, the associated exchange rate flexibility should provide an incentive for the private sector to manage its financial risks better. Third, the transparency features of inflation targeting should aid in reducing uncertainty and policy miscalculations that sometimes contribute to crises.

Nevertheless, it would be unwise to conclude that countries employing inflation targeting are immune to crises, even when they have been associated, as in Brazil, with a substantial degree of exchange rate flexibility. If a full-blown international financial crisis develops in Brazil, the exchange rate will be a symptom, but not the principal cause, of the crisis precisely because the exchange rate is floating and has been allowed to float relatively freely (figure 5.5). The principal locus of any crisis in Brazil almost certainly would be in the scale of its government debt relative to GDP, resulting from a lack of confidence in the Brazilian government to have the will and the way to continue to service that debt on market terms. A secondary locus could be the country's external debt. In both cases, a further substantial depreciation of the real could be an important contributing factor. John Williamson (2002b) and Morris Goldstein (2003a) offer contrasting views about the likelihood of such a crisis as of late 2002 and early 2003.

One can only hypothesize about the circumstances in which an inflation targeter might experience a crisis: build-up of unsustainable internal and/or external debt by the government or the country as a whole, which might be associated with widespread problems in its domestic financial system or with political (and, hence, policy) uncertainty and, perhaps, a large downward adjustment in its exchange rate accompanied by domestic capital flight and a withdrawal of foreign capital.[1] Under such circumstances, the monetary authorities will be challenged to make difficult judgments in the context of their inflation-targeting framework, should they choose to retain it. Upward pressure on inflation and downward pressure on economic activity—a conflict situation—would normally be expected. Whether a country is a maintainer, converger, or squeezer is also relevant to its policy choices.

The situations in the United Kingdom in 1992 and Brazil in 1999 may illustrate the possible circumstances of inflation-targeting maintainers in the wake of an international financial crisis. They were not inflation targeters at the time of their crises and, aside from their low inflation rates, were not identical in several respects—for example, the United Kingdom at no point lost access to international capital markets although the adjustment in its external accounts over the following two years (1993 and 1994) was substantial. Economic activity increased in both countries in the wake of their crises. In the United Kingdom, year-over-year inflation, which was 3.7 percent in 1992 (with growth at 0.2 percent) and 5.9 percent in 1991 (with growth at minus 1.4 percent), declined to 1.6 percent in 1993 (with growth at 2.5 percent) before rising to 2.5 percent in 1994 (with growth at 4.7 percent).

In Brazil, year-over-year inflation was 3.2 percent in 1998 (with growth at 0.2 percent) and 6.9 percent the year before (with growth at 3.3 percent). Inflation rose to only 4.9 percent in 1999 (with growth at 0.8 percent) and to 7 percent in 2000 (with growth again at 0.8 percent). Brazil's performance was remarkable, especially on the inflation side, but not quite as remarkable in absolute terms as that of the United Kingdom (table 5.1).

Comparing the experiences of these two economies, one might reasonably conclude that inflation targeting can aid in the return to stability of a country in crisis but that the challenges for an emerging-market economy appear to be substantially greater.

The experience of the Czech Republic comes closest to that of an inflation-targeting converger. In 1997—the year the Czech Republic abandoned its exchange rate peg in the middle of the year and adopted an inflation-targeting framework for its monetary policy at the end of the year—year-over-year inflation was 8.5 percent and real GDP declined 0.8 percent; the year before, inflation was 8.8 percent and growth 4.3 percent. In 1998, inflation rose to 10.6 percent, above the central bank's target range for "net inflation, excluding regulated prices and the effects of changes in taxes" of 5.5 to 6.5 percent, and the real economy contracted by 1 percent. In 1999,

---

1. Brazil is not the only inflation-targeting country that might experience an international financial crisis in the next few years. Others include Poland, Hungary, the Czech Republic (as was discussed implicitly in chapter 5), Colombia, Mexico, the Philippines, and South Africa, each of which faced in 2003 one or more difficult economic and financial problems that could potentially reach crisis proportions.

inflation dropped to 2.1 percent, substantially below the central bank's target range of 4 to 5 percent, and growth was negligible at 0.5 percent.

This evidence suggests that inflation-targeting convergers, in the wake of international financial crises, can achieve substantial inflation convergence but at a nontrivial sacrifice in terms of economic growth, and their success may be short-lived. However, the Czech situation was not a full crisis because the central bank took preemptive action to abandon the exchange rate peg in 1997.

Turkey offers the first case of a possible inflation-targeting squeezer in the context of an international financial crisis. Turkey's authorities intend to adopt inflation targeting in due course. But the parameters of its framework have not yet been set, nor has a date for initial implementation been set. However, following inflation of 55 percent in 2000 and 2001 along with a 6.2 percent contraction of real GDP in 2001 and inflation of 45 percent in 2002 along with growth of 6.3 percent, the authorities have their proverbial work cut out for them, especially in light of an external debt at the end of 2002 of 55 percent of GDP and a government debt of 82 percent of GDP. Argentina, another possible inflation-targeting squeezer, is in an even more demanding and precarious position.

This discussion leads naturally to the question of the extent to which the IMF should advocate or support inflation targeting as a framework for monetary policy among its members, either in general or specifically in the context of IMF-supported adjustment programs. As discussed in chapter 3, the IMF staff in their writings on this subject—for example, IMF (2001) and Khan (2003)—have tended to stress that inflation targeting is a demanding framework for the conduct of monetary policy, without offering a full comparison with the alternatives, which generally include ad hoc discretion (perhaps constrained by the central bank's formal mandate), targeting a monetary aggregate, or some type of relatively fixed exchange rate regime, ranging from a tightly managed exchange rate or a peg to a currency board or dollarization.

As was discussed in chapter 6, a country's choice of inflation targeting as a framework for the conduct and evaluation of monetary policy is linked to its choice of an exchange rate arrangement. The traditional posture of the IMF is to treat the latter choice as one for the member to make. Unfortunately, the wrong choice often contributes to financial crises. Nevertheless, if a country chooses an exchange rate arrangement other than a hard peg or a very heavily managed rate, then it should also be free to choose inflation targeting as its framework for monetary policy. The IMF should support that choice. I recognize that it is possible for a country to choose floating and an ad hoc policy framework for monetary policy, which is also unfortunate.

Three considerations appear to drive the IMF's reluctance to be enthusiastic about the choice of inflation targeting by some countries, in particular following crises or when they otherwise have high inflation rates.

First, in the case of a country emerging from a crisis, the IMF may feel that the situation is too chaotic to make a rational choice; this normally would be a period of six months at the most. Second, the IMF is often of the view that some countries do not satisfy certain institutional preconditions or lack adequate skills to implement inflation targeting; these arguments generally have little merit and can be exaggerated. Finally, the IMF may be concerned that the authorities lack the credibility as well as the capacity to implement inflation targeting; this argument also has little merit and can be exaggerated.

The theoretical case for inflation targeting rests on the view that its successful implementation increases the central bank's credibility, which translates into more effective policy in achieving an inflation objective at lower economic cost. A systematic failure to achieve an inflation target means that the central bank will not build up such credibility and therefore will not achieve the associated boost to the effectiveness of its policy. However, such a failure does not render inflation targeting useless as a monetary policy framework; inflation targeting still provides constructive focus for monetary policy as in the case of Brazil in the 2001–03 period.

Moreover, if the IMF does not favor the choice of inflation targeting by a particular country, it has to favor something else. If it favors a hard peg, not only is there the heightened risk of crisis associated with such regimes but also the authorities, perhaps with the help of the IMF, have to pick the right, sustainable exchange rate, and it is far from clear that to do so is any easier technically than to implement inflation targeting. Targeting monetary aggregates as an alternative more than likely is not relevant to the macroeconomic performance of the economy, with the exception of cases of very high inflation.

In this context, it is refreshing that Berg et al. (2003, 44) conclude in an IMF study, "Targeting of monetary aggregates will rarely serve as a coherent framework for floats; informal or formal inflation targeting offers more promise." They wrote in the context of postcrisis situations. However, the point applies more generally, although I would argue that the distinction between formal and informal inflation targeting, which can be traced again to issues of whether certain preconditions are met, is not helpful. Institutional and intellectual capacities develop over time, as has been the case with most inflation targeters.

As was noted in chapter 2, 46 nonindustrial economies were included in this study's sample of inflation targeters and potential targeters of some significance to the world economy, where the crude test of significance is whether Consensus Economics has included these economies in its *Consensus Forecasts* for some years. Thirteen are inflation targeters; three of them (Brazil, Colombia, and Peru) are conducting their policies with IMF-supported adjustment programs, and the Philippines, as of the end of 2002, was implementing its policies under postprogram monitoring by the IMF. Nine of the 33 remaining nonindustrial-country potential targeters, as of the end of 2002, had IMF-supported adjustment programs.[2] In addition, based on the classification of Levy-Yeyati and Sturzenegger (2001a and 2001b), six of the 33 economies had de facto floating exchange rates as far back as the end of 2000 and therefore could be called countries in search of a monetary anchor.[3]

One view is that inflation targeting is not an appropriate monetary policy framework for countries with inflation rates above 20 percent or, perhaps, in double digits. Instead, they should at least be convergers. However, as was noted in chapter 3 (see also appendix table A.2), 23 of the 33 potential nonindustrial-country inflation targeters had inflation rates of less than 10 percent in 2002. These 23 countries included four (Bulgaria, Guatemala, Pakistan, and Vietnam) of the nine countries with IMF-supported adjustment programs; two (Indonesia and Uruguay) of the remaining five had inflation rates in 2002 of less than 15 percent.[4]

Following is a more detailed discussion of inflation targeting and the design and operation of IMF-supported adjustment programs.

IMF Adjustment Programs

Mario Blejer et al. (2002) provide an excellent overview of the tensions and challenges posed by the potential interaction of inflation targeting and IMF conditionality. As they explain, the IMF imposes conditions to establish safeguards to increase the certainty that its resources are used only temporarily as the member reaches or returns to a viable balance-of-payments position. This conditionality is enforced through performance criteria, which normally are formal quantitative targets on defined variables, subject to verification, such as the level of or changes in the central bank's net international reserve (NIR) position and net domestic assets (NDA).[5] A floor on NIR prevents the central bank from intervening excessively to resist currency depreciation, and a ceiling on NDA is designed to prevent too much sterilized intervention—to force a tightening of monetary policy if the central bank runs down its reserves too far or too fast. In addition, of course, a country's program is intended to achieve cer-

---

2. The nine are Argentina, Bulgaria, Guatemala, Indonesia, Pakistan, Romania, Turkey, Uruguay, and Vietnam.

3. The six are Paraguay, Romania, Russia, Sri Lanka, Turkey, and Ukraine. In addition, Taiwan, which was not included in the Levy-Leyati and Sturzenegger results, also has a floating exchange rate regime but is not an IMF member.

4. Argentina, Turkey, and Romania had inflation rates above 15 percent.

5. Net international reserves (NIR) are normally defined as gross international assets less credit advanced by the IMF and any other official short-term credit to the central bank or finance ministry. Net domestic assets (NDA) are normally defined as the difference between reserve money (currency plus bank deposits at the central bank) and NIR.

tain macroeconomic results, and monetary policy, therefore, is a central part of any program.

The potential incompatibility of traditional IMF conditionality with inflation targeting arises, in the words of Blejer et al. (2002, 3), "because the actual implementation of inflation targeting is largely based on the premise that an independent central bank can use, at its discretion, its various policy instruments, in the proportions considered appropriate in each particular circumstance, so as to ensure the attainment of its inflation goal." This situation does not leave the IMF with much to monitor or constrain with respect to the central bank's use of policy instruments.

The underlying tension between inflation targeting and monitoring of central bank performance by the IMF, the financial markets, or the general public was present at the time the New Zealand authorities adopted inflation targeting in 1989, although it was not operating with IMF financial support. In the context of the ongoing reform of public-sector management in New Zealand at that time, some viewed inflation targeting as a second-best framework for monetary policy because (a) the performance of the central bank could not be continuously monitored and (b) it was recognized that even the most skillful and dedicated central banker would not have the technical capacity to achieve a precise inflation target because inflation in the short term and often the medium term is affected by forces beyond a central banker's control that cannot be fully anticipated.

Thus, by the standard of "trust but verify," a country employing an inflation-targeting framework for the conduct and evaluation of its monetary policy must, at least in the short run, rely more on trust and less on verification. In the context of IMF-supported adjustment programs, two other potential issues arise beyond the challenge of monitoring or verification. First, IMF support for many countries' adjustment programs consists of one-year standby arrangements. This means that policies and policy outcomes are reviewed only for a 12-month period, perhaps with a short period of postprogram monitoring. Given that monetary policy works with a lag that in many countries is thought to be at least six to eight quarters, this means that the results of policy actions taken during the period of the IMF-supported program will not be known until after the program is ended, and inflation during the program period may be the uncertain result of policy actions prior to the agreement on the program between the country's authorities and the IMF.

Second, an important component of traditional IMF conditionality focuses on the balance sheet of the central bank and the level of or changes in the central bank's holdings of international reserves and its extension of credit to the domestic economy. The rationale is the IMF's concern that the central bank should not excessively intervene in the foreign exchange market using its reserves, which have been in part borrowed from the IMF, to support an unrealistic exchange rate, or that if the central bank does reduce its reserves through intervention, it tightens its monetary policy at the same time by bringing about an overall contraction of the asset side of its balance sheet and thereby the liability side. In other words, beyond a certain point, foreign exchange market intervention should not be sterilized. This approach to monetary policy implies a focus on the balance sheet of the central bank in order to safeguard the resources that the IMF has lent to the country. However, there is no assurance that the monetary policy actions triggered by such IMF conditionality will produce the desired inflation outcome for the country. In other words, the balance sheet of the central bank is the locus for monitoring progress in achieving two potentially conflicting objectives: limiting a country's loss of reserves and achieving its target for inflation.

As a further complication, the link between achieving an inflation target that supports maximum sustainable economic growth and realizing a viable balance-of-payments position is one that is not well established either in theory or in practice, nor in the rationale for the IMF's interactions with its members. The IMF's Articles of Agreement (1993, Article I) state the IMF's purposes. Article I mentions the temporary availability of IMF resources to members "under adequate safeguards"[6] to provide them with "the opportunity to correct maladjustments in their balance of payments without resorting to measures destructive of national or international prosperity" and thereby "to shorten the duration and lessen the degree of disequilibrium in the international balances of payments of members." The closest that the language in Article I comes to mentioning low inflation is a reference to the "promotion and maintenance of high levels of employment and real income" in its members. IMF programs almost always have something to say about inflation, but it is often difficult to distinguish (a) an assumption about inflation that is needed to achieve a coherent overall macroeconomic framework for the program, (b) a forecast about inflation that is a hoped-for outcome, or (c) a target of inflation that is central to the program's success or failure.

Supporters of the IMF's involvement with its members' anti-inflation policies might reasonably argue that the IMF is a monetary institution and that monetary institutions should be concerned about inflation regardless of what their charters state to be their mandates. In support of this view, Article IV (of the IMF Articles of Agreement) governing members' obligations regarding exchange rate arrangements states that a member "undertakes to collaborate with the Fund and other members . . . [and] shall endeavor to direct its economic and financial policies toward the objective of fostering orderly economic growth with reasonable price stability, with due regard to its circumstances." It also could be argued that low global inflation contributes to the better functioning of the international financial system and, therefore, is fully consistent with the purposes of the IMF.

---

6. This is the link to the IMF's conditionality to protect its loans.

The IMF also has a reason to have an interest in the instruments and manifestations of a member's monetary policy—interest rates and central bank credit—and how they are used to help reestablish a sustainable balance-of-payments position, inclusive of its capital account, via the reestablishment of macroeconomic stability, once a sustainable position has been lost.

The sensitive point, for example, in Turkey's experience with the IMF, dating back to late 1999, is that Turkey did not initially face a balance-of-payments problem in the sense that those problems are conventionally understood—that is, downward pressure on its exchange rate and difficulty financing its current account deficit, which was less than 1 percent of GDP in 1999. One could reasonably argue, in terms of the stability of the international financial system, that Turkey in 1999 was an accident waiting to happen because of the country's large budget deficits, rising stocks of government and external debt, and weak banking system as well as its high inflation that was never less than 60 percent per year from 1987 through 1999. From this perspective, the IMF was justified in supporting preemptive action by Turkey to bring down inflation and establish macroeconomic stability especially when the objective of bringing down inflation and the approach to doing so enjoyed the strong support of the Turkish government.

The exchange rate regime that the IMF supported to reduce Turkish inflation was high-risk; the IMF endorsed an exchange rate–based disinflation strategy with a decelerating crawling peg within a narrow band exiting after 18 months into a gradually widening band. In hindsight, the program that the IMF supported brought on the crisis that the Turkish authorities, and the IMF, were trying to avoid. Inflation did not decline as rapidly as expected, while real interest rates declined more rapidly than expected; the Turkish lira became overvalued; the economy boomed; the current account went into substantial deficit; and the banking system collapsed. It would appear that a rethinking of the IMF's rationale for intervention in such cases could usefully be undertaken.

By the time of the first Turkish program in late 1999, the IMF had already begun to adapt its traditional policies on conditionality to the reality that inflation targeting is the preferred monetary policy framework for some members with IMF-supported adjustment programs. Starting with the Brazilian case—at the time an inflation-targeting maintainer, not a converger or a squeezer—the IMF had to find an approach to blend its traditional instruments of conditionality that placed constraints on intervention and monetary policy by the central bank with Brazil's inflation-targeting framework for the conduct of that policy. What the IMF management proposed, the Brazilian authorities accepted, and the IMF executive board approved—as described by Blejer et al. (2001) and Bogdanski et al. (2002)—was an approach to IMF conditionality that retained a limit on the NIR level—to ensure that the central bank held onto enough resources to repay the IMF and guard against a reversion to exchange rate fixity, perhaps due to an underlying fear of floating—and quarterly reviews of the central bank's progress in meeting its 12-month inflation targets, but without a restriction on the expansion of domestic assets on the central bank's balance sheet.[7]

Finally, notwithstanding the fact that Brazil's inflation targets were stated in terms of the December-to-December rates, the IMF's quarterly reviews of the central bank's progress in achieving its inflation target were based on interpolated 12-month inflation rates with a deviation of plus or minus 1 percent, triggering an informal consultation with the IMF staff, and a deviation of plus or minus 2 percent, triggering a formal review involving the IMF executive board. In principle, if Brazil failed to pass this review, IMF support for its program could be suspended.

The IMF's procedure in Brazil's case was associated with reasonable results in 1999 and 2000, but inflation in 2001 at 7.7 percent (December to December) exceeded the central bank's target of 4 percent plus a margin of 2.5 percent. In early 2002, Arminio Fraga, governor of the Banco Central do Brasil, sent an open letter to Pedro Malan, Brazil's minister of finance, describing the causes of missing the target, the measures the central bank had taken to get back on track, and the time period for doing so. Conditional on the real remaining stable at its level in early 2002 and reduced pressure on inflation from increases in administered prices, Fraga expected that inflation would be back within its target band by the end of 2002. In the event, he was disappointed, and Brazil not only missed its inflation target in 2002 but it did by a wide margin, as discussed in chapter 5.

Although the IMF should be commended for its imagination and flexibility with respect to conditionality in the Brazilian and other two Latin American cases, this aspect of the three programs should be considered as experiments for both the IMF and the three countries. These programs have established one model for how the IMF should blend its need to protect its resources through conditionality and respond constructively to sovereign decisions by members with adjustment programs it is supporting to employ inflation targeting as their frameworks for monetary policy. The model should be reviewed and developed in light of experience.

In addition to considering both the role of limits on the use of international reserves or on the central bank's holding of domestic assets and the rationale for IMF involvement in support of anti-inflation programs, it would be reasonable for the IMF to consider or, in some cases, to revisit its consideration of a range of other possible models or approaches to conditionality in IMF-supported programs for inflation targeters. Alternative

---

7. In April 2001, the IMF applied essentially the same procedure to Colombia, a converger, and in February 2002 to Peru, a maintainer. The Philippines also adopted inflation targeting but only in January 2002, after the end of its most recent IMF program, when the Philippines was subject only to postprogram monitoring.

approaches can be arrayed under three headings: intrusiveness, monitoring, and indicators.

Intrusiveness (in decreasing degree)

- The IMF, through its resident representative or her agent, runs central bank policy; a broad guideline (an inflation target) might be agreed between the country and the IMF, but all operational decisions about how to conduct policy in light of that target would be subject to prior approval or nondisapproval by the resident representative.[8]
- Quarterly reviews based on quantitative inflation targets.
- Trust the central bank and review performance only annually.
- Trust the central bank, review performance annually, but provide that if the executive board were not satisfied with the central bank's performance, it could ask for early repayment of some or all IMF disbursements.

Monitoring (depending on the indicator or indicators chosen)

- On a biweekly, monthly, quarterly, or semiannual basis.
- Conducted by (a) IMF staff; (b) IMF staff and the executive board as is now the case for Brazil, Colombia, and Peru; (c) IMF staff with the executive board reserving the right to ask for a formal review if it became concerned; (d) a group of independent experts who might or might not have the discretion to refer their findings or concerns to the executive board.

Indicators (one or more of the following)

- Inflation bands as is now the case for Brazil, Colombia, and Peru, but consideration might be given to wider bands or widening of the bands under some circumstances such as a lower level of initial inflation.
- A guideline for the minimum level of a real short-term interest rate based on the observed level of the particular real interest rate on average over a preprogram period.[9]
- An exchange rate guideline such as one based on the BBC (band, basket, and crawl) approach.
- An intervention guideline based on the intensity (for example, amount per period of time) and/or cumulative amount of net operations.

---

8. This might be called the Indonesian model used in the spring of 1998; it was adopted on a de facto basis after two failed attempts by the government and the central bank of Indonesia to abide by mutually agreed monetary policy guidelines.

9. Some inflation-targeting central banks employ such a guideline in their internal deliberations.

- An agreed rule for the implementation of changes in monetary policy such as the Taylor rule or a variant thereof.[10]
- Independent forecasts of inflation—for example, surveys of expected inflation such as are conducted by a number of inflation-targeting central banks in emerging-market economies.
- Forecasts of inflation and their inputs as prepared by the inflation-targeting central bank—for example, the exchange rate, money growth, output gaps, inflation, the term structure of interest rates, and the spread on external debt.[11]

Further work and experimentation is appropriate on the structure of conditionality for inflation targeters that are receiving IMF support for their programs and also on the underlying rationale for the IMF's involvement in monetary policy implementation. The potential elements listed under these three headings are intended to be illustrative rather than definitive or exhaustive.

Going forward, a number of considerations are relevant for constructing an optimal approach to designing the conditionality for and associated monitoring of IMF-supported adjustment programs of inflation-targeting countries. I propose that in its future work on this issue, the IMF should apply the following five criteria:

First, the approach should recognize that inflation targeting is an appropriate framework for the conduct and evaluation of monetary policy for a range of different countries in different circumstances.

Second, the IMF's approach to inflation targeting should seek to build on the key elements of the framework, in particular the inclusiveness of its information base, the forward-looking analytical structure that it usually employs, and its stress on both transparency and accountability. Conversely, the IMF should expect the member to be candid about its monetary policy procedures, for example, with respect to constructing its inflation forecasts.

Third, the IMF should seek to differentiate between its conditions on monetary policy that are primarily designed to safeguard the resources it lends and its reviews of monetary policy that are primarily designed to help the country achieve its macroeconomic objectives. This is particularly important when both aspects come together on the central bank's balance sheet.

---

10. Blejer et al. (2002) and Bogdanski et al. (2002) have investigated the application of a Taylor rule approach to monitoring the Banco Central do Brasil's execution of monetary policy and have not found that it provides much improvement in terms of better outcomes or less binding constraints on the central bank. This finding is consistent with the skeptical view of the usefulness of Taylor rules as guides for actual monetary policy (see footnote 16 in chapter 1).

11. It is reasonable in cases where inflation is a key element in an IMF-supported adjustment program that the IMF have full knowledge of the model, framework, or process by which the central bank constructs its own forecasts of inflation.

Fourth, there should be a strong presumptive case in favor of "IMF lite," at least for inflation-targeting maintainers if not inflation-targeting convergers. For inflation-targeting convergers and squeezers, in cases where controlling or reducing inflation is a central element of the country's program, a tighter approach employing a wider array of indicators or guidelines of success or potential failure may be justified. In this area, judgment has to be applied with respect to the seriousness of the authorities in trying to achieve their inflation objective (assuming it is central to the program's success) as well as with respect to their capacity to do so.

Fifth, on the basis of a positive assessment of a member's overall performance in the IMF-supported program, the conditionality surrounding the implementation of its inflation-targeting framework for the conduct of monetary policy should be relaxed, consistent with the transparency and accountability ingredients of that framework. Similarly, where there has been deterioration in performance, a tightening of the conditionality is justified.

One consideration that is not directly relevant is the issue whether IMF conditionality in this area is central to the IMF's core mission, as opposed to being forced by mission creep or the ambitions of some IMF members to get the IMF involved in areas of so-called structural conditionality, as criticized by Morris Goldstein (2003b and 2001). Views may differ about the extent to which IMF programs should focus on an inflation objective, in particular in cases where a member's authorities do not share the IMF's concern, but monetary policy and a country's monetary policy framework remain central to the IMF's work.

Conclusions

Four broad conclusions emerge from this discussion. First, inflation targeting does not offer protection from external financial crises. Nevertheless, depending on how one interprets Brazil's situation as it evolves, no inflation targeter to date has experienced a crisis after it has adopted such a framework. Inflation-targeting frameworks for monetary policies are likely to be somewhat less crisis-prone than more rigid monetary frameworks, but the jury is still out on this issue.

Second, inflation targeting as a framework for monetary policy offers potential benefits to those countries emerging from external financial crises that want to float their currencies and for whom targeting some monetary aggregate is not attractive.

Third, the IMF should endeavor to project a more supportive attitude toward its members, whether receiving IMF financial support or not, that choose to adopt inflation targeting as their monetary policy framework.

Fourth, with respect to IMF conditionality, the IMF is to be commended for seeking to adapt its procedures for countries with IMF-supported adjustment programs that also have adopted inflation targeting. Further modifications and experimentation are desirable in this area, including the clarification of the role IMF conditionality is intended to play and an enhanced use of forward-looking indicators and alternative monitoring approaches in cases where inflation is or may become, in the view of the country's authorities, a serious problem. The IMF should employ the five criteria I have suggested in its evolving work on this topic.

7

Challenges and Opportunities

This study has investigated inflation targeting as a framework for the conduct and evaluation of national monetary policies and the challenges and opportunities it offers to benefit the world economy. Inflation targeting is now a fixture in the international financial system. In the 13 years from the end of 1989, when New Zealand first adopted inflation targeting, to the end of 2002, 21 countries have followed its lead (table 2.3). Together these 22 countries account for more than 20 percent of world GDP. Finland and Spain abandoned inflation targeting when they joined the euro area at the end of 1998, but five other members or aspiring members of the European Union and the euro area are currently inflation targeters.

In practice, inflation targeting is a flexible framework for the conduct and evaluation of monetary policy. The framework emphasizes the central bank's achievement of an inflation target while allowing scope for the central bank both to take account of other factors, such as the level of economic activity, and to choose the time horizon over which the target is first achieved and again achieved if there has been a departure.

Inflation-targeting frameworks include four principal elements:

- price stability as a principal, if not the sole, explicit or implicit goal of monetary policy;
- a numerical target or sequence of targets for inflation to make the goal of price stability operational;
- a time horizon to reach the target or return to the target; and
- an evaluation approach for the ongoing review of whether the target will be or has been met.

As discussed in chapter 3, inflation-targeting frameworks of countries vary considerably in practice. The central bank's mandate setting forth its monetary policy goals may be somewhat vague; the numerical inflation target sometimes is fuzzy as well. More often than not, the time frame for returning to the target is unspecified, and transparency and accountability mechanisms are both varied and not unique to inflation-targeting frameworks for the conduct and evaluation of monetary policy (tables 3.1 and 3.2). Nevertheless, countries that are considering the adoption of inflation targeting as the framework for their monetary policy should find it useful to organize their thinking around these four elements.

Although the objective of this study was not to be prescriptive about inflation-targeting frameworks, the information and analysis suggest a few broad generalizations.

What is a reasonable inflation target? For industrial countries, a point or midpoint target between 2 and 3 percent is appropriate, with or without a range of plus and minus one percentage point in order to avoid the risk of deflation. For nonindustrial countries that are concerned about facing a volatile external environment, a somewhat higher point or midpoint, say, between 2 and 4 percent, and a somewhat wider range, say, up to plus and minus 3 percentage points, should not be rejected. Too much can be made of the argument that central banks must establish their credibility by hitting their targets and should choose their inflation targets or avoid inflation targeting according to their capacity to deliver on their commitments. Performance helps build reputations, but demonstrated serious effort that falls short of perfection is also an important contributor to credibility.[1]

What is a reasonable time horizon to achieve or return to an inflation target? The answer depends in part on whether a country is in transition to, or has achieved, price stability. In the first case, excessive ambition should be avoided unless there is a broad political consensus supporting the inevitable large short-run sacrifice of growth. In the second case, once reasonable price stability has been achieved, the most appropriate time horizon for maintaining it is continuously—for example, every month or quarter relative to the previous 12 months or four quarters. My view is that it is unnecessary and potentially too demanding for an inflation targeter to decide in advance how rapidly to return to price stability once it has missed its target. On the other hand, complete discretion is inconsistent with the basic framework. Therefore, I would counsel as a reasonable alternative an ex ante commitment by the central bank to announce via a

---

1. In this connection, it is sometimes argued that inflation targeters should focus on core measures of inflation, excluding volatile components such as food and energy prices, because a scaled-back target is easier to hit, and it is important to achieve the target to build credibility. I find this argument unconvincing because it tends to lose sight of the basic objective of the framework—the achievement of a reasonable degree of price stability over time.

letter or some other public communication, after a deviation has occurred, its trajectory for returning to the target and its associated reasoning.

What can be said about the evaluation of the monetary policies of inflation targeters? Transparency is an important element of this and other monetary policy frameworks and contributes to the accountability of the central bank for its actions. I do not share the view that an absence of goal independence is a necessary component of an inflation-targeting framework for a democratic society. On the other hand, it is important that inflation targeters, in particular central banks with dual or hierarchical mandates, pay attention to those aspects of their mandates other than price stability. One way to do so is to include in the central bank's inflation report, or the equivalent documents, forecasts—as distinct from targets—for growth and commentary on the risks to growth as well as risks of inflation or deflation.

For purposes of this study, actual and potential inflation-targeting countries were grouped into four categories:

- Maintainers have essentially achieved whatever they have decided is an appropriately low level of inflation, sometimes referred to as stationary inflation, normally less than 5 percent per year.
- Convergers are well on their way to achieving stationary inflation, for example, with inflation rates of more than 5 percent but less than double digits.
- Squeezers have embarked on longer-term projects to bring inflation rates down to single digits from rates that are 20 percent or higher.
- Reversers have inflation rates of less than zero, and are seeking to raise inflation to a low positive rate on a sustained basis.

Based on their inflation rates at the time of adopting inflation targeting (table 3.3), most countries were either maintainers (11) or convergers (7), a few were squeezers (4), and to date there have been no examples of reversers. Japan would be the first if, as is recommended in this study, it were to adopt inflation targeting.

The intellectual origins of inflation targeting as a framework for the conduct and evaluation of monetary policy, reviewed in chapter 2, can be found in a number of strands of experience, analysis, and policy debate over the past several decades. The most important strand is the search for a better anchor for monetary policy under conditions in which intermediate targets have proved unreliable, exchange rate–based regimes have proved to be brittle, and increased transparency about policy intentions has received growing analytical and political attention.

The choice of inflation targeting is also supported by empirical evidence on the negative influence of high inflation on growth despite the fact that there is less than full agreement on the channels of that influence, whether some inflation is better than no inflation, and at what level of inflation the negative effects of inflation on growth kick in. The empirical literature on inflation and growth derives, in part, from an older literature on the costs of inflation as well as from political dissatisfaction with inflation, initially in the industrial countries in the late 1970s and early 1980s.

Inflation targeting as an attractive framework for monetary policy has also been supported by analytical work on the performance of alternative monetary policy regimes and on the implications of different rules to guide monetary policies; this work has provided some of the theoretical underpinnings to inflation targeting and guidance in implementing the framework. The largely successful implementation of inflation targeting by a growing number of countries was also aided over the past decade by a general decline in inflation not only among industrial countries, where the decline began two decades ago, but also among nonindustrial countries, where average inflation has been close to or in single digits for more than five years.

The most recent development contributing to the attraction of inflation targeting has been the emergence of the specter of deflation, in particular in Japan, but also similar concerns in a number of other countries. Increased recognition of the higher probability and challenges of deflation has led to increased attention to the lower bound associated with any inflation-targeting framework, replacing and to some extent relaxing the traditional focus on the upper bound.

Chapter 2 reports empirical work on the economic, structural, and institutional factors that have been systematically and generally sensibly associated with countries' choices of inflation targeting.[2] Yifan Hu and I found a negative coefficient on real growth, which is consistent with a view that one motivation for the adoption of inflation targeting is to improve overall economic performance; in other words, the better a country's growth rate the less likely it is to adopt inflation targeting to further improve that performance. A similar interpretation, with the opposite sign, can be made about the (positive) influence of high real short-term interest rates on the choice of inflation targeting. However, higher inflation was negatively associated with the choice of inflation targeting, as one might expect on the basis of the comment earlier about the number of countries in each of the four categories of inflation targeters when they made their choices.

An expected result was that external financial crises, or exchange rate pressures, were positively associated with the choice of inflation targeting. The only structural factor that stood out in the results was the absence of fiscal pressures, which is interpreted as a factor contributing to the suc-

---

2. Yifan Hu and I collaborated on this empirical work. She assembled a database for 68 economies, including 22 inflation targeters and 46 potential targeters. Her sample included most of the countries that are significant enough for Consensus Economics to collect forecasts for them for at least six years. Based on the classification in the IMF's *International Financial Statistics*, 22 economies are industrial and 46 are nonindustrial.

cess of inflation targeting. The lack of significance of openness to trade or terms-of-trade variability is informative in light of the view of some that economies with these structural features should avoid inflation targeting because they are likely to undermine the capacity of the authorities to control inflation with any precision.

Inflation Targeting by the G3

Inflation targeting by the Group of Three (G3)—the United States, Euroland, and Japan—would be a net plus for the world economy (chapter 4). It should help the G3 economies as a group to produce better economic outcomes; the improvement in clarity and transparency of monetary policies would tend to outweigh any risk of excessive rigidity. More generally, the quality of G3 monetary cooperation should improve, which would be desirable.

Although it is difficult to make a very strong case that the collective G3 adoption of inflation targeting is essential to improve the functioning of the international financial system, it likely would make a positive contribution to the performance of the global economy and the functioning of the system. Moreover, the downside risks are insignificant. Quite the reverse, inflation targeting by the G3 in the form of *antideflation targeting*, in effect, would serve as a potentially valuable insurance policy for the global economy.

If the United States alone were to adopt inflation targeting as its framework for monetary policy, the evidence from theory and practice is that the benefits in terms of somewhat better US economic performance would outweigh any costs in the form of reduced policy flexibility. If the Federal Reserve were to adjust the framework under which it conducts and evaluates its policy, the transparency and accountability of its policy would be improved. The world economy would benefit from better US economic performance and, in particular, from more clarity about US monetary policy given its substantial global influence.

In addition, the neighborhood benefit to Canada and Mexico might be substantial, comparable to the direct benefit to the world economy as a whole if the entire G3 adopted inflation targeting. The indirect benefit to the international financial system from US leadership in this area would be more substantial if US adoption of inflation targeting induced the European Central Bank (ECB) and the Bank of Japan (BOJ) to do so.

If the ECB alone were to adopt inflation targeting for Euroland, the benefits in the form of better economic performance, under the ECB's hierarchal mandate with price stability as the principal goal, would outweigh the costs by a larger margin than in the case of the United States because the improvement in policy transparency will be larger. The improved economic performance would have a positive economic and demonstration effect on its current EU partners and on aspiring EU members. Inflation targeting would enhance the transparency and accountability of policy, and therefore economic performance, even if the ECB did no more than adopt an inflation target of 1 to 2 percent, building on its recent clarification that its goal of price stability is inflation less than but close to 2 percent over the medium term.

Additional benefits would flow if the ECB chose a higher point or midpoint for its range, for example, 2.5 percent. Such a target would allow more scope for euro area growth, limit the risk of deflation in some constituent economies, and not involve a large deviation from the ECB's actual behavior today, which has tended to tolerate, if not endorse, inflation somewhat above 2 percent in recent years. Further benefits under inflation targeting would result if the ECB's policy deliberations, public statements about monetary policy, and actual policy that would draw upon the forward-looking features of inflation targeting led to a more proactive policy posture and contributed to the achievement of the subsidiary elements of the ECB's mandate, in particular "a balanced development of economic activities" in the euro area.

Japan today faces more complex economic and financial problems than either the United States or Euroland. The evidence reviewed in chapter 4 on Japanese monetary policy leads to the conclusion that the Japanese economy and the world economy would benefit substantially from a more aggressive strategy of quantitative easing by the BOJ. The BOJ at the same time should adopt inflation targeting not because it would be a panacea but because it would provide the bank with scope to act more flexibly and imaginatively in implementing its policy of quantitative easing.

If Japan had adopted an inflation-targeting framework in the early 1990s, when other countries and their central banks did so, Japan's economic performance would have been better. The forward-looking feature of the inflation-targeting framework should have aided the bank in anticipating the risks of deflation and in acting preemptively to deal with them; the transparency feature of the framework should have reinforced the effectiveness of the BOJ's policy actions and increased its accountability. Today, the inflation-targeting framework would protect the bank from the only real risk it faces at present: being too easy for too long. Even if Japan acted alone to adopt inflation targeting, the benefits to the world economy would be substantial. It should help rescue Japan from its decade of stagnation and deflation and provide the assurance that the BOJ in the future is willing and able to follow a responsible domestic monetary policy.

Each G3 central bank enjoys substantial independence in choosing its policy objectives in addition to its independence in choosing the policy instruments to achieve those goals. I have proposed, in chapter 4, procedures each of the G3 central banks could follow to adopt inflation targeting. Those procedures would preserve their goal independence and build on the transparency and accountability of inflation targeting.

The process of adopting inflation targeting might take a year for the Federal Reserve or ECB to implement. However, one might imagine an accelerated process in which the BOJ sets a good example for its other G3 partners by moving more expeditiously, in part because there has already been extensive debate about inflation targeting within and outside the BOJ, as well as within and outside Japan. The Japanese process might be completed in six months, for example, by March 31, 2004. Of course, changes in the G3 inflation-targeting frameworks could be made later based on experience, as long as their rationale was clearly communicated to the public.

Is Inflation Targeting Broadly Applicable?

Inflation targeting may not be optimal for all countries because no framework for monetary policy can promise to be the best for all countries in all circumstances. Beyond the G3, the case for adoption of inflation targeting to improve the functioning of the international financial system rests on the contribution inflation targeting can make to global economic and financial stability. For those countries that have rejected hard pegs for their exchange rates and therefore are floating in some form, inflation targeting is probably the best monetary policy framework because it not only is flexible but also provides a focus for the central bank's policy.

An inflation-targeting framework may not be the best for every economy because economic and financial conditions may not be conducive or the authorities may not have the political support to implement such a framework. Successful implementation requires political will to focus with some degree of seriousness on achieving a reasonable degree of price stability even though the target itself can be specified in a number of different forms.

On the other hand, the analysis in chapter 3 rejects the view of some skeptics that a long list of preconditions must be satisfied before a country adopts inflation targeting. The goal of a country's inflation-targeting framework should be well defined and broadly supported, which may or may not involve a precise or narrow mandate for the central bank; the country's fiscal position should not be one of fiscal dominance in which the central bank is obligated to finance the government because it cannot do so through tax revenues or by floating securities on the domestic capital market; financial stability is certainly desirable but can be overstressed; and the central bank should be reasonably equipped and motivated to achieve its objective, including with a substantial degree of instrument autonomy, if not full independence, in the implementation of policy. The country should be serious about controlling inflation, but beyond that it is unwise and unjustified to be very prescriptive.

In particular, this study argues that the importance of the institutional and technical preconditions for the success of inflation targeting is frequently exaggerated. It is both arbitrary and arrogant to suggest that industrial countries can successfully implement inflation targeting and that nonindustrial countries cannot because the former can draw upon their longer histories, stronger institutions, and greater technical expertise.

This study concludes that inflation targeting, in principle, is broadly applicable to a wide range of countries; I found no evidence to support the view that many economies are too small, vulnerable, or unprepared to successfully implement an inflation-targeting framework. Even by the criterion of initial inflation rates that are not excessive, only four of the potential inflation targeters among the 33 nonindustrial countries had inflation rates in 2002 of more than 20 percent (chapter 3). It is not clear that this is a reasonable criterion or cutoff for the adoption of inflation targeting; the point is that a large number of countries might reasonably consider adopting the framework.

Looking at the experience of inflation targeters and other countries, the empirical analysis presented in chapter 3 identified a number of economic, financial, and structural factors that are associated with either the level or variability of inflation, more successfully for the level. Those results support the view that inflation targeting has had a beneficial effect in reducing levels of inflation without significant negative effects on growth rates.

Little empirical support was found for the proposition that nonindustrial countries with open economies and greater vulnerability to external influences have higher or more variable inflation rates and, therefore, are less likely to be successful with an inflation-targeting framework. There do appear to be significant differences between industrial and nonindustrial countries in the factors affecting the level and variability of inflation. However, the factors identified with the external environment do not figure prominently in explaining those differences. This is not to say that emerging-market and other nonindustrial countries may not face greater volatility, which may reduce their capacity to achieve their inflation targets and reduce some of the benefits from inflation targeting in boosting the central banks' credibility and reputation. However, even under such circumstances, which need not necessarily pertain, inflation targeting can still play an important role as a monetary policy focus, as Brazil's experience in 2001–03 demonstrated.

With respect to whether the adoption of inflation targeting affects the trade-off between inflation and growth or the variability of inflation and growth, the results from the empirical analyses presented in chapter 3 provide no support for the view that inflation targeting involves the choice by a country of a different point on a stationary Phillips Curve—less inflation at the expense of less growth. They provide some support for the view that following the adoption of inflation targeting, the targeters' Phillips Curves shift toward the origin. At the same time, the results provide little or no support for the view that inflation targeting involves the choice by a country of a different point on a stationary Taylor Curve—less inflation volatility and more growth volatility. The results provide some support for the view that following the adoption of inflation targeting, the targeters' Taylor Curves shift toward the origin. In other words, there is some evidence of overall improvement in macroeconomic performance on average for those countries that have adopted inflation targeting.

The case for inflation targeting presumes that a country has some scope to exercise an independent monetary policy and that the economy will generally perform at a higher level over a sustained period if the authorities are in a position to exploit that independence, at least occasionally. The successful exercise of an independent monetary policy requires that in an open economy there be a meaningful difference in the behavior of the prices of traded and nontraded goods so that adjustment of real exchange rates has the potential for offering a lower-cost means of adjusting to disturbances than economywide inflation or deflation. In addition, in an open or closed economy, there must be some short-run elasticity of output to inflation. Monetary policy needs a fulcrum on which to operate. Moreover, the authorities must be willing, or see it as potentially advantageous on balance, to use monetary policy as an instrument of adjustment. If they are content to have the economy's interest rates and its price level determined entirely by the interaction of the real economy with monetary conditions as set, or at least strongly influenced, by the authorities of another country, or if they see no alternative, then inflation targeting is not for them.

Implications for Exchange Rate Policies

The adoption of inflation targeting as an economy's monetary policy framework does not guarantee exchange rate stability and does not eliminate the potential for wide swings in exchange rates, over short periods of a few months or over longer periods of several years whether or not their targets were the same (chapter 5). On the margin, if inflation targeting contributes to better economic performance, including reduced inflation variability, this should make a small contribution to more stable exchange rates.

It follows that the implications of G3 inflation targeting for the behavior and management of G3 exchange rates might be a very small net plus (chapter 4). The adoption of inflation targeting might contribute to greater underlying stability in the G3 economies, in particular the Japanese economy, but most critics of the medium-term swings in G3 exchange rates do not cite macroeconomic instability or, in particular, differences in inflation rates among the G3 economies as the principal cause.

More broadly, the inflation-targeting framework is compatible with a variety of exchange rate regimes ranging from free floating to regimes envisaging more active concern about exchange rate movements, such as managed floating in the context of wide bands (chapter 5) of at least plus or minus 10 percent. Inflation targeters need to choose a compatible exchange rate regime, but under some circumstances a regime or policy that involves relatively heavy management of the exchange rate may be not only viable but also appropriate. At the same time, the greater the clarity about the relationship between the inflation-targeting framework and exchange rate policy, the better. In particular, hybrid frameworks may be viable or desirable under some conditions, but it is preferable that the hierarchy of objectives be understood in advance and departures clearly explained.

However, inflation targeting does not remove either the incentive or the need for the authorities to think about movements in exchange rates and their impacts on the economy. These judgments are more difficult in conflict situations. Both John Williamson's "band, basket, and crawl" (BBC) approach to viewing exchange rates and Morris Goldstein's "managed floating plus" approach to worrying about the implications of exchange rate movements for the size of currency mismatches and effects on balance sheets offer some potentially useful guidance to the authorities of inflation-targeting countries.

Implications for the International Financial Architecture

The widespread adoption of inflation targeting will not free the international financial system from financial crises (chapter 6). Depending on how one interprets Brazil's situation as it evolves, no inflation targeter to date has experienced a crisis after it has adopted such a framework.

Inflation-targeting frameworks for monetary policies are likely to be less crisis-prone than policy frameworks that rely on rigid exchange rate arrangements to impose macroeconomic discipline because the associated exchange rate policies are less brittle and promote better risk management practices. In addition, the increased transparency normally associated with the framework supports other trends in crisis prevention. Inflation targeting also has some promise of being useful to countries emerging from crises that want to float their currencies and for whom targeting some monetary aggregate is not attractive.

The IMF has been constructive in adapting its apparatus of policy conditionality to IMF-supported adjustment programs by members that are inflation targeters, but it should be more proactive in this area.

Recommendations

Five policy recommendations follow from this study of inflation targeting in the world economy.

1. The G3 economies should adopt inflation targeting, preferably collectively or, as a second best, individually to improve their economic performance and to reduce the risk of deflation. The IMF should actively encourage the G3 to do so because of the benefits to the performance of the global economy and the international financial system. The IMF has taken some partial and tentative steps in this direction with respect to the United States and Japan, but it needs to go further. In May 2003, the IMF staff made a substantive and tactical mistake to bless prematurely the ECB's half-baked clarification of its definition of price stability.

2. With respect to other potential targeters, the IMF should endeavor to project a more benign and constructive attitude toward those of its members, whether receiving IMF financial support or not, that choose to adopt inflation targeting as their monetary policy framework. In its explicit and implicit policy advice, the IMF and its staff should place greater stress on the potential benefits and limited risks of inflation targeting and less stress on barriers or preconditions to successful use of the framework.

3. Potential inflation-targeting squeezers like Argentina, Russia, and Turkey should seriously consider adopting the framework. It may well be that for many countries and their central banks there is no realistic alternative to an eclectic approach to monetary policy, to rigidly fixed exchange rates, or to the abandonment of their currencies, and in some cases such regimes have produced reasonable results. However, critics of inflation targeting combined with more flexible exchange rate regimes, though not necessarily free floating regimes, need to be more honest in their criticisms, including the critics within the squeezers. They should state more clearly what they are for as well as what they are against.

4. Inflation targeting should not be rejected on the grounds that countries will be unable or unwilling to implement the framework because of a "fear of floating." The fact that a country's authorities may react to and seek to transparently influence exchange rate movements does not necessarily manifest such fear. Their attitude is better seen as a reasonable focus of policy attention that does not disqualify the country from adopting inflation targeting if it wants to and as long as it is reasonably clear about its priorities. Hybrid inflation-targeting frameworks and experimentation should be tolerated and encouraged as long as they are transparent.

5. The IMF should further modify and experiment with the application of its policy conditionality to inflation targeters with IMF-supported ad-

justment programs by applying the criteria laid out in chapter 6. The IMF should clarify the role its conditionality is intended to play in programs supporting such countries, distinguishing more clearly between conditions designed to project the IMF's resources and those designed to produce better policy outcomes. The enhanced use of forward-looking indicators and alternative monitoring approaches should be promoted in cases where inflation is or may become, in the view of the country's authorities, a serious problem. The use of those devices and the intensity and intrusiveness of IMF monitoring should be calibrated to the country's inflation performance and the inflation objective that the country has chosen for its stabilization program.

Concluding Thoughts

Inflation targeting offers both challenges and opportunities for the world economy. Inflation targeting should not be treated as a monetary policy rule, a fixed formula, or a straitjacket. It is a flexible framework for the conduct and evaluation of monetary policy. It is neither a panacea nor a poison pill for an individual economy or the world economy.

The framework is broadly adaptable and offers promise to a range of economies in different circumstances. Adaptation may involve hybrids that place different weights on various considerations, such as exchange rate movements, while retaining a primary focus on reasonable price stability. However, one challenge is to be clear about the nature of the hybrid and avoid randomized eclecticism.

Inflation targeting has considerable promise not only for inflation maintainers such as the G3 economies but also for other countries as long as they are serious about their use of the framework. That qualification applies to any successful monetary policy framework.

Inflation targeting provides an opportunity for inflation convergers as long as they understand that the framework involves discipline, not magic, and that the associated credibility has to be earned. The short-run economic costs of reducing inflation are not likely to be lowered, but it may be easier and less costly gradually to reduce inflation and maintain it at a low level.

With respect to inflation squeezers, the applicability of inflation targeting without any supporting mechanisms is more open to debate. However, some squeezers have employed inflation-targeting frameworks with reasonable success, and further use by countries with double-digit inflation rates should not be ruled out.

For potential inflation-targeting reversers like Japan, the framework offers some protection in the context of forceful unconventional policy implementation, but the adoption of inflation targeting alone will not end deflation.

Inflation targeting as a framework for the conduct and evaluation of monetary policy should be employed flexibly; experimentation is appropriate. The evidence to date, including that presented in this study as well as that assembled by other researchers, does not support concerns that the widespread adoption of inflation targeting would distort policy priorities in the direction of fighting inflation excessively and neglecting economic growth. Inflation targeting may improve overall economic performance in many but not all cases, but the evidence on this point is not fully conclusive.

I conclude this study as an inflation targeting sympathizer, not a proselytizer.

Appendix

Table A.1 Countries excluded from empirical analysis

Country	Table 2.4	Tables 3.4 and 3.5	Tables 3.6, 3.8, and 3.9	Table 3.7 and figure 3.2 (a)	(b)	Figure 3.1 (a)	(b)
Inflation targeters (22)							
Australia							
Brazil		X	X				
Canada				X	X		
Chile				X	X		
Colombia			X			X	X
Czech Republic			X				
Finland							
Hungary			X	X	X	X	X
Iceland			X	X	X	X	X
Israel		X	X	X	X		
Korea			X				
Mexico		X	X				
New Zealand				X	X		
Norway			X	X	X	X	X
Peru	X	X	X	X	X	X	X
Philippines	X			X	X	X	X
Poland		X	X				
South Africa			X			X	X
Spain							
Sweden							
Thailand			X			X	X
United Kingdom							
Subtotal							
Excluded	2	5	13	9	9	8	8
Included	20	17	9	13	13	14	14
Potential inflation targeters (46)							
Argentina		X	X	X	X	X	X
Austria							
Bangladesh				Xa	Xa		
Belgium							
Bolivia		X	X	Xa	Xa		
Bulgaria		X	X	X	X	X	X
China				Xa	Xa		
Costa Rica				Xa	X		X
Denmark							
Dominican Republic			X	Xa	Xa		X
Ecuador		X	X	X	X	X	X
Egypt				Xa	X		
France							
Germany							
Greece				X	X		X
Guatemala				X	X		X
Honduras				X	X		X
Hong Kong	X	X	X			Xa	Xa
India				Xa	Xa		
Indonesia			X		X		X
Ireland							
Italy							
Japan							
Malaysia							

(table continues next page)

Table A.1 *(continued)*

Country	Table 2.4	Tables 3.4 and 3.5	Tables 3.6, 3.8, and 3.9	Table 3.7 and figure 3.2 (a)	(b)	Figure 3.1 (a)	(b)
Morocco				X	X		
Netherlands							
Nigeria		X	X	X	X	X	X
Pakistan				Xa	Xa		
Panama				Xa	Xa		
Paraguay				Xa	X		X
Portugal				X			X
Romania		X	X	X	X	X	X
Russia			X	X	X	X	X
Saudi Arabia				Xa	Xa		
Singapore							
Slovak Republic			X	Xa	X	Xa	X
Slovenia			X	X	X	X	X
Sri Lanka				Xa	X		X
Switzerland							
Taiwan	X	X	X				
Turkey		X	X	X	X	X	X
Ukraine		X	X	X	X	X	X
United States							
Uruguay		X	X	X	X	X	X
Venezuela		X	X	X	X	X	X
Vietnam			X	Xa	X	Xa	X
Subtotal							
Excluded	2	12	18	15	23	11	22
Included	44	34	28	31	23	35	24
Total (all countries)							
Excluded	4	17	31	24	32	19	30
Included	64	51	37	44	36	49	38

Note: Countries excluded from table 2.4 because of lack of economic data or because they chose inflation targeting after mid-2001; from tables 3.4 and 3.5 because of lack of economic data or average 1980–2000 inflation rates were greater than 25 percent; from tables 3.6, 3.8, and 3.9 because of lack of economic data or average 1985–2000 inflation rates were greater than 50 percent or greater than 50 percent in any year between 1985 and 1994. In the case of table 3.7 and figure 3.2, (a) countries excluded because of lack of data or average 1990–2001 inflation rates were greater than 20 percent ("Xa" indicates countries also excluded from control group for Mexico because of lack of data; they appear in the totals as included countries), and (b) countries excluded from restricted control groups because average 1990–2001 inflation rates were greater than 5 percent for industrial countries or greater than 10 percent for nonindustrial countries ("Xa" indicates countries also excluded from restricted control group for Mexico because of lack of data; they appear in the totals as included countries). In the case of figure 3.1, (a) countries excluded because of lack of data or average 1990–2001 inflation rates were greater than 20 percent ("Xa" indicates countries also excluded from control groups for Chile and Israel; they appear in the totals as included countries), and (b) countries excluded from restricted control groups because average 1990–2001 inflation rates were greater than 5 percent for industrial countries or greater than 10 percent for nonindustrial countries ("Xa" indicates countries also excluded from restricted control groups for Chile and Israel; they appear in the totals as included countries).

Table A.2   Inflation in 2002, mean of annual inflation rates and standard deviation, 1990–2002

Country	2002	Mean of annual inflation rates	Standard deviation
Australia	3.00	2.84	1.88
Brazil[a]	12.55	507.58	764.09
Canada	2.25	2.27	1.41
Chile[a]	2.80	9.05	6.96
Colombia[a]	7.00	18.61	7.63
Czech Republic[b]	1.79	8.32	5.10
Finland	1.55	2.22	1.49
Hungary	5.73	18.95	8.44
Iceland	5.17	4.56	3.62
Israel	5.69	9.25	5.25
Korea	2.77	5.11	2.35
Mexico[a]	5.70	17.01	12.68
New Zealand[c]	2.68	2.18	1.35
Norway	1.28	2.45	0.81
Peru[a]	1.50	618.01	2,056.27
Philippines	3.11	8.34	3.81
Poland	1.88	65.23	143.12
South Africa	10.60	9.27	3.29
Spain	3.07	4.02	1.50
Sweden	2.16	2.95	3.21
Thailand	0.60	4.12	2.33
United Kingdom[d]	2.20	3.34	2.05
Average			
All inflation targeters	3.87	60.26	138.12
10 with inflation mean < 5 percent	2.39	3.09	1.96
6 with inflation mean 5–10 percent	4.46	8.22	4.46
3 with inflation mean 10–20 percent	6.14	18.19	9.58
3 with inflation mean > 20 percent	5.31	396.94	987.83
Potential inflation targeters			
Argentina[a]	25.87	114.11	356.41
Austria	1.82	2.38	1.02
Bangladesh	2.82	4.81	2.37
Belgium	1.64	2.16	0.74
Bolivia[a]	2.45	7.88	4.90
Bulgaria	5.81	146.90	276.93
China	−0.80	5.95	7.69
Costa Rica[a]	9.67	15.34	6.14
Denmark	2.43	2.22	0.39
Dominican Republic[a]	8.40	12.80	19.59
Ecuador[a]	12.48	40.32	20.71
Egypt	2.74	8.68	5.93
France	1.92	1.86	0.80
Germany	1.31	2.23	1.25
Greece	3.61	9.33	6.11
Guatemala	8.03	13.02	10.60
Honduras	7.70	17.37	8.24
Hong Kong[e]	−3.04	4.07	5.48
India[f]	4.39	8.25	3.37
Indonesia	11.88	13.25	13.35
Ireland	4.67	2.94	1.31

(table continues next page)

Country	2002	Mean of annual inflation rates	Standard deviation
Italy	2.47	3.77	1.60
Japan	−0.91	0.75	1.33
Malaysia	1.81	3.18	1.15
Morocco	2.80	3.84	2.38
Netherlands	3.49	2.69	0.71
Nigeria	12.88	26.53	22.33
Pakistan	1.56	8.17	3.64
Panama[a]	1.01	1.01	0.68
Paraguay[a]	10.51	14.22	9.75
Portugal	3.59	5.44	3.49
Romania[e]	22.54	105.60	83.50
Russia[b,g]	15.79	270.33	419.99
Saudi Arabia	−0.52	0.84	1.94
Singapore	−0.39	1.64	1.26
Slovak Republic[g]	3.32	9.85	5.07
Slovenia[g]	7.48	25.69	41.99
Sri Lanka	9.71	10.96	4.24
Switzerland	0.64	2.07	1.92
Taiwan	−0.20	2.30	1.65
Turkey	44.96	71.28	16.27
Ukraine[g]	0.80	671.22	1,344.08
United States	1.58	2.91	0.99
Uruguay[a]	13.97	36.67	35.55
Venezuela[a]	31.20	40.04	23.98
Vietnam[e]	3.83	14.61	22.92
Average			
All potential targeters	6.73	38.51	60.99
19 with inflation mean < 5 percent	1.33	2.51	1.52
8 with inflation mean 5–10 percent	2.61	7.94	5.02
8 with inflation mean 10–20 percent	8.72	13.95	11.85
11 with inflation mean > 20 percent	17.62	140.79	240.16

a. For all years, December-to-December, not year-over-year, inflation data used in order to match *Consensus Forecasts*.
b. Inflation data available only since 1992.
c. For New Zealand, the CPI excludes housing and interests since third quarter of 1999. *Consensus Forecasts* take this into account.
d. For the United Kingdom, retail price index excluding mortgage interest payments (RPIX) used since 1998, not CPI. *Consensus Forecasts* take this into account.
e. Inflation data available only since 1991.
f. For India, year-over-year inflation given for fiscal year in order to match *Consensus Forecasts*. Indian fiscal year t starts in April t and ends in March $t+1$.
g. For Russia, December-to-December, not year-over-year, inflation data used since 1998 in order to match *Consensus Forecasts*.

Note: Based on average CPI, year-over-year, 1990–2002, except as noted.

Sources: IMF, *International Financial Statistics;* Consensus Economics, *Consensus Forecasts;* and selected government statistics.

Table A.3 GDP growth in 2002, mean of annual GDP growth rates and standard deviation, 1990–2002

Country	2002	Mean of annual GDP growth rates	Standard deviation
Australia	3.80	3.64	1.99
Brazil	1.55	2.54	2.01
Canada	3.37	2.46	1.94
Chile	2.10	5.60	3.46
Colombia	1.50	2.63	2.54
Czech Republic[a]	1.95	1.10	3.20
Finland	1.63	1.83	3.58
Hungary	3.30	0.97	4.63
Iceland	−1.87	2.21	2.74
Israel	−0.20	4.28	2.61
Korea	6.35	6.23	4.29
Mexico	0.90	3.15	3.32
New Zealand	4.40	2.72	2.17
Norway	1.30	3.27	1.31
Peru	5.20	3.26	4.21
Philippines	5.20	3.11	2.10
Poland	1.30	2.40	16.26
South Africa	3.12	1.79	1.86
Spain	2.01	2.61	1.51
Sweden	1.90	2.09	1.96
Thailand	5.20	4.95	5.53
United Kingdom	1.80	2.16	1.48
Average			
All inflation targeters	2.54	2.96	3.40
10 with inflation mean < 5 percent	2.35	2.79	2.42
6 with inflation mean 5–10 percent	3.09	3.69	2.92
3 with inflation mean 10–20 percent	1.90	2.25	3.50
3 with inflation mean > 20 percent	2.68	2.73	7.49
Potential inflation targeters			
Argentina	−10.80	1.93	6.16
Austria	1.00	2.26	1.26
Bangladesh[b]	4.60	4.97	0.83
Belgium	0.70	2.02	1.31
Bolivia	2.10	3.51	1.62
Bulgaria	3.90	−1.19	6.15
China	8.00	9.48	2.71
Costa Rica	2.40	4.57	2.81
Denmark	1.61	2.11	1.34
Dominican Republic	4.10	4.63	3.69
Ecuador	3.40	2.32	3.07
Egypt	2.96	4.28	1.34
France	1.51	1.87	1.16
Germany	0.35	2.63	3.42
Greece	3.95	2.38	1.71
Guatemala	2.25	3.76	0.89
Honduras	2.54	2.92	2.47
Hong Kong[c]	2.25	4.02	3.42
India[d]	4.37	5.54	1.62
Indonesia	3.70	4.23	5.42
Ireland	6.30	7.17	3.07
Italy	0.74	1.56	0.96

(table continues next page)

Table A.3 *(continued)*

Country	2002	Mean of annual GDP growth rates	Standard deviation
Japan	0.30	1.55	1.58
Malaysia	4.20	6.57	4.82
Morocco	3.20	2.92	5.50
Netherlands	0.27	2.59	1.21
Nigeria	2.70	3.09	1.81
Pakistan[b]	4.40	4.31	1.23
Panama	0.80	4.16	2.79
Paraguay	−3.60	1.69	2.14
Portugal	0.47	2.75	1.97
Romania[c]	4.90	−0.83	6.00
Russia[a]	4.30	−3.77	11.66
Saudi Arabia	1.20	2.73	3.28
Singapore	2.20	6.78	4.16
Slovak Republic[a]	4.40	2.47	4.11
Slovenia[a]	3.18	2.15	4.30
Sri Lanka	2.95	4.59	2.05
Switzerland	0.08	1.03	1.34
Taiwan	3.50	5.25	2.37
Turkey	7.79	3.57	5.59
Ukraine[a]	4.30	−7.04	13.56
United States	2.45	2.81	1.47
Uruguay	−10.50	1.35	4.97
Venezuela	−8.90	1.69	5.10
Vietnam[c]	7.05	7.29	1.55
Average			
All potential targeters	2.03	2.97	3.28
19 with inflation mean < 5 percent	1.96	3.42	2.38
8 with inflation mean 5–10 percent	3.83	4.34	2.04
8 with inflation mean 10–20 percent	2.67	4.21	2.63
11 with inflation mean > 20 percent	0.39	0.30	6.22

a. GDP growth data available only since 1992.
b. For Bangladesh and Pakistan, annual GDP growth rate given for fiscal year in order to match *Consensus Forecasts*, except for 1990 when not available. For both countries, fiscal year *t* starts in July *t* and ends in June *t*+1.
c. GDP growth data available only since 1991.
d. For India, annual GDP growth rate given for fiscal year in order to match *Consensus Forecasts*. Indian fiscal year *t* starts in April *t* and ends in March *t*+1.

Sources: IMF, *International Financial Statistics;* Consensus Economics, *Consensus Forecasts;* and selected government statistics.

Table A.4 Industrial countries: Mean of annual inflation rates (IM), standard deviation (SD), average inflation forecast error (AFE), root mean squared error (RMSE), and mean of standard deviation reported in inflation forecasts

Country	Actual inflation (1990–2001)		One-year-ahead forecast (1990–2001)			Two-year-ahead forecast (1991–2001)		
	IM	SD	AFE	RMSE	Mean SD of forecasts	AFE	RMSE	Mean SD of forecasts
Group of Three (G3)								
Germany	2.30	1.27	−0.13	0.83	0.21	−0.40	1.08	0.32
Japan	0.89	1.29	0.02	0.50	0.32	−0.47	0.82	0.51
United States	3.02	0.95	−0.03	0.53	0.32	−0.55	0.78	0.46
Average								
G3 (all inflation mean < 5 percent)	2.07	1.17	−0.05	0.62	0.29	−0.47	0.89	0.43
Inflation targeters (IT)								
Australia	2.82	1.96	−0.80	1.28	0.49	−1.74	2.42	0.79
Canada	2.27	1.46	−0.23	0.68	0.31	−0.74	1.17	0.45
Finland	2.28	1.54	−0.75	1.24	n.a.	−1.43	1.81	n.a.
Iceland	4.51	3.76	n.a.	n.a.	n.a.	n.a.	n.a.	n.a.
New Zealand[a]	2.14	1.39	−0.36	1.23	0.56	−0.82	1.58	0.57
Norway	2.55	0.76	−0.51	0.88	0.13	−1.01	1.27	0.20
Spain	4.10	1.54	0.04	0.66	0.24	−0.18	0.83	0.33
Sweden	3.02	3.33	−0.41	1.61	0.36	−1.21	2.06	0.39
United Kingdom[b]	3.43	2.11	−0.07	0.97	0.42	−0.82	1.18	0.70
Average								
All inflation targeters (all inflation mean < 5 percent)	3.01	1.98	−0.39	1.07	0.36	−0.99	1.54	0.49
Potential inflation targeters (PIT)								
Austria	2.43	1.05	−0.02	0.64	n.a.	−0.34	0.91	n.a.
Belgium	2.21	0.75	−0.19	0.63	n.a.	−0.61	0.87	n.a.

Denmark	2.20	0.40	-0.44	0.70	n.a.	-0.74	0.98	n.a.
France	1.85	0.83	-0.19	0.44	0.20	-0.63	0.80	0.28
Germany	2.30	1.27	-0.13	0.83	0.21	-0.40	1.08	0.32
Greece	9.80	6.12	-0.38	0.87	n.a.	-1.10	1.33	n.a.
Ireland	2.79	1.26	-0.29	1.20	n.a.	-0.67	1.48	n.a.
Italy	3.88	1.62	0.07	0.65	0.26	-0.16	1.01	0.42
Japan	0.89	1.29	0.02	0.50	0.32	-0.47	0.82	0.51
Netherlands	2.63	0.70	0.03	0.44	0.19	-0.16	0.80	0.25
Portugal	5.59	3.59	0.03	1.11	n.a.	-0.63	1.47	n.a.
Switzerland	2.19	1.95	-0.14	0.97	0.33	-0.65	1.62	0.25
United States	3.02	0.95	-0.03	0.53	0.32	-0.55	0.78	0.46

Average

All potential targeters (all inflation mean < 10 percent)	3.21	1.68	-0.13	0.73	0.26	-0.55	1.07	0.36
11 with inflation mean < 5 percent	2.40	1.10	-0.12	0.69	0.26	-0.49	1.01	0.36
Two with inflation mean 5 to 10 percent	7.70	4.85	-0.17	0.99	n.a.	-0.86	1.40	n.a.
Average of industrial IT and PIT								
All (all inflation mean < 10 percent)	3.13	1.80	-0.23	0.86	0.31	-0.72	1.25	0.42
20 with inflation mean < 5 percent	2.68	1.50	-0.23	0.85	0.31	-0.70	1.23	0.42
Two with inflation mean 5 to 10 percent	7.70	4.85	-0.17	0.99	n.a.	-0.86	1.40	n.a.

n.a. = not available

a. For New Zealand, the CPI excludes housing and interests since third quarter of 1999. *Consensus Forecasts* take this into account.
b. For the United Kingdom, retail price index excluding mortgage interest payments (RPIX) used since 1998, not CPI. *Consensus Forecasts* take this into account.

Note: Average CPI, year-over-year, 1999–2001, except as noted.

Sources: IMF, *International Financial Statistics;* and Consensus Economics, *Consensus Forecasts.*

Table A.5 Nonindustrial countries: Mean of actual annual inflation rates (IM), standard deviation (SD), average inflation forecast error (AFE), root mean squared error (RMSE), and mean of standard deviation reported in inflation forecasts

Country	Actual inflation (1990–2001)		One-year-ahead forecast (1990–2001)			Two-year-ahead forecast (1991–2001)		
	IM	SD	AFE	RMSE	Mean SD of forecasts	AFE	RMSE	Mean SD of forecasts
Inflation targeters (IT)								
Brazil[a]	548.83	781.26	−106.43	1,318.35	1,013.06	225.18	807.48	83.67
Chile[a]	9.57	7.00	−0.58	1.09	0.51	−0.82	1.16	0.60
Colombia[a]	19.58	7.13	−0.58	2.50	0.83	−1.44	3.56	1.07
Czech Republic[b]	8.98	4.89	−0.19	1.33	0.70	−0.68	3.23	1.05
Hungary	20.05	7.84	1.62	3.57	0.80	3.65	7.37	0.85
Israel	9.55	5.36	−1.06	1.82	n.a.	−1.61	2.77	n.a.
Korea	5.30	2.35	−0.60	1.62	0.80	−0.48	2.32	0.87
Mexico[a]	17.95	12.75	1.98	8.84	1.48	4.21	14.78	2.23
Peru[a]	669.39	2,132.20	−3.44	5.46	0.60	−3.40	5.42	0.90
Philippines	8.77	3.64	−0.57	1.13	n.a.	−0.36	1.67	n.a.
Poland	70.51	147.75	3.99	10.85	0.73	2.33	5.17	0.70
South Africa	9.16	3.40	−0.69	1.18	n.a.	−1.54	1.73	n.a.
Thailand	4.41	2.18	−0.76	1.51	0.97	−1.06	3.18	1.57
Average								
All inflation targeters	107.85	239.83	−8.25	104.56	102.05	17.23	66.14	9.35
One with inflation mean < 5 percent	4.41	2.18	−0.76	1.51	0.97	−1.06	3.18	1.57
Six with inflation mean 5 to 10 percent	8.56	4.44	−0.62	1.42	0.75	−0.93	2.35	0.96
Two with inflation mean 10 to 20 percent	18.76	9.94	0.70	4.97	0.99	1.69	7.97	1.41
Four with inflation mean > 20 percent	327.20	767.26	−20.97	268.15	203.20	45.27	165.80	17.44
Potential inflation targeters (PIT)								
Argentina[a]	121.47	370.01	−1.61	1.73	0.68	−2.43	2.75	0.71
Bangladesh	4.99	2.35	−1.00	3.40	n.a.	−0.89	3.44	n.a.
Bolivia[a]	8.33	4.83	−1.23	1.76	n.a.	−1.27	3.60	n.a.

(table continues next page)

Bulgaria	158.65	285.10	129.81	325.58	n.a.	175.99	419.96	n.a.
China	6.51	7.74	-2.80	3.58	1.11	-6.09	7.23	1.63
Costa Rica[a]	15.81	6.16	1.46	4.62	n.a.	0.84	5.26	n.a.
Dominican Republic[a]	13.16	20.35	0.02	2.33	n.a.	-0.55	2.88	n.a.
Ecuador[a]	42.64	19.86	12.44	22.93	n.a.	19.66	28.90	n.a.
Egypt	9.18	5.90	-1.13	4.06	n.a.	-2.26	2.74	n.a.
Guatemala	13.44	10.93	n.a.	n.a.	n.a.	n.a.	n.a.	n.a.
Honduras	18.17	8.07	n.a.	n.a.	n.a.	n.a.	n.a.	n.a.
Hong Kong[c]	4.71	5.27	-1.29	2.17	0.83	-2.52	3.87	0.78
India[d]	8.58	3.31	-0.98	4.11	1.13	-1.51	3.62	1.10
Indonesia	13.37	13.88	4.04	13.36	2.47	5.40	16.57	2.43
Malaysia	3.30	1.13	-0.78	0.94	0.79	-0.93	1.67	1.20
Morocco	3.92	2.46	n.a.	n.a.	n.a.	n.a.	n.a.	n.a.
Nigeria	27.67	22.87	-3.19	9.38	n.a.	-2.74	3.22	n.a.
Pakistan	8.72	3.23	-2.97	4.11	n.a.	-2.92	4.53	n.a.
Panama[a]	1.01	0.70	-0.76	1.18	n.a.	-0.83	1.27	n.a.
Paraguay[a]	14.53	10.09	-3.59	5.87	5.37	-5.33	7.33	5.85
Romania[c]	113.15	83.20	18.25	48.00	17.40	33.91	57.17	16.05
Russia[b,e]	295.79	432.32	-0.12	37.34	n.a.	-2.27	40.58	n.a.
Saudi Arabia	0.95	1.98	-2.24	3.15	0.54	-2.09	2.47	0.48
Singapore	1.81	1.16	-0.72	1.18	1.37	-1.11	1.47	2.40
Slovak Republic[b]	10.51	4.86	-0.46	1.60	n.a.	-0.13	2.74	n.a.
Slovenia[b]	27.52	43.62	0.95	2.01	n.a.	0.74	2.57	n.a.
Sri Lanka	11.07	4.40	-0.62	4.26	0.44	-0.91	4.64	0.50
Taiwan	2.51	1.54	-1.04	1.32	7.57	-1.08	1.60	9.80
Turkey	73.47	14.98	13.07	16.28	7.10	14.12	22.33	4.85
Ukraine[b]	738.26	1,392.04	-39.50	82.84	n.a.	-46.10	93.02	n.a.
Uruguay[a]	38.57	36.37	-3.52	5.16	n.a.	-7.53	8.84	n.a.
Venezuela[a]	40.77	24.82	2.37	16.92	6.74	1.78	23.73	13.47
Vietnam[c]	15.59	23.69	-5.48	6.87	n.a.	-6.36	7.78	n.a.
Average								
All potential targeters	56.61	86.95	3.58	21.30	3.82	5.15	26.26	4.38
Eight with inflation mean < 5 percent	2.90	2.07	-1.12	1.91	0.65	-1.35	2.26	0.74
Five with inflation mean 5 to 10 percent	8.26	5.00	-1.60	3.37	1.20	-2.38	4.09	1.71

Table A.5 Nonindustrial countries: Mean of actual annual inflation rates (IM), standard deviation (SD), average inflation forecast error (AFE), root mean squared error (RMSE), and mean of standard deviation reported in inflation forecasts *(continued)*

Country	Actual inflation (1990–2001)		One-year-ahead forecast (1990–2001)			Two-year-ahead forecast (1991–2001)		
	IM	SD	AFE	RMSE	Mean SD of forecasts	AFE	RMSE	Mean SD of forecasts
Nine with inflation mean 10 to 20 percent	13.96	11.38	–0.69	6.22	2.47	–1.15	7.41	2.43
11 with inflation mean > 20 percent	152.54	247.75	11.72	51.65	7.47	16.83	63.91	8.46
Average nonindustrial IT and PIT								
All	71.09	130.15	0.00	46.47	44.75	8.80	38.32	6.45
Nine with inflation mean < 5 percent	3.07	2.09	–1.07	1.86	0.71	–1.31	2.37	0.91
11 with inflation mean 5 to 10 percent	8.42	4.70	–1.15	2.48	1.02	–1.72	3.30	1.41
11 with inflation mean 10 to 20 percent	14.83	11.12	–0.35	5.90	1.49	–0.44	7.55	1.75
15 with inflation mean > 20 percent	199.12	386.28	1.51	119.31	96.44	25.72	95.75	12.54

n.a. = not available

a. For all years, December-to-December, not year-over-year, inflation data used in order to match *Consensus Forecasts*.
b. Inflation data available only since 1992.
c. Inflation data available only since 1991.
d. For India, year-over-year inflation given for fiscal year in order to match *Consensus Forecasts*. Indian fiscal year *t* starts in April *t* and ends in March *t*+1.
e. For Russia, December-to-December, not year-over-year, inflation data used since 1998 in order to match *Consensus Forecasts*.

Note: Based on average CPI, year-over-year, 1990–2001, except as noted.

Sources: IMF, *International Financial Statistics*; Consensus Economics, *Consensus Forecasts*; and selected government statistics.

Table A.6 Industrial countries: Mean of annual GDP growth rates (GM), standard deviation (SD), average growth forecast error (AFE), root mean squared error (RMSE), and mean of standard deviation reported in growth forecasts, 1990–2001

Country	Actual growth (1990–2001)		One-year-ahead forecast (1990–2001)			Two-year-ahead forecast (1991–2001)		
	GM	SD	AFE	RMSE	Mean SD of forecasts	AFE	RMSE	Mean SD of forecasts
Group of Three (G3)								
Germany	2.81	3.50	0.76	3.20	0.31	0.20	3.53	0.45
Japan	1.60	1.59	-0.04	1.17	0.63	-1.15	1.92	0.62
United States	2.84	1.53	0.50	1.28	0.38	0.54	1.75	0.56
Average								
G3 (all inflation mean < 5 percent)	2.42	2.21	0.41	1.88	0.44	-0.14	2.40	0.55
Inflation targeters (IT)								
Australia	3.66	2.05	1.33	1.99	0.46	1.31	2.17	0.68
Canada	2.38	2.00	-0.24	1.40	0.46	-0.35	1.82	0.51
Finland	1.96	3.80	-0.79	3.27	n.a.	-0.34	3.55	n.a.
Iceland	2.56	2.48	n.a.	n.a.	n.a.	n.a.	n.a.	n.a.
New Zealand	2.55	2.23	0.16	2.03	0.59	-0.34	2.27	0.57
Norway	3.10	1.35	0.66	1.34	0.53	0.69	1.55	0.45
Spain	2.66	1.57	-0.19	1.13	0.24	-0.59	1.83	0.37
Sweden	1.59	2.21	-0.11	1.44	0.66	-0.51	2.13	0.57
United Kingdom	2.18	1.54	0.23	1.11	0.43	-0.14	1.53	0.52
Average								
All inflation targeters (all inflation mean < 5 percent)	2.52	2.14	0.13	1.71	0.48	-0.03	2.10	0.52
Potential inflation targeters (PIT)								
Austria	2.31	1.16	0.35	0.82	n.a.	-0.34	1.28	n.a.
Belgium	2.19	1.32	-0.09	1.31	n.a.	-0.37	1.60	n.a.

(table continues next page)

Table A.6 Industrial countries: Mean of annual GDP growth rates (GM), standard deviation (SD), average growth forecast error (AFE), root mean squared error (RMSE), and mean of standard deviation reported in growth forecasts, 1990–2001 *(continued)*

Country	Actual growth (1990–2001)		One-year-ahead forecast (1990–2001)			Two-year-ahead forecast (1991–2001)		
	GM	SD	AFE	RMSE	Mean SD of forecasts	AFE	RMSE	Mean SD of forecasts
Denmark	2.10	1.41	−0.09	1.35	n.a.	−0.15	1.44	n.a.
France	1.94	1.27	−0.37	1.06	0.28	−0.74	1.55	0.30
Germany	2.81	3.50	0.76	3.20	0.31	0.20	3.53	0.45
Greece	2.25	1.72	0.45	0.60	n.a.	0.37	0.76	n.a.
Ireland	7.24	3.21	2.57	3.47	n.a.	3.07	4.24	n.a.
Italy	1.63	0.97	−0.41	0.86	0.24	−0.86	1.41	0.30
Japan	1.60	1.59	−0.04	1.17	0.63	−1.15	1.92	0.62
Netherlands	3.18	1.94	0.69	2.09	0.26	0.55	2.06	0.32
Portugal	3.02	1.90	0.13	1.75	n.a.	−0.21	2.00	n.a.
Switzerland	1.14	1.34	−0.57	1.40	0.23	−1.28	1.79	0.20
United States	2.84	1.53	0.50	1.28	0.38	0.54	1.75	0.56
Average								
All potential targeters (all inflation mean) < 10 percent)	2.63	1.76	0.30	1.57	0.33	−0.03	1.95	0.39
11 with inflation mean < 5 percent	2.63	1.75	0.30	1.64	0.33	−0.05	2.05	0.39
Two with inflation mean 5 to 10 percent	2.64	1.81	0.29	1.18	n.a.	0.08	1.38	n.a.
Average industrial IT and PIT								
All (all inflation mean) < 10 percent)	2.59	1.91	0.24	1.62	0.41	−0.03	2.01	0.46
20 with inflation mean < 5 percent	2.58	1.92	0.23	1.67	0.41	−0.04	2.07	0.46
Two with inflation mean 5 to 10 percent	2.64	1.81	0.29	1.18	n.a.	0.08	1.38	n.a.

n.a. = not available

Sources: IMF, *International Financial Statistics;* and Consensus Economics, *Consensus Forecasts.*

Table A.7 Nonindustrial countries: Mean of actual annual GDP growth rates (GM), standard deviation (SD), average growth forecast error (AFE), root mean squared error (RMSE), and mean of standard deviation reported in growth forecasts, 1990–2001

Country	Actual growth (1990–2001)		One-year-ahead forecast (1990–2001)			Two-year-ahead forecast (1991–2001)		
	GM	SD	AFE	RMSE	Mean SD of forecasts	AFE	RMSE	Mean SD of forecasts
Inflation targeters (IT)								
Brazil	2.14	1.96	−0.02	2.25	0.70	−1.17	2.72	1.14
Chile	5.91	3.90	−0.01	3.25	0.45	−0.60	4.32	0.53
Colombia	2.73	2.63	−1.46	2.50	0.50	−2.49	3.87	0.70
Czech Republic[a]	1.03	3.36	−0.86	2.64	0.43	−2.43	3.55	0.85
Hungary	0.78	4.76	−1.13	3.64	0.47	−0.42	3.55	0.55
Israel	5.26	1.79	1.16	2.31	n.a.	−0.65	2.66	n.a.
Korea	6.22	4.47	0.58	3.85	0.97	0.01	5.40	0.75
Mexico	3.34	3.40	−0.01	2.37	0.56	−0.51	3.85	0.71
Peru	3.10	4.34	0.12	3.70	0.73	−1.39	3.79	0.73
Philippines	2.94	2.09	−0.35	1.59	n.a.	−1.39	2.85	n.a.
Poland	2.49	16.92	−0.14	16.36	0.53	0.78	17.40	0.45
South Africa	1.63	1.87	−0.38	1.09	n.a.	−1.13	1.77	n.a.
Thailand	4.93	5.75	−1.67	3.95	0.90	−2.47	6.49	0.93
Average								
All inflation targeters	3.27	4.40	−0.32	3.81	0.62	−1.07	4.62	0.74
One with inflation mean < 5 percent	4.93	5.75	−1.67	3.95	0.90	−2.47	6.49	0.93
Six with inflation mean 5 to 10 percent	3.83	2.91	0.03	2.30	0.70	−1.12	3.25	0.80
Two with inflation mean 10 to 20 percent	3.03	3.01	−0.01	2.81	0.51	−0.56	4.08	0.62
Four with inflation mean > 20 percent	2.13	7.00	−0.53	5.69	0.59	−0.94	5.83	0.72

(table continues next page)

Table A.7 Nonindustrial countries: Mean of actual annual GDP growth rates (GM), standard deviation (SD), average growth forecast error (AFE), root mean squared error (RMSE), and mean of standard deviation reported in growth forecasts, 1990–2001 (continued)

Country	Actual growth (1990–2001)		One-year-ahead forecast (1990–2001)			Two-year-ahead forecast (1991–2001)		
	GM	SD	AFE	RMSE	Mean SD of forecasts	AFE	RMSE	Mean SD of forecasts
Potential inflation targeters (PIT)								
Argentina	2.99	5.15	-1.63	3.84	0.86	-2.35	5.89	0.93
Bangladesh[b]	5.04	0.91	0.54	1.18	n.a.	0.12	0.53	n.a.
Bolivia	3.63	1.64	-0.82	1.64	n.a.	-0.87	2.18	n.a.
Bulgaria	-1.62	6.21	-1.01	5.72	n.a.	-3.35	7.07	n.a.
China	9.60	2.78	0.17	1.09	0.59	-0.98	1.70	0.95
Costa Rica	4.77	2.84	0.59	3.18	n.a.	0.86	3.37	n.a.
Dominican Republic	4.66	3.84	1.39	2.62	n.a.	2.11	3.04	n.a.
Ecuador	2.23	3.17	-0.79	3.27	n.a.	-2.42	4.52	n.a.
Egypt	4.43	1.38	0.64	1.49	n.a.	0.77	1.62	n.a.
Guatemala	3.88	0.80	n.a.	n.a.	n.a.	n.a.	n.a.	n.a.
Honduras	2.95	2.57	-0.04	3.71	0.73	-0.34	4.65	0.78
Hong Kong[c]	3.99	3.62	0.26	1.59	0.47	-0.22	1.29	0.72
India[d]	5.59	1.69	-0.69	4.09	1.09	-2.00	6.67	1.03
Indonesia	4.27	5.63	-0.34	4.08	0.86	0.16	5.86	0.88
Malaysia	6.77	4.96	n.a.	n.a.	n.a.	n.a.	n.a.	n.a.
Morocco	2.89	5.75	-1.30	2.58	n.a.	-0.51	2.80	n.a.
Nigeria	3.12	1.88	-0.07	2.19	n.a.	-0.85	1.37	n.a.
Pakistan[b]	4.40	1.33	-0.93	1.50	n.a.	-0.91	2.26	n.a.
Panama	4.44	2.72	-1.46	1.99	n.a.	-2.09	2.52	n.a.
Paraguay	2.13	1.56	-0.84	4.91	n.a.	-3.97	6.19	n.a.
Romania[c]	-1.31	6.01	-1.13	12.03	0.93	-1.00	13.88	0.95
Russia[a]	-4.58	11.94	-0.02	1.19	1.23	-0.07	2.30	1.20
Saudi Arabia	2.85	3.38	1.13	4.62	n.a.	1.62	5.00	n.a.
Singapore	7.17	4.11	1.44	2.04	0.84	0.65	1.84	0.73
Slovak Republic[a]	2.71	4.40	0.10	1.07	0.83	-0.10	0.97	0.80
Slovenia[a]	2.05	4.48	-0.96	2.62	n.a.	-0.58	3.08	n.a.
Sri Lanka	4.73	2.08						

Taiwan	5.42	2.33	−0.67	2.13	0.41	−0.26	2.58	0.37
Turkey	3.22	5.68	−0.53	5.14	1.10	−0.32	6.73	1.20
Ukraine[a]	−8.17	13.72	0.02	6.45	1.07	−2.94	7.48	0.80
Uruguay	2.33	3.76	−0.63	4.02	n.a.	−1.52	4.55	n.a.
Venezuela	2.57	4.25	−0.51	2.93	1.19	−1.18	4.51	1.83
Vietnam[c]	7.31	1.61	0.16	1.25	n.a.	−0.95	1.76	n.a.
Average								
All potential targeters	3.23	3.88	−0.27	3.21	0.87	−0.78	3.94	0.94
Eight with inflation mean								
< 5 percent	4.82	3.47	−0.05	2.63	0.71	0.05	3.31	0.69
Five with inflation mean								
5 to 10 percent	5.53	1.76	0.27	1.67	0.63	−0.25	1.66	0.82
Nine with inflation mean								
10 to 20 percent	4.16	2.81	−0.17	2.63	1.09	−0.44	3.41	1.03
11 with inflation mean								
> 20 percent	0.26	6.02	−0.75	4.72	1.06	−1.79	5.87	1.15
Average nonindustrial IT and PIT								
All	3.24	4.03	−0.28	3.39	0.77	−0.87	4.15	0.86
Nine with inflation mean								
< 5 percent	4.83	3.72	−0.25	2.79	0.75	−0.27	3.71	0.74
11 with inflation mean								
5 to 10 percent	4.60	2.39	0.16	1.96	0.66	−0.64	2.38	0.81
11 with inflation mean								
10 to 20 percent	3.95	2.85	−0.13	2.67	0.70	−0.47	3.58	0.76
15 with inflation mean								
> 20 percent	0.76	6.28	−0.68	5.03	0.85	−1.52	5.86	0.95

n.a. = not available

a. GDP growth data available only since 1992.
b. For Bangladesh and Pakistan, annual GDP growth rate given for fiscal year in order to match *Consensus Forecasts*, except for 1990 when not available. For both countries, fiscal year t starts in July t and ends in June $t+1$.
c. GDP growth data available only since 1991.
d. For India, year-over-year GDP growth rate given for fiscal year in order to match *Consensus Forecasts*. Indian fiscal year t starts in April t and ends in March $t+1$.

Sources: IMF, International Financial Statistics; Consensus Economics, *Consensus Forecasts;* and selected government statistics.

References

Agénor, Pierre-Richard. 2002. Monetary Policy under Flexible Exchange Rates: An Introduction to Inflation Targeting. In *Ten Years of Inflation Targeting: Design, Performance, Challenges*, ed. Norman Loayza and Raimundo Soto. Santiago: Central Bank of Chile.

Ahearne, Alan, Joseph Gagnon, Jane Haltmaier, and Steve Kamin. 2002. Preventing Deflation: Lessons from Japan's Experience in the 1990s. *International Finance Discussion Papers* 729. Washington: Board of Governors of the Federal Reserve System.

Ahmed, Shaghil, Christopher J. Gust, Steven B. Kamin, and Jonathan Huntley. 2002. Are Depreciations as Contractionary as Devaluations? A Comparison of Selected Emerging and Industrial Economies. *International Finance Discussion Papers* 737. Washington: Board of Governors of the Federal Reserve System.

Ahmed, Shaghil, Andrew Levin, and Beth Anne Wilson. 2002. Recent U.S. Macroeconomic Stability: Good Policies, Good Practices, or Good Luck? *International Finance Discussions Papers* 730 (July). Washington: Board of Governors of the Federal Reserve System.

Akerlof, George A, William F. Dickens, and George L. Perry. 1996. The Macroeconomics of Low Inflation. *Brookings Papers on Economic Activity* 1: 1–59. Washington: Brookings Institution.

Akerlof, George A, William F. Dickens, and George L. Perry. 2000. Near-Rational Wage and Price Setting and the Long-Run Phillips Curve. *Brookings Papers on Economic Activity* 1: 1–60. Washington: Brookings Institution.

Amato, Jeffrey D., and Stefan Gerlach. 2002. Inflation Targeting in Emerging Market and Transition Economies: Lessons After a Decade. *European Economic Review* 46: 781–90.

Ammer, John, and Richard T. Freeman. 1995. Inflation Targeting in the 1990s: The Experiences of New Zealand, Canada, and the United Kingdom. *Journal of Economics and Business* 47, no. 2 (May): 165–92.

Archer, David. 1997. The New Zealand Approach to Rules and Discretion in Monetary Policy. *Journal of Monetary Economics* 39: 3–15.

Archer, David. 2000. Inflation Targeting in New Zealand. Paper presented at a seminar at the International Monetary Fund, Washington, March 20–21. Photocopy.

Baig, Taimur. 2003. Monetary Policy in a Deflationary Environment. In *Japan's Lost Decade: Policies for Economic Revival*, ed. Timothy Callen and Jonathan Ostry. Washington: International Monetary Fund.

Ball, Laurence. 1992. Why Does High Inflation Raise Inflation Uncertainty? *Journal of Monetary Economics* (June): 371–88.

Ball, Laurence. 1996. Disinflation and the NAIRU. *NBER Working Paper* 5520. Cambridge, MA: National Bureau of Economic Research. (Also published in *Reducing Inflation: Motivation and Strategy*, 1997, ed. Christine Romer and David Romer. Chicago: University of Chicago Press.)

Ball, Laurence. 1999a. Efficient Rules for Monetary Policy. *International Finance* 2: 63–83.

Ball, Laurence. 1999b. Policy Rules for Open Economies. In *Monetary Policy Rules*, ed. John B. Taylor. Chicago: University of Chicago Press.

Ball, Laurence, N. Gregory Mankiw, and Ricardo Reis. 2002. Monetary Policy for Inattentive Economies. Harvard University. Photocopy (December).

Ball, Laurence, and Niamh Sheridan. 2003. Does Inflation Targeting Matter? Paper prepared for NBER Conference on Inflation Targeting, Bal Harbour, Florida, January 23–25. Photocopy.

Baltensperger, Ernst, Andreas M. Fischer, and Thomas J. Jordan. 2002. Abstaining from Inflation Targets: Understanding the Importance of Strong Goal Independence. Swiss National Bank. Photocopy (October).

Banco Central do Brasil (research department). 2000. Issues in the Adoption of an Inflation Targeting Framework in Brazil. In *Inflation Targeting in Practice: Strategic and Operational Issues and Application to Emerging Market Economies*, ed. Mario I. Blejer, Alain Ize, Alfredo M. Leone, and Sergio Werlang. Washington: International Monetary Fund.

Banco Central do Brasil. 2002. *Inflation Targeting in Brazil: A Collection of Working Papers*. Brasilia: Banco Central do Brasil.

Bank of Canada. 2000. *Price Stability and the Long-Run Target for Monetary Policy: Proceedings of a Seminar at the Bank of Canada*. Ottawa: Bank of Canada.

Barro, Robert J. 1991. Economic Growth in a Cross Section of Countries. *Quarterly Journal of Economics* 106: 407–44.

Barro, Robert J. 1995. Inflation and Economic Growth. *Bank of England Quarterly Bulletin* 35 (May): 166–76.

Barro, Robert J., and Xavier Sala-i-Martin. 1990. Economic Growth and Convergence Across the United States. *NBER Working Paper* 3419. Cambridge, MA: National Bureau of Economic Research.

Batini, Nicoletta, and Andrew G. Haldane. 1999. Forward-Looking Rules for Monetary Policy. In *Monetary Policy Rules*, ed. John B. Taylor. Chicago: University of Chicago Press.

Begg, David, Barry Eichengreen, László Halpern, Jürgen von Hagen, and Charles Wyplosz. 2002. Sustainable Regimes of Capital Movements in Accession Countries. *CEPR Policy Paper* 10. London: Centre for Economic Policy Research.

Berg, Andrew, Sean Hagen, Christopher Jarvis, Bernhard Steinki, Mark Stone, and Alessandro Zanello. 2003. Reestablishing a Credible Nominal Anchor After a Financial Crisis. In *Managing Financial Crises: Recent Experience and Lessons for Latin America*, ed. Charles Collyns and G. Russel Kincaid. Washington: International Monetary Fund.

Berg, Claes. 2000. Inflation Forecast Targeting: The Swedish Experience. In *Inflation Targeting in Practice: Strategic and Operational Issues and Application to Emerging Market Economies*, ed. Mario I. Blejer, Alain Ize, Alfredo M. Leone, and Sergio Werlang. Washington: International Monetary Fund.

Berg, Claes, and Lars Jonung. 1999. Pioneering Price Level Targeting: The Swedish Experience Since 1931–1937. *Journal of Monetary Economics* 43 (June): 525–51.

Bergsten, C. Fred, Takatoshi Ito, and Marcus Noland. 2001. *No More Bashing: Building a New Japan–United States Economic Relationship*. Washington: Institute for International Economics.

Bernanke, Ben S. 2000. Japanese Monetary Policy: A Case of Self-Induced Paralysis. In *Japan's Financial Crisis and Its Parallels to US Experience*, ed. Ryoichi Mikitani and Adam Posen. Washington: Institute for International Economics.

Bernanke, Ben S. 2002a. Asset-Price Bubbles and Monetary Policy. Remarks before the New York Chapter of the National Association for Business Economists, October 15. Photocopy.

Bernanke, Ben S. 2002b. Deflation: Making Sure It Doesn't Happen Here. Remarks before the National Economists Club, Washington, November 21. Photocopy.

Bernanke, Ben S. 2002c. Statement at Confirmation Hearings (July 30). Committee on Banking, Housing, and Urban Affairs. Washington: US Senate. Photocopy.

Bernanke, Ben S. 2003a. A Perspective on Inflation Targeting. Remarks at the Annual Washington Policy Conference of the National Association of Business Economists, March 25. Board of Governors of the Federal Reserve System. Photocopy.

Bernanke, Ben S. 2003b. Some Thoughts on Monetary Policy in Japan. Remarks before the Japan Society of Monetary Economists, Tokyo, May 31. Board of Governors of the Federal Reserve System. Photocopy.

Bernanke, Ben S., and Mark Gertler. 1999. Monetary Policy and Asset Volatility. *Federal Reserve Bank of Kansas City Economic Review* 84, no. 4 (fourth quarter): 17–52.

Bernanke, Ben S., and Mark Gertler. 2001. Should Central Banks Respond to Movements in Asset Prices? *American Economic Review* 91, no. 2 (May): 253–57.

Bernanke, Ben S., Thomas Laubach, and Frederic S. Mishkin, and Adam S. Posen. 1999. *Inflation Targeting: Lessons from International Experience.* Princeton, NJ: Princeton University Press.

Bernanke, Ben S., and Frederic S. Mishkin. 1997. Inflation Targeting: A New Framework for Monetary Policy? *Journal of Economic Perspectives* 11, no. 2 (spring): 97–116.

Bhundia, Ashok. 2002. An Empirical Investigation of Exchange Rate Pass-Through in South Africa. *IMF Working Paper* WP/02/165. Washington: International Monetary Fund.

Bjorksten, Nils, and Anne-Marie Brook. 2002. Exchange Rate Strategies for Small Open Economies Such as New Zealand. *Reserve Bank of New Zealand Bulletin* 65, no. 1: 14–27.

Blanchard, Olivier. 2003. Comment on Inflation Targeting in Transition Economies: Experience and Prospects by Jiri Jonas and Frederic Mishkin. Paper prepared for the NBER Conference on Inflation Targeting, Bal Harbour, Florida, January 23–25. Photocopy.

Blanchard, Olivier, and John Simon. 2001. The Long and Large Decline in U.S. Output Volatility. *Brookings Papers on Economic Activity* 1: 135–74.

Blanchard, Olivier, and Justin Wolfers. 2000. The Role of Shocks and Institutions in the Rise of European Unemployment: The Aggregate Evidence. *Economic Journal* 110 (March): 1–33.

Bleaney, Michael. 2001. Exchange Rate Regimes and Inflation Persistence. *IMF Staff Papers* 47, no. 3: 387–402.

Blejer, Mario I., Alain Ize, Alfredo M. Leone, and Sergio Werlang, ed. 2000. *Inflation Targeting in Practice: Strategic and Operational Issues and Application to Emerging Market Economies.* Washington: International Monetary Fund.

Blejer, Mario I., and Alfredo M. Leone. 2000. Introduction and Overview. In *Inflation Targeting in Practice: Strategic and Operational Issues and Application to Emerging Market Economies*, ed. Mario I. Blejer, Alain Ize, Alfredo M. Leone, and Sergio Werlang. Washington: International Monetary Fund.

Blejer, Mario I., Alfredo M. Leone, Pau Rabanal, and Gerd Schwartz. 2002. Inflation Targeting in the Context of IMF-Supported Adjustment Programs. In *Ten Years of Inflation Targeting: Design, Performance, Challenges*, ed. Norman Loayza and Raimundo Soto. Santiago: Central Bank of Chile.

Blinder, Alan, Charles Goodhart, Philipp Hildebrand, David Lipton, and Charles Wyplosz. 2001. How Do Central Banks Talk? *Geneva Reports on the World Economy* 3. Geneva: International Center for Monetary and Banking Studies.

Bogdanski, Joel, Paulo Springer de Freitas, Ilan Goldfajn, and Alexandre Antonio Tombini. 2002. Inflation Targeting in Brazil: Shocks, Backward-Looking Prices, and IMF Conditionality. In *Ten Years of Inflation Targeting: Design, Performance, Challenges*, ed. Norman Loayza and Raimundo Soto. Santiago: Central Bank of Chile.

Bogdanski, Joel, Alexandre Antonio Tombini, and Sérgio Ribeiro C. Werlang. 2000. Implementation of Inflation Targeting in Brazil. *Central Bank of Brazil Working Paper* 1 (July). Brasilia: Banco Central do Brasil. (Reprinted in Banco Central do Brasil. 2002. *Inflation Targeting in Brazil: A Collection of Working Papers*. Brasilia: Banco Central do Brasil.)

BOJ (Bank of Japan). 2003a. Minutes of the Monetary Policy Meeting on March 23, 2003. Bank of Japan, Tokyo. Photocopy (May 6).

BOJ (Bank of Japan). 2003b. Minutes of the Monetary Policy Meeting on April 30, 2003. Bank of Japan, Tokyo. Photocopy (June 16).

BOJ (Bank of Japan). 2003c. Minutes of the Monetary Policy Meeting on May 19–20, 2003. Bank of Japan, Tokyo. Photocopy (June 30).

BOJ (Bank of Japan). 2003d. Minutes of the Monetary Policy Meeting on June 10–11, 2003. Bank of Japan, Tokyo. Photocopy (July 18).

BOJ (Bank of Japan). 2003e. The Output Gap and the Potential Growth Rate: Issues and Applications as an Indicator of Price Change. Tokyo: Bank of Japan. Photocopy (May 9).

Bomfim, Antulio, and Glenn D. Rudebusch. 2000. Opportunistic and Deliberate Disinflation Under Imperfect Credibility. *Journal of Money Credit and Banking* 32, part I (November): 707–21.

Bordo, Michael D., and Olivier Jeanne. 2002. Monetary Policy and Asset Prices: Does Benign Neglect Make Sense? *IMF Working Paper* WP/02/225. Washington: International Monetary Fund. (Also published in *International Finance* 5, no. 2 [summer]: 139–64.)

Borensztein, Eduardo, Jeromin Zettelmeyer, and Thomas Philippon. 2001. Monetary Independence in Exchange Markets: Does the Exchange Rate Regime Make a Difference? *IMF Working Paper* 01/1. Washington: International Monetary Fund.

Borio, Claudio, and Philip Lowe. 2002. Asset Prices, Financial and Monetary Stability: Exploring the Nexus. *BIS Working Papers* 114. Basel, Switzerland: Bank for International Settlements.

Borio, Claudio, William English, and Andrew Filardo. 2003. A Tale of Two Perspectives: Old or New Challenges for Monetary Policy? *BIS Working Papers* 127. Basel, Switzerland: Bank for International Settlements.

Brash, Donald T. 1998. New Zealand's Economic Reform: A Model For Change? *Reserve Bank of New Zealand Bulletin* 61, no. 2 (June): 160–69.

Brash, Donald T. 2002. Inflation Targeting 14 Years On. Speech delivered at the American Economic Association, January 5. Photocopy.

Brenner, Meachem, and Meir Sokoler. 2003. Inflation Targeting and Exchange Rate Regimes: Evidence from the Financial Markets. New York University and the Bank of Israel. Photocopy (February).

Bruno, Michael, and William Easterly. 1996. Inflation and Growth: In Search of a Stable Relationship. *Federal Reserve Bank of St. Louis Review* 78 (May/June): 139–46.

Bryant, Ralph C. 1996. Central Bank Independence, Fiscal Responsibility, and the Goals of Macroeconomic Policy: An American Perspective on the New Zealand Experience. *Brookings Discussion Papers in International Economics* 126. Washington: Brookings Institution (June).

Bryant, Ralph C. 2000. Economic Policy When the Short-term Nominal Interest Rate Is Stuck at the Lower Bound of Zero. *Journal of Money, Credit and Banking* 32, part II (November): 1036–50. (Also published in 1999. Economic Policy When the Short-term Nominal Interest Rates Is Stuck at the Lower Bound of Zero. *Brookings Discussion Papers in International Economics* 151. Washington: Brookings Institution [November].)

Bryant, Ralph C. 2003. *Turbulent Waters: Cross-Border Finance and International Governance*. Washington: Brookings Institution.

Bryant, Ralph C., Peter Hooper, Dale W. Henderson, Gerald Holtham, Peter Hooper, and Steven A. Symansky, ed. 1988. *Empirical Macroeconomics for Interdependent Economies*. Washington: Brookings Institution.

Bryant, Ralph C., Gerald Holtham, and Peter Hooper. 1988. *External Deficits and the Dollar: The Pit and the Pendulum*. Washington: Brookings Institution.

Bryant, Ralph C., Peter Hooper, and Catherine L. Mann, eds. 1993. *Evaluating Policy Regimes: New Research in Empirical Macroeconomics.* Washington: Brookings Institution.

Burger, John D., and Francis E. Warnock. 2003. Diversification, Original Sin, and International Bond Portfolios. *International Finance Discussion Papers* 755. Washington: Board of Governors of the Federal Reserve System.

Burns, Arthur F. 1979. *The Anguish of Central Banking.* Washington: International Monetary Fund, Per Jacobsson Foundation.

Caballero, Ricardo, and Arvind Krishnamurthy. 2003. Inflation Targeting and Sudden Stops. Paper prepared for the NBER Conference on Inflation Targeting, Bal Harbour, Florida, January 23–25. Photocopy.

Calvo, Guillermo A., and Frederic S. Mishkin. 2003. The Mirage of Exchange Rate Regimes for Emerging Market Economies. Inter-American Development Bank and Columbia University. Photocopy (March).

Calvo, Guillermo A., and Carmen M. Reinhart. 2000. Fear of Floating. *NBER Working Paper* 7993. Cambridge, MA: National Bureau of Economic Research.

Calvo, Guillermo A., and Carmen M. Reinhart. 2001. Fixing for Your Life. In *Brookings Trade Forum 2000*, ed. Susan Collins and Dani Rodrik. Washington: Brookings Institution.

Carare, Alina, Andrea Schaechter, Mark Stone, and Mark Zelmer. 2002. Establishing Initial Conditions in Support of Inflation Targeting. *IMF Working Paper* WP/02/102. Washington: International Monetary Fund.

Carare, Alina, and Mark Stone. 2003. Inflation Targeting Regimes. *IMF Working Paper* WP/03/9. Washington: International Monetary Fund.

Carson, Carol S., Charles Enoch, and Claudia Dziobek, ed. 2002. *Statistical Implications of Inflation Targeting.* Washington: International Monetary Fund.

Carstens, Agustin G., and Alejandro M. Werner. 2000. Mexico's Monetary Policy Framework Under a Floating Exchange Rate Regime. In *Inflation Targeting in Practice: Strategic and Operational Issues and Application to Emerging Market Economies*, ed. Mario I. Blejer, Alain Ize, Alfredo M. Leone, and Sergio Werlang. Washington: International Monetary Fund.

Catão, Luis, and Marco E. Terrones. 2003. Fiscal Deficits and Inflation. *IMF Working Paper* WP/03/65. Washington: International Monetary Fund.

Cecchetti, Stephen G., and Michael Ehrmann. 2002. Does Inflation Targeting Increase Output Volatility? An International Comparison of Policymakers' Preferences and Outcomes. In *Monetary Policy Rules and Transmission Mechanisms*, ed. Norman Loayza and Klaus Schmidt-Hebbel. Santiago: Central Bank of Chile.

Cecchetti, Stephen G., Hans Genberg, and Sushil Wadhwani. 2002. Asset Prices in a Flexible Inflation Targeting Framework. *NBER Working Paper* 8970. Cambridge, MA: National Bureau of Economic Research.

Cecchetti, Stephen G., Hans Genberg, John Lipsky, and Sushil Wadhwani. 2000. Asset Prices and Central Bank Policy. *Geneva Report on the World Economy* 2. Geneva: International Center for Monetary and Banking Studies.

Cecchetti, Stephen G., and Junhan Kim. 2003. Inflation Targeting, Price-Path Targeting and Output Variability. Paper prepared for the NBER Conference on Inflation Targeting, Bal Harbour, Florida, January 23–25. Photocopy.

Chortareas, Georgios, David Stasavage, and Gabriel Sterne. 2002. Does It Pay to Be Transparent? International Evidence from Central Bank Forecasts. *Federal Reserve Bank of St. Louis Review* 84, no. 4 (July/August): 99–118.

Choudhri, Ehsan U., and Dalia S. Hakura. 2001. Exchange Rate Pass-Through to Domestic Prices: Does the Inflationary Environment Matter? *IMF Working Paper* 01/194. Washington: International Monetary Fund.

Christoffersen, Peter F., and Peter Doyle. 1998. From Inflation to Growth: Eight Years of Transition. *IMF Working Paper* 98/99. Washington: International Monetary Fund.

Clarida, Richard, Jordi Galí, and Mark Gertler. 1998. Monetary Policy Rules in Practice: Some International Evidence. *European Economic Review* 42: 1033–67.

Clarida, Richard, Jordi Galí, and Mark Gertler. 1999. The Science of Monetary Policy: A New Keynesian Perspective. *Journal of Economic Literature* 37 (December): 1661–1707.

Clarida, Richard, Jordi Galí, and Mark Gertler. 2000. Monetary Policy Rules and Macroeconomic Stability: Evidence and Some Theory. *Quarterly Journal of Economics* 115 (February): 147–80.

Clarida, Richard, Jordi Galí, and Mark Gertler. 2001. Optimal Monetary Policy in Open versus Closed Economies: An Integrated Approach. *American Economic Review* 91, no. 2 (May): 248–52.

Clouse, James, Dale Henderson, Athanasios Orphanides, David Small, and Peter Tinsley. 2000. Monetary Policy When the Nominal Short-Term Interest Rate Is Zero. *Finance and Economic Discussion Series* 2000-51. Washington: Board of Governors of the Federal Reserve System.

Coats, Warren, Douglas Laxton, and David Rose, ed. 2003. *The Czech National Bank's Forecasting and Policy Analysis System*. Prague: Czech National Bank.

Coenen, Günter, and Volker Wieland. 2002. The Zero-Interest-Rate Bound and the Role of the Exchange Rate for Monetary Policy in Japan. Paper prepared for the Conference on the Tenth Anniversary of the Taylor Rule, November 22–23, 2002, and published in the *Carnegie-Rochester Conference Series on Public Policy*. Photocopy (March).

Cooper, Richard. 1984. A Monetary System for the Future. *Foreign Affairs* 63, no. 1 (fall): 166–84.

Corbo, Vittorio, Oscar Landerretche, and Klaus Schmidt-Hebbel. 2002. Does Inflation Targeting Make a Difference? In *Inflation Targeting: Design, Performance, Challenges*, ed. Norman Loayza and Raimundo Soto. Santiago: Central Bank of Chile.

Corbo, Vittorio, and Klaus Schmidt-Hebbel. 2001. Inflation Targeting in Latin America. *Central Bank of Chile Working Papers* 105. Santiago: Banco Central de Chile.

Corrigan, E. Gerald. 2001. Monetary Policy and Financial Market Volatility. Speech delivered to The Money Marketeers of New York University, April 4. Photocopy.

Corsetti, Giancarlo, John Flemming, Seppo Honkapohja, Willi Leibfritz, Gilles Saint-Paul, Hans-Werner Sinn, and Xavier Vives. 2002. *Report on the European Economy 2002*. Munich: Ifo Institute for Economic Research.

Cottarelli, Carlo, and Gurzio Giannini. 1997. Credibility Without Rules? Monetary Policy Frameworks in the Post-Bretton Woods Era. *IMF Occasional Paper* 154. Washington: International Monetary Fund.

Cukierman, Alex, Geoffrey Miller, and Bilin Neyapti. 2001. Central Bank Reform, Liberalization, and Inflation in Transition Economies: An International Perspective. *Centre for Economic Policy Research Discussion Paper* 2808. London: Centre for Economic Policy Research. (Also published in the *Journal of Monetary Economics*, March 2002.)

Debelle, Guy. 1997. Inflation Targeting in Practice. *IMF Working Paper* 97/35. Washington: International Monetary Fund.

Debelle, Guy. 2000. Inflation Targeting and Output Stabilization in Australia. In *Inflation Targeting in Practice: Strategic and Operational Issues and Application to Emerging Market Economies*, ed. Mario I. Blejer, Alain Ize, Alfredo M. Leone, and Sergio Werlang. Washington: International Monetary Fund.

Debelle, Guy. 2001. The Case for Inflation Targeting in East Asian Countries. Paper prepared for Reserve Bank of Australia Conference on Future Directions in Monetary Policy in East Asia, July. Photocopy.

Debelle, Guy, and Stanley Fischer. 1994. How Independent Should a Central Bank Be? In *Goals, Guidelines, and Constraints Facing Monetary Policymakers*, ed. Jeffrey C. Fuhrer. Boston: Federal Reserve Bank of Boston.

Debelle, Guy, and Jenny Wilkinson. 2002. Inflation Targeting and the Inflation Process: Lessons from an Open Economy. In *Ten Years of Inflation Targeting: Design, Performance, Challenges*, ed. Norman Loayza and Raimundo Soto. Santiago: Central Bank of Chile.

Decressin, Anja, and Jörg Decressin. 2002. On Sand and the Role of Grease in Labor Markets: How Does Germany Compare? *IMF Working Paper* WP/02/164. Washington: International Monetary Fund.

De Grauwe, Paul. 2002. Central Banking as Art or Science: Lessons from the Fed and the ECB: Review of Bob Woodward's *Maestro* and Otmar Issing, Victor Gaspar, Ignazio Angeloni and Oreste Tristani's *Monetary Policy in the Euro Area*. *International Finance* 5, no. 1: 129–37.

De Gregorio, Jose. 1993. Inflation Taxation, and Long-Run Growth. *Journal of Monetary Economics* 31: 271–98.

Devereux, Michael. 1989. Positive Theory of Inflation and Inflation Variance. *Economic Inquiry* 27 (January): 105–16.

Dornbusch, Rudiger. 2001. Fewer Monies, Better Monies. *American Economic Review* 91, 2 (May): 238–42.

Drew, Aaron. 2002. Lessons from Inflation Targeting in New Zealand. In *Ten Years of Inflation Targeting: Design, Performance, Challenges*, ed. Norman Loayza and Raimundo Soto. Santiago: Central Bank of Chile.

Duisenberg, Willem F. 2001. Reply to the letter by Mrs. Randzio-Plath, Chairperson of the Committee on Economic and Monetary Affairs of the European Parliament. European Central Bank, Frankfurt. Photocopy (December 15).

Duisenberg, Willem F., and Lucas Papademos. 2002. Introductory Statement and Transcript of Press Conference. European Central Bank, Frankfurt (December 5).

Easterly, William, and Stanley Fischer. 2001. Inflation and the Poor. *Journal of Money, Credit and Banking* 33, no. 2, part I (May): 160–78.

ECB (European Central Bank). 2001. *A Guide to Eurosystem Staff Macroeconomic Projection Exercises*. Frankfurt: European Central Bank (June).

ECB (European Central Bank). 2003a. The Dispersion of Inflation across the Euro Area Countries and the US Metropolitan Areas. *European Central Bank Monthly Bulletin* (April): 22–24.

ECB (European Central Bank). 2003b. Overview of the Background Studies for the Reflections on the ECB's Monetary Policy Strategy. European Central Bank, Frankfurt. Photocopy (May 8).

Eggertsson, Gauti, and Michael Woodford. 2003. The Zero Bound on Interest Rates and Optimal Monetary Policy. *Brookings Papers on Economic Activity* 1: 139–211. Photocopy (March 19).

Eichengreen, Barry. 2001. Should Emerging Markets Float? Can They Inflation Target? University of California, Berkeley. Photocopy (June).

Eichengreen, Barry, Paul Masson, Miguel Savastano, and Sunil Sharma. 1999. Transition Strategies and Nominal Anchors on the Road to Greater Exchange-Rate Flexibility. *Essays in International Finance* 213. Princeton, NJ: International Finance Section, Department of Economics, Princeton University.

Eichengreen, Barry, and Alan M. Taylor. 2003. The Monetary Implications of a Free Trade Area of the Americas. University of California, Berkeley. Photocopy (March).

Eijffinger, Sylvester C. W., and Petra M. Geraats. 2003. How Transparent Are Central Banks. Center for Economic Research, Tuborg University, and University of Cambridge. Photocopy (April).

Eijffinger, Sylvester C. W., and Marco Hoeberichts. 2002. Central Bank Accountability and Transparency: Theory and Some Evidence. *International Finance* 5, no. 1 (spring): 73–96.

Elkayam, David, Ofer Klein, and Edward Offenbacher. 2002. Estimating a Central Bank's Reaction Function During Gradual Disinflation. Bank of Israel. Photocopy (December).

Erceg, Christopher J. 2002. The Choice of an Inflation Target Range in a Small Open Economy. *American Economic Review* 92, no. 2 (May): 85–89.

Faust, Jon, John H. Rogers, and Jonathan W. Wright. 2001. An Empirical Comparison of Bundesbank and ECB Monetary Policy Rules. *International Finance Discussion Papers* 705. Washington: Board of Governors of the Federal Reserve System.

Faust, Jon, and Lars E. O. Svensson. 1998. Transparency and Credibility: Monetary Policy with Unobservable Goals. *International Finance Discussion Papers* 605. Washington: Board of Governors of the Federal Reserve System.

Federal Reserve Bank of Cleveland. 2000. Inflation and Prices. *Economic Trends* (July). www.clevelandfed.org/research/et2000/0700/trends.pdf.

Federal Reserve Bank of Cleveland. 2001. Inflation and Prices. *Economic Trends* (July). www.clevelandfed.org/research/et2001/0701/trends.pdf.

Federal Reserve System. 2002. *Alternative Instruments for Open Market and Discount Window Operations.* Washington: Board of Governors of the Federal Reserve System.

Feldstein, Martin, ed. 1997. *The Costs and Benefits of Price Stability.* Chicago: The University of Chicago Press.

Fels, Joachim. 2001. In Defense of the ECB. *Economic Trends.* Morgan Stanley Dean Witter (July 14).

Ferguson, Roger W., Jr. 2002. Why Central Banks Talk. Remarks at the Graduate Institute of International Studies, Geneva, January 8. Photocopy.

Ferguson, Roger W., Jr. 2003. Uncertain Times: Economic Challenges Facing the United States and Japan. Remarks before the Japan Society, New York, June 11. Photocopy.

Fischer, Stanley. 1993. The Role of Macroeconomic Factors in Growth. *Journal of Monetary Economics* 32: 485–512.

Fischer, Stanley. 1996. Why Are Central Banks Pursuing Long-Run Price Stability? In *Achieving Price Stability*: 7–34. Federal Reserve Bank of Kansas City.

Fischer, Stanley. 2001. Exchange Rate Regimes: Is the Bipolar View Correct? *Journal of Economic Perspectives* 15, no. 2: 3–24.

Fischer, Stanley, Ratna Sahay, and Carlos Végh. 2002. Modern Hyper- and High Inflations. *IMF Working Paper* WP/02/197. Washington: International Monetary Fund. (Forthcoming in the *Journal of Economic Literature.*)

Fitoussi, Jean-Paul, and Jérôme Creel. 2002. *How to Reform the European Central Bank.* London: Centre for European Reform.

Flood, Robert P., and Michael Mussa. 1994. *Issues Concerning Nominal Anchors for Monetary Policy.* NBER Working Papers 4850. Cambridge, MA: National Bureau of Economic Research.

FOMC (Federal Open Market Committee). 1995. Transcript of Discussion on Inflation Targeting, January 31–February 1: 38–59. Washington: Board of Governors of the Federal Reserve System.

FOMC (Federal Open Market Committee). 1996a. Transcript of Discussion on Inflation Targeting, January 30–31: 37–50. Washington: Board of Governors of the Federal Reserve System.

FOMC (Federal Open Market Committee). 1996b. Transcript of Discussion on Inflation Targeting, July 2–3: 41–68. Washington: Board of Governors of the Federal Reserve System.

FOMC (Federal Open Market Committee). 2002. Minutes of the Federal Open Market Committee meeting, November 6. Washington: Board of Governors of the Federal Reserve System.

Fraga, Arminio. 2000. Monetary Policy During the Transition to a Floating Exchange Rate: Brazil's Recent Experience. *Finance and Development* 37, no. 1 (March): 16–18. Washington: International Monetary Fund. (Also published in *New Challenges for Monetary Policy: A Symposium Sponsored by the Federal Reserve Bank of Kansas City* (August 26–28, 1999): 149–54. Kansas City: Federal Reserve Bank of Kansas City.)

Frankel, Jeffrey A. 1999. No Single Currency Regime Is Right for All Countries or at All Times. *Essays in International Finance* 215. Princeton, NJ: International Finance Section, Princeton University.

Frankel, Jeffrey A., and Menzie Chinn. 1995. The Stabilizing Properties of a Nominal GNP Rule. *Journal of Money Credit and Banking* 27, no. 2 (May): 318–34.

Frankel, Jeffrey A., and Peter R. Orzag, eds. 2002. *American Economic Policy in the 1990s.* Cambridge, MA: MIT Press.

Freeman, Richard T., and Jonathan I. Willis. 1995. Targeting Inflation in the 1990s. *International Finance Discussion Papers* 525. Washington: Board of Governors of the Federal Reserve System.

Friedman, Benjamin M. 2001. The Use and Meaning of Words in Central Banking: Inflation Targeting, Credibility, and Transparency. *NBER Working Paper* 8972. Cambridge, MA: National Bureau of Economic Research. (Also presented at the Conference in Honor of Charles Goodhart, November 15–16, 2001, and published in *Central Banking, Monetary Theory and Practice: Essays in Honor of Charles Goodhart* 1, ed. Paul Mizen. London: Edward Elgar.)

Friedman, Milton. 1968. The Role of Monetary Policy. *American Economic Review* 58: 1–17.

Friedman, Milton. 2003. Should the European Central Bank Change its Two Percent Inflation Ceiling? *The International Economy* 17, no. 1 (winter): 46–50.

Fry, Maxwell, Deanne Julius, Lavan Mahadeva, Sandra Roger, and Gabriel Sterne. 2000. Key Issues in the Choice of Monetary Policy Framework. In *Monetary Policy Frameworks in a Global Context*, ed. Lavan Mahadeva and Gabriel Sterne. London: Routledge.

Fuhrer, Jeffrey C., and Mark S. Sniderman, ed. 2000. Monetary Policy in a Low Inflation Environment: A Conference Sponsored by the Federal Reserve Banks of Boston, New York, Cleveland, Richmond, Atlanta, St. Louis, Minneapolis, and the Board of Governors of the Federal Reserve System, October 18–20, 1999. *Journal of Money, Credit, and Banking* 32, part 2 (November): 845–69.

Fujiki, Hiroshi, Kunio Okina, and Shigenori Shiratsuka. 2001. Monetary Policy under Zero Interest Rate: Viewpoints of Central Bank Economists. *Monetary and Economic Studies* 19 (February): 89–130. Tokyo: Institute for Monetary and Economic Studies, Bank of Japan.

Fukui, Toshihiko. 2003. Challenges for Monetary Policy in Japan. Speech at the Spring Meeting of the Japan Society of Monetary Economics, Tokyo, June 1. Photocopy.

Gagnon, Joseph E., and Jane E. Ihrig. 2002. Monetary Policy and Exchange Rate Pass-Through. *International Finance Discussion Papers* 704. Washington: Board of Governors of the Federal Reserve System.

Gaspar, Vitor, and Frank Smets. 2002. Monetary Policy, Price Stability and Output Gap Stabilization. *International Finance* 5, no. 2 (summer): 193–211.

Genberg, Hans. 2001. Inflation Targeting: The Holy Grail of Monetary Policy? Graduate Institute of International Studies, Geneva. Photocopy (September 26).

Geraats, Petra M. 2002. Central Bank Transparency. *The Economic Journal* 112 (November): 532–65.

Gerlach, Stefan. 1999. Who Targets Inflation Explicitly? *European Economic Review* 43, no. 7: 1257–77.

Ghosh, Atish R. 2000. Inflation and Growth. *IMF Research Bulletin* 1, no. 1: 1–3. Washington: International Monetary Fund.

Ghosh, Atish R., Anne-Marie Gulde, Jonathan D. Ostry, and Holger C. Wolf. 1997. Does the Nominal Exchange Rate Regime Matter? *NBER Working Papers* 5874. Cambridge, MA: National Bureau of Economic Research.

Ghosh, Atish R., and Steven Phillips. 1998. Warning: Inflation May be Harmful to Your Growth. *IMF Staff Papers* 45, no. 4: 672–710. Washington: International Monetary Fund.

Goldfajn, Ilan, and Sérgio Ribeiro da Costa Werlang. 2000. The Pass-through from Depreciation to Inflation: A Panel Study. *Central Bank of Brazil Working Paper* 5 (September). Brasilia: Banco Central do Brasil. (Reprinted in *Inflation Targeting in Brazil: A Collection of Working Papers*. Brasilia: Banco Central do Brasil.)

Goldstein, Morris. 2001. IMF Structural Conditionality: How Much Is Too Much? *Institute for International Economics Working Papers* 01-4. Washington: Institute for International Economics.

Goldstein, Morris. 2002. *Managed Floating Plus.* Washington: Institute for International Economics.

Goldstein, Morris. 2003a. Debt Sustainability, Brazil, and the IMF. *Institute for International Economics Working Papers* 03-1. Washington: Institute for International Economics.

Goldstein, Morris. 2003b. IMF Structural Programs. In *Economic and Financial Crises in Emerging Market Economies,* ed. Martin Feldstein. Chicago: University of Chicago Press.

Golob, John E. 1994. Does Inflation Uncertainty Increase with Inflation? *Federal Reserve Bank of Kansas City Working Paper*: 27–38. Kansas City: Federal Reserve Bank of Kansas City.

Gómez, Javier, José Darío Uribe, and Hernando Vargas. 2002. The Implementation of Inflation Targeting in Colombia. Paper presented at a Bank of Mexico conference, March 4–5. Photocopy.

Goodfriend, Marvin. 2000. Maintaining Low Inflation: Rationale and Reality. In *Inflation Targeting in Practice: Strategic and Operational Issues and Application to Emerging Market Economies*, ed. Mario I. Blejer, Alain Ize, Alfredo M. Leone, and Sergio Werlang. Washington: International Monetary Fund.

Goodfriend, Marvin. 2003. Inflation Targeting in the United States? Paper prepared for the NBER Conference on Inflation Targeting, Bal Harbour, Florida, January 23–25. Photocopy.

Gramlich, Edward M. 2000. Inflation Targeting. Remarks before the Charlotte Economics Club. Charlotte, North Carolina, January 13. Photocopy.

Gramlich, Edward M. 2003. Conducting Monetary Policy. Remarks at a Joint Meeting of the North American Economic and Finance Association and the Allied Social Science Association, Washington, January 4. Photocopy.

Green, Edward J. 2001. Central Banking and the Economics of Information. *Federal Reserve Bank of Chicago Economic Perspectives* 2Q: 28–37.

Greenspan, Alan. 1989. Statement before the Committee on Finance, January 26. Washington: US Senate.

Greenspan, Alan. 1994. Statement before the Subcommittee on Economic Growth and Credit Formulation of the Committee on Banking, Finance, and Urban Affairs, February 22. Washington: US House of Representatives.

Greenspan, Alan. 2001. Transparency in Monetary Policy. Remarks at the Federal Reserve Bank of St. Louis Economic Policy Conference, October 11. Photocopy.

Greenspan, Alan. 2002a. Economic Volatility. Remarks at a symposium sponsored by the Federal Reserve Bank of Kansas City, August 30. Photocopy.

Greenspan, Alan. 2002b. Testimony before the US Congress, Joint Economic Committee, November 13. Washington.

Groshen, Erica L., and Mark E. Schweitzer. 1999. Identifying Inflation's Grease and Sand Effects in the Labor Market. In *The Costs and Benefits of Price Stability*, ed. Martin Feldstein. Chicago: University of Chicago Press.

Groshen, Erica L., and Mark E. Schweitzer. 2000. The Effects of Inflation on Wage Adjustments in Firm-Level Data: Grease or Sand? Federal Reserve Bank of New York. Photocopy (June).

Gutiérrez, Eva. 2003. Inflation Performance and Constitutional Central Bank Independence: Evidence from Latin America and the Caribbean. *IMF Working Paper* WP/03/53. Washington: International Monetary Fund.

Haldane, Andrew. 2000. Targeting Inflation: The United Kingdom in Retrospect. In *Inflation Targeting in Practice: Strategic and Operational Issues and Application to Emerging Market Economies*, ed. Mario I. Blejer, Alain Ize, Alfredo M. Leone, and Sergio Werlang. Washington: International Monetary Fund.

Hamann, A. Javier, and Alessandro Prati. 2002. Why Do Many Disinflations Fail? The Importance of Luck, Timing and Political Institutions. *IMF Working Paper* WP/02/228. Washington: International Monetary Fund.

Hampton, Tim. 2001. How Much Do Import Price Shocks Matter for Consumer Prices? *Discussion Paper Series* DP2001/06. Wellington: Reserve Bank of New Zealand.

Hausmann, Ricardo, Michael Gavin, Carmen Pagés, and Ernesto Stein. 1999. Financial Turmoil and the Choice of Exchange Rate Regime. *Research Department Working Paper* 400. Washington: Inter-American Development Bank.

Hausmann, Ricardo, Ugo Panizza, and Ernesto Stein. 2000. Why Do Countries Float the Way They Float? *Research Department Working Paper* 418. Washington: Inter-American Development Bank.

Heikensten, Lars, and Anders Vredin. 1998. Inflation Targeting and Swedish Monetary Policy: Experience and Problems. *Quarterly Review* 4: 5–33. Stockholm: Swedish Riksbank.

Ho, Corrinne, and Robert N. McCauley. 2003. Living with Flexible Exchange Rates: Issues and Recent Experience in Inflation Targeting Emerging Market Economies. *BIS Working Papers* 130. Basel, Switzerland: Bank for International Settlements.

Hori, Masahiro, Toshiyuki Tanabe, Makoto Yamane, and Daiju Aoki. 2002. Monetary Policy and the Liquidity. Trap: Simulations Using a Short-Run Macro Economic Model of the Japanese Economy. *ESRI Discussion Paper Series* 23. Tokyo: Economic and Social Research Institute, Cabinet Office (December)

Hu, Yifan. 2003a. Empirical Investigations of Inflation Targeting in Essays on Monetary Policy and International Finance. Unpublished Ph.D. dissertation. Georgetown University, Washington.

Hu, Yifan. 2003b. Empirical Investigations of Inflation Targeting. *Institute for International Economics Working Papers* 03-6. Washington: Institute for International Economics.

Hunt, Benjamin, and Douglas Laxton. 2001. The Zero Interest Rate Floor (ZIF) and its Implications for Monetary Policy in Japan. *IMF Working Paper* WP/01/186. Washington: International Monetary Fund. (Also published in *Japan's Lost Decade: Policies for Economic Revival*, ed. Timothy Callen and Jonathan Ostry. Washington: International Monetary Fund.)

IMF (International Monetary Fund). 1993. *Articles of Agreement of the International Monetary Fund*. Washington: International Monetary Fund.

IMF (International Monetary Fund). 2001. The Decline of Inflation in Emerging Markets: Can It Be Maintained? Chapter IV of *World Economic Outlook* (May): 116–44.

IMF (International Monetary Fund). 2002a. Japan: 2002 Article IV Consultation—Staff Report; Staff Statement; and Public Information Notice on the Executive Board Discussion. *IMF Country Report* 02/175 (August). Washington: International Monetary Fund.

IMF (International Monetary Fund). 2002b. Monetary Policy in a Low Inflation Era. Third of three essays in chapter II of *World Economic Outlook* (April): 85–103.

IMF (International Monetary Fund). 2003a. Concluding Statement of the IMF Mission on Euro Area Policies. Washington: International Monetary Fund (May 28).

IMF (International Monetary Fund). 2003b. Deflation: Determinants, Risks, and Policy Options. Washington: International Monetary Fund (April 30).

IMF (International Monetary Fund). 2003c. Hungary—2003 Article IV Consultation Discussions Preliminary Conclusions. Washington: International Monetary Fund (February 6).

IMF (International Monetary Fund). 2003d. Statement of the Fund Mission—2003 Article IV Consultation with the United States of America. Washington: International Monetary Fund (June 16).

IMF (International Monetary Fund). 2003e. Statement of the Fund Mission—2003 Article IV Consultation with Poland. Washington: International Monetary Fund (March 10).

IMF (International Monetary Fund). 2003f. When Bubbles Burst. *World Economic Outlook*. Washington: International Monetary Fund.

IMF (International Monetary Fund). 2003g. Japan 2003 Article IV Consultation—Staff Report. *IMF Country Report* 03/281 (August). Washington: International Monetary Fund.

Isard, Peter, Douglas Laxton, and Ann-Charlotte Eliasson. 2001. Inflation Targeting with NAIRU Uncertainty and Endogenous Policy Credibility. *IMF Working Paper* WP/01/7. Washington: International Monetary Fund.

Issing, Otmar. 2000. Europe's Challenges after the Establishment of Monetary Union: A Central Banker's View. Speech at CES-IFO Conference on the Issues of Monetary Integration in Europe, Munich, December 1. Photocopy.

Issing, Otmar. 2001a. The Euro and the ECB: Successful Start—Challenges Ahead. Speech at Market News Seminar, London, May 3. Photocopy.

Issing, Otmar. 2001b. The Challenge for Monetary Policy: A European Perspective. Speech to the German British Forum, London, October 17. Photocopy.

Issing, Otmar. 2001c. The Single Monetary Policy of the European Central Bank: One Size Fits All. *International Finance* 4, no. 3: 441–62.

Issing, Otmar. 2002. Monetary Policy and the Role of the Price Stability Definition. Speech to ECB Watchers Conference, Milan, June 10. Photocopy.

Issing, Otmar, Vitor Gaspar, Ignazio Angeloni, and Oreste Tristani. 2001. *Monetary Policy in the Euro Area: Strategy and Decision-Making at the European Central Bank.* Cambridge, England: Cambridge University Press.

Ito, Takatoshi, and Tomoko Hayashi. 2003. Inflation Targeting in Asia. University of Tokyo and Japan Bank for International Cooperation. Photocopy (March 28).

Jaeger, Albert. 2003. The ECB's Monetary Pillar: An Assessment. *IMF Working Paper* WP/03/82. Washington: International Monetary Fund.

Jensen, Henrik. 2002. Targeting Nominal Income Growth or Inflation? *American Economic Review* 92, no. 4 (September): 928–56.

Jinushi, Toshiki, Yoshihiro Kuroki, and Ryuko Miyao. 2000. Monetary Policy in Japan Since the Late 1980s: Delayed Policy Actions and Some Explanations. In *Japan's Financial Crisis and Its Parallels to US Experience,* ed. Ryoichi Mikitani and Adam Posen. Washington: Institute for International Economics.

Johnson, David. 2002. The Effect of Inflation Targeting on the Behavior of Expected Inflation: Evidence from an 11 Country Panel. *Journal of Monetary Economics* 49: 1521–38.

Johnson, Karen, David Small, and Ralph Tryon. 1999. Monetary Policy and Price Stability. *International Finance Discussion Papers* 641. Washington: Board of Governors of the Federal Reserve System.

Jonas, Jiri, and Frederic S. Mishkin. 2003. Inflation Targeting in Transition Economies: Experience and Prospects. Paper prepared for the NBER Conference on Inflation Targeting, Bal Harbour, Florida, January 23–25. Photocopy.

Jones, Larry E., and Rodolfo E. Manuelli. 1993. Growth and the Effects of Inflation. *NBER Working Papers* 4523. Cambridge, MA: National Bureau of Economic Research.

Judson, Ruth, and Athanasios Orphanides. 1999. Inflation, Volatility and Growth. *International Finance* 2, no. 1: 117–38.

Kahn, George A., and Klara Parrish. 1998. Conducting Monetary Policy with Inflation Targets. *Federal Reserve Bank of Kansas City Economic Review* (third quarter): 5–32.

Kamin, Steven B. 1998. A Multi-Country Comparison of the Linkages between Inflation and Exchange Rate Competitiveness. *International Finance Discussion Papers* 603. Washington: Board of Governors of the Federal Reserve System.

Kamin, Steven B., John W. Schindler, and Shawna L. Samuel. 2001. The Contribution of Domestic and External Factors to Emerging Market Devaluation Crises: An Early Warning Systems Approach. *International Finance Discussion Papers* 711. Washington: Board of Governors of the Federal Reserve System.

Khan, Mohsin S. 2003. Current Issues in the Design and Conduct of Monetary Policy. *IMF Working Paper* WP/03/56. Washington: International Monetary Fund.

Khan, Mohsin S., and Abdelhak S. Senhadji. 2001. Threshold Effects in the Relationship Between Inflation and Growth. *IMF Staff Papers* 48, no. 1: 1–21. Washington: International Monetary Fund.

Khan, Mohsin S., Abdelhak S. Senhadji, and Bruce D. Smith. 2001. Inflation and Financial Depth. *IMF Working Paper* WP/01/44. Washington: International Monetary Fund.

Kieler, Mads. 2003. The ECB's Inflation Objective. *IMF Working Paper* WP/03/91. Washington: International Monetary Fund.

Kim, Jinill, and Dale W. Henderson. 2002. Inflation Targeting and Nominal Income Growth Targeting: When and Why Are They Suboptimal? *International Finance Discussion Papers* 719. Washington: Board of Governors of the Federal Reserve System.

King, Mervyn. 1997a. Changes in UK Monetary Policy: Rules and Discretion in Practice. *Journal of Monetary Economics* 39: 81–87.

King, Mervyn. 1997b. The Inflation Target Five Years On. *Bank of England Quarterly Bulletin* (November).

King, Mervyn. 1999a. Challenges for Monetary Policy: New and Old. In *New Challenges for Monetary Policy: A Symposium Sponsored by the Federal Reserve Bank of Kansas City* (August 26–28, 1999): 11–57. Kansas City: Federal Reserve Bank of Kansas City.

King, Mervyn. 1999b. The MPC Two Years On. Speech delivered to the Queen's University, Belfast, May 17, and published in *Bank of England Quarterly Bulletin* (August).

King, Mervyn. 2002. The Inflation Target Ten Years On. Speech delivered to the London School of Economics, November 19 and published in *Bank of England Quarterly Bulletin* (winter).

Kohn, Donald L. 2000. Report to the Non-Executive Directors of the Court of the Bank of England on Monetary Policy Processes and the Work of Monetary Analysis, Bank of England. www.bankofengland.co.uk/kohn.pdf

Kohn, Donald L. 2002. Thirty-Two Years of Monetary Policy—Some Lessons Learned. Remarks delivered to The Money Marketeers of New York University, June 6. Photocopy.

Kohn, Donald L. 2003. Comment on Marvin Goodfriend's paper entitled Inflation Targeting in the United States? Prepared for the NBER Conference on Inflation Targeting, Bal Harbour, Florida, January 23–25. Photocopy.

Kozicki, Sharon. 1999. How Useful Are Taylor Rules for Monetary Policy? Federal Reserve Bank of Kansas City *Economic Review* (second quarter): 1–33.

Krueger, Anne. 2003. Statement by IMF First Deputy Managing Director in Tokyo. Washington: International Monetary Fund. Photocopy (June 4).

Krugman, Paul R. 1998. Further Notes on Japan's Liquidity Trap. http://web.mit.edu/krugman/www/liquid.html.

Kumhof, Michael. 2002. A Critical View of Inflation Targeting: Crises, Limited Sustainability, and Aggregate Shocks. In *Ten Years of Inflation Targeting: Design, Performance, Challenges*, ed. Norman Loayza and Raimundo Soto. Santiago: Central Bank of Chile.

Kuttner, Kenneth N., and Adam S. Posen. 1999. Does Talk Matter After All? Inflation Targeting and Central Bank Behavior. *Federal Reserve Bank of New York Staff Report* (October): 88.

Kuttner, Kenneth N., and Adam S. Posen. 2000. Inflation, Monetary Transparency, and G3 Exchange Rate Volatility. *Institute for International Economics Working Papers* 00-6. Washington: Institute for International Economics.

Kuttner, Kenneth N., and Adam S. Posen. 2001. Beyond Bipolar: A Three-Dimensional Assessment of Monetary Frameworks. *International Journal of Finance and Economics* 6: 369–87.

Lane, Philip. 1995. Inflation in Open Economies. *Journal of International Economics* 42: 327–47.

Laubach, Thomas, and Adam S. Posen. 1997. Some Comparative Evidence on the Effectiveness of Inflation Targeting. *Research Paper* 9714. New York: Federal Reserve Bank of New York.

Laxton, Douglas, and Papa N'Diaye. 2002. Monetary Policy Credibility and the Unemployment-Inflation Trade-Off: Some Evidence from 17 Industrial Countries. *IMF Working Paper* WP/02/220. Washington: International Monetary Fund.

Laxton, Douglas, and Paolo Pesenti. 2002. Monetary Rules for Small, Open, Emerging Economies. Paper presented at the Conference on the Tenth Anniversary of the Taylor Rule, November 22–23, 2002, and published in the *Carnegie-Rochester Conference Series on Public Policy.*

Lebow, David, and Jeremy B. Rudd. 2003. Measurement Error in the Consumer Price Index: Where Do We Stand? *Journal of Economic Literature* 41 (March): 159–201.

Leiderman, Leonardo, and Gil Bufman. 2000. Inflation Targeting Under a Crawling Band Exchange Rate Regime: Lessons from Israel. In *Inflation Targeting in Practice: Strategic and Operational Issues and Application to Emerging Market Economies*, ed. Mario I. Blejer, Alain Ize, Alfredo M. Leone, and Sergio Werlang. Washington: International Monetary Fund.

Levin, Andrew, and John C. Williams. 2002. Robust Monetary Policy with Competing Reference Models. Paper presented at the Conference on the Tenth Anniversary of the Taylor Rule, November 22–23, 2002, and published in the *Carnegie-Rochester Conference Series on Public Policy*.

Levin, Andrew, Volker Wieland, and John C. Williams. 2003. The Performance of Forecast-Based Monetary Policy Rules under Model Uncertainty. *American Economic Review* 93, No. 3: 622–645.

Levin, Andrew, Volker Wieland, and John C. Williams 1999. Robustness of Simple Monetary Policy Rules under Model Uncertainty. In *Monetary Policy Rules*, ed. John B. Taylor. Chicago: University of Chicago Press.

Levine, Ross, and David Renelt. 1992. A Sensitivity Analysis of Cross-Country Growth Regression. *American Economic Review* 82, no. 4 (September): 942–63.

Levine, Ross, and Sara Zervous. 1993. What Have We Learned about Policy and Growth from Cross-Country Analysis? *American Economic Review Papers and Proceedings* 83 (May): 426–30.

Levy-Yeyati, Eduardo, and Federico Sturzenegger. 2001a. Exchange Rate Regimes and Economic Performance. *IMF Staff Papers* 47 (special issue): 62–98. Washington: International Monetary Fund.

Levy-Yeyati, Eduardo, and Federico Sturzenegger. 2001b. To Float or to Trail: Evidence on the Impact of Exchange Rate Regimes. Universidad Torcuato Di Tella, Argentina. Photocopy (January).

Lindsay, David L. 1995. Multi-Year Inflation Targets. Memorandum to the Federal Open Market Committee. Photocopy (January 20).

Loayza, Norman, and Raimundo Soto. 2002. Inflation Targeting: An Overview. In *Ten Years of Inflation Targeting: Design, Performance, Challenges*, ed. Norman Loayza and Raimundo Soto. Santiago: Central Bank of Chile.

Loboguerrero, Ana Maria, and Ugo Panizza. 2003. Inflation and Labor Market Flexibility: It Is the Squeaky Wheel that Gets the Grease. Inter-American Development Bank. Photocopy.

Longworth, David. 2000. The Canadian Monetary Transmission Mechanism and Inflation Projections. In *Inflation Targeting in Practice: Strategic and Operational Issues and Application to Emerging Market Economies*, ed. Mario I. Blejer, Alain Ize, Alfredo M. Leone, and Sergio Werlang. Washington: International Monetary Fund.

Mahadeva, Lavan, and Gabriel Sterne. 2000. *Monetary Policy Frameworks in a Global Context*. London: Routledge.

Mankiw, N. Gregory. 2002. U.S. Monetary Policy in the 1990s. In *American Economic Policy in the 1990s*, ed. Jeffrey A. Frankel and Peter R. Orzag. Cambridge, MA: MIT Press.

McCallum, Bennett T. 2000. Theoretical Analysis Regarding a Zero Bound on Nominal Interest Rates. *Journal of Money, Credit and Banking* 32: 870–904.

McCallum, Bennett. T. 2002. Inflation Targeting and the Liquidity Trap. In *Ten Years of Inflation Targeting: Design, Performance, Challenges*, ed. Norman Loayza and Raimundo Soto. Santiago: Central Bank of Chile.

Meltzer, Allan H. 2002a. Japan's Monetary and Economic Policy. *World Economics* 3, no. 3 (July–September): 85–103.

Meltzer, Allan H. 2002b. New International Financial Arrangements. *IMES Discussion Paper* 2002-E-11. Tokyo: Institute for Monetary and Economic Studies, Bank of Japan.

Meyer, Laurence H. 2001. Inflation Targets and Inflation Targeting. Paper presented at the University of California at San Diego Economics Roundtable, San Diego, July 17. Photocopy.

Mikitani, Ryoichi, and Adam S. Posen, eds. 2000. *Japan's Financial Crisis and its Parallels to US Experience*. Washington: Institute for International Economics.

Mishkin, Frederic S. 1998. Central Banking in a Democratic Society: Implications for Transition Countries. Graduate School of Business, Columbia University. Photocopy (May).

Mishkin, Frederic S. 1999. International Experiences with Different Monetary Regimes. *Journal of Monetary Economics* 43, no. 3 (June): 579–606.

Mishkin, Frederic S. 2000a. Inflation Targeting for Emerging Market Countries. *American Economic Review: Papers and Proceedings* 90: 2 (May): 105–09.

Mishkin, Frederic S. 2000b. What Should Central Banks Do? *Federal Reserve Bank of St. Louis Review* (November/December): 1–13.

Mishkin, Frederic S. 2002a. Commentary on Neumann and von Hagen. *Federal Reserve Bank of St. Louis Review* (July/August): 149–63.

Mishkin, Frederic S. 2002b. The Role of Output Stabilization in the Conduct of Monetary Policy. *International Finance* 5, no. 2 (summer): 213–27.

Mishkin, Frederic S. 2003. Overview. In *Rethinking Stabilization Policy: A Symposium Sponsored by the Federal Reserve Bank of Kansas City,* August 29–31, 2002. Kansas City: Federal Reserve Bank of Kansas City.

Mishkin, Frederic S., and Adam S. Posen. 1997. Inflation Targeting: Lessons from Four Countries. *Federal Reserve Bank of New York Economic Policy Review* (August): 9–110.

Mishkin, Frederic S., and Miguel A. Savastano. 2001. Monetary Policy Strategies for Latin America. *Journal of Development Economics* 66, no. 2 (December): 415–44.

Mishkin, Frederic S., and Klaus Schmidt-Hebbel. 2002. A Decade of Inflation Targeting in the World: What Do We Know and What Do We Need to Know? In *Ten Years of Inflation Targeting: Design, Performance, Challenges,* ed. Norman Loayza and Raimundo Soto. Santiago: Central Bank of Chile.

Morandé, Felipe, and Klaus Schmidt-Hebbel. 2000. Monetary Policy and Inflation Targeting in Chile. In *Inflation Targeting in Practice: Strategic and Operational Issues and Application to Emerging Market Economies,* ed. Mario I. Blejer, Alain Ize, Alfredo M. Leone, and Sergio Werlang. Washington: International Monetary Fund.

Morsink, James, and Tamim Bayoumi. 2001. A Peek Inside the Black Box: The Monetary Transmission Mechanism in Japan. *IMF Staff Papers* 48, no. 1: 22–57.

Nadal-De Simone, Francisco. 2001. An Investigation of Output Variance Before and During Inflation Targeting. *IMF Working Paper* WP 01/215. Washington: International Monetary Fund.

Neumann, Manfred J. M., and Jürgen von Hagen. 2002. Does Inflation Targeting Matter? *Federal Reserve Bank of St. Louis Review* (July/August): 127–48.

Obstfeld, Maurice, and Kenneth Rogoff. 1995. The Mirage of Fixed Exchange Rates. *Journal of Economic Perspectives* 9, no. 4 (fall): 73–96.

Okina, Kunio, Masaaki Shirakawa, and Shigenori Shiratsuka. 2001. The Asset Price Bubble and Monetary Policy: Japan's Experience in the Late 1980s and the Lessons. *Monetary and Economic Studies* (special edition, February): 395–450.

Orphanides, Athanasios, and David W. Wilcox. 2002. The Opportunistic Approach to Disinflation. *International Finance* 5, no. 1 (spring): 47–71.

Orphanides, Athanasios, and John C. Williams. 2003. Imperfect Knowledge, Inflation Expectations, and Monetary Policy. Paper prepared for the NBER Conference on Inflation Targeting, Bal Harbour, Florida, January 23–25. Photocopy.

Papaioannou, Michael G. 2003. Determinants of the Choice of Exchange Rate Regimes in Six Central American Countries: An Empirical Analysis. *IMF Working Paper* WP/03/59. Washington: International Monetary Fund.

Phelps, Edmund S. 1968. Money-Wage Dynamics and Labor Market Equilibrium. *Journal of Political Economy* 76, no. 4 (part 2): 678–711.

Posen, Adam S. 1998. *Restoring Japan's Economic Growth.* Washington: Institute for International Economics.

Posen, Adam S. 2002. Six Practical Views of Central Bank Transparency. In *Central Banking, Monetary Theory and Practice: Essays in Honor of Charles Goodhart* 1, ed. Paul Mizen. London: Edward Elgar.

Posen, Adam S. 2003. Is Germany Turning Japanese? *Institute for International Economics Working Papers* 03-2. Washington: Institute for International Economics.

Reinhart, Carmen M. 2000. The Mirage of Floating Exchange Rates. *American Economic Review* 90, no. 2 (May): 65–70.

Reinhart, Carmen M., and Kenneth S. Rogoff. 2002. The Modern History of Exchange Rate Arrangements: A Reinterpretation. *NBER Working Paper* 8963. Cambridge, MA: National Bureau of Economic Research.

Reserve Bank of New Zealand. 2000. *Independent Review of the Operation of Monetary Policy: Reserve Bank and Non-Executive Directors' Submissions.* Wellington: Reserve Bank of New Zealand.

Reserve Bank of New Zealand. 2002. *Policy Targets Agreement: Reserve Bank Briefing Note and Related Papers.* Wellington: Reserve Bank of New Zealand.

Rich, Georg. 2000. Monetary Policy Without Central Bank Money: A Swiss Perspective. *International Finance* 3, no. 3: 439–69.

Rich, Georg. 2001. Inflation and Money Stock Targets: Is There Really a Difference? Revised version of paper presented at the International Conference on the Conduct of Monetary Policy, Taipei, Taiwan, June 12–13, 1998.

Rivlin, Alice M. 2002. Comment on U.S. Monetary Policy in the 1990s by N. Gregory Mankiw. In *American Economic Policy in the 1990s,* ed. Jeffrey Frankel and Peter R. Orzag. Cambridge, MA: MIT Press.

Roach, Stephen. 2001. The Case Against the ECB. *Economic Trends* (June 8). Morgan Stanley Dean Witter.

Rogoff, Kenneth. 1985. The Optimal Degree of Commitment to an Intermediate Monetary Target. *Quarterly Journal of Economics* 100, no. 4: 1169–89.

Rogoff, Kenneth. 2001. Why Not a Global Currency? *American Economic Review* 91, no. 2 (May): 243–47.

Romer, David. 1993. Openness and Inflation: Theory and Evidence. *Quarterly Journal of Economics* 108 (November): 869–903.

Ross, Kevin. 2002. Market Predictability of ECB Monetary Policy Decisions: A Comparative Examination. *IMF Working Paper* WP/02/233. Washington: International Monetary Fund.

Rudebusch, Glenn D., and Lars E. O. Svensson. 1999. Policy Rules for Inflation Targeting. In *Monetary Policy Rules,* ed. John B. Taylor. Chicago: University of Chicago Press.

Rudebusch, Glenn D., and Carl E. Walsh. 1998. U.S. Inflation Targeting: Pro and Con. *FRBSF Economic Letter* 98-18 (May 29). San Francisco: Federal Reserve Bank of San Francisco.

Sabbán, Verónica Cohen, Martín Gonzalez Rozada, and Andrew Powell. 2003. A New Test for the Success of Inflation Targeting. Universidad Torcuato Di Tella, Buenos Aires. Photocopy (January).

Santomero, Anthony M. 2003. Flexible Commitment or Inflation Targeting for the U.S.? Speech delivered to The Money Marketeers of New York University, June 10. Photocopy.

Sarel, Michael. 1996. Nonlinear Effects of Inflation on Economic Growth. *IMF Staff Papers* 43 (March): 199–215. Washington: International Monetary Fund.

Schaechter, Andrea, Mark R. Stone, and Mark Zelmer. 2000. Adopting Inflation Targeting: Practical Issues for Emerging Market Countries. *IMF Occasional Paper* 202. Washington: International Monetary Fund.

Schellekens, Philip. 2003. Deflation in Hong Kong SAR. *IMF Working Paper* WP/03/77. Washington: International Monetary Fund.

Schmidt-Hebbel, Klaus, and Matías Tapia. 2002. Monetary Policy Implementation and Results in Twenty Inflation-Targeting Countries. *Central Bank of Chile Working Papers* 166 (June). Santiago: Central Bank of Chile.

Scott, Graham C. 1996. Government Reform in New Zealand. *IMF Occasional Paper* 140. Washington: International Monetary Fund.

Sherwin, Murray. 2000. Strategic Choices in Inflation Targeting: The New Zealand Experience. In *Inflation Targeting in Practice: Strategic and Operational Issues and Application to Emerging Market Economies,* ed. Mario I. Blejer, Alain Ize, Alfredo M. Leone, and Sergio Werlang. Washington: International Monetary Fund.

Shirakawa, Masaaki. 2001. Monetary Policy Under a Zero-Interest Rate Boundary and Balance Sheet Adjustment. *International Finance* 4, no. 3: 463–89.

Shirakawa, Masaaki. 2002. One Year Under "Quantitative Easing." *IMES Discussion Paper* 2002-E-3. Tokyo: Institute for Monetary and Economic Studies, Bank of Japan.

Siebert, Horst. 2000. The Japanese Bubble: Some Lessons for International Macroeconomic Policy Coordination. *Aussenwirtschaft* 55, no. 2: 233–50.

Siklos, Pierre L. 1999. Inflation-Target Design: Changing Inflation Performance and Persistence in Industrial Countries. *Federal Reserve Bank of St. Louis Review* 81, no. 2 (March/April): 46–58.

Simes, Ric. 2002. The New Target for the RBA: Financial Stability. Policy Comment for ICAP. Photocopy. On file with author.

Sims, Christopher. 2003. Limits to Inflation Targeting. Paper prepared for NBER Conference on Inflation Targeting, Bal Harbour, Florida, January 23–25. Photocopy

Smyth, David J. 1994. Inflation and Growth. *Journal of Macroeconomics* 6 (spring): 261–70.

Solans, Eugenio Domingo. 2000. Monetary Policy Under Inflation Targeting. Speech at the Fourth Annual Conference of Banco Central de Chile, December 1. Photocopy.

Sterne, Gabriel. 2002. Inflation Targets in a Global Context. In *Ten Years of Inflation Targeting: Design, Performance, Challenges*, ed. Norman Loayza and Raimundo Soto. Santiago: Central Bank of Chile.

Stockton, David J. 1996. The Price Objective for Monetary Policy: An Outline of the Issues. Report to the Federal Open Market Committee. Photocopy (June).

Stone, Mark R. 2003a. The Costs and Benefits of Greater Monetary Policy Transparency for the G3: Lessons from the International Experience with Full-Fledged Inflation Targeting. Remarks delivered at the Board of Governors of the Federal Reserve System, April 24. International Monetary Fund, Washington. Photocopy.

Stone, Mark R. 2003b. Inflation Targeting Lite. *IMF Working Paper* WP/03/12. Washington: International Monetary Fund.

Summers, Lawrence. 1991. How Should Long-Term Monetary Policy Be Determined? *Journal of Money, Credit and Banking* 23, no. 3: 625–31.

Summers, Lawrence. 1996. Commentary: Why Are Central Banks Pursuing Long-Run Price Stability? Comment on Stanley Fischer, Why Are Central Banks Pursuing Long-Run Price Stability? In *Achieving Price Stability*: 35–41. Kansas City: Federal Reserve Bank of Kansas City.

Sun, Yan. 2003. Do Fixed Exchange Rates Induce More Fiscal Discipline? *IMF Working Paper* WP 03/78. Washington: International Monetary Fund.

Svensson, Lars E. O. 1999. Inflation Targeting as a Monetary Rule. *Journal of Monetary Economics* 43: 607–54.

Svensson, Lars E. O. 2001a. Independent Review of Monetary Policy in New Zealand: Report to the Minister of Finance. February.

Svensson, Lars E. O. 2001b. The Zero Bound in an Open Economy: A Foolproof Way of Escaping from a Liquidity Trap. *Monetary and Economic Studies* 19 (S-1): 277–312 (February).

Svensson, Lars E. O. 2002a. Escaping from a Liquidity Trap and Deflation: The Foolproof Way and Others. Forthcoming in *Journal of Economic Perspectives*. Photocopy (February).

Svensson, Lars E. O. 2002b. Inflation Targeting: Should It Be Modeled as an Instrument Rule or a Targeting Rule? *European Economic Review* 46: 771–80.

Svensson, Lars E. O. 2003a. Monetary Policy and Real Stabilization. In *Rethinking Stabilization Policy: A Symposium Sponsored by the Federal Reserve Bank of Kansas City*, August 29–31, 2002. Kansas City: Federal Reserve Bank of Kansas City.

Svensson, Lars E. O. 2003b. What is Wrong with Taylor Rules? Using Judgment in Monetary Policy Through Targeting Rules. *Journal of Economic Literature* 61, no. 2 (June): 426–77.

Svensson, Lars E. O., and Michael Woodford. 2003. Implementing Optimal Policy through Inflation Targeting. Paper prepared for NBER Conference on Inflation Targeting, Bal Harbour, Florida, January 23–25. Photocopy.

Swiss National Bank. 1999. Monetary Policy Decisions of the Swiss National Bank for 2000. *Quarterly Review* (December): 19–23.

Taylor, John B. 1993. Discretion Versus Policy Rules in Practice. *Carnegie-Rochester Conference Series on Public Policy* 39 (December): 195–214.

Taylor, John B. 1999a. Commentary: Challenges for Monetary Policy: New and Old. In *New Challenges for Monetary Policy: A Symposium Sponsored by the Federal Reserve Bank of Kansas City*, August 26–28. Kansas City: Federal Reserve Bank of Kansas City.

Taylor, John B., ed. 1999b. *Monetary Policy Rules*. Chicago: University of Chicago Press.

Taylor, John B. 2001. The Role of the Exchange Rate in Monetary-Policy Rules. *American Economic Review* 91, no. 2 (May): 263–67.

Tetlow, Robert J. 2000. Inflation Targeting and Target Instability. *Finance and Economics Discussion Series* 2000–01. Washington: Board of Governors of the Federal Reserve System.

Thiessen, Gordon. 1998. The Canadian Experience with Targets for Inflation Control. The Gibson Lecture, Queen's University, Kingston, Ontario, October 15. Photocopy.

Truman, Edwin M. 2002a. How Far Have We/They Come? Performance Scorecard for Major Emerging Market Economies. Paper presented at Bretton Woods Committee Scorecard Symposium, New York, April 19.

Truman, Edwin M. 2002b. Economic Policy and Exchange Rate Regimes: What Have We Learned in the Ten Years Since Black Wednesday? Paper presented at European Monetary Symposium, London School of Economics, September 16.

Truman, Edwin M. 2003a. A Critical Review of Coordination Efforts in the Past. Paper presented at the Kiel Week Conference on Macroeconomic Policies in the World Economy, Kiel, Germany, June 23–24.

Truman, Edwin M. 2003b. The Limits of Exchange Market Intervention. In *Dollar Overvaluation and the World Economy*, ed., C. Fred Bergsten and John Williamson. Washington: Institute for International Economics.

Volcker, Paul A. 1983. Can We Survive Prosperity? Speech at the Joint Meeting of the American Economic Association and American Finance Association, San Francisco, December 28. Photocopy.

Volcker, Paul A. 2001. Globalization and the World of Finance. 2001 Hutchinson Lecture, University of Delaware, April 30. Photocopy.

Wadhwani, Sushil. 2000. The Exchange Rate and the MPC: What Can We Do? Speech to the Senior Business Forum at the Centre for Economic Performance, London, May 31. Photocopy.

Werner, Alejandro. 2002. Some Reflections on Inflation Targeting from a Mexican Perspective. Remarks at a meeting on Three Years of Inflation Targeting in Brazil, Rio de Janeiro, May 17. Photocopy.

Williamson, John. 2000. *Exchange Rate Regimes for Emerging Markets: Reviving the Intermediate Option*. Washington: Institute for International Economics.

Williamson, John. 2002a. The Evolution of Thought on Intermediate Exchange Rate Regimes. *The Annals of the American Academy of Political and Social Science* 579 (January): 73–86.

Williamson, John. 2002b. Is Brazil Next? *International Economics Policy Briefs* PB 02-7. Washington: Institute for International Economics (August).

Woodford, Michael. 2000. Pitfalls of Forward-Looking Monetary Policy. *American Economic Review* 90, no. 2 (May): 100–109.

Wyplosz, Charles. 2001. Do We Know How Low Inflation Should Be? *NBER Working Papers* 2722. Cambridge, MA: National Bureau of Economic Research.

Index

Other Publications from the Institute for International Economics

* = out of print

Measuring the Costs of Visible Protection in Korea* Namdoo Kim
November 1996 ISBN 0-88132-236-9

The World Trading System: Challenges Ahead
Jeffrey J. Schott
December 1996 ISBN 0-88132-235-0

Has Globalization Gone Too Far? Dani Rodrik
March 1997 ISBN cloth 0-88132-243-1

Korea-United States Economic Relationship*
C. Fred Bergsten and Il SaKong, editors
March 1997 ISBN 0-88132-240-7

Summitry in the Americas: A Progress Report
Richard E. Feinberg
April 1997 ISBN 0-88132-242-3

Corruption and the Global Economy
Kimberly Ann Elliott
June 1997 ISBN 0-88132-233-4

Regional Trading Blocs in the World Economic System Jeffrey A. Frankel
October 1997 ISBN 0-88132-202-4

Sustaining the Asia Pacific Miracle: Environmental Protection and Economic Integration Andre Dua and Daniel C. Esty
October 1997 ISBN 0-88132-250-4

Trade and Income Distribution William R. Cline
November 1997 ISBN 0-88132-216-4

Global Competition Policy
Edward M. Graham and J. David Richardson
December 1997 ISBN 0-88132-166-4

Unfinished Business: Telecommunications after the Uruguay Round
Gary Clyde Hufbauer and Erika Wada
December 1997 ISBN 0-88132-257-1

Financial Services Liberalization in the WTO
Wendy Dobson and Pierre Jacquet
June 1998 ISBN 0-88132-254-7

Restoring Japan's Economic Growth
Adam S. Posen
September 1998 ISBN 0-88132-262-8

Measuring the Costs of Protection in China
Zhang Shuguang, Zhang Yansheng, and Wan Zhongxin
November 1998 ISBN 0-88132-247-4

Foreign Direct Investment and Development: The New Policy Agenda for Developing Countries and Economies in Transition
Theodore H. Moran
December 1998 ISBN 0-88132-258-X

Behind the Open Door: Foreign Enterprises in the Chinese Marketplace
Daniel H. Rosen
January 1999 ISBN 0-88132-263-6

Toward A New International Financial Architecture: A Practical Post-Asia Agenda
Barry Eichengreen
February 1999 ISBN 0-88132-270-9

Is the U.S. Trade Deficit Sustainable?
Catherine L. Mann
September 1999 ISBN 0-88132-265-2

Safeguarding Prosperity in a Global Financial System: The Future International Financial Architecture, Independent Task Force Report Sponsored by the Council on Foreign Relations
Morris Goldstein, Project Director
October 1999 ISBN 0-88132-287-3

Avoiding the Apocalypse: The Future of the Two Koreas Marcus Noland
June 2000 ISBN 0-88132-278-4

Assessing Financial Vulnerability: An Early Warning System for Emerging Markets
Morris Goldstein, Graciela Kaminsky, and Carmen Reinhart
June 2000 ISBN 0-88132-237-7

Global Electronic Commerce: A Policy Primer
Catherine L. Mann, Sue E. Eckert, and Sarah Cleeland Knight
July 2000 ISBN 0-88132-274-1

The WTO after Seattle Jeffrey J. Schott, editor
July 2000 ISBN 0-88132-290-3

Intellectual Property Rights in the Global Economy Keith E. Maskus
August 2000 ISBN 0-88132-282-2

The Political Economy of the Asian Financial Crisis Stephan Haggard
August 2000 ISBN 0-88132-283-0

Transforming Foreign Aid: United States Assistance in the 21st Century Carol Lancaster
August 2000 ISBN 0-88132-291-1

Fighting the Wrong Enemy: Antiglobal Activists and Multinational Enterprises Edward M.Graham
September 2000 ISBN 0-88132-272-5

Globalization and the Perceptions of American Workers
Kenneth F. Scheve and Matthew J. Slaughter
March 2001 ISBN 0-88132-295-4

World Capital Markets: Challenge to the G-10
Wendy Dobson and Gary C. Hufbauer, assisted by Hyun Koo Cho
May 2001 ISBN 0-88132-301-2

Prospects for Free Trade in the Americas
Jeffrey J. Schott
August 2001 ISBN 0-88132-275-X

Lessons from the Old World for the New: Constructing a North American Community
Robert A. Pastor
August 2000 ISBN 0-88132-328-4

Measuring the Costs of Protection in Europe: European Commercial Policy in the 2000s
Patrick A. Messerlin
September 2001 ISBN 0-88132-273-3

Job Loss from Imports: Measuring the Costs
Lori G. Kletzer
September 2001 ISBN 0-88132-296-2

DISTRIBUTORS OUTSIDE THE UNITED STATES

Australia, New Zealand,
and Papua New Guinea
D.A. Information Services
648 Whitehorse Road
Mitcham, Victoria 3132, Australia
tel: 61-3-9210-7777
fax: 61-3-9210-7788
email: service@adadirect.com.au
http://www.dadirect.com.au

Canada
Renouf Bookstore
5369 Canotek Road, Unit 1
Ottawa, Ontario KlJ 9J3, Canada
tel: 613-745-2665
fax: 613-745-7660
http://www.renoufbooks.com

United Kingdom and Europe
(including Russia and Turkey)
The Eurospan Group
3 Henrietta Street, Covent Garden
London WC2E 8LU England
tel: 44-20-7240-0856
fax: 44-20-7379-0609
http://www.eurospan.co.uk

India, Bangladesh, Nepal, and Sri Lanka
Viva Books Pvt.
Mr. Vinod Vasishtha
4325/3, Ansari Rd.
Daryaganj, New Delhi-110002
India
tel: 91-11-327-9280
fax: 91-11-326-7224
email: vinod.viva@gndel.globalnet.
ems.vsnl.net.in

Japan and the Republic of Korea
United Publishers Services, Ltd.
KenkyuSha Bldg.
9, Kanda Surugadai 2-Chome
Chiyoda-Ku, Tokyo 101 Japan
tel: 81-3-3291-4541
fax: 81-3-3292-8610
email: saito@ups.co.jp
For trade accounts only.
Individuals will find IIE books in
leading Tokyo bookstores.

Southeast Asia (Brunei, Cambodia,
China, Malaysia, Hong Kong, Indonesia,
Laos, Myanmar, the Philippines, Singapore,
Taiwan, and Vietnam)
Hemisphere Publication Services
1 Kallang Pudding Rd. #0403
Golden Wheel Building
Singapore 349316
tel: 65-741-5166
fax: 65-742-9356

Thailand
Asia Books
5 Sukhumvit Rd. Soi 61
Bangkok 10110 Thailand
tel: 662-714-07402 Ext: 221, 222, 223
fax: 662-391-2277
email: purchase@asiabooks.co.th
http://www.asiabooksonline.com

Visit our Web site at:
www.iie.com
E-mail orders to:
orders@iie.com